Corporate Valuation: A Guide for Managers and Investors

Phillip R. Daves
University of Tennessee
Michael C. Ehrhardt
University of Tennessee
Ronald E. Shrieves
University of Tennessee

Australia · Canada · Mexico · Singapore · Spain · United Kingdom · United States

Corporate Valuation: A Guide for Managers and Investors

Phillip R. Daves, Michael C. Ehrhardt, and Ronald E. Shrieves

VP/Editorial Director:
Jack W. Calhoun

VP/Editor-in-Chief:
Michael P. Roche

Executive Editor:
Michael R. Reynolds

Developmental Editor:
Elizabeth Thomson

Editorial Assistant:
Joe Squance

Senior Marketing Manager:
Charlie Stutesman

Senior Production Editor:
Kara ZumBahlen

Media Developmental Editor:
John Barans

Media Production Editor:
Mark Sears

Manufacturing Coordinator:
Sandee Milewski

Production House/ Compositor:
DPS Associates, Inc.

Printer:
Phoenix Color
Hagerstown, MD

Design Project Manager:
Bethany Casey

Internal Designer:
Anne Marie Rekow

Cover Designer:
Bethany Casey

Cover Images:
© PhotoDisc, Inc.

Printed in the United States of America
1 2 3 4 5 06 05 04 03

ISBN: 0-324-27428-9 (package)
ISBN: 0--324-29073-X (text-only)

Library of Congress Control Number:
2003108932

For more information contact South-Western,
5191 Natorp Boulevard,
Mason, Ohio 45040.
Or you can visit our Internet site at:
http://www.swlearning.com

Corporate Valuation: A Guide for Managers and Investors

Contents

PART 4 Valuing Actual Companies with the Corporate Valuation Spreadsheet 153

About the Authors

Phillip Daves received his B.A. in Economics from Davidson College and his M.S. in Mathematics and Ph.D. in Finance from the University of North Carolina at Chapel Hill. He is currently an Associate Professor of Finance at the University of Tennessee in Knoxville. His research interests are in health care finance, asset pricing, derivative securities, and market microstructure. He has published papers in such journals as *The Journal of Finance*, *The International Journal of Finance*, *Financial Review*, *Applied Financial Economics*, *Journal of Financial Practice and Education*, and *The Journal of Financial and Strategic Decisions*. He is also coauthor of the popular text *Intermediate Financial Management*. Dr. Daves' teaching interests are in health care finance, investments, financial management, and asset pricing. He teaches these at the undergraduate, MBA and Ph.D. levels. Dr. Daves' consulting interests are in business valuation, compensation, value based management, and health care policy, and he has consulted for a range of large and small companies and the State of Tennessee.

Mike Ehrhardt is the Paul and Beverly Castagna Professor of Investments at the University of Tennessee at Knoxville. Dr. Ehrhardt did his undergraduate work in Civil Engineering at Swarthmore College. After working several years as an engineer, he returned to graduate school and received an M.S. in Operations Research and a Ph.D. in Finance from the Georgia Institute of Technology. He has taught extensively at the undergraduate, masters, and doctoral levels in the areas of investments, corporate finance, and capital markets. He has directed and served on numerous dissertation committees. He is a member of the team that developed and delivers the integrative first year of the MBA program. Dr. Ehrhardt was the winner of the Allen G. Keally Outstanding Teacher Award in the College of Business in 1989, the Tennessee Organization of MBA Students Outstanding Faculty Member in 1998, the College of Business Administration Research & Teaching Award in 1998, and the John B. Ross Outstanding Teaching Award in the College of Business in 2003. Much of his research is in the areas of corporate valuation and asset pricing models, including pricing models for interest-rate sensitive instruments. His work has been published in numerous journals including *The Journal of Finance*, *Journal of Financial and Quantitative Analysis*, *Journal of Applied Corporate Finance, Financial Management*, *The Financial Review*, *The Journal of Financial Research*, and *Journal of Banking and Finance*. He is the author of T*he Search for Value: Measuring the Company's Cost of Capital*, published by the Harvard Business School Press. He is a coauthor of *Financial Management: Theory and Practice*, the market-leading MBA finance textbook, and *Corporate Finance: A Focused Approach*, a more focused textbook that can be covered in a single semester. Dr. Ehrhardt teaches in executive education programs and consults in the areas of corporate valuation, value-based compensation plans, financial aspects of supply-chain management, and the cost of capital.

Ronald E. Shrieves is the William Voigt Professor of Business and Finance at the University of Tennessee at Knoxville. He received his Ph.D. in Business Economics from UCLA, where his Ph.D. thesis dealt with the determinants of inter-industry differences in research and development efforts. Dr. Shrieves was a finalist for the John B. Ross Award for Outstanding Teaching in the College of Business in 1993–94 and for the College of Business Administration Teaching and Research Award in 1998–99. He has published widely in finance and economics journals including the *Journal of Empirical Finance*, *Review of Economics and Statistics*, *Journal of Financial and Quantitative Analysis*, *Financial Management*, *Journal of Banking and Finance*, and *Journal of Financial Services Research*. Dr. Shrieves has received two best paper awards for academic journal articles. In 1993, along with coauthor Drew Dahl, he was honored with the Iddo Sarnat Award for the best paper in the *Journal of Banking and Finance*. In 2001, he and coauthor John Wachowicz received the Eugene L. Grant Award for the best paper in the *Engineering Economist*. Dr. Shrieves' primary current research interests are in the areas of the corporate governance and the impact of organization structure and regulation on commercial bank performance. In addition to teaching responsibilities in the undergraduate, MBA, and Ph.D. programs, Dr. Shrieves has also taught in two executive MBA programs: the Taiwan Executive MBA and the Professional MBA. The executive MBA programs have an interdisciplinary perspective, involving an integrated team-teaching approach to executive education.

Preface

We believe corporate valuation is important for all finance students, all managers, all financial analysis, and all individual investors. We especially believe that our focus on "fundamental" valuation analysis is vitally important because the process of projecting financial statements and cash flows requires the analyst to identify and understand a company's fundamental value-drivers. Thus, the insights gained through fundamental analysis are exactly those needed by investors who are searching for undervalued stocks and by corporate managers who are striving to maximize their company's value.

There are other books on corporate valuation, but they are extremely difficult to read and apply unless you already have a strong knowledge of accounting and finance. Our objective in *Corporate Valuation: A Guide for Managers and Investors* is to create a book that can be understood by someone with only a modest background in accounting and finance. We accomplish this through an iterative approach in which we first provide the reader with a complete valuation framework as applied to a very simple company. We then build the reader's skills by extending the analysis to value a series of increasingly complex companies. Finally, we lead the reader through a valuation of an actual company with the user-friendly spreadsheet-based valuation model that is available at the book's web site, **http://daves.swlearning.com**.

The valuation model is structured to guide the user through the entire valuation process, beginning with the input of actual historical financial statements from a variety of sources. The model then guides the user through an in-depth analysis of the company's current and historical financial position. After this analysis, the model provides a structured framework for estimating the cost of capital and the inputs required to project financial statements. Using the projected statements, the model calculates expected future free cash flows and discounts them to find the current estimated fundamental stock price.

We provide detailed explanations throughout the analysis for accessing and using data available on the Internet, especially the data provided through the Thomson ONE-Business School Edition, available to purchasers of this book.

Intended Market and Use

Corporate Valuation can be used as a supplement for investment and corporate finance courses, at both the graduate and undergraduate levels. It can also be used by general managers and finance professionals, as well as individual investors.

Investment and Corporate Finance Courses

Our book is ideally suited for investment courses that emphasize fundamental valuation or corporate finance courses that cover corporate valuation, merger analysis, financial strategies, or value-based management. Its strength relative to standard texts is its emphasis on understanding and using financial information to provide insights into the way corporate strategic choices affect a company's value.

Managers and Finance Professionals

General managers can use the book's model to estimate the impact their decisions have on the value of their company, particularly with respect to decisions that affect more than one functional area in the company, such as supply chain management. For example, it is easy to measure the costs but not the benefits of many strategic initiatives, because the costs are usually incurred by a particular operating unit whereas the benefits accrue to the entire company. The corporate valuation model explained in this book is an especially useful tool for evaluating such situations having localized costs but global benefits.

Financial managers can use the spreadsheet model to estimate the value of potential acquisitions and divestures, conduct long-term financial planning, identify future capital requirements, and evaluate potential compensation systems.

Financial analysts who are charged with making buy/sell recommendations can use the valuation spreadsheet as a part of their analyses. The model can also be used by any other analysts who must estimate the value of a company, including accountants who estimate the value of privately held companies for tax purposes.

Individual Investors

Finally, *Corporate Valuation* is ideally suited for individual investors who wish to use their own judgment in picking stocks for their portfolios. With our emphasis on building the necessary financial skills and accessing the relevant data, individual investors can use the same techniques as professional analysts.

Key Features of the Text

Following are some key features:

1. **Corporate Valuation Spreadsheet Model.** As described earlier, *Corporate Valuation's* web site has user-friendly corporate valuation Excel spreadsheet models that allow students to conduct their own valuation analyses.
2. **Thomson ONE-Business School Edition.** Purchasers of the book receive access to Thomson ONE-Business School Edition, provided by Thomson Financial, a global leader in financial information. Thomson ONE provides downloadable financial statements in Excel worksheets for 500 well-known companies, which can be pasted into the book's valuation model. Thomson ONE also provides I/B/E/S earnings estimates, ratio comparisons with peer companies, Datastream stock prices, Thomson Financial market data, Worldscope market data, and current company news.
3. **End-of-Chapter Excel Spreadsheet Projects.** The first eight chapters have a series of Excel spreadsheet projects that develop students' spreadsheet skills as well as valuation expertise. The remaining chapters have spreadsheet projects that lead students through the valuation of actual companies.
4. **PowerPoint Presentations.** PowerPoint presentations are available for each chapter. These presentations provide a structured way for an instructor to cover each chapter's material.

5. **Instructional Audio/Video Files.** The book's web site has a series of instructional audio/video files that lead the viewer through a complete valuation analysis using the book's spreadsheet valuation model. These files are available in two formats, either as stand-alone files that may be viewed without any additional software or as AVI files that may be viewed through widely available software such as Windows Media® Player or RealPlayer®.
6. **Supplementary Web Materials.** The book's web site has resources to help readers conduct their own valuation analyses. These include answers to *Frequently Asked Questions* and a section containing *Tips and Advice for Using the Corporate Valuation Model.*
7. **Instructor's Resources.** In addition to the previously described features that are available to all students, the book's web site has additional resources available only for instructors, including solutions to all end-of-chapter spreadsheet projects.

Acknowledgments

We are grateful to our colleagues and students at the University of Tennessee who have given us many useful suggestions. The South-Western and DPS Associates staffs—especially Mike Reynolds, Elizabeth Thomson, Kara ZumBahlen, Vicky True, John Barans, Mark Sears, Charlie Stutesman, and Crystal Bullen—helped greatly with all phases of text development, production, and marketing.

We especially want to thank our families, who have supported us during the many, many hours we have worked on this project.

Conclusion

Corporate valuation, with its importance to investment analysts and corporate managers, plays a vital role in promoting well-functioning financial markets and economically healthy business firms. Because it is so important, corporate valuation should be thoroughly understood by all investors and managers. However, this is easier said than done, because the topic is relatively complex and requires specialized skills and knowledge. We sincerely hope that *Corporate Valuation: A Guide for Managers and Investors* will help readers understand and conduct their own valuation analyses.

Phillip R. Daves
The University of Tennessee
PDaves@utk.edu

Michael C. Ehrhardt
The Paul and Beverly Castagna Professor of Investment
The University of Tennessee
Ehrhardt@utk.edu

Ronald E. Shrieves
William Voigt Professor of Business and Finance
University of Tennessee
RShrieve@utk.edu

August 2003

PART 1

Basic Concepts of Corporate Valuation

Chapter 1

Why Corporate Valuation?

Introduction

You make financial decisions every day. If you're an individual investor, you make daily decisions to buy, sell, or hold stock. If you're a senior executive, you make critical strategic choices. If you're a manager, you make and implement operating decisions. If you are on the financial staff, you regularly evaluate potential acquisitions and divestitures. In each case, the success or failure of your decisions depends on whether you correctly identify, measure, and evaluate a firm's underlying sources of value. In a nutshell, your success depends on understanding corporate valuation.

Despite its obvious importance to individual investors and corporate managers, corporate valuation was until recently an arcane science, limited to a select few at investment banks and brokerage firms. If you're old enough to remember the movie *Wall Street* or the book *Barbarians at the Gate*, then you probably remember investment banker analysts portrayed as quantitative whizzes running sophisticated computer programs that sifted through mountains of data to determine an offer price. Stock analysts employed by brokerage firms used the same complex set of analytic methods to produce their buy and sell recommendations. Whether conducted by financial analysts or investment bankers, valuation analysis required long years of training in quantitative methods, sophisticated computer technology, and access to large, proprietary databases. These requirements formed an insurmountable barrier to ordinary investors and corporate managers, preventing them from performing their own analyses.

But we have good news for you. Almost all individual investors, executives, and managers now have desktop computers or laptops with more power than the mainframe supercomputers of a decade ago. Powerful but easy-to-use spreadsheet software is standard on these computers, and financial data and information are now just a click away on the Internet. Many web sites are free, but because you bought this book, you have access to Thomson ONE-Business School Edition. This combination of hardware, software, and data levels the playing field and makes it possible for you to conduct an in-depth corporate valuation. If you are an individual investor, you can now do your own valuations, identifying the upside potential and downside risk of your investments. You can also evaluate the management teams behind your stocks, and vote with your feet if performance is not what it should be.

If you are a manager, you can now easily use the same analytic tools that Wall Street uses. You can quickly analyze all of your decisions with the same attention that was once reserved only for high-profile mergers and acquisitions. Not only will corporate valuation tools help you improve your decisions and increase the value of your firm, but your own wealth may also increase, if you are among the many managers today who are compensated with stock options or bonuses that mirror stock performance.

Whether you are an analyst, an individual investor, or a corporate manager, don't get too excited just yet! Acquiring the skills explained in this book will take a bit of serious effort on your part. But don't get discouraged, either, because we have made this as easy as possible for you by presenting the concepts and tools in a step-by-step approach with lots of examples.

Our Goals

Corporate valuation techniques have progressed at a rapid pace over the last three decades. Within the last few years, the financial community has reinvented investment valuation, creating new analytical measurements such as free cash flow, return on invested capital, and economic value added. Of course, there is vigorous competition among investment bankers and various consulting groups, each promoting its own trademarked variation of valuation analysis, and each claiming to offer the best approach.

Our objective in writing this book is to provide investors and managers with the basic knowledge necessary to value an entire company or a division of a company using a model that is nonproprietary, understandable, and, most importantly, easily implemented by any financial manager or investor.[1] To accomplish this, we focus on the free cash flow (FCF) valuation framework and implement it in Microsoft® Excel. No model is useful without accurate data for inputs, so throughout our discussion we incorporate references to easily accessible online data sources, particularly Thomson ONE-Business School Edition. Our examples demonstrate how these sources can be used to identify a company's underlying sources of value, determine its "leverage points," and estimate its fundamental value.

The model we develop can be used in a variety of ways. Investors can use it for identifying undervalued stocks and those with the most growth potential. They can also use it to critically assess the quality of any professional investment advice they receive. Managers can use this model to make better business decisions for their companies, performing useful "what if" analyses of alternative decisions. And by applying it to their customers or suppliers, managers can also use it to gain insight into the companies with which they negotiate.

In summary, our goals are to explain the concepts underlying corporate valuation and to develop a comprehensive spreadsheet-based valuation model that you can use for investment analysis and financial decision-making. We'll begin slowly, explaining the concepts and the spreadsheet applications one step at a time. With this approach, you'll understand how the model is designed, programmed, and implemented from the ground up. This comprehensive model, combined with a knowledgeable user, is a powerful tool and will enable you to make better investment and business decisions.

[1]As we stated in the Preface, the same valuation principles apply to all companies, even financial institutions and start-up companies. However, the application is more complicated, and so we focus on nonfinancial companies that have matured beyond the start-up stage.

Our Approach: One Step at a Time

One of the most difficult things about learning finance is that you need to know finance in order to learn finance. In other words, studying finance involves what may be called "circular" learning. There are two reasons why this is true. First, it is very difficult to actually apply financial analysis to a specific problem, such as valuation, if you don't already know how to perform financial analyses on other problems. For example, analyzing a firm's decision about how much debt to use in financing its assets requires that you know something about securities markets and how investors value corporate bonds (usually covered in investments courses). On the other hand, understanding how investors value a firm's bonds requires that you understand something about how its bond ratings are determined, which, in turn, depend on the firm's financing decision (usually covered in finance courses).

This circularity is both good news and bad news. It's good news, because mastering financial analysis for one type of problem really moves you up the learning curve when it comes to solving other types of problems. But it's bad news in the sense that you really need some breadth in your knowledge of finance in order to solve any problem in finance.

The second cause of circularity in learning finance is that a proper financial analysis of a particular problem, such as valuation, requires considerable attention to detail. This means you must have in-depth knowledge and skills. But it is really tough to develop the in-depth knowledge needed to address the details of a problem if you don't already know the basic outline for solving that type of problem. Don't get discouraged: By the time you finish this book, you will have the breadth and depth to conduct a proper valuation of a company. But you will build your knowledge the same way an artist paints a picture. First, she sketches the entire painting in a rough outline. Then she begins filling in the painting with broad strokes, without spending time on details. Finally, she zooms in on particular parts of the painting, such as the subject's eyes, and finishes them in meticulous detail.[2]

This is exactly the way you will learn how to conduct a valuation analysis. You will start with a very rough, but complete, outline of the process and apply it in Chapter 2 to MPR, Inc., the simplest company imaginable. In Chapters 3 and 4 you will learn and apply some more advanced skills to a slightly more complicated company, ACME General Corporation. In Chapters 5 through 8 you will learn even more advanced skills, and apply those skills to the valuation of an even more complicated company, Van Leer, Inc. By the time you complete this iterative process, you'll be able handle the complexities of valuing an actual company, Home Depot, in Chapters 9 through 13.

Before starting Chapter 2, let's take a few minutes to survey some broad valuation issues and to identify three specific areas in which you will develop investment expertise: discounted cash flow techniques, accounting skills, and technology skills.

Discounted Cash Flow Techniques

When investors decide to buy a firm's stock, they do so in anticipation of eventually recovering their investment, plus a premium to compensate for investment risk and

[2]Unless, of course, she is an abstract artist, in which case she just throws a couple of buckets of paint on the canvas and calls it quits!

to reward them for investing rather than consuming. The "calculus" of investment decisions, therefore, involves evaluating the trade-off between dollars spent or invested today and future income that is expected to result from investing. For evaluating this "time value" trade-off, virtually all modern valuation techniques rely on the **discounted cash flow (DCF)** method. In its simplest form, the discounted cash flow method simply makes use of the observation that a dollar to be received today is worth more than a dollar to be received at some time in the future. In other words, the **present value** of a dollar in the future is less than a dollar. The **discount rate** is the interest rate, r, which penalizes the dollar to be received in the future. For example, if the discount rate is 9%, the present value of $1 to be received in one year is

$$\text{Present value} = \$1/(1 + r) = \$1/(1 + 0.09) = \$0.917.$$

So in this example, a dollar to be received in one year is worth only about 91.7 cents today if the discount rate is 9%. (The idea, of course, is that if you had 91.7 cents today, and if you could invest it at 9%, then it would grow to $1.00 in one year.)

The rigorous treatment of DCF dates back almost four thousand years to the Babylonians.[3] While first used as a tool for analyzing compound interest problems, modern business has broadened the application of DCF techniques to capital budgeting and security valuation, including valuing initial public offerings, sale of a closely-held firm or a division of a publicly-held firm, mergers, and acquisitions.

These techniques also play a major role in evaluating managerial performance using the concept of residual income, also known as **Economic Value Added (EVA™)**.[4] It is important to be able to measure reliably a manager's performance, because if you pay managers more when they perform well and less when they perform worse, then you might expect them to improve their performance. But how do you tell whether a manager is doing a good job? Traditional measures such as quarterly earnings per share are badly flawed because they are subject to manipulation, as recently illustrated by Enron and WorldCom. Even worse, quarterly earnings may not be highly correlated with actions that increase the value of a company, and poorly conceived compensation plans may incentivize managers to make decisions that harm the company. However, EVA, whose calculation is based on the technique of **free cash flow valuation**, solves many of the measurement problems and is now commonly used in corporate compensation packages. This fact alone has vastly increased corporate interest in understanding the sources of value creation and destruction and in the analytical tools that investors use to assess value.

These applications, however, have also raised a number of practical concerns about applying DCF methods. Chiefly, is the financial information that DCF techniques use readily available, and is this information reliable? One of our objectives is to show how publicly available financial information can be used intelligently to value a business and, at the same time, point out the potential pitfalls in standard accounting data. Indeed, much of our discussion deals with how to adjust accounting information so it is useful for financial management and can be used to implement free cash flow valuation.

---

[3]See Parker, R. H., "Discounted Cash Flow in Historical Perspective," *Journal of Accounting Research*, Spring 1968, 58–71.

[4]See Stewart, G. Bennett III, *The Quest for Value* (New York: HarperBusiness, 1991).

Accounting Skills

We are not accountants, and it is not our objective to make you into an accountant. However, the fundamental resource available to analysts, whether inside or outside the firm being valued, is the historical financial information contained in the firm's accounting statements. We use this information as one of the most important inputs to the valuation model we develop, and you must understand how the accounting statements work in order to use them in valuation. Therefore, we'll cover the most important basic accounting principles in this book, starting with very simple hypothetical firms and working our way up to the complexities of actual firms.

Publicly listed firms are required under the provisions of the Securities Act of 1933 and the Securities Exchange Act of 1934 to make much of their accounting information available to potential investors in the form of numerous "filings." The best known and generally most useful filing is the annual report, filed with the Securities and Exchange Commission and affectionately known as the "10-K." As a reader of this book, you have access to Thomson ONE-Business School Edition, which provides 10-K statements in an easy-to-use format. We'll show you how to use it in Chapter 9.

Technology Skills

In today's world, analysts have faster and cheaper access to greater quantities of information than ever before, and you need the skills to locate, access, and process the available information. In particular, you need the capability to find and download information to a personal computer and then to process that information efficiently. Throughout this book we will show you how to access useful Internet resources, such as Thomson ONE-Business School Edition, EDGAR (via the Securities and Exchange Commission), Zack's, Disclosure, Yahoo!, Lexis-Nexis, the Federal Reserve Bank, and others. You don't have to be a spreadsheet guru to use the software that accompanies this book, but we'll help you to develop your spreadsheet skills as we develop the corporate valuation model.

Preview of What's Ahead

As an investor, you are confronted with the problem of selecting from among thousands of individual assets, ranging from certificates of deposit and Treasury securities at one end of the spectrum to exotic financial derivatives at the other end. Somewhere in between these extremes lies the basic challenge of valuing the equity of a privately or publicly-held firm, or valuing a division of a firm. We will provide you a set of tools to meet this challenge.

A proper corporate valuation requires considerable attention to detail, and in-depth knowledge and skills. But as we noted earlier, it is really tough to develop the in-depth knowledge needed to address the details of a problem if you don't already know the basics for solving that type of problem. A similar circular problem is present when learning a foreign language. To communicate in a foreign language you need to know vocabulary, but you have to use the words in actual speaking or reading before they make sense to you. So in learning a foreign language, you first speak and read simple sentences in order to build up your vocabulary. Similarly, in order to do corporate valuation, you have to know the language of finance. But to understand the language of finance, you have to use it in a financial analysis. Therefore, we'll teach you corporate valuation by developing simple, but complete, financial models that illustrate the concepts, and then we'll add more detail to make them more applicable to everyday situations.

Let's get started!

Summary

Recent improvements in computer hardware, software, and data accessibility now make it possible for managers and investors to conduct in-depth corporate valuations. Managers can now analyze all their decisions with techniques once reserved only for high-profile mergers and acquisitions, resulting in better decisions that increase their firms' values. Individual investors can now perform their own valuations, identifying the upside potential and downside risk of stock investments.They can also evaluate the performance of the management teams running those companies.

As you progress through the book, you will learn basic accounting and financial concepts, plus you will develop the computer skills necessary to apply these concepts. Cash flows form the foundation for corporate valuation, and we will show you how to forecast and evaluate cash flows.

Chapter 2 A Complete Corporate Valuation for a Simple Company

Introduction

As we said in Chapter 1, you will build your expertise in valuation analysis one step at a time, starting with an analysis of the simplest company imaginable. Although the company is simple, the analysis will be comprehensive in the sense that it covers all the issues that you will apply to much more complicated situations in later chapters. But first, let's be clear about what we mean when we use the term "value." There are three kinds of values that may be used in various ways by investors or analysts. First, **book value** is a company's historical value as shown on its financial statements. Second, **market value** is the current price at which an asset may be bought or sold. Third, **intrinsic value** is the estimate of value that a particular buyer places on an asset.

What makes life interesting, of course, is that estimates of intrinsic value differ among investors, and for any particular investor, intrinsic value may differ rather substantially from market value. Our main concern in this book is to provide a sound structure for estimating intrinsic value for shares of a company's common stock. In using this structure, however, you must understand the general principles and techniques of valuation, including their application to other types of assets, such as corporate bonds or bank loans. Because the techniques require a basic knowledge of the state of the economy, the nature of the industry in which a firm operates, and the current financial conditions of the firm, they are often referred to as "fundamental" valuation techniques, and the resulting estimate of intrinsic value that results may be referred to as the **fundamental value**.

Warren Buffett is perhaps the most respected investor in the world, and he takes a **fundamental valuation** approach. This means that he estimates the fundamental value of a company, compares it with the company's market value, and then buys stock in the company (or sometimes he buys the *entire* company!) if the fundamental value is greater than the market value. The key to his success is his ability to correctly determine a company's fundamental value. We cannot turn you into the next Warren Buffett (since we, unfortunately, are not the next Warren Buffett ourselves), but we can teach you the techniques for estimating a company's fundamental value, starting with the basic concepts of valuation.

The Basic Concepts of Valuation

Let's start with the three most basic concepts in valuation. First, investors can only spend cash, and more cash is better than less cash. Second, cash today is more valuable than cash in the future. Third, a risky potential cash flow is less valuable than a certain cash flow. Therefore, the value of a company depends upon the size, timing, and risk of its expected future cash flows. In a nutshell, here is all there is to valuing a company: Estimate the size and timing of its future cash flows, and then determine how much those future cash flows are worth today, after adjusting for risk.

Like the portrait painter, we have just completed our initial sketch. Now it's time to begin putting in color. Keep in mind that we are only using broad brushstrokes now; we'll get to the fine details later in this book.

Valuing a Very Simple Company

Let's start with a very simple company, Mayberry Personal Receivers, Inc., a company that manufactures Internet capable pagers. Before plunging into accounting, we'll take a look at MPR's investors.

Investors

Most companies must spend money to make money, and MPR is no exception. For example, it must build a factory and buy raw materials before it ever receives a single dollar from sales. MPR gets the money for these expenditures from two types of investors, debtholders and stockholders.

Debtholders and the Value of Debt

Because debt is usually easier to value than equity, we'll start with a debtholder who owns a bond. Later we'll fill in more details, but a bond is simply an IOU issued by the company. MPR printed bond certificates and sold them to investors, called debtholders. The investors got the bonds, and MPR got the cash.

Why would an investor want a bond? Well, a bond issued by MPR promises to pay its owner $90 per year for 10 years; this bond will also pay $1,000 at the end of the tenth year. Because the payments end in 10 years, this bond has a 10-year maturity. The $90 is called a **coupon payment**, and the $1,000 is called the **face value**, or the maturity value. Since $90/$1,000 = 9%, we say that this bond pays a 9% **coupon rate**. Why would MPR promise 9% interest to investors? The answer is competition. MPR has to compete in a financial marketplace where many firms (and the federal government) are simultaneously trying to attract funds. If potential MPR debtholders could earn 9% on other securities of equivalent risk, then MPR will have to offer at least 9% to attract investors to its bonds. Therefore, the **required rate of return** by MPR's debtholders, which is called r_D, is 9%.[1]

[1] We say "required rate of return" to express the rate that an investor feels is commensurate with the risk of the investment. If they don't have an expectation of earning that rate going in, they don't invest. Of course, the rate that is actually earned when the investment is liquidated will generally be higher or lower than the required rate (otherwise, where's the risk?). But, on average, the investor expects to earn at least this required rate of return.

How much is the bond worth to the debtholder? Like any investment, the value of the bond depends on the size, timing, and risk of its cash flows. In particular, the value of this bond is the present value of its cash flows, when discounted at r_D, the rate that reflects the risk of the bond.[2] As we show in Appendix 2, the value of the bond is $1,000. In other words, an investor would be willing to pay $1,000 for this bond, after taking into account the size, timing, and risk of the bond's cash flows. (As we discuss in the appendix, the value of a bond is not necessarily equal to its maturity value.)

From the corporate perspective, because purchasers of MPR bonds require a 9% return on their investment, it *costs* MPR 9% to raise capital by issuing bonds. We say that the cost of debt financing for MPR is 9%, at least before we consider the fact that interest is a tax-deductible expense. We'll deal with the tax issue later in this chapter.

Stockholders and the Value of Stock

What about the other type of investor, the stockholders? MPR printed shares of stock and sold them to investors, called stockholders or shareholders. We'll fill in the details later, but the stockholders are the owners of the firm. The value of being an owner depends upon the value of the asset that is owned, minus the value of any debt. For example, you might own a house worth $200,000. But if you owe the bank $150,000, the value of your ownership, called home equity, is only $200,000 – $150,000 = $50,000.

The same reasoning applies to companies. For example, suppose MPR is worth a total of about $501 million, but owes the debtholders $150 million. The remaining value of the company, about $501 – $150 = $351 million, belongs to the stockholders and is called **stockholders' market value of equity**. Think of it this way: The total value of all the future cash flows that the company will provide is $501 million, but the portion of future cash going to creditors is worth $150 million, so the remaining portion of future cash flows must be worth $351 million. This leaves us with one way to find the value of equity: If we know the total value of the company and the value of the debt, then the value of the equity is the total value of the company less the value of the debt. Another way to value equity is to estimate directly the cash flows equity holders receive, and then find the value of these cash flows, as we did with debt. We'll address both of these techniques below and compare them.

Let's start off by estimating directly the cash flows that equity holders receive and then finding their value. Stockholders often receive a cash payment from the company called a **dividend**. For example, MPR's most recent dividend, D_0, was $2.34 per share. Unlike a bond, the stock has no maturity date. In other words, the dividends will continue to be paid as long as the company exists. Also, unlike the interest payments on a bond, the dividend payments are not fixed. In fact, for most firms the dividends can be expected to grow. Let's suppose MPR's investors expect its dividends to grow at a rate of 5% per year. Finally, because the stockholders get paid only after the bondholders are paid, stock is riskier than debt. MPR's stockholders

[2]We're assuming that you already know a little about the time value of money; that is, you know how to find the present value of a dollar that will be received in the future. If this is completely new to you, then you should read the chapter on time value of money in a finance book. Our recommendation, perhaps not surprisingly, is *Financial Management: Theory and Practice*, written by E. Brigham and M. Ehrhardt, available at your college's bookstore or Amazon.com.

require a return of 12% to compensate them for the higher risk of MPR's stock. This **required return on equity** (or stock) is called r_S. We'll explain in a later chapter how to estimate r_S, the return that stockholders require, but for now simply notice that $r_S = 12\%$, which is greater than $r_D = 9\%$ for MPR, consistent with the fact that MPR's stockholders bear more financial risk than its bondholders.

Other than these three differences (no maturity date, a dividend that grows over time, and greater risk), we can apply the same approach to valuing the stock as we apply to valuing debt: the value of the stock is the present value of all its cash flows, which are the growing dividend payments. In MPR's case, the dividends are $2.34 per share, and are expected to grow at 5%. If you want to see the calculations, look in the appendix. Otherwise, you can take our word that this present value is $35.10 per share. As with the case of MPR's debt financing, we say that the rate of return that equity investors require represents the cost to MPR of raising new equity capital.

If we can forecast the dividends of a company, then we can find the value of its stock. However, this dividend valuation approach may not be very helpful to a manager. For example, a manager would like to know how improving her company's profitability or reducing the amount of inventory would affect the value of its stock. Also, how can we find the value of a company that doesn't pay dividends? Or what about the value of a division within a company? Fortunately, we have another way to find the value of a company. It is called the **corporate valuation model**.[3]

The Corporate Valuation Model

To find the value of a corporation, we will use the same approach as for debt and equity. But instead of finding the present value of the cash flows that a particular class of investor expects (such as bond payments to debtholders or dividends to stockholders), we will find the present value of the cash flows that are available for distribution to *all* of the company's investors. And instead of discounting them at the rate of return required by a particular class of investors (such as r_D for debtholders or r_S for stockholders), we will discount them at the average rate of return required by *all* investors, which represents the average cost of each dollar of financing for MPR's assets.

We call the cash flows that are available for distribution to all investors **free cash flows (FCF)**, and we call the average rate of return required by all investors the **weighted average cost of capital (WACC)**. In the next sections we'll explain how to calculate the WACC and FCF for MPR.

The Weighted Average Cost of Capital

For our simple company, MPR, there were only two types of investors, debtholders and stockholders. We know that MPR's debtholders require a return of 9% and that its stockholders require a return of 12%. So from the perspective of MPR, these are costs; that is, MPR's cost of debt is 9% and its cost of equity is 12%. Therefore, its weighted average cost of capital, WACC, is an average of its cost of debt and its cost

[3]Sometimes this is called the **entity valuation model**, since it finds the value for the entire entity (i.e., the whole corporation) instead of the value of the individual investments (i.e., debt or equity).

of equity. Because we already know MPR's costs of debt and equity, there are only two issues we need to resolve: taxes and targets.

First, how do taxes affect MPR's cost of debt? Even though MPR's bondholders require a return of 9%, after we consider the impact of corporate income taxes, it does not cost MPR 9% to provide that return. This is because MPR can deduct interest expenses from its taxable income. In other words, for every dollar of interest it pays, MPR reduces its tax payments by the amount of tax it would have paid on that dollar. Suppose MPR has a total federal, state, and local tax rate of about 40%. If MPR pays a dollar of interest, it saves 40 cents of taxes. Thus, MPR's total cost of providing a dollar of interest to a bondholder is just 60 cents, or just 60% of its interest payments. We can write the after-tax cost of debt as $r_D(1 - T)$, where T is the tax rate. For MPR, this is 9%(1 – 0.4) = 5.4%; it costs MPR 5.4% to provide a 9% return to its debtholders. In contrast, companies may not deduct dividend payments from taxable income, so we don't need to adjust the cost of equity for taxes. In other words, it costs MPR 12% to provide a 12% return to its shareholders.

The second issue faced in estimating the average cost of capital involves the mixture of debt and equity. Since we are going to use this cost of capital to discount a series of future cash flows, the relevant mixture of debt and equity capital is the mixture that is expected to prevail in the future. This is the company's **target capital structure**. In other words, when a company raises debt and equity in the foreseeable future, what percentage will be debt (called w_D) and what percentage will be stock (called w_S)? These percentages, or weights, define the target capital structure and allow us to calculate the weighted average cost of capital using the following formula.

$$\text{WACC} = (1 - T)r_D w_D + r_S w_S \qquad \textbf{(2-1)}$$

MPR's target percentages are 30% debt and 70% stock. Using MPR's target capital structure and its costs of debt and equity, its weighted average cost of capital is

$$\text{WACC} = (1 - T)r_D w_D + r_S w_S = (1 - 0.4)(9\%)(0.3) + 12\%(0.7) = 10.02\%. \qquad \textbf{(2-1a)}$$

This 10.02% is the average after-tax cost of all of MPR's capital.

Calculating Free Cash Flows

Recall that free cash flow (FCF) is the amount of cash available for distribution to all of the firm's investors. In calculating FCF, we begin with the firm's operations, which include the activities associated with factories, equipment, workers, sales force, and managers—basically, all the activities the firm needs to make and sell its products. These operations generate a profit. Unfortunately, some of the profit goes to the IRS in the form of taxes. We call what is left **net operating profit after taxes**, or **NOPAT**.

However, not all NOPAT can be distributed to investors, because the company must invest in new capital such as factories, machines, and raw materials if it is to support its growth in sales. We call this an **investment in operating capital** because this capital is used to support the firm's operations. If we subtract this investment in capital from NOPAT, we get free cash flow. In other words, this is the amount of cash available for distribution to investors, *after* taking into account the investments needed to support the firm's growing operations.

We have put it off as long as possible, but now we must do some accounting before we can calculate free cash flows. Let's take a look at MPR's financial statements.

An Overview of Financial Statements

We cannot make you into an expert accountant unless you already are one. The good news is that you do not need to be an expert in accounting to calculate the value of a company, but you do need to know a few of the basics. We'll cover the basics in this chapter and add more details later as you need them. Let's start with a quick look at some simple financial statements.

The Balance Sheet

Exhibit 2-1 is a simple balance sheet for MPR, covering three years of operations. The balance sheet shows the types and amounts of **assets** the firm has purchased, as well as a summary of its funding sources. These sources are classified either as **liabilities** or **owners' equity**. In other words, it is a snapshot on a specific date of what the company owns, how much it owes, and how much the stockholders have invested in it since it was founded.

All of MPR's assets are directly related to the company's basic operations. For example, companies buy raw materials and process them in factories using machines. The raw materials and the machines are all examples of **operating assets**.[4]

Accountants divide assets into two major categories, current assets and long-term assets. Current assets are expected to be sold or "converted" to cash within one year. Obviously, this includes cash, but it also includes accounts receivable and inventory.[5] To keep the calculations simple, we have lumped all of MPR's short-term assets into a category called **operating current assets**.

MPR also has some long-term assets, which are its investments in **property, plant, and equipment (PPE)**. To keep the calculations simple, we are only showing net PPE, which is the amount of PPE remaining after depreciation. We'll explain this in more detail in Chapter 3, but for now you can think of net PPE as the amount of remaining PPE, given the wear and tear since it was purchased. For MPR, total assets are just the sum of current assets and net PPE.[6] Notice that MPR is growing and added \$18.858 million (\$18.858 = \$396.900 – \$378.042) in assets during 2003.

Accountants divide liabilities into short-term liabilities and long-term liabilities. Like current assets, current liabilities must be paid off (i.e., "converted") within one year. Some of these liabilities are directly related to the firm's operations. For example, most companies buy some of their raw materials on credit—they do not have to pay their suppliers as soon as they take delivery of the goods. The amount they owe on these credit purchases is called accounts payable. To keep our calculations simple, we have lumped all of MPR's operating current liabilities into a single account.

---

[4]Some companies have assets that are not related to operations. We explain these nonoperating assets in Chapter 5.

[5]When a company extends credit to a customer, the customer takes possession of the product but doesn't pay the company immediately. Instead, the customer promises to pay the company. This promise is called an account receivable. Chapter 3 provides a more detailed explanation of current assets.

[6]We explain more complex balance sheets, such as those with ownership interests in other companies, in Chapter 10 and its appendix.

Exhibit 2-1 MPR's Balance Sheet (thousands of dollars, as of December 31)

Assets	2001	2002	2003
Operating current assets	$162,000.0	$168,000.0	$176,400.0
Total current assets	$162,000.0	$168,000.0	$176,400.0
Net PPE	199,000.0	210,042.0	220,500.0
Total assets	$361,000.0	$378,042.0	$396,900.0
Liabilities and Shareholders' Equity			
Operating current liabilities	$ 57,911.5	$ 62,999.7	$ 66,150.0
Total current liabilities	$ 57,911.5	$ 62,999.7	$ 66,150.0
Long-term debt	136,253.0	143,061.0	150,223.0
Total liabilities	$194,164.5	$206,060.7	$216,373.0
Total common equity	166,835.5	171,981.3	180,527.0
Total liabilities and equity	$361,000.0	$378,042.0	$396,900.0

Long-term debt is the total principal amount of outstanding debt that is not due during the upcoming year. In MPR's case, the $150.223 million long-term debt shown for 2003 is an issue of 150,223 bonds that MPR issued in various years, each of which carries a $1,000 principal payment obligation. Notice that debt is reported at its book value, which may differ from its current market value.

The final section, total common equity, summarizes the amount that shareholders have invested in the firm over the years. Some of this is a direct investment, made when MPR sold stock to the shareholders. Some of it is an indirect investment from the shareholders, which happens every time MPR reinvests some of its profits instead of giving the profits to its shareholders. To keep our calculations simple, we are only going to show total common equity, which is the total of the direct and indirect investments made by shareholders. This figure is a book value, which represents the cumulative amount that shareholders have invested in the firm, and it may be quite different from the current market value of equity.

The Income Statement

Exhibit 2-2 shows the income statements for MPR. Unlike the balance sheet, which is a snapshot of the firm's assets and liabilities as of the last day of the year, the income statement summarizes the results of the firm's income generating activities during the year. The income statement starts with sales; as shown in Exhibit 2-2, MPR had $441 million in sales during 2003.

Naturally, MPR had costs, including direct costs such as the labor and materials that went into producing the product that it sold, and overhead costs such as salaries of managers. We'll break costs into more categories later, but for now let's keep it simple and consider only one category. The total of these costs for MPR was $374.8816 million in 2003.

Exhibit 2-2 MPR's Income Statement (thousands of dollars for year ending December 31)

	2001	2002	2003
Sales	$400,000.0	$420,000.0	$441,000.0
Costs	344,000.0	361,994.2	374,881.6
Operating profit	$ 56,000.0	$ 58,005.8	$ 66,118.4
Interest expense	11,678.9	12,262.8	12,875.5
Earnings before taxes	$ 44,321.1	$ 45,743.0	$ 53,242.9
Taxes	17,728.4	18,297.2	21,297.2
Net income	$ 26,592.7	$ 27,445.8	$ 31,945.7
Dividends	$ 21,200.0	$ 22,300.0	$ 23,400.0

The difference between sales and costs is **operating profit,** because it is directly related to MPR's operations. Nonoperating expenses, such as the $12.8755 million in interest MPR paid on its debt, are then deducted from operating income to arrive at **earnings before taxes (EBT)**. For MPR, EBT was $53.2429 million in 2003. Of course, there is still the little matter of income taxes. At a combined federal, state, and local tax rate of 40%, MPR reported taxes of $21.2972 million. After subtracting taxes, MPR had a net income of $31.9457 million. Out of this amount, MPR paid $23.4 million in dividends and used the remainder ($31.9457 – $23.4000 = $8.5457 million) to purchase some of the $18.858 million in new assets that it added in 2003. In total, MPR used $8.5457 million of its reinvested net income, $7.162 million in new debt ($7.162 = $150.223 – $143.061), and $3.1503 million in new current liabilities ($3.1503 = $66.15 – $62.9997) to fund the $18.858 in new assets.

Calculating Free Cash Flows

Now that you understand the basics of financial statements, you are ready to calculate free cash flow. First calculate the net operating profit after taxes (NOPAT), and then calculate the amount of operating capital. Finally, deduct the year-to-year investment in operating capital from NOPAT to calculate free cash flow.

Calculating NOPAT

If two otherwise identical companies have different amounts of debt, then they will have identical operating performance but different net incomes, because they will have different interest payments. This demonstrates that net income does not always accurately reflect a company's true operating performance or the effectiveness of its managers and employees. A better measure is the net operating profit after taxes, or NOPAT. In a nutshell, NOPAT is the amount of net income that a company would generate if it had no debt. We can define NOPAT as

$$\text{NOPAT} = \text{Operating profit}(1 - \text{Tax rate}). \quad \textbf{(2-2)}$$

Using data from the income statement of Exhibit 2-2, the 2003 NOPAT for MPR was

$$\text{NOPAT} = \$66.1184(1 - 0.4) = \$39.67104 \text{ million.} \quad \textbf{(2-2a)}$$

Calculating Operating Capital

Total operating capital, sometimes just called **operating capital** or even just **capital**, is the amount of assets required to support a company's operations, less the liabilities that arise from those operations. Operating capital consists of two components, short-term and long-term. The short-term component is called **net operating working capital (NOWC)**. Net operating working capital is defined as

$$\text{NOWC} = \text{Operating current assets} - \text{Operating current liabilities.} \quad \textbf{(2-3)}$$

The operating current assets are the short-term assets that a company needs to support its operations. For example, all companies must carry some cash balance to grease the wheels of their operations. Companies continuously cash checks from their customers and write checks to their suppliers, employees, and others. They also face contingencies such as equipment failures that require cash reserves. Because they cannot predict perfectly when these checks will clear the bank, they must maintain a certain balance of cash with the bank. In other words, a certain amount of cash is required if companies are to conduct their operations. Inventory and accounts receivable are also a part of normal operations. For a simple company like MPR, operating current assets are equal to the sum of cash, inventory, and accounts receivable. As noted earlier, we have lumped them into one category, operating current assets, on the balance sheet in Exhibit 2-1.

Some current liabilities, such as accounts payable, are also a normal part of operations. Each dollar's worth of these operating current liabilities is a dollar that the company doesn't have to fund itself. Therefore, when finding the amount of net operating working capital, we subtract these operating current liabilities from the operating current assets.

Using the balance sheets of Exhibit 2-1, MPR's net operating working capital for 2003 was

$$\begin{aligned}\text{NOWC} &= \text{Operating current assets} - \text{Operating current liabilities} \quad \textbf{(2-3a)}\\ &= \$176.40 - \$66.15 = \$110.25 \text{ million.}\end{aligned}$$

The long-term operating capital for a simple company like MPR is just the amount of net plant, property, and equipment (PPE). The total operating capital is

$$\text{Total operating capital} = (\text{Net operating working capital}) + (\text{Net PPE}). \quad \textbf{(2-4)}$$

For MPR, the total operating capital is

$$\begin{aligned}\text{Total operating capital} &= (\text{Net operating working capital}) + (\text{Net PPE}) \quad \textbf{(2-4a)}\\ &= \$110.25 + \$220.50\\ &= \$330.75 \text{ million.}\end{aligned}$$

What do these calculations tell us? In 2003, MPR had tied up $330.75 million in capital that it needed to support its operations. In other words, investors had supplied

$330.75 million, which MPR used to purchase things like buildings, equipment, and inventory. Because this cash is tied up, it is not available for distribution to investors.

Because MPR already had some investments in total operating capital at the beginning of 2003, it did not have to purchase the entire $330.75 million worth of operating capital during 2003. How much did it have to spend in 2003 to end up with $330.75 million? First, let's see how much total operating capital MPR had at the beginning of 2003, which is the same as the end of 2002.

MPR had $168 million in operating current assets and $62.9997 million in operating current liabilities in 2002, for NOWC of $105.0003 million ($168 – $62.9997 = $105.0003). With its $210.042 million of net PPE in 2002, MPR had total operating capital of $315.0423 million ($105.0003 + $210.042 = $315.0423). Since MPR started the year with $315.0423 million and ended the year with $330.75 million, it must have made a net investment in operating capital of $15.7077 million in 2003 ($330.75 – $315.0423 = $15.7077).

Free Cash Flow

At long last, we can calculate free cash flow (FCF). We have just seen that MPR generated $39.67104 million in NOPAT in 2003. But MPR also spent $15.7077 million to purchase net operating capital during the year. Therefore, its free cash flow, which is the amount available for distribution to investors, is the difference between NOPAT and the net investment in total operating capital.

$$\begin{aligned} \text{FCF} &= \text{NOPAT} - \text{Net investment in total operating capital} \\ &= \text{NOPAT} - (\text{Total operating capital for this year} \\ &\qquad - \text{Total operating capital for last year}) \end{aligned} \tag{2-5}$$

For MPR, the free cash flow for 2003 is

$$\begin{aligned} \text{FCF} &= \text{NOPAT} - \text{Net investment in total operating capital} \\ &= \$39.67104 - (\$330.75 - \$315.0423) \\ &= \$39.67104 - \$15.7077 \\ &= \$23.96334 \text{ million.} \end{aligned} \tag{2-5a}$$

In other words, MPR generated FCF of $23.96334 million in 2003, which was available for distribution to its investors. But just being *available* for distribution to investors does not mean that this amount of cash was actually distributed. What did MPR actually do with its free cash flow?

Recall that FCF is the amount of cash that is available for distribution to all investors, including shareholders and debtholders. There are five ways for a company to use FCF:

1. Pay interest expenses to debtholders; keep in mind that the net cost to the company is the after-tax interest expense.
2. Repay debtholders; that is, pay off some of the debt.
3. Pay dividends to shareholders.
4. Repurchase stock from shareholders.
5. Buy marketable securities or make other investments in nonoperating assets. Recall that the company does not have to use FCF to purchase operating assets

because FCF already takes into account the company's purchase of operating assets needed to support its growth.

In practice, most companies combine the five uses of FCF in such way that the total is equal to FCF. The appendix shows how MPR spent its FCF. In fact, MPR paid \$7.7253 million in after-tax interest payments to its bondholders and \$23.4 million in dividends to its common stockholders. Since this total of \$31.1253 million exceeds the free cash flow, it is natural to ask how MPR managed to make the payments to investors. The answer is that MPR's payments to bondholders were negative since it borrowed the additional \$7.162 million!

Exhibit 2-3 provides a summary of the calculations for FCF.

Corporate Valuation

The next step is to forecast MPR's future financial statements, and then use them to calculate projected FCF.[7] We'll cover all the details of projecting financial statements later in the book, but for now let's just assume that all the items on the financial statements will grow at a constant rate of 5%. For MPR, this means that its FCF will also grow at a constant rate of 5%. Exhibit 2-4 gives the expected FCF for MPR for the next several years, assuming that the 5% growth is maintained. For example, in 2004, FCF = \$23,963.34(1.05) = \$25,161.5 thousand.

The value of a company's operations, V_{op}, is the present value of all its expected future free cash flows, discounted at the company's weighted average cost of capital.[8]

---

[7]These projected financial statements are sometimes called **pro forma statements**.

[8]The expression $\sum_{t=1}^{\infty} \frac{FCF_t}{(1+WACC)^t}$ means to take the sum of $\frac{FCF_t}{(1+WACC)^t}$ for t starting at 1 and continuing forever:

$$\frac{FCF_1}{(1+WACC)^1} + \frac{FCF_2}{(1+WACC)^2} + \frac{FCF_3}{(1+WACC)^3} + \cdots$$

Exhibit 2-3 Calculating Free Cash Flow (thousands of dollars)

	2001	2002	2003
NOPAT	\$ 33,600.00	\$ 34,803.48	\$ 39,671.04
Operating CA	\$162,000.00	\$168,000.00	\$176,400.00
Operating CL	\$ 57,911.50	\$ 62,999.70	\$ 66,150.00
NOWC	\$104,088.50	\$105,000.30	\$110,250.00
Net PPE	\$199,000.00	\$210,042.00	\$220,500.00
Total net operating capital	\$303,088.50	\$315,042.30	\$330,750.00
Investment in capital		\$ 11,953.80	\$ 15,707.70
FCF		\$ 22,849.68	\$ 23,963.34

Exhibit 2-4 Projecting Free Cash Flow (thousands of dollars)

	2004	2005	2006	2007	2008
FCF	$25,161.5	$26,419.6	$27,740.6	$29,127.6	$30,584.0

$$V_{op} = \sum_{t=1}^{\infty} \frac{FCF_t}{(1 + WACC)^t} \quad \textbf{(2-6)}$$

Of course, you have probably noticed that this equation isn't particularly helpful. The pattern shown in Exhibit 2-4 continues *ad infinitum,* and so we have to find the present value of an infinite number of cash flows. But keep in mind that the free cash flows in this example are expected to grow at a constant growth rate of g. A very useful short-cut formula that can be used for calculating the present value of such a constant growth infinite stream of cash flows is

$$V_{op} = \sum_{t=1}^{\infty} \frac{FCF_t}{(1 + WACC)^t} = \frac{FCF_1}{WACC - g} = \frac{FCF_0(1 + g)}{WACC - g}. \quad \textbf{(2-7)}$$

Even though this formula does not explicitly include all the future free cash flows, it does in fact equal the present value of all the future free cash flows. This formula, called the **constant growth model**, provides a nice, simple way to find the present value of all the future growing free cash flows. Also, even though the formula uses the current free cash flow, FCF_0, to help us estimate the next free cash flow, the value of operations depends only upon the future cash flows, which are linked to FCF_0 through the growth rate assumption.

Substituting the most recent FCF, the expected growth rate, and the WACC for MPR gives us its value of operations.

$$V_{op} = \frac{FCF_0(1 + g)}{WACC - g} = \frac{\$23.96334(1 + 0.05)}{0.1002 - 0.05} = \$501.225 \text{ million} \quad \textbf{(2-7a)}$$

V_{op} ignores future cash flows from any nonoperating assets that the firm might own, such as stocks or bonds in other companies, other short-term investments, or perhaps land held for speculative purposes. In general, the value of such assets must be added in when determining the total value of the enterprise.

$$\text{Total value} = \text{Value of operations} + \text{Value of nonoperating assets} \quad \textbf{(2-8)}$$

MPR has no nonoperating assets, so its total value is the same as its value of operations, $501.225 million. To find the value of its equity, we subtract any obligations that MPR has to investors other than stockholders.

$$\text{Value of equity} = \text{Total value} - \text{Value of obligations to non-equity investors} \quad \textbf{(2-9)}$$

For MPR, the only obligation to other investors is the $150.223 million that it owes to its debtholders. It is true that MPR has obligations to those who provided the operating current liabilities, such as the suppliers who sold to MPR on credit.

But we already accounted for these obligations when we deducted the change in operating capital from NOPAT.[9] Therefore, the value of MPR's equity is

$$\text{Value of equity} = \$501.225 - \$150.223 = \$351.002 \approx \$351 \text{ million.} \quad \textbf{(2-9a)}$$

Finally, we can divide the value of equity by the number of shares of stock to get the value of a single share of stock, V_S.

$$V_S = \text{Value of equity}/\#\text{ shares of stock} \quad \textbf{(2-10)}$$

MPR has 10 million shares of stock. Therefore, the value of a share of MPR's stock is

$$V_S = \$351/10 = \$35.10. \quad \textbf{(2-10a)}$$

Exhibit 2-5 provides a summary of these calculations. If you look in the appendix, you will see that $35.10 is exactly the same price as calculated by discounting the expected future dividends at the rate of return expected by shareholders. Even though the discounted dividend model (shown in the chapter appendix) results in the same value as the corporate valuation model, we prefer the corporate valuation model because: (1) it can be used to find the value of companies that do not pay dividends; (2) it can be used to find the value of privately held companies or divisions of publicly traded companies; and (3) managers and investors can learn a lot about a company in the process of building a corporate valuation model.

Congratulations! You have now covered every issue in corporate valuation, albeit for a very simple company:

- Estimation of the WACC;
- Preparation of financial forecasts;
- Calculation of FCF;
- Application of discounted cash flow methods to value FCF; and
- Determination of per share value of stock.

You now have a complete framework for corporate valuation, and the rest of the book will fill in the details so that you can use this framework for valuing actual companies.

Corporate Performance: The Return on Invested Capital

The same data that we used to find the value of MPR can also be used to evaluate its performance. The **return on invested capital (ROIC)** is defined as a year's net operating profit divided by the amount of capital that the company had in place at

[9]Think of it in the following way. The change in NOWC represents an investment of cash resources in current assets, net of the amounts borrowed in the form of current liabilities, that will be needed to carry on the business in the coming year. We develop this concept in more depth in the next chapter.

Exhibit 2-5 Application of the Corporate Valuation Model (millions of dollars, except per share data)

	2003
FCF	$23.96334
Value of operations	$ 501.225
Plus the value of nonoperating assets	0.000
= Total value of the corporation	$ 501.225
Minus value of debt	150.223
= Value of equity	$ 351.002
Divided by number of shares	10
= Price per share	$ 35.10

the beginning of the year. In other words, how much did the company earn on the capital it had? ROIC is defined as

$$ROIC_t = \frac{NOPAT_t}{Capital_{t-1}}. \quad \textbf{(2-11)}$$

MPR's 2003 ROIC is

$$ROIC_{2003} = \frac{NOPAT_{2003}}{Capital_{2002}} = \frac{\$39.67104 \text{ million}}{\$315.0423 \text{ million}} = 0.125923 = 12.6\%. \quad \textbf{(2-11a)}$$

Is a 12.6% return good or bad? It all depends upon the return that investors require. MPR has a WACC of 10.02%, so its investors require a return of 10.02%. Therefore, MPR's actual return of 12.6% is better than the investors' required return.

Another key measure of operating performance is **Economic Value Added (EVA™)**. Although the concepts underlying EVA have been around for decades, the specific calculations were first defined by the consulting firm Stern Stewart and Co. Since its calculations are proprietary, we will use the generic version, **economic profit (EP)**. The basic idea is to find the amount of profit a company generates above and beyond the profit that its investors require. Recall that NOPAT is the operating profit that the company generates. WACC is the rate of return that investors require and operating capital is the amount of capital that investors have tied up in the company. So the amount of profit investors require is equal to the WACC multiplied by the capital that the investors have tied up at the beginning of the year. Therefore, economic profit is

$$EP_t = NOPAT_t - WACC(Capital_{t-1}). \quad \textbf{(2-12)}$$

MPR's economic profit is

$$\begin{aligned} EP_{2003} &= \$39.67104 - 0.1002(\$315.0423) \\ &= \$39.67104 - \$31.56724 \\ &= \$8.1038 \text{ million.} \end{aligned}$$

This shows that MPR's investors required an operating profit of \$31.56724 million, but MPR actually generated an operating profit of \$39.67104 million. In other words, MPR had superior performance by generating \$8.1038 million more than its investors required.

We can also calculate economic profit this way:

$$\begin{aligned} EP_t &= (\text{ROIC} - \text{WACC})\text{Capital}_{t-1} \\ &= (0.125923 - 0.1002)\$315.0423 \\ &= \$8.1038 \text{ million.} \end{aligned} \quad \textbf{(2-13)}$$

The difference between the return on invested capital and the WACC is called the **spread**. This provides a quick and dirty way to evaluate a company's performance. If the spread is positive, then the company is generating value above and beyond its investor's requirements. If the spread is negative, then the company is destroying value, in the sense that its investors would be better off investing elsewhere.

Applications of the Corporate Valuation Model

Let's look at three typical uses for the corporate valuation model: (1) analysis of mergers and acquisitions, (2) value-based management, and (3) fundamental investing.

Mergers and Acquisitions

Suppose another firm were interested in acquiring MPR. The acquiring firm believes that with its existing sales force it could bump up the sales (and FCF) growth rate from the current value of 5% to 6%. What is the most the acquiring firm should pay for MPR?

To answer this question, we can go back to the fundamental valuation Equation 2-7 and replace the old 5% growth rate with 6%.

$$V_{op} = \frac{FCF_0(1+g)}{WACC - g} = \frac{\$23.96334(1+0.06)}{0.1002 - 0.06} = \$631.869 \text{ million} \quad \textbf{(2-7b)}$$

Since MPR already owes about \$150.233 million in debt, the raider would be willing to pay \$631.869 – \$150.223 = \$481.646 million for MPR's stock. This works out to be \$481.646/10 = \$48.16 per share. Thus, if the raider could acquire MPR's stock for less than \$48.16 per share and successfully implement its growth plans, then the raider could reap a significant reward.

Now suppose that MPR is considering selling one of its divisions. MPR could calculate the FCF, growth rate, and WACC for the division and then use the fundamental valuation equation to determine the value of the division. If another company is willing to pay more than this amount, then MPR should strongly consider selling the division.

As these examples illustrate, the corporate valuation model plays a key role in the analysis of mergers, acquisitions, and divestitures.

Value-Based Management

Managers should make decisions that increase the value of their companies, and firms that operate with this as a stated objective are said to employ **value-based management**. The corporate valuation model is an important tool in value-based management because it can help managers evaluate strategic alternatives. For example, suppose MPR's managers could invest $5 million in new information technology that would reduce costs and decrease inventory so that next year's projected free cash flow (ignoring the $5 million investment) would be $26 million rather than 23.96334(1.05) = $25.1615 million without the investment. The expected growth rate in FCF would remain at 5%. The fundamental valuation equation shows the impact on value.

$$V_{op} = \frac{FCF_1}{WACC - g} = \frac{\$26}{0.1002 - 0.05} = \$518 \text{ million} \quad \text{(2-7c)}$$

Since this increase in value ($518 – $501 = $17 million) is greater than the $5 million cost of the system, MPR's managers should implement the project. As this example shows, the corporate valuation model is a valuable tool for firms that use value-based management.[10]

Fundamental Investing

In fundamental investing, the analyst or investor tries to identify firms that are worth more than their current stock price; Warren Buffet is perhaps the most famous investor to employ this style of investing. It's easy to identify the current stock price (market value) of a company, but how can you determine its fundamental (intrinsic) value? This is where the corporate valuation model comes in. For example, the model gives a fundamental value of $35.10 per share for MPR. If the current market price were only $25, then a fundamental investor would strongly consider purchasing stock in MPR.

Summary

Starting with an analysis of the simplest company imaginable, MPR, this chapter provided a framework for estimating a stock's intrinsic value and took you through all the basic steps in a valuation analysis. We emphasized the three most basic concepts in valuation. First, investors value cash flow instead of accounting profit. Second, cash today is more valuable than cash in the future. Third, a risky potential cash flow is less valuable than a certain cash flow. In a nutshell, valuation requires that you estimate the size and timing of future cash flows, and then determine how much those future cash flows are worth today after adjusting for risk.

Companies have two major types of investors; debtholders and stockholders. The rate of return required to satisfy these investors is called the weighted average cost of capital (WACC). The cash flows available for distribution to all investors are called free cash flows (FCF). We illustrated the free cash flow calculation using the

[10] Readers with some finance background will recognize that the $12 million difference between the value improvement and the cost of the project is called the project's net present value.

financial statements for our hypothetical firm MPR. Free cash flow is defined as net operating profit after tax (NOPAT) minus the investment in new operating working capital (NOWC) and net property plant and equipment (net PPE).

The value of operations is the present value of the expected future free cash flows, discounted at the weighted average cost of capital. Adding the value of nonoperating assets gives the total value of the firm. Subtracting the claims held by debtholders gives the value of equity. The intrinsic stock price is the value of equity divided by the numbers of shares outstanding.

Our objectives were to introduce vocabulary, define a framework for valuation, and illustrate a comprehensive valuation analysis. Subsequent chapters will take these basic concepts and apply them to successively more complicated companies, ending with an analysis of an actual company.

Spreadsheet Problems

2-1 Mayberry Personal Receivers

The *Original* worksheet in the spreadsheet, ***Prob 02-01.xls*** shows data for Mayberry Personal Receivers (MPR) as described in this chapter, including the financial statements, calculations of free cash flow, and calculations of stock price per share.

Now suppose instead that in 2002 MPR had been able to make improvements in its supply chain. In particular, MPR was able to modify its processes in such a way that improved quality, shortened cycle time, shortened delivery time, reduced inventories, and reduced the amount of net plant, property, and equipment (PPE) needed to support sales. The result was an increase in its sales growth rate from 5% to 6% (which is expected to be maintained indefinitely), a reduction in its ratio of costs/sales, a reduction in its ratio of inventory/sales, and a reduction in its ratio of net PPE/sales. The financial statements for this improved situation are shown in the *Improved Template* worksheet in the file ***Prob 02-01.xls***. These statements assume that MPR kept the same debt levels it would have had in its original situation.

Using the data for the improved situation, answer the following questions.

a. What impact did the changes have on NOPAT in 2002? In 2003?

b. What impact did the changes have on net operating working capital in 2002? In 2003?

c. What impact did the changes have on total operating capital in 2002? In 2003?

d. What impact did the changes have on free cash flow in 2002? In 2003? What happened to disbursements to shareholders (i.e., dividend payments) in 2002? In 2003?

e. What is the value of operations at 2003 in the improved scenario? How does this compare with the value of operations in the original scenario?

f. What is the stock price at 2003 in the improved scenario? How does this compare with the original scenario?

g. What are the return on invested capital and economic profit for 2003 in the improved scenario? How do these compare with the original scenario?

2-2 Maggie Mountain Software

The file ***Prob 02-02.xls*** shows financial statements for Maggie Mountain Software. Answer the following questions.

a. What is the FCF for 2003?
b. If the expected growth rate in FCF is 6% and the WACC is 9%, what is the stock's intrinsic share value?

Appendix 2

Comparing Bond and Stock Valuation Models with the Corporate Valuation Model

Perhaps some of you are already familiar with other valuation techniques such as bond valuation or stock valuation using discounted dividends. In this appendix we show that these techniques give the same value for a firm as does the corporate valuation model. We start with the basics of bond pricing.

Bond Pricing

As stated in the chapter, the MPR bond has a 9% coupon rate and a 10-year maturity; MPR's debtholders expect a 9% return for a security that has the same risk as MPR's bonds. The value of this bond, V_B, is the present value of its cash flows, when discounted at a rate that reflects the risk of the bond. If we let M stand for the maturity value, n stand for the number of payments, r_c denote the coupon rate, and r_D denote the rate of return that a debtholder expects for an investment of this risk, then the value of a bond is[1]

$$V_B = \sum_{t=1}^{n} \frac{r_c M}{(1 + r_D)^t} + \frac{M}{(1 + r_D)^n}. \quad \textbf{(2A-1)}$$

For the bond issued by MPR, the value is

$$\begin{aligned} V_B &= \sum_{t=1}^{10} \frac{\$90}{(1 + 0.09)^t} + \frac{\$1{,}000}{(1 + 0.09)^{10}} \\ &= \$577.59 + \$422.41 = \$1{,}000.00. \end{aligned} \quad \textbf{(2A-2)}$$

The value of the bond is $1,000. In other words, an investor would be willing to pay $1,000 for this bond, after taking into account the size, timing, and risk of the bond's cash flows. Notice that if MPR had offered the bonds with a 10% coupon rate, the size of the interest payments would be $100 per year, but if the risk

[1]The expression $\sum_{t=1}^{n} \frac{r_c M}{(1 + r_D)^t}$ means to take the sum of $\frac{r_c M}{(1 + r_D)^t}$ for t starting at 1 and ending at n. If n is 10, then this becomes $\frac{r_c M}{(1 + r_D)^1} + \frac{r_c M}{(1 + r_D)^2} + \frac{r_c M}{(1 + r_D)^3} + \dots \frac{r_c M}{(1 + r_D)^{10}}$.

remained unchanged, so that investors still require a 9% return, the value of the bond would be $1,064.18.

$$V_B = \sum_{t=1}^{10} \frac{\$100}{(1+0.09)^t} + \frac{\$1{,}000}{(1+0.09)^{10}} = \$1{,}064.18 \quad \textbf{(2A-3)}$$

If the cash flows remained at the original level, but the risk of the bond increased due to adverse developments in the electronics or communications industry, then the return required by debtholders would increase. Suppose r_D increased to, say, 11%. Then the value of the bond would fall to $882.22.

$$V_B = \sum_{t=1}^{10} \frac{\$90}{(1+0.11)^t} + \frac{\$1{,}000}{(1+0.11)^{10}} = \$882.22 \quad \textbf{(2A-4)}$$

The total cash received by the bondholder is $1,900 (the sum of the ten payments of $90 and the final payment of $1,000). Suppose the bond contract was originally written so that MPR did not make any annual payments, but paid the entire $1,900 at Year 10. If the risk is the same as the original scenario (r_D = 9%), what is the value of the bond?

$$V_B = \sum_{t=1}^{10} \frac{\$0}{(1+0.09)^t} + \frac{\$1{,}900}{(1+0.09)^{10}} = \$802.58 \quad \textbf{(2A-5)}$$

Notice that the value of the bond is less than its value when the coupon payments are spread out over time. Even though the total cash flow of the bonds has not changed, most of the cash flow occurs later, and this makes the bond less valuable.

As these examples show, the size, timing, and risk of the cash flows determine the value of the investment.

The Discounted Dividend Model of Stock Pricing

As stated in the chapter, MPR paid a $2.34 dividend per share, and it is expected to grow at a constant rate of 5%. (This is reasonable, given the assumption that sales, earnings, and free cash flow will all grow at 5%.) MPR's stockholders expect a return of 12% to compensate them for the risk of its stock. The value of the stock, V_S, is the present value of all its cash flows. If we let D_t stand for the dividend we expect to be paid at time t, and r_S denote the appropriate rate to discount those dividends, the value of a share of stock is

$$V_S = \sum_{t=1}^{\infty} \frac{D_t}{(1+r_S)^t}. \quad \textbf{(2A-6)}$$

Because the dividends in this example are expected to grow at a constant growth rate of g, we can use a short-cut version of Equation 2A-6 called the constant growth formula.

$$V_S = \frac{D_1}{r_S - g} = \frac{D_0(1+g)}{r_S - g} \quad \textbf{(2A-7)}$$

This model is similar to the constant growth model we used in the chapter to find the value of operations. But instead of discounting FCF (the cash flows available to all investors) at the WACC (the return expected by all investors), we discount the cash flows going to shareholders (dividends) at the return expected by shareholders.

For MPR, the expected growth rate is 5% and the most recent dividend was \$2.34 per share. MPR's stockholders require a return of 12%. Using Equation 2A-7, a share of stock in MPR is worth

$$V_S = \frac{D_0(1+g)}{r_S - g} = \frac{\$2.34(1+0.05)}{0.12-0.05} = \$35.10. \qquad \textbf{(2A-7a)}$$

Notice that this is exactly the same price per share that we calculated in the chapter using the corporate valuation model.

The Uses of Free Cash Flow

The source of a company's free cash flow is its operations, and the uses are various distributions to investors. Let's see how MPR used its free cash flow in 2003. First, MPR paid an after-tax interest expense of \$12.8755(1 – 0.4) = \$7.7253 million. Second, MPR issued new debt of \$7.162 million, because its balance sheets show that debt increased from \$143.061 million in 2002 to \$150.223 million in 2003. Third, MPR paid dividends of \$23.4 million. MPR did not issue any new stock, and MPR didn't invest in any nonoperating assets.

We can summarize the total uses of FCF (the signs of the cash flows reflect the perspective of the investors):

$$\begin{aligned} \text{FCF} = {} & \text{After-tax interest payments} + \text{Old debt paid off} \\ & - \text{New debt issued} + \text{Dividends paid} \\ & + \text{Old stock repurchased} - \text{New stock issued} \\ & + \text{Purchase of nonoperating financial assets} \\ & - \text{Sales of nonoperating financial assets.} \end{aligned} \qquad \textbf{(2A-8)}$$

For MPR, the uses of the FCF in 2003 were paying interest, paying dividends, and issuing new debt:

$$\begin{aligned} \text{FCF} &= \text{After-tax interest payments} - \text{New debt issued} \\ &\quad + \text{Dividends paid} \\ &= \$12.8755(1-0.4) - \$7.162 + \$23.4 \\ &= \$23.9633 \text{ million.} \end{aligned} \qquad \textbf{(2A-8a)}$$

Notice that the value of FCF calculated by adding up its uses (i.e., using Equation 2A-8) is the same value as the FCF calculated from operations (i.e., using Equation 2-5 in the text.). In other words, to calculate free cash flow we could use either the operating approach (as we did in the chapter) or the financing approach (as we did in the appendix). Because our focus as managers or investors is usually upon how proposed or announced changes in corporate strategy will affect the operations of a company, we generally estimate FCF using the operating approach of Equation 2-5 in the chapter. In addition, the operating approach is the only approach that is feasible when calculating the FCF of a division.

PART 2

Intermediate Concepts of Corporate Valuation

Chapter 3

Financial Statements and Free Cash Flow

Introduction

One of the golden rules of finance is "Cash is king;" another is "Timing is everything." You might say these are the guiding principles of free cash flow valuation. Cash is king for the simple reason that an investment usually costs money up front, and investors won't pay out money up front without an expectation of getting back their initial investment, plus a premium reflecting the risk and duration of their investment.

In the last chapter you saw the simplified financial statements for Mayberry Personal Receivers (MPR) and estimated its value. This chapter will cover financial statements in a bit more depth for a different (but still hypothetical) firm, and we will again calculate the free cash flows that are available for distribution to the firm's investors. We don't intend to make you into accounting experts, but you need this increased detail to reach the ultimate goal of evaluating actual companies.

As "outsiders," the most comprehensive information most stockholders can get about a company's financial condition is from the information filed under the U.S. securities acts of 1933–1934. U.S. securities law requires, among other things, that firms subject to the law file periodic statements of financial results with the Securities and Exchange Commission (SEC). Since 1993, these filings have been in electronic format. They are available free of charge from the SEC's Electronic Data Gathering, Analysis, and Retrieval system, better known as EDGAR (**http://www.sec.gov/edgarhp.htm**). There are a number of filings that firms are required to submit, but we will be most interested in the 10-K and 10-Q filings, which are the annual and quarterly financial reports.

A firm's annual report has four parts, which summarize its financial condition: (1) balance sheet, (2) income statement, (3) statement of cash flow, and (4) statement of shareholders' equity. Footnotes to these statements provide additional information.

Unlike footnotes found in many books (and especially in academic journals), the footnotes accompanying a financial report are not superfluous![1] They often contain

[1] Of course, all of our footnotes are very important, including this one.

information that has significant bearing on the value of a company because accountants sometimes bury important information there.[2] The four parts of financial statements and the footnotes provide the (hopefully objective) information by which we track the financial condition and performance of a company, and all contain information important for corporate valuation.

For many "outsiders," these financial statements are the only source of financial information on the company. Because companies must follow the same rules when publishing their financial statements, they are consistent from company to company. This is good news for outsiders because understanding the accounting rules for one company usually means that you understand the rules for another company. It is good news for this textbook, too, because when we develop useful adjustments to the accounting statements for one company, the adjustments make sense for other companies as well. "Insiders" who perform internal valuation analyses will also find much that is useful in the firm's financial statements. The financial statements represent an objective historical record of the corporate business experience and, as such, can provide an important source of data for internal benchmarking (e.g., the likely profit margin for a new product) that may be used in assessing the likely performance of new projects and new strategies. Such benchmarks are indispensable in predicting the results of proposed new strategies or operating policies. Therefore, insiders also need to know basic accounting principles and their firm's specific internal accounting procedures.

In this chapter, we discuss accounting principles in the context of corporate valuation. We extend Chapter 2's coverage of rudimentary accounting, so that you can begin to read financial statements and understand how to use them. After discussing the four components of the annual report, we use them to help estimate the value of the firm's stock using the free cash flow framework. As you will see, we make intensive use of the firm's financial statements, but our focus on cash flow is different from that of accountants. We think (hope!) you will find that our focus makes accounting much more intuitive, and much more useful to you.

What Is Cash Flow, Anyway?

Most valuations are carried out using information from a firm's financial accounting records, which are prepared under **Generally Accepted Accounting Principles (GAAP)**. Statements prepared in this way are reasonably consistent from firm to firm, due to the fairly strict accounting rules that govern the financial reporting process. These rules are a double-edged sword for the financial analyst, though. The traditional accounting measures like net income, earnings per share, net change in cash, and return on equity are not adequate for valuation purposes. The accountants' rules were designed more to show where a company has been, rather than

[2]For example, Enron Corporation's March 31, 2001, 10-Q quarterly filing had the following information in footnote 16. "In 2000 and 1999, Enron entered into transactions with limited partnerships (the Related Party) whose general partner's managing member is a senior officer of Enron. The limited partners of the Related Party are unrelated to Enron. Management believes that the terms of the transactions with the Related Party were reasonable compared to those which could have been negotiated with unrelated third parties." These "reasonable," but otherwise unreported, terms contributed to the largest bankruptcy in history.

where it is going, and to show how much profit the firm has earned in each period, rather than how much cash flow has resulted from its operations. Valuation, on the other hand, is forward looking in nature, and we have to modify the firm's accounting statements to focus on cash flow in order to be able to use them.

When Do You Record It? A "Cruel" Rule

The biggest problem with GAAP accounting statements from the perspective of cash flow valuation is that some of the items recorded as income don't have corresponding cash inflows, and some of the items recorded as expenses don't require any actual payments. And to make it more complicated, sometimes actual cash expenses incurred cannot be reported as expenses, and actual cash inflows cannot be reported as income. You can see why this might lead to confusion if what we really care about is cash and all we have are accounting statements! This is because most companies prepare financial statements on what is known as the **accrual basis**. ("Accrual" = "a cruel"—get it? Well, what do you expect from accounting humor?) Accrual, in turn, relies on the recognition and matching principles. Entire courses and degrees are devoted to the ins and outs of accrual accounting, but in short, the basic premise is that revenue and most costs should be recognized when the sale of the good or service occurs, rather than when the cash is received or when expenses are paid. Most firms implement this standard by using the date of shipment of the product to the customer as the point of recognition. The **matching principle** holds that, irrespective of when cash payments for costs of producing goods are actually made, the costs cannot be incorporated as expenses into income until the goods are sold and shipped. For example, a firm that produces computers may not include the cost of the units still in inventory as expenses for that year. Hence, for a firm that has accumulated significant inventory in a given year, cost of goods sold reported on the income statement may be much less than actual cash production costs for that year. And since we care more about cash flow than we do about accounting profit, we must take this into account in our valuation analyses.

A few industries and firms use other bases for recognizing revenue. For example, in the construction business, the percentage-of-completion method might be used to report income prior to completion of a long-term project. Some other recognition methods are completed contract, installment, cost recovery, and proportional performance. Although the vast majority of firms base recognition on sale/shipment of the product to the customer, the analyst must be aware of the recognition method employed in the industry or firm being analyzed and make adjustments accordingly.

In using accounting information to construct cash flow, we will incorporate a number of "corrections" to accounting income and/or assets. Most of these adjust for GAAP's recognition and matching principles. In addition, firms have some discretion over how they account for certain transactions, such as last-in-first-out (LIFO) versus first-in-first-out (FIFO) inventory accounting. These choices affect accounting income and/or cash flow and also require adjustments to make consistent comparisons between firms. We will consider only the most basic adjustments now, and defer the more complex or infrequently encountered adjustments to later chapters.

The Balance Sheet

Exhibit 3-1 illustrates the basic format of the balance sheet (sometimes referred to as a "position statement") for ACME General Corporation. The balance sheet provides investors with a cumulative statement of the types and amounts of assets in which the firm has invested since its inception, as well as a summary of the sources of invested capital, which are classified either as liabilities or owners' equity. Note that we have provided 3 years worth of data on ACME's position, which is useful for checking for the presence of obvious trends.

Assets

Assets are divided into two major categories, current assets and long-term assets. Current assets include cash or other assets expected to be sold or otherwise converted to cash within one year. For example, **accounts receivable (AR)** consists of money owed to ACME by those customers who purchased on credit terms. These accounts receivable will convert to cash as ACME's customers pay them. Inventory is raw materials, partially completed goods, or finished goods. It represents ACME's investment in the labor and materials required to bring its product to the stage

Exhibit 3-1 Balance Sheet for ACME General
(Year ending December 31, millions of dollars)

	2001	2002	2003
Assets			
Cash	$ 37.30	$ 41.40	$ 45.12
Inventory	522.14	579.58	631.74
Accounts receivable	932.40	1,034.96	1,128.11
Total current assets	$ 1,491.84	$ 1,655.94	$ 1,804.97
Gross PPE	2,619.28	3,031.40	3,443.32
Accumulated depreciation	754.48	961.47	1,187.09
Net PPE	$ 1,864.80	$ 2,069.93	$ 2,256.23
Total assets	$ 3,356.64	$ 3,725.87	$ 4,061.20
Liabilities and Shareholders' Equity			
Accounts payable	$ 372.96	$ 413.99	$ 451.24
Accrued expenses	186.48	206.99	225.62
Short-term debt	183.19	285.90	381.71
Total current liabilities	$ 742.63	$ 906.88	$ 1,058.57
Long-term debt	1,000.00	1,000.00	1,000.00
Total liabilities	$ 1,742.63	$ 1,906.88	$ 2,058.57
Common stock	500.00	600.00	600.00
Retained earnings	1,114.01	1,218.99	1,402.63
Total common equity	$ 1,614.01	$ 1,818.99	$ 2,002.63
Total liabilities and equity	$ 3,356.64	$ 3,725.87	$ 4,061.20

where it can be sold. Inventory is considered a current asset because it is expected to be sold within a year.

Long-term assets, which for ACME are its investments in property, plant, and equipment (PPE), are assets expected to be held by ACME for a period longer than one year. Gross PPE is the total of the original purchase prices for all long-term assets that ACME now owns. Some of those assets are depreciable, such as buildings and equipment.[3] Under the matching principle, the initial cost of these assets is not expensed in the year the asset is purchased. Instead, it will be counted as an expense against revenues over a number of years after their purchase. Each year during the predetermined "life" of these assets, a fraction of their purchase price will be charged as an expense against revenues during that year. This charge is called **depreciation**. The fraction is determined under guidelines that are part of GAAP. For example, suppose a machine was purchased on January 1, 2001, for $20 million, and we were going to use the method known as "straight-line" depreciation over a period of 10 years. The depreciation "expense" of $20/10 = $2 million per year would appear on ACME's income statement each year from 2001 through 2010. It's important for you to note that even though the $2 million per year is included as an expense, no cash is actually paid out after the original purchase! The company eventually gets to deduct from income the entire $20 million purchase price that was paid out in 2001, but it does so over a 10-year period rather than in the year the asset was purchased.

The cumulative depreciation charged against assets since their purchase is recorded in the accumulated depreciation account on the balance sheet, and this is deducted from gross PPE to get net book value of PPE or simply net PPE. For example, the machine purchased for $20 million in 2001 would have accumulated depreciation by year-end 2003 of $2 × 3 = $6 million, and a net book value of $20 − $6 = $14 million.[4]

For ACME, total assets equal the sum of current assets and net PPE. More complex balance sheets will involve other categories of assets, such as ownership interests in other companies. We discuss these other assets in Chapter 10.

One of the first points to keep in mind about balance sheets is that by-and-large the asset and liability amounts are recorded at historical cost, that is, they are not adjusted for any gains or losses in actual market value since the assets were purchased or the liabilities were incurred.[5] For example, suppose ACME's PPE investment of $20 million in 2001 is primarily in some type of machinery that has become technologically obsolete since it was purchased. The actual resale value of that equipment by year-end 2003 may be less than its recorded net book value of $14 million.[6] On

[3]Land may not be depreciated.

[4]**Depletion** and **amortization** are similar to depreciation, except that depletion is the allocation of the cost of natural resources, such as oil and timber; amortization is the allocation of the cost of intangible assets, such as patents and copyrights.

[5]Note the by-and-large qualification in this statement. There are exceptions to the historical cost rule, some of which we cover in subsequent chapters. Most exceptions follow the principle of conservatism and require recording the market value of an asset when it is lower than historical cost.

[6]Since 1995, firms are required under FASB 121 to report the lower of cost or market value on long-lived assets, but it is difficult to objectively determine market values for many assets, so it is doubtful that this requirement is adhered to faithfully.

the other hand, perhaps ACME owns land where its facilities are located, and this land may have appreciated substantially since it was purchased, in which case its market value may be substantially more than its historical, or book value. Given these reporting problems, the $4,061 million given in the balance sheet as a "value" for ACME's total assets as of year-end 2003 may either overstate or understate the market value of ACME's assets.

Liabilities

On the liabilities and owners' equity part of the balance sheet for ACME General, current liabilities total $1,059 million in 2003 and include accounts payable, accrued expenses, and short-term debt. Like current assets, ACME expects to convert these items within one year, which means paying them off. Accounts payable (AP) of $451 million represent the amounts that ACME owes to suppliers who have sold parts, materials, or services to ACME on credit terms. Accrued expenses (in ACME's case, $226 million), are amounts owed for expenses reported on the income statement, but not yet paid, such as labor, mortgage interest, or taxes. The reason the expenses haven't been paid is simply that the payment cycle for some expenses lags behind the period during which the expense is incurred. **Short-term debt** of $382 million is the amount of any loans payable within one year, including the principal portion of any long-term debt that is scheduled for repayment within the year.

Long-term debt represents the aggregate principal amount of long-term obligations to creditors such as banks, insurance companies, or other financial institutions, or the total principal owed to individual investors who bought bonds issued in a public offering. In ACME's case, the $1,000 million in 2003 debt is a bond issue that was sold to investors in a public offering. Details about the bond issue appear in the footnotes to the financial statements, as we describe in Chapter 4.

Probably the most complex portion of the balance sheet is the section relating to owners' equity, or stockholders' equity, as it is often called. This section reports the amount of capital that has been invested by the stockholders (also called the "owners") of ACME. For now, we need only consider a relatively simple breakdown of the equity account into two components: common stock and retained earnings. **Common stock** records the amount of capital that ACME has raised by selling its shares to stockholders. ACME has actually received $600 million from the sale of its shares at various times (most recently, a sale of $100 million in 2002).

Retained earnings are the cumulative amount, over ACME's existence, of net income earned but not distributed to shareholders as dividends. The net income that is not paid out as a dividend is reinvested in inventory, net PPE, and other assets. As of 2003, ACME has reinvested a cumulative $1,403 million.

The Income Statement

Unlike the balance sheet, which represents a cumulative account of a firm's position since it came into existence, the income statement summarizes the results of the firm's operating and nonoperating activities for a single calendar period, usually a year or a quarter. In the most basic terms, the income statement shows the various sources of revenue and the various expenses. The difference between revenue and all expenses is usually called **net income (NI)**, although it is sometimes called **earnings**.

Sales

Exhibit 3-2 contains the 2001–2003 income statements for ACME General Corporation. Remember that the income statement also reflects the twin principles of recognition and matching, so the **sales** figure reflects only products or services recognized as being sold in the current period, net of any items that were returned. ACME's income statement shows sales of $4,512 million in 2003.

Expenses

The expenses reported directly under the net sales entry are divided into two major categories. The first, totaling $2,798 million, is **cost of goods sold (COGS)**, which is the direct costs of producing the products or services reported as sold during the period. For example, labor and materials that went into the manufacture of the products that ACME sold would be included in COGS. The $902 million in **sales, general and administrative expenses (SGA)** are expenditures that are difficult or impossible to attribute to specific units of the product or services sold. Examples are marketing expenses, insurance, and salaries of senior executives. As we discussed earlier, the $226 million in depreciation charges does not reflect money that ACME actually had to pay out in 2003. Instead, it is the recognition as an expense of money that ACME paid for depreciable assets in 2003 and in earlier years.[7]

Operating profit is defined as sales minus COGS, SGA, and depreciation. Nonoperating expenses, such as the $106 million in interest expense, are then deducted from operating income to arrive at earnings before taxes (EBT), which for ACME in 2003 was $481 million. Of course, ACME must render unto Caesar what is due to Caesar and pay income taxes, which amounted to a whopping $192 million—maybe ACME should hire some of Enron's former accountants!

[7]Some income statements don't show a separate line for depreciation, but include it as a part of COGS. For those situations, you can find depreciation in the statement of cash flows, which we discuss in a later section.

Exhibit 3-2 Income Statement for ACME General (millions of dollars)

	2001	2002	2003
Sales	$ 3,729.60	$ 4,139.86	$ 4,512.44
Costs of goods sold	2,312.35	2,566.71	2,797.71
Sales, general and administrative	745.92	827.97	902.49
Depreciation	186.48	206.99	225.62
Operating profit	$ 484.85	$ 538.19	$ 586.62
Interest expense	88.05	96.49	105.73
Earnings before taxes	$ 396.80	$ 441.70	$ 480.89
Taxes	158.72	176.68	192.36
Net income	$ 238.08	$ 265.02	$ 288.53

The "bottom line" is that ACME reported earnings, or net income (NI), of $289 million in 2003. Although it is not shown on the income statement, ACME paid about $105 million in dividends to its common stockholders in 2003. As indicated earlier, the amount of net income that is left after dividends are paid is added to the retained earnings account on the balance sheet. As we shall see in the following section, this ties the balance sheet and income statement together.

The Statement of Shareholders' Equity

The retained earnings balance is an important linkage between the firm's income statement and its balance sheet. Retained earnings in each year equal the prior year's retained earnings, plus the current year's net income (net profit after tax) less any dividends paid to stockholders. ACME's retained earnings in 2002 were $1,219 million, and they were $1,403 million in 2003. The difference is $184 million, which means that ACME plowed $184 million of its 2003 profits back into the company.

This is shown on the statement of shareholders' equity. This statement reconciles the equity balance with the prior year's balance and the transactions or events that occurred during the year. Exhibit 3-3 shows that ACME earned net income, paid dividends, and issued stock (had ACME repurchased stock, it would have been shown here as well).[8]

The Statement of Cash Flows

When a company uses the accrual basis for accounting, the amounts shown on the income statement do not generally correspond to its cash receipts and expenditures. Sales do not necessarily reflect cash coming in, and expenses do not necessarily correspond to cash paid out. To reconcile the actual cash flows into and out of the firm during a given reporting period with the income statement and balance sheet, a number of adjustments have to be made, which are summarized in the statement of cash flows.

[8]More complicated transactions that might be encountered, such as comprehensive income and foreign exchange translation adjustments, are addressed in the appendix to Chapter 10.

Exhibit 3-3 ACME General Statement of Shareholders' Equity (millions of dollars)

	2002	2003
Balance as of December 31 of previous year	$1,614.01	$1,818.99
Net income	265.02	288.53
Dividends on common stock	(160.04)	(104.88)
Issuance of common stock	100.00	0.00
Common stock repurchases	0.00	0.00
Balance as of December 31	$1,818.99	$2,002.62

These adjustments fall into three broad categories—cash flow from operating activities, cash flow from investing activities, and cash flow from financing activities. Recall that the balance sheet reconciles assets and liabilities so that total assets always equal total liabilities and equity. The statement of cash flows, on the other hand, reconciles the sources and uses of cash so that they explain the change in the company's cash balance from the beginning of the period to the end of the period. Exhibit 3-4 shows ACME's statement of cash flows for 2002 and 2003.

Cash Flow from Operating Activities

The basic source of operating cash flow is net income. However, because most firms use accrual accounting, they usually have some costs reported in their income statements that do not have a corresponding cash outflow. As discussed earlier, this occurs when expenditures, although recorded this period, actually took place in a different time period. The most common example of such a cost is depreciation expense. The depreciation line in Exhibit 3-4 tells us that ACME's reported depreciation for 2003 was $226 million. Depreciation is an expense charged for capital goods that were purchased in prior periods, so the $226 million is not "out of pocket" during 2003 (although the entire purchase of a depreciable asset was certainly a cash outflow in

Exhibit 3-4 Statement of Cash Flows for ACME General (millions of dollars)

	2002	2003
Operating activities		
Net income	$ 265.02	$ 288.53
Depreciation	206.99	225.62
Change in inventory	(57.44)	(52.16)
Change in accounts receivable	(102.56)	(93.15)
Change in accounts payable	41.03	37.25
Change in accruals	20.51	18.63
Net cash from operating activities	$ 373.55	$ 424.72
Investing activities		
Investment in PPE	(412.12)	(411.92)
Net cash from investing activities	$(412.12)	$(411.92)
Financing activities		
Change in short-term debt	102.71	95.81
Change in long-term debt	0.00	0.00
Change in common stock	100.00	0.00
Common dividends	(160.04)	(104.89)
Net cash from financing activities	$ 42.67	$ (9.08)
Net change in cash	4.10	3.72
Starting cash	37.30	41.40
Ending cash	$ 41.40	$ 45.12

the year it was purchased). To correct for this "noncash expense," we must add depreciation back to net income. Unfortunately, there is a great deal of variability in how firms report depreciation. Some firms report a depreciation line item on their income statements, as does ACME. Other firms "bury" the depreciation expense in cost of goods sold and selling, general, and administrative expenses, and do not report a depreciation line item on the income statement. Still other firms report some of the depreciation charges on a depreciation line item on the income statement and bury the rest in COGS or SGA. The statement of cash flows contains all of the depreciation charges, so you must look there to determine the actual depreciation expenses, even if a depreciation expense line item is reported on the income statement. For ACME, the depreciation charge on the income statement is the same as the depreciation listed on the statement of cash flows.

Because most firms sell on credit, the reported sales figure does not necessarily correspond to the cash received. To adjust the revenue figure from an accrual basis to a cash basis, we must correct for the change in accounts receivable. ACME's balance sheet for 2002 in Exhibit 3-1 shows accounts receivable of $1,035 million. This means that as of the end of 2002, $1,035 million still needed to be collected. Another way to look at it is that in 2003, $1,035 million was collected in cash for sales made in 2002—these collections are *not* included in the sales for 2003. To put the 2003 sales on a cash basis, this $1,035 million would have to be added to net income for 2003.

However, the 2003 balance sheet shows accounts receivable of $1,128 million. These are sales that have been included in the reported sales figure, but for which cash has not been collected. The adjustment for these amounts to be collected is to deduct it from net income for 2003.

Here's a summary of the effect that credit sales have on the 2003 cash flow. First, you should add the 2002 accounts receivable of $1,035 million, because ACME collected it in 2003. Second, you should subtract the 2003 accounts receivable of $1,128 million, because ACME has not yet collected it. The combined effect of these two adjustments is a negative $93 million impact on cash flow.

This can be confusing, so here is how we keep it straight. Suppose you did not own a DVD player last year, but now you do. In other words, the amount of "stuff" you owned got "bigger." However, what happened to your cash when you purchased the DVD player? It went down. Similarly, suppose you owned a car last year, but you sold it and no longer own it. The amount of stuff you own got "smaller," but your cash went up. So our rule of thumb is this: if the amount of stuff you own gets bigger, then it is a negative cash flow (i.e., you had to "buy" it); if the amount of stuff you own gets smaller, it is a positive cash flow (i.e., you "sold" it).

Notice that accounts receivable is an asset, so it is something the company owns. Notice also that accounts receivable got bigger by $93 million during 2003. Using our rule, something the company owned got bigger, so that is a negative cash flow of $93 million.

The same type of argument applies to inventories. The cost of goods sold on the income statement usually does not reflect actual cash outlays for raw materials during 2003. In fact, COGS incorporates only the raw materials that were used in production *and* then sold. So it doesn't include the raw materials that were purchased but not yet used, nor does it reflect the new finished goods that were produced but not sold. The balance sheet in Exhibit 3-1 shows that ACME's inventory (the combination of raw materials, finished goods, and work in progress) increased from $580 million to $632 million, or by $52 million during 2003. Since the $52 million of added inventory did not contribute anything to ACME's revenue (because the inventory has not yet been sold), the matching principle prevents us from including the inventory production costs in the reported COGS for 2003. But you had to pay for producing them in 2003, even if you don't get to report the costs as an expense. So, putting production costs on a cash basis instead of an accrual basis requires adding the increase in inventory to COGS—or more simply, subtracting it from net income. To put it in the context of our "rules," inventory is something you own, and it increased by $52 million in 2003, which means it is a negative cash flow.

Liabilities are treated in the opposite way as assets. Here is how we remember whether a change in liabilities is a positive or negative cash flow. Suppose you borrowed $1,000 and signed a promissory note to repay the loan over the next three years. The note is a liability to you: it represents something you "owe." In this case, the amount you owe went up by $1,000, and so did your cash (at least until you spend the borrowed money). Or suppose you began the year owing $80,000 on your house, but finished the year owing $75,000. The amount you owe went down by $5,000, but you had to pay $5,000 to make it go down. Here is our rule: If the amount you owe gets bigger, then you have a positive cash flow; if the amount you owe gets smaller, you have a negative cash flow.

Consider ACME. In 2003, accounts payable increased from $414 million to $451 million, or by $37 million. ACME, like most other firms, takes advantage of trade credit from its suppliers, and this is reflected in the accounts payable balance. In 2003, $451 million was still owed to suppliers—even though some of this had been reported as an expense. Therefore, COGS overstates cash payments to suppliers by $451 million. The 2002 accounts payable balance of $414 million says that in 2003 ACME paid $414 million out in cash for expenses it recognized in 2002, so COGS in 2003 understates cash payments by $414 million. The net effect is that COGS is understated by $37 million, which is the increase in accounts payable, so this amount should be added to net income. In terms of our "rules," accounts payable increased by $37 million in 2003. Something ACME owed got larger, and so it reflects a positive cash flow.

The statement of cash flows in Exhibit 3-4 has only one additional item under the operating activities heading, change in accruals. This is something ACME "owes," and it increased from $207 million in 2002 to $226 million in 2003. Therefore, this is a positive cash flow of $19 million in 2003.

The sum of all of these adjustments represents the cash that is generated from the company's operations. It is called **net cash from operating activities**, or sometimes the **net cash flow from operations**. These adjustments can be summarized as

Net cash from operations (CFO) = net income
+ depreciation
− net change in current operating assets and liabilities (excluding cash).

In 2003, this was

$$CFO_{2003} = \$288.53 + \$225.63 - \$89.43 = \$424.72 \text{ million.}$$

Cash Flow from Investing Activities

Firms engage in a variety of other activities that are not operating activities but which affect their cash flows. Accountants categorize the purchase of equipment or other long-term assets as an investment, and the effects of such purchases appear under the section called "cash flow from investing activities." In ACME's case, the balance sheet shows that gross PPE increased from $3,031 million to $3,443 million, or by $412 million in 2003. This change in PPE appears on the statement of cash flows under the investing activities category, and since it is an increase in something ACME owns, it is a negative cash flow. If ACME had sold equipment, land, or other long-term assets, then something ACME owned would have decreased during 2003, and it would have been a positive cash flow.

Cash Flow from Financing Activities

The final section on the statement of cash flows shows the effects of ACME's financing activities. Issuing common stock, long-term debt and short-term debt are sources of cash (remember, this makes ACME owe more, which is a positive cash flow). ACME issued $100 million in common stock in 2002, but none in 2003. In 2002, ACME borrowed $103 million in short-term debt (as shown by the increase in the short-term debt account from $183 million in 2001 to $286 million in 2002). In 2003, ACME borrowed $96 million in short-term debt. ACME did not change its level of long-term debt in either 2002 or 2003. Paying dividends is another use of cash for ACME. In 2002, ACME used $160 million in cash to pay dividends, and it used $105 million in cash in 2003 for dividends.[9] The net cash flow from financing activities in 2003 is negative $9 million ($96 million in new debt minus $105 million in dividends).

Net Change in Cash

The total of the three categories (cash flow from operating activities, cash flow from investing activities, and cash flow from financing activities) is the net change in cash. During 2003 ACME generated $424.73 million from its operations. It spent $411.92 million of this on new equipment, leaving $12.81 million. After increasing short-term debt by $95.80 million and paying dividends of $104.89 million, ACME had a net use of $9.09 million from financing activities, leaving $3.72 million, which is its net change in cash. This $3.72 million plus the previous cash balance of $41.40 million gives the ending cash balance of $45.12. This is reflected in its cash account shown on the balance sheet. For 2003, ACME's cash balance is

Beginning cash balance	$41.40
Net change in cash	+ 3.72
Ending cash balance	$45.12.

[9]You may be wondering about ACME's volatile dividend payments. We'll have a lot more to say about dividends in Chapter 7 when we discuss financial policies.

ACME's Free Cash Flow

From an analyst's perspective, there are some deficiencies in the financial statements prepared under GAAP. Historically, investors and analysts have placed great emphasis on the "bottom line" (net income or earnings per share) reported in the income statement. But analysts today need a better indication of how investors are affected by the firm's financial performance, and net income doesn't always accurately depict this. The problem is that traditional measures of earnings do not adequately account for the reinvestment in the company that is required to sustain growth.

Rather than focusing on NI, the free cash flow approach asks: What cash flows are available for distribution to investors? This definition of free cash flow recognizes that net income diverges from cash available for distribution to investors for three reasons. The first reason, as discussed in prior sections, is due to the use of accrual-basis accounting. Reported net income does not accurately reflect the actual cash flows associate with operations.

The second reason is that, for a firm with debt, NI is a "contaminated" measure of operating performance since it includes interest payments as an expense. You can see how interest expense contaminates NI by considering two firms that are exactly the same—they have the same sales, the same markets, the same operating costs, the same technology, and the same assets, except one firm has chosen to use more debt to finance these assets, while the other firm has chosen to use more equity. The firm with more debt will report a lower net income, since it has more interest expense. But the two firms actually have the same ability to make pre-tax payments to all investors, including debtholders. It is just that the firm with more debt allocates more of the total payments to debtholders, while the firm with more equity allocates more to the stockholders. It's not that their operating performance is different—they just chose different financing mixes.

The third reason why NI is a poor metric for assessing the firm's performance is that the firm must reinvest some of its cash flows in new or replacement assets if it wants to continue to exist. Not all of the cash from operations is "free" for distribution to investors—that portion of cash flow needed for reinvestment in the company should be held back. This leaves us with the "free" cash available for making payments to stockholders and creditors being cash from operations calculated as if the firm had no debt, less the amount of cash needed for profitable investments.

Traditional financial statements do not *directly* measure the cash flows available for distribution to investors. The remainder of this section explains how to calculate free cash flow from the information provided in the financial statements.

Defining Free Cash Flow

Free cash flow (FCF) for a given period is defined as cash *potentially* available for distribution to both stockholders and creditors. This consists of

- potential payments to equity investors as dividends or stock repurchases; and
- potential payments to creditors as interest or principal payments.

The intuition behind the concept of free cash flow is that it measures the cash "thrown off" by operations, less the amount that must be reinvested in order to generate future growth in cash flows. This reinvestment is in both long-term assets like plant and equipment, as well as in working capital.

We say that FCF is cash potentially available for distribution because most firms distribute less, that is, pay less in dividends (and stock repurchases), than they can afford to pay. Often cited reasons are

- Managers prefer to hold liquid reserves in order to meet contingencies.
- Managers want to retain funds in anticipation of large capital expenditures at a future date because it is less expensive to use internally generated cash to fund future investments than it is to raise capital by issuing new securities.
- Liquidity gives managers valuable flexibility (options).

Thus, many firms often "park" a portion of their free cash flow by purchasing short-term investments, such as Treasury bills. We address this in more detail in Chapter 5, but for now we will assume that all free cash flows are distributed to investors.[10]

Recall from Chapter 2 that free cash flow is equal to a firm's net operating profit after taxes (NOPAT) minus its investment in operating capital. The following sections show how to calculate FCF for ACME.

Calculating Free Cash Flow

Exhibit 3-5 summarizes the calculations of free cash flow for ACME in 2003.

In Chapter 2 we defined NOPAT as net operating profit after taxes. This is the operating profit less the taxes on operating profit. For ACME, the 2003 NOPAT is

$$\text{NOPAT}_{2003} = \$586.62(1 - 0.4) = \$351.97 \text{ million}$$

Recall from Chapter 2 that net operating working capital (NOWC) is

$$\text{NOWC} = \text{Operating current assets} - \text{Operating current liabilities.}$$

For ACME, the operating current assets are cash, accounts receivable, and inventory. The operating current liabilities are accounts payable and accruals. Note that the operating current liabilities do not include short-term debt, since this is a financing decision rather than a part of operations. For ACME, this means that

$$\text{NOWC} = (\text{Cash} + \text{Inventory} + \text{AR}) - (\text{AP} + \text{Accrued expenses})$$
$$\text{NOWC}_{2003} = (\$45.12 + \$631.74 + \$1{,}128.11) - (\$451.24 + \$225.62) = \$1{,}128.11.$$

[10]Unfortunately, there is another use of free cash flow. Many studies have shown that companies with lots of free cash flow often use it to acquire other companies, often at inflated prices. In other words, managers with lots of free cash flow are willing to pay more for acquisitions than they are worth. Obviously, this harms the shareholders of the acquiring firm. Why, then, would managers be willing to do this? We believe that most peculiarities in finance can be attributed to either the tax code or compensation plans. In this case, many studies have shown that a manager's compensation is highly correlated with the size of the company. Therefore, a manager might well decide to keep the company large by using the free cash flow to make an acquisition, rather than reducing the company's size by returning the free cash flow to investors. The solution to this problem is to more closely link a manager's compensation with improvement in the value of the firm, and not just its size. As we noted in Chapter 1, this is exactly the objective of some performance-based executive compensation plans, such as those based on EVA™.

Exhibit 3-5 ACME General's Free Cash Flow (millions of dollars)

	2001	2002	2003
Operating profit	$ 484.85	$ 538.19	$ 586.62
Tax on operating profit	193.94	215.28	234.65
NOPAT	$ 290.91	$ 322.91	$ 351.97
Operating current assets	1,491.84	1,655.94	1,804.97
Operating current liabilities	559.44	620.98	676.86
NOWC	$ 932.40	$ 1,034.96	$ 1,128.11
Net PPE	$ 1,864.80	$ 2,069.93	$ 2,256.23
Total operating capital	$ 2,797.20	$ 3,104.89	$ 3,384.34
Investment in total net operating capital		$ 307.69	$ 279.45
FCF		$ 15.22	$ 72.52

We combine net operating working capital with the net long-term operating assets (for ACME, this is just net PPE) to find total operating capital.

$$\text{Total operating capital} = \text{NOWC} + \text{Net long-term operating capital}$$

For ACME, this is

$$\text{Total operating capital 2003} = \$1{,}128.11 + \$2{,}256.23 = \$3{,}384.34.$$

Recall that free cash flow is NOPAT minus the net investment in total operating capital. The net investment in total operating capital is the change in total operating capital from the previous year. For ACME, the 2003 FCF is

$$\begin{aligned}\text{FCF} &= \text{NOPAT} - \text{Net investment in total operating capital}\\ \text{FCF} &= \$351.97 - (\$3{,}384.34 - \$3{,}104.89)\\ \text{FCF} &= \$351.97 - \$279.45 = \$72.52 \text{ million.}\end{aligned}$$

Although ACME earned $289 million in profits in 2003 and had NOPAT of $352 million, it had to reinvest $279 million to support its future operations. This left about $73 million in free cash flow available for distribution to all investors. ACME paid $106 million to debtholders in the form of interest, but its after-tax cost was only about $64 million because ACME was able to deduct the interest expense when computing its taxable income. In other words, of the $106 million, ACME paid $64 million and the government subsidized the other $42 million. After paying the $64 million in after-tax interest payments, ACME was left with FCF of about $8.52 million ($8.52 = $72.52 – $64). However, if you look at the statement of cash flows, ACME also paid $105 million in dividends to shareholders, even though it didn't have the free cash flow to do so. Where did this money come from? Just like a household that spends more than it takes in or a deficit-running government, ACME borrowed almost $96 million to enable it to make these payments. This is where the "extra" money came from!

An Alternative Approach to Calculating Free Cash Flow: The Financing Approach

One of the nice things about accounting is that there are often several equivalent ways to calculate something of interest. In our experience, students wouldn't exactly use the word "nice" to describe this characteristic, but often these alternate calculations can shed additional light on what is going on behind the numbers. Along these lines, an alternative approach to finding free cash flow is the **financing approach**. Since free cash flow is the amount of cash flow distributed to investors, we can calculate it quickly using the statement of cash flows. The third section in the statement of cash flows, financing activities, shows the net amount of cash paid as dividends, raised by issuing stock, spent on repurchasing stock, raised by borrowing, or spent in paying back debt. For ACME, Exhibit 3-4 shows that this amounted to a negative \$9.08 million in 2003 (ACME paid \$105 million in dividends and raised \$96 million in new debt). Since this part of the statement of cash flows is calculated from the perspective of ACME and not from the perspective of the investors, the cash flow being distributed to investors is the negative of the net cash flow (to ACME) from financing activities. In other words, if ACME spent \$9 million in its financing activities, then investors received \$9 million.

In addition to the financing activities, the income statement in Exhibit 3-2 shows that ACME had an interest expense of \$105.73 in 2003. Since interest is deductible for tax purposes, ACME's actual after-tax interest expense was \$105.73(1 – 0.4) = \$63.44. Thus, ACME's free cash flow using this approach is its after-tax interest expense plus the negative of its cash flow from financing activities (from the statement of cash flows).

$$\text{FCF} = \text{After-tax interest expense} - \text{Net CF from financing activities}$$
$$\text{FCF}_{2003} = \$63.44 - (-\$9.08) = \$72.52$$

The insight this gives is that free cash flow is the negative of the net amount contributed from financing activities, plus after-tax interest expense—investors and the company view free cash flow symmetrically. However, even though the financing approach makes it quite easy to calculate FCF, it isn't very helpful in projecting free cash flow, as you will see in Chapter 5. See the Chapter 3 appendix for more discussion of the relationship between free cash flow and the statement of cash flows.

ACME's Operating Performance

Recall from Chapter 2 that we can measure operating performance by the return on invested capital (ROIC), and that ROIC is defined as NOPAT divided by the amount of operating capital available at the beginning of the year.

$$\text{ROIC}_t = \frac{\text{NOPAT}_t}{\text{Capital}_{t-1}}$$

ACME's 2002 and 2003 ROIC's are shown below.

$$\text{ROIC}_{2002} = \frac{\text{NOPAT}_{2002}}{\text{Capital}_{2001}} = \frac{\$322.91}{\$2,797.2} = 0.115 = 11.5\%$$

$$ROIC_{2003} = \frac{NOPAT_{2003}}{Capital_{2002}} = \frac{\$351.97}{\$3,104.89} = 0.113 = 11.3\%$$

Is 11.5% a good or a bad ROIC? To answer that question, we need to know the rate of return that ACME's investors expect. Recall from Chapter 2 that this return is called the weighted average cost of capital (WACC). We'll calculate this in Chapter 4, but we can tell you now that ACME's WACC is 10%. ACME's investors expect a return of 10%, but ACME's ROIC is over 11%. Therefore, ACME is earning more than its investors require, and this means it has had superior operating performance.

Summary

This chapter reviews key basic principles underlying the four major components of a firm's annual report. We explain the principles of accrual-basis accounting, revealing the differences between reported profits and cash flow, and we show how the income statement and balance sheet may be reconciled through the statement of cash flows. We also show how an analyst may use publicly available financial statements to calculate the free cash flow available for distribution to the firm's investors. In the next chapter we will show how to use projections of free cash flow to calculate the corporate value of ACME and the price of ACME's stock.

Spreadsheet Problems

3-1 ACME General Corp.

The financial statements for ACME General Corporation are shown in the worksheet in the file ***Prob 03-01.xls***.

a. Complete the shaded cell entries in the 2001–2003 income statements and balance sheets. (These simply require subtotaling or totaling the entries in various categories on the financial statements.)
b. Using the information from the completed balance sheets and the income statements for ACME, construct a statement of shareholders' equity and a statement of cash flows for 2002 and 2003. A template is provided in the worksheet, and hints are given in the cells with comments.
c. Calculate the free cash flow for ACME for 2002 and 2003. Also calculate ACME's return on invested capital for 2002 and 2003.

3-2 Benziger Corp.

The financial statements for Benziger Corporation are shown in the worksheet in the file ***Prob 03-02.xls***.

a. Complete the shaded cell entries in the 2003 balance sheet and income statement. (These simply require subtotaling or totaling the entries in various categories on the financial statements.)
b. Using the information from the completed 2002 and 2003 balance sheet and the 2003 income statement for Benziger, construct a statement of cash

flows for 2003. A template is provided in the worksheet, but you will need to supply the formulas.

c. As a check on your cash flow statement, see if the ending cash balance equals the figure in the 2003 balance sheet. If not, you have made a mistake somewhere in you calculations, and you need to recheck them.
d. After completing the statement of cash flows, compute the free cash flow and return on invested capital for Benziger for 2003. (Hint: for free cash flow, you should get $57 million.)

Appendix 3

Reconciling Free Cash Flow with the Statement of Cash Flows

With a couple of modifications, the information contained in the statement of cash flows in Exhibit 3-4 can be altered to make calculating free cash flow quite simple. The first modification corrects for the "contamination" of earnings by interest payments as discussed earlier in the chapter. We correct for interest payments by restating income as if the firm had no interest expense, that is, as if the firm were entirely equity financed. Recall that this is the definition of net operating profit after-tax (NOPAT). The adjustment amounts to removing the interest expense and its associated impact on income taxes from the income statement. Let's start with ACME's 2003 net income. If we eliminate the \$105.73 million in interest charges paid by ACME, its taxes would increase by about \$105.73(0.40) = \$42.29 million since ACME's tax rate is 40%. Therefore, the after-tax interest expense is \$105.73 – \$42.29 = \$105.73(1 – 0.40) = \$63.44 million. This first correction amounts to adding the after-tax interest expense back to net income.

$$\begin{aligned} \text{NOPAT} &= \text{NI} + \text{Interest} - (\text{T} \times \text{Interest}) \\ &= \text{NI} + \text{Interest}(1 - \text{T}) \qquad \textbf{(3A-1)} \\ \text{NOPAT}_{2003} &= \$288.53 + \$105.73(1 - .40) = \$351.97 \end{aligned}$$

Note that this calculation of NOPAT looks a little different from the calculation in Chapter 2.

$$\text{NOPAT} = (\text{Operating profit})(1 - \text{Tax rate}) \qquad \textbf{(2-11)}$$

For a simple company, the calculation is the same, however.

$$\text{NI} = (\text{Operating profit} - \text{Interest})(1 - \text{T})$$

so

$$\begin{aligned} \text{NOPAT} &= \text{NI} + \text{Interest}(1 - \text{T}) \\ &= (\text{Operating profit} - \text{Interest})(1 - \text{T}) + \text{Interest}(1 - \text{T}) \\ &= (\text{Operating profit})(1 - \text{T}) \end{aligned}$$

For some companies it is easier to start with operating profit and remove taxes, as in (2-11), while for others it is easier to start with net income and remove the effects of interest as in (3A-1).

Although we have "corrected" for the effects of financial structure by calculating NOPAT, this still does not measure cash flow from operations because of the accrual accounting principles discussed earlier in this chapter. Recall that in constructing the statement of cash flows, we added back depreciation and deducted the change in operating working capital in order to convert net income to a cash basis. We apply the same principle here to our corrected income measure, NOPAT, but with one modification. The modification we make is in the definition of working capital. We will take the arguably "unaccounting" stance and recognize that cash balances are themselves necessary for the normal operation of the firm and that cash balances, like other long- and short-term operating assets, must grow as the business grows. This is important since investors in a growing business need to realize that they will have to invest more in cash balances as the firms grows, leaving less cash available for distribution to investors. So our modified definition of cash from operations considers cash balances as an operating current asset and will include the change in cash balances along with the changes in other operating current assets.[1]

$$\text{NOWC} = \text{Operating current assets} - \text{Operating current liabilities}$$
$$\text{NOWC} = (\text{Cash} + \text{Inventory} + \text{A/R}) - (\text{A/P} + \text{Accrued expenses})$$

For ACME in 2003, this means that

$$\text{NOWC}_{2003} = (\$45.12 + \$631.74 + \$1{,}128.11) - (\$451.24 + \$225.62) = \$1{,}128.11$$
$$\text{NOWC}_{2002} = (\$41.40 + \$579.58 + \$1{,}034.96) - (\$413.99 + \$206.99) = \$1{,}034.96.$$

The change in operating working capital from 2002 to 2003 was

$$\begin{aligned} \Delta\text{NOWC} &= \Delta\text{Operating current assets} - \Delta\text{Operating current liabilities} \\ \Delta\text{NOWC}_{2003} &= \text{NOWC}_{2003} - \text{NOWC}_{2003} \\ \Delta\text{NOWC}_{2003} &= \$1{,}128.11 - \$1{,}034.96 = \$93.15 \end{aligned}$$

where the Δ symbol means "change in."

The final element of FCF is the deduction of investment in operating long-term assets necessary to sustain and improve cash flow in the future. Such investment represents a reduction in the cash that the firm can "afford" to distribute to its investors. In equation form, free cash flow boils down to net operating profit after-tax, plus depreciation, less the investments in operating working capital and long-term assets:

$$\text{FCF} = \text{NI} + \text{After-tax interest} + \text{Depreciation} - \Delta\text{NOWC} - \Delta\text{Long-term investments.}$$

From the statement of cash flows shown in Exhibit 3-4, ACME's expenditures for long-term assets in 2003 were $411.92 million. Therefore, ACME's free cash flow for 2003 is

$$\begin{aligned} \text{FCF} &= \text{NI} + \text{After-tax interest} + \text{Depreciation} - \Delta\text{NOWC} - \Delta\text{Long-term investments} \\ &= \$288.53 + \$63.44 + \$225.62 - \$93.15 - \$411.92 = \$72.52. \end{aligned}$$

[1]Later on, we will change this definition as well and include only the minimum amount of cash necessary to "grease the wheels of commerce" in operating working capital. Any cash balance over this minimal cash balance will be a nonoperating asset.

Now that you see the steps, we can use the statement of cash flows to find free cash flow more quickly. Start with the subtotal from the first section, the cash flow from operations. Add to this the after-tax interest expense (which we have to derive from the income statement, as shown above). At this point, we have the equivalent of NOPAT plus the change in all components of net operating working capital except the change in cash, which is an operating current asset. But we can get this directly from the bottom line of the statement of cash flows, which is the net change in cash. Finally, all we have to do is subtract the investment in fixed assets, which is shown in the second section of the statement of cash flows. Summarizing, we have

$$\text{FCF} = \text{Net cash from operations} + \text{Interest}(1 - \text{T}) - \text{Net change in cash} - \\ \text{Net cash used in investing activities.}$$

For 2003, ACME's FCF is

$$\text{FCF}_{2003} = \$424.73 + \$105.73(1 - 0.40) - \$3.72 - \$411.92 = \$72.52.$$

Chapter 4

Estimating the Value of ACME

Introduction

Chapter 2 explained the basic steps in valuation: estimate the weighted average cost of capital (WACC), estimate the future free cash flows (FCF), and discount the FCFs at the weighted average cost of capital (WACC). Now we will apply those steps to ACME, starting with the WACC.

The Weighted Average Cost of Capital

Recall that the weighted average cost of capital (WACC) is the rate of return that a company's investors, including both stockholders and debtholders, expect to receive in return for their investment in the company. In Chapter 2, we showed you how to calculate the WACC if you already know the cost of debt (r_D), the tax rate (T), the cost of equity (r_S), and the target weights for the percentages of the firm that will be financed with debt (w_D) and equity (w_S).

$$WACC = (1 - T)r_D w_D + r_S w_S \quad \textbf{(4-1)}$$

But how do you estimate the cost of debt and the cost of equity? How do you estimate the target weights? We'll show you how in this chapter.

Risk and Return

One of the fundamental ideas in finance is that risk and return are related: an investor will buy a high-risk security only if the expected return is correspondingly high. In other words, the more risk an investment has, the higher its expected return must be to induce an investor to invest in it rather than in a less risky security. Therefore, if we know how risky a security is and if we understand the "risk-return trade-off," then we can estimate the rate of return required to induce an investor to buy it.

The following sections explain how to estimate the rates of return required by ACME's debtholders and common shareholders. The appendix to this chapter has a more technical treatment.[1]

[1]For even more details on calculating the WACC, see E. Brigham and P. Daves, *Intermediate Financial Management*, 8th edition, South-Western, or M. Ehrhardt, *The Search for Value*, 1994, Oxford Press.

Estimating the Cost of Debt

ACME has two types of debt, as shown on its financial statements from Chapter 3: short-term debt and long-term debt. The short-term debt is a loan from a bank, with a current interest rate of 9%. This is called a **floating rate** loan because the bank changes the rate periodically to reflect prevailing interest rates in the economy. For example, when the Federal Reserve Board cuts interest rates, the bank will also cut the rate on its loan to ACME. When the Fed increases interest rates, so will ACME's bank. Since the interest rate changes to reflect market conditions, the interest rate reflects the rate of return required by the bank. This is a cost from ACME's perspective, and so the cost of debt for ACME's short-term debt is 9%.

What about the long-term debt? ACME's annual report has footnotes that describe the long-term debt; these are shown in the appendix to this chapter. These bonds were originally issued in 1999 with a maturity of 30 years, a coupon rate of 8% payable semiannually, and a face value of $1,000 per bond. Unlike the bank loan, the coupon rate on the bonds is fixed by the underlying contract between ACME and the bondholders. To find the size of the annual payment for each bond, you just multiply the 8% coupon by the $1,000 face value, which gives an $80 annual payment. However, ACME, like virtually all companies that issue bonds, pays interest semiannually, so it makes a $40 payment every 6 months. It will do this until the bonds mature on December 31, 2029, when it will also make a $1,000 principal payment to each of the bondholders. ACME sold 1 million of these bonds to investors in 1999 for $1,000 per bond, raising a total of $1 billion. At the time ACME issued these bonds, the appropriate interest rate was 8%, which is why the bonds have an 8% coupon. Therefore, ACME's cost of debt in 1999 was 8%.[2]

However, we're going to use the WACC to find the present value of the company's *future* free cash flows, so we want to know the rate the company will pay on its debt in the future, not the historical rate it paid on previously issued debt. In other words, the pre-tax cost of debt, r_D, is the rate at which a company could issue *new* debt. If you work for a company, its CFO might know this (or could possibly find the answer by calling the company's investment bankers). But if you don't work at the company you're analyzing, then you must use one of the following methods: (1) use the current price of the company's existing bonds to calculate the rate of return that its investors expect, or (2) find the yield on the debt of a similar company. These methods work because we know that any new bonds issued by ACME will have to compete for investors' funds in the broader capital market. In particular, new bonds would compete against ACME's existing bonds and with similar bonds issued by other companies. Therefore, any new bonds that ACME issues must provide investors a rate of return similar to those provided by its existing bonds or other companies' similar bonds. Since ACME's debt is publicly traded, we can observe its current price and then use the first method. If the bond isn't publicly traded, then you must use the second method, which we apply to Home Depot in Chapter 11.

[2]Those of you with a strong background in finance may realize that the compounded annual rate is a little higher than 8%. However, it is common practice to simply use the 8% as the annual cost. See this chapter's appendix for a more detailed explanation.

You might be asking yourself, wouldn't the price on ACME's old bonds always be $1,000? The short answer is *no*.[3] The reason is that interest rates fluctuate over time because of changes in the economy (e.g., inflation, Federal Reserve Board monetary policy), political developments (e.g., the size of the federal deficit), and changes in how investors perceive the risk of ACME. As a result of such changes, investors update the amount they are willing to pay for an ACME bond that pays $40 every 6 months plus $1000 when it matures. For example, suppose interest rates for bonds of similar risk have fallen to 7%, as a result of developments in the economy since the bonds were first issued. Would you rather own a new bond with a 7% coupon, or ACME's bond with an 8% coupon? Obviously, if they were the same price and same risk, you, and every other investor, would rather have ACME's bond because you would be earning 8% instead of the lowly 7% yield on new bonds. Since many investors will try to buy ACME's bond, its price will be "bid up" from its original price of $1,000. But if you pay more than $1,000 for ACME's bond with its $80 annual payments, then your rate of return will be less than 8%. In fact, investor demand will drive up the price on ACME's bond until its rate of return falls to 7%.

The reverse will occur if interest rates rise, say to 9%. The current owners of ACME's bonds will see that they could buy a new bond with a 9% coupon, which is better than the 8% rate on the ACME bonds that they own. If the two prices are the same, then they will all try to sell their ACME bonds, which will drive down their price below $1,000. If you can buy ACME's bond for less than $1,000, but still get the $80 payment, then your rate of return will be higher than 8%. In fact, ACME's bond owners will continue trying to sell their ACME bonds until their price falls enough so that investors can get the same 9% return on ACME's bond that they can get on a comparable new bond.

The appendix to this chapter explains bond pricing in more detail, but the basic idea is pretty simple: a bond's value is the present value of all its future cash flows, discounted at the cost of debt (i.e., at the investor's required rate of return). For a given bond, we know the future cash payments to the bondholder, so if we observe the current selling price (market value) of the bond, we can deduce the discount rate that investors are using to value the bond. This discount rate is the bondholders' required rate of return, and the rate of return ACME will have to pay if it wants to compete for investors' funds.

If r_c is the coupon rate and M is the face value, then the annual coupon payment is r_c times M. For a bond with semiannual payments, such as ACME's, each payment is equal to $r_cM/2$. If the bond has n remaining payments, then the value of the bond, V_B, is

$$V_B = \sum_{t=1}^{n} \frac{(r_c M/2)}{(1 + r_D)^t} + \frac{M}{(1 + r_D)^n}. \tag{4-2}$$

As of December 31, 2003, the date of our analysis, ACME's bonds have 26 years until maturity, which means they have 52 remaining payments. The semiannual

[3]The long answer is also *no*. This is a very common misconception.

payment is \$40 and the face value is \$1,000. At the end of 2003, ACME's bond had a market price of \$900.15 per bond. We can substitute these values into Equation 4-2.

$$\$900.15 = \sum_{t=1}^{52} \frac{\$40}{(1 + r_D)^t} + \frac{\$1{,}000}{(1 + r_D)^{52}} \quad \textbf{(4-2a)}$$

To find the cost of debt, r_D, we only need to solve this equation. This is actually pretty difficult, unless you have a financial calculator or a computer. The spreadsheet for this chapter shows you how to do this in Excel, and that's how we determined that r_D is 4.5%. But this is a semiannual rate, so we need to multiply it by 2 to get the annual cost of debt of 9%.

The bottom line is that ACME has a 9% cost for its long-term debt.

Estimating the Cost of Common Stock

For stocks, risk and return are defined by the **Capital Asset Pricing Model (CAPM)**. In particular, a stock's risk is measured by something called its "beta." At the risk of oversimplification, the CAPM states that investors should hold portfolios and not just single stocks, since this helps diversify away risk. Therefore, the relevant measure of stock risk is the amount of risk that the stock contributes to the portfolio. This is exactly what beta measures.[4]

But beta also has a more intuitive interpretation, because it also measures the sensitivity of the rate of return on a particular stock to the overall returns experienced in the stock market. More precisely, beta is an estimate of how much the return on a particular stock will change when the return on stocks *generally* changes by 1%. So a stock with a beta of 1.0 has the same amount of relevant risk as the stock market itself, and investors will require the same return on this stock as they require from the stock market, on average. A stock with a beta greater than 1.0 has more risk than the stock market, so investors will require a higher return on this stock than they require from the stock market, on average. Conversely, stock with a beta less than 1.0 has less risk than the stock market, so investors will require a lower return that the overall stock market.

Naturally, investors expect that over a fairly long period the average return they will get from investing in stocks will be higher than the return from investing in safe investments like Treasury bonds. The return on Treasury bonds is often referred to as the "risk-free" rate, because such bonds are generally considered to be the safest investment. The difference between the expected return on the stock market and the risk-free rate is called the **market risk premium (RP_M)**. Although there is no way to prove it, most analysts and professors think the market risk premium is fairly stable and is somewhere around 5.0% to 6.5%. We typically use 5.5% to 6% as an estimate of RP_M, the market risk premium. When the stock market is at a relatively high level, we use 5.5%. When the market is down, we use 6%.

[4]For more details on CAPM, see the appendix to this chapter. Also, see Chapters 6 and 7 in E. Brigham and M. Ehrhardt, *Financial Management: Theory and Practice*, 10th edition, South-Western Publishing. There are alternative theories for the relationship between risk and return, and these are discussed in Chapter 7 of *Financial Management: Theory and Practice*.

For example, suppose the risk-free rate is 5.4% (we'll show you some easy Internet sources for Treasury bond rates in Chapter 11) and the stock market is down. Then the expected return on the stock market is about 11.4% = 5.4% + 6%. If the risk-free interest rate were 8% and the market were still down, then the expected market return would be around 14% = 8% + 6%.

The Capital Asset Pricing Model is a conceptual representation of the relationship between investors' required returns and beta risk. Here is the equation for the CAPM.

$$r_S = r_{RF} + \text{Beta}(RP_M) \quad \textbf{(4-3)}$$

The CAPM says that the required rate of return on a stock equals the risk-free rate, *plus* an adjustment based on the stock's risk. This adjustment scales up or down the market risk premium, depending on whether the stock is more or less risky than the stock market as a whole. We explain in the appendix how to measure beta if you want to do it yourself, but estimates of betas are readily available on the Internet. In Chapter 11, we show how to get an estimate of beta from the Internet, but for now you can just trust us that ACME's beta is about 1.1. In other words, ACME is just slightly riskier than the average company.

What's the cost of equity for ACME based on the CAPM? Given a beta of 1.1, a market risk premium of 6%, and a risk-free rate of 5.4%, we can use Equation 4-3 to find ACME's cost of equity.

$$\begin{aligned} r_S &= r_{RF} + \text{Beta}(RP_M) \\ r_S &= 5.4\% + 1.1(6\%) = 12\% \end{aligned} \quad \textbf{(4-3)}$$

This means that ACME's shareholders must get a return of around 12% in order to compensate them for the risk they bear.[5]

Estimating the Target Weights

To calculate the WACC, we need to estimate the percentage of the firm that we think will be financed with debt (w_D) and the percentage that will be financed with stock (w_S). These are the target weights that ACME will shoot for, not the current weights it may have. We will show you how to estimate these for Home Depot in Chapter 11, but for now let's just assume that ACME's target weights are 30% debt (w_D = 30%) and 70% equity (w_S = 70%).

Putting the Pieces Together: Calculating the WACC

Now that we've done the hard part, it's pretty easy to actually calculate the WACC. Recall from Chapter 2 that even though investors receive their required

[5]Be careful in interpreting our meaning when we speak of the required rate of return. We are not saying that the investor really expects to earn 12% *each and every year*, but rather that the investor knows the return will fluctuate from year to year, and that it will fluctuate somewhat more than the market return (its beta is greater than 1), but that its return should *average* 12% over a multiyear holding period.

return on debt, it doesn't cost the company the full amount of the interest payments, since the company can deduct them when calculating its taxes. For example, in Chapter 3, Exhibit 3-2, we saw that ACME's interest payments were \$105.73 million, reducing their taxable income by that amount. This, in turn, reduced their taxes by \$42.29 = 0.4 × \$105.73. So the net after-tax cost of the debt financing was only \$63.44 million. This tax-deductibility feature of interest payments means the cost of debt is actually the after-tax required return. Since ACME's tax rate, T, is 40%, ACME's cost of debt is (1 – 0.4)9%, and their WACC is

$$\text{WACC} = w_D(1 - T)r_D + w_S r_S$$
$$\text{WACC} = 0.3(1 - 0.40)(9\%) + 0.7(12\%) = 10.0\%.$$

Estimating the Future Expected Free Cash Flows

We calculated the past free cash flows of ACME in the last chapter, but how do we estimate the future free cash flows? And how do we estimate ACME's value if its free cash flows aren't presently growing at a constant rate? Chapter 5 will explain the nuts and bolts of forecasting free cash flows, but for now we'll simply assume that your trusty assistant has projected ACME's financial statements.

Exhibit 4-1 shows the financial statements for the most recent year and the projected statements for the next 4 years. Even though your assistant is trusty, it never hurts to do a quick check to see if the projections have any obvious errors. In particular, let's look at the first projected year, 2004, and compare it with the most recent actual year, 2003. Sales are growing modestly, so let's check operating profits. If operating profits skyrocketed or fell sharply from 2003, we probably would be skeptical of the projections, unless you had some specific reason to expect a dramatic change. But sales and operating profits both seem to be growing at about the same rate, so, in the absence of expectations of a dramatic change, there isn't an obvious mistake in either the assumptions or arithmetic underlying the projections. In general, we apply this same logic to all the categories, and none seem out of line for ACME. Always perform this check for plausibility of projections in light of the information that you may have about the company.

In addition to comparing the year-to-year changes in all the individual accounts, we should also compare the income statement with the balance sheet. Notice also that sales are growing modestly, and total assets are growing at roughly the same rate. Again, in the absence of specific knowledge as to why ACME's future assets shouldn't grow apace with their sales projections, this makes sense. Based on this "quick and dirty" examination of the projections, we can't find any obvious errors.

The next step in valuation is to calculate the projected free cash flows. We took the free cash flows for the most recent year, 2003, from Chapter 3, and then calculated the projected free cash flows for the remaining years using the same methods as in Chapter 3. Exhibit 4-2 shows these projections.

Exhibit 4-1 ACME General Projected Financial Statements (millions of dollars)

Income Statements	Actual 2003	Projected 2004	Projected 2005	Projected 2006	Projected 2007
Sales	$4,512.44	$4,873.44	$5,165.84	$5,475.80	$5,804.34
Costs of goods sold	2,797.71	3,021.53	3,202.82	3,394.99	3,598.69
Sales, general & administrative	902.49	974.69	1,033.17	1,095.16	1,160.87
Depreciation	225.62	243.67	258.29	273.80	290.22
Operating profit	$ 586.62	$ 633.55	$ 671.56	$ 711.85	$ 754.56
Interest on original debt	80.00	80.00	80.00	80.00	80.00
Interest expense on new debt	25.73	34.35	42.84	50.18	57.95
Interest expense	105.73	114.35	122.84	130.18	137.95
Earnings before taxes	$ 480.89	$ 519.20	$ 548.72	$ 581.67	$ 616.61
Taxes	192.36	207.68	219.49	232.67	246.65
Net income	$ 288.53	$ 311.52	$ 329.23	$ 349.00	$ 369.96
Dividends	$ 104.89	$ 135.10	$ 191.43	$ 202.90	$ 215.05
Additions to retained earnings	$ 183.64	$ 176.41	$ 137.80	$ 146.11	$ 154.91

Balance Sheets	Actual 2003	Projected 2004	Projected 2005	Projected 2006	Projected 2007
Assets					
Cash	$ 45.12	$ 48.73	$ 51.66	$ 54.76	$ 58.04
Inventory	631.74	682.28	723.22	766.61	812.61
Accounts receivable	1,128.11	1,218.36	1,291.46	1,368.95	1,451.09
Total current assets	$1,804.97	$1,949.38	$2,066.34	$2,190.32	$2,321.74
Gross PPE	3,443.32	3,867.49	4,271.98	4,700.75	5,155.24
Accumulated depreciation	1,187.09	1,430.77	1,689.06	1,962.85	2,253.07
Net PPE	$2,256.23	$2,436.72	$2,582.92	$2,737.90	$2,902.17
Total assets	$4,061.20	$4,386.09	$4,649.26	$4,928.22	$5,223.91
Liabilities and Shareholders' Equity					
Accounts payable	$ 451.24	$ 487.34	$ 516.58	$ 547.58	$ 580.43
Accrued expenses	225.62	243.67	258.29	273.79	290.22
Short-term debt	381.71	476.04	557.55	643.90	735.40
Total current liabilities	$1,058.57	$1,207.05	$1,332.42	$1,465.27	$1,606.05
Long-term debt	1,000.00	1,000.00	1,000.00	1,000.00	1,000.00
Total liabilities	$2,058.57	$2,207.05	$2,332.42	$2,465.27	$2,606.05
Common stock	600.00	600.00	600.00	600.00	600.00
Retained earnings	1,402.63	1,579.04	1,716.84	1,862.95	2,017.86
Total common equity	$2,002.63	$2,179.04	$2,316.84	$2,462.95	$2,617.86
Total liabilities and equity	$4,061.20	$4,386.09	$4,649.26	$4,928.22	$5,223.91

Note: The projections were made using a spreadsheet model. Due to rounding, sums may not total exactly.

Exhibit 4-2 ACME's Projected Free Cash Flows (millions of dollars)[g]

	Actual 2003	Projected 2004	Projected 2005	Projected 2006	Projected 2007
Operating profit	$ 586.62	$ 633.55	$ 671.56	$ 711.85	$ 754.56
Tax on operating profit	234.65	253.42	268.62	284.74	301.82
NOPAT[a]	$ 351.97	$ 380.13	$ 402.94	$ 427.11	$ 452.74
Operating current assets	1,804.97	1,949.37	2,066.34	2,190.32	2,321.74
Operating current liabilities	676.86	731.01	774.87	821.37	870.65
NOWC[b]	$1,128.11	$1,218.36	$1,291.47	$1,368.95	$1,451.09
Total operating capital[c]	3,384.34	3,655.08	3,874.39	4,106.85	4,353.26
Investment in total operating capital[d]	$ 279.45	$ 270.74	$ 219.31	$ 232.46	$ 246.41
FCF[e]	$ 72.52	$ 109.39	$ 183.63	$ 194.65	$ 206.33
ROIC[f]	11.3%	11.2%	11.0%	11.0%	11.0%
Growth in Sales	9.0%	8.0%	6.0%	6.0%	6.0%
Growth in NOPAT	9.0%	8.0%	6.0%	6.0%	6.0%
Growth in total net op. cap.	9.0%	8.0%	6.0%	6.0%	6.0%
Growth in FCF	376.6%	50.8%	67.9%	6.0%	6.0%
Growth in dividends	-34.5%	28.8%	41.7%	6.0%	6.0%

Notes:

[a]NOPAT is net operating profit after taxes.

[b]Net operating working capital, NOWC, is equal to operating current assets minus operating current liabilities.

[c]Total operating capital is equal to NOWC plus net PPE.

[d]The investment in total net operating capital is the difference in total net operating capital from one year to the next.

[e]FCF is NOPAT minus the investment in total net operating capital.

[f]ROIC is the return on invested capital, defined as NOPAT for a year divided by the total net operating capital as of the beginning of the year (which is the capital at the end of the previous year).

[g]All projections and calculations were made in a spreadsheet model. Due to rounding, sums may not total exactly.

Below the calculation of free cash flow in Exhibit 4-2 is the return on invested capital (ROIC). To calculate ROIC, take the NOPAT for a given year and divide it by the amount of total operating capital at the beginning of the year (which is the total operating capital shown for the end of the previous year). The ROIC tells how well the company performed in a particular year, and it also gives us another way to verify the plausibility of the projections. We can see that ACME's ROIC for the most recent year was about 11.3%. If the ROICs for the projected years are substantially different from this, then it means we have either made an arithmetic mistake in projecting the statements or we have assumed that the future performance will be very different than the past performance. For ACME, the projected ROICs are similar to the 2003 ROIC, which once again makes us think that the projections are reasonable. Also, notice that ACME's projected ROICs are a little larger than its WACC of 10%. In other words, ACME has been providing a rate of return greater than the return required by ACME's investors, and the projections assume that this will continue.

As Chapter 2 explained, a firm's value depends on *all* its future free cash flow. In particular, it is the present value of the free cash flows when discounted at the WACC.

$$V_{op} = \sum_{t=1}^{\infty} \frac{FCF_t}{(1 + WACC)^t} \tag{4-4}$$

In Chapter 2 we made the simplifying assumption that free cash flows would grow at a constant rate, starting with the current year. However, if you look back at Exhibit 4-2 you will see that the expected future free cash flows grow at a 50.8% rate in 2004 and at 67.9% rate in 2005. But as we look at 2006 and 2007, the growth rate has dropped to 6%, and it appears to be steady.[6] In fact, you can see that the growth rate in FCF lags the growth rate in sales, since sales growth has also dropped down to a level 6%. We'll talk about the economic factors that drive sales growth in Chapter 5, but the fact is that the most plausible assumption regarding long-term sales growth for any company is that it should eventually level off due to a combination of market saturation and the forces of competition. After sales growth levels off, free cash flows will soon level off.

Since free cash flow doesn't grow at a constant rate throughout the entire forecast period, but does begin growing at a constant rate by the end of the forecast period, we can break the calculation of value into two steps. First, we'll find the present value as of December 31, 2007, of all the free cash flows beyond December 31, 2007. It's as if we got into a time machine and transported ourselves into the future, stopping at December 31, 2007, and then asked "What is the present value of the free cash flows from this point forward." We call this the **horizon value** because it represents the value of the company at the end of the forecast period.[7] Second, we discount the horizon value and all of the free cash flows in the forecast period back to the current period, resulting in the present value of all future free cash flows, which is the value of operations.

To find the horizon value at Year N, HV_N, we use a modified version of the constant growth valuation equation from Chapter 2, Equation (2-7).

[6]Changes in free cash flow are generally very sensitive the year-to-year changes in the sales growth rate. This is because the change in investment in operating capital is usually sensitive to changes in sales growth (even small changes). The 376.6% change in ACME's FCF for 2003 resulted from a 2-percentage-point decline in the year-on-year growth rate in sales from 11% in 2002 (see Exhibit 3-1), to 9% in 2003. This decline in the rate of growth of sales has a much more dramatic effect on investment in operating capital than it has on NOPAT, so the difference between NOPAT and investment gets pretty big. As the changes in sales growth rates get smaller, as they do when the projections approach the steady-state, the percentage changes in FCF "settle down" to the steady-state growth rate (we'll say more on this in later chapters).

[7]The horizon value is sometimes called the **continuing value**, since it represents the value of the company if it continues to operate beyond the forecast period, and it is sometimes called the **terminal value**, since it is at the end of the forecast period.

$$V_{op} = \frac{FCF_1}{WACC - g} = \frac{FCF_0(1 + g)}{WACC - g} \quad \textbf{(2-7)}$$

The modified equation just changes some notation, replacing V_{op} with HV_N and FCF_0 with FCF_N.

$$HV_N = \frac{FCF_{N+1}}{WACC - g} = \frac{FCF_N(1 + g)}{WACC - g} \quad \textbf{(4-5)}$$

For ACME, the horizon value at 2007 is

$$HV_{2007} = \frac{FCF_{2007}(1 + g)}{WACC - g} = \frac{\$206.33(1 + 0.06)}{0.100 - 0.06} = \$5{,}467.75 \text{ million.} \quad \textbf{(4-5)}$$

To find the current value of operations, as of December 31, 2003, we find the present value of the forecasted free cash flows and the present value of the 2006 horizon value.

$$V_{op} = \frac{\$109.38}{(1 + 0.10)} + \frac{\$183.63}{(1 + 0.10)^2} + \frac{\$194.65}{(1 + 0.10)^3} + \frac{\$206.33}{(1 + 0.10)^4} + \frac{\$5{,}467.75}{(1 + 0.10)^4}$$
$$= \$4{,}272.92 \text{ million}$$

ACME had no nonoperating assets on December 31, 2003, so its total value is equal to its value of operations. To find the value of equity, we must subtract the debt that ACME had on December 31, 2003. At that time, ACME had $381.71 million in short-term debt. Recall that ACME also had one million bonds with a market price of $900.15 per bond as of December 31, 2002, for total long-term debt of $900.15 million. Therefore, the total market value of ACME's debt was: $1,281.86 million ($1,281.86 = $381.71 + $900.15). Subtracting the $1,281.86 million in debt from the $4,272.92 value of operations results in a $2,991 million value of equity.

ACME had 100 million shares of stock. Therefore, the estimated price per share is $29.91 = $2,991/100. Exhibit 4-3 summarizes these calculations.

Exhibit 4-3 Application of the Corporate Valuation Model (millions of dollars, except per share data)

	2003
Value of operations	$4,272.92
Plus the value of nonoperating assets	0
= Total value of the corporation	$4,272.92
Minus value of debt	1,281.86
= Value of equity	$2,991.06
Divided by number of shares	100
= Price per share	$ 29.91

Alternative Valuation Approaches: The Method of Multiples

Academic studies have shown that the corporate valuation model is more accurate than other methods.[8] Surveys show that when evaluating potential acquisitions, more corporate managers believe the discounted cash flow model is the best valuation approach. We certainly favor the corporate valuation model, not only for its relative accuracy and popularity among sophisticated practitioners, but also because the process of forecasting free cash flow provides so much insight into how a company is operating and the sources of value for the company. However, there are other valuation methods, and we would be remiss if we did not mention them. Following is a brief description of one popular class of methods, called comparative valuation methods.

If you have ever consulted a real estate agent about selling your home, the agent probably provided an analysis of its likely sales price. For example, suppose you have a 2,500 square-foot home with three bedrooms, two baths, a detached garage, and a large deck. The agent would search a database for similar homes that have sold in your neighborhood during the recent past. The agent would calculate the average sales price for these similar homes, and this would be a pretty good estimate of the price at which you could sell your home.

Comparative valuation methods attempt to do the same for a company. Although no two homes are exactly identical, it is much easier to find two similar homes than it is to find two similar companies. Therefore, most analysts define similar companies as those that compete in the same line of business and that are approximately the same size. So the first step is to find a group of companies that are similar to the one that you want to value.

The next step is to choose a comparison criterion. The most widely used criterion is EBITDA. This is pronounced "e-bit-dah," and it is an acronym for Earnings Before Interest, Taxes, Depreciation, and Amortization. Another widely used criterion is earnings per share, or EPS. Given a criterion and a price, the analyst divides the price by the criterion. A high price-to-criterion ratio implies that investor will pay more for a dollar of the criterion than when the ratio is low.

Given a comparison criterion, the analyst must decide whether the appropriate "price" is the stock price per share or the total value of the company (i.e., the total value of debt plus the total value of equity, defined as the stock price multiplied by the price per share). For example, if the criterion is earnings per share, then the price should be the stock's price per share, because the earnings "belong" to common stockholders. In a real sense, when an investor buys a share of the firm's stock, she is buying right to the per share earnings. But if the criterion is EBITDA, then the price should be the total market value of the firm, since EBITDA represents the combined returns for both stockholders and creditors. Two firms could have the same EBITDA, but may have financed their assets with very different proportions

[8]For example, see S. N. Kaplan and R. S. Ruback, 1995, "The Valuation of Cash Flow Forecasts: An Empirical Analysis," *Journal of Finance*, (Vol. 50, No. 4, September), 1059–1093.

of debt and equity capital. Hence, while we might expect the total of the values of debt and equity to be similar, the value of the equity component in the two companies could be quite different.

For example, suppose the analyst wants to value ACME using the EBITDA criterion. After identifying an appropriate comparison group of companies, say other widget manufacturers of comparable size, the analyst would divide the total value of each company's debt and equity by its EBITDA, and calculate the average Price/EBITDA for the group of companies. Suppose this average ratio is 6. The analyst then finds the EBITDA for ACME and multiplies it by 6. The result is an estimated value for the company. If ACME's own value-to-EBITDA ratio is less than six, the implication is that ACME's securities are selling at bargain prices relative to the EBITDA that the company is generating, and that investing in the company is suggested. If on the other hand, ACME's ratio is above the comparison-group average, then the implication is that ACME's securities are being overvalued by investors, and selling the company's securities is suggested.

Although the price/EBITDA ratio is the most widely used comparative valuation ratio, analysts frequently use other ratios as well. These include the price/net income, which is often called the P/E ratio (where P stands for price per share and E stands for earnings per share, which is the same as net income per share). Some analysts even use price/sales (where price is the total value). In some industries they even use nonfinancial comparisons, such as price/subscriber in the cellular phone industry and price/eyeball in many Internet companies (where eyeball is the number of hits).

Some analysts use the current EBITDA, some use the average of the past several years, and some use the average of the projected EBITDA for several future years. The point is that there are many, many variations of this criterion value approach to valuation.

Of course, when you look at the actual ratios for a sample of companies, the average may be 6, but the ratios may range from 2 to 18. Why should companies have such a range in ratios? In other words, why would two companies with identical EBITDAs have such different prices? The answer can best be understood by thinking about this in the context of the corporate valuation model. For example, two companies with identical EBITDAs can have very different free cash flows. One company could be very capital intensive, which reduces its free cash flows (sales growth implies relatively high levels of operating investment for the more capital intensive firm, hence lower FCF for a given NOPAT). So the corporate valuation model would show that this company would have a low price due to low free cash flows, and this would give it a lower price/EBITDA ratio.

Another reason that two companies with identical EBITDAs might have very different stock prices is that one company might have a much higher growth rate in sales and free cash flow than the other. If the comparison criterion approach only looks at the *current* level of the criterion (or at most, looks one or two years ahead), it does not give appropriate consideration to the expected growth differential, which would give a higher price, and a higher price/EBITDA ratio, to the faster growing firm.

Yet a third reason that the simple criterion ratio approaches might fail to give accurate signals of value is that they ignore potential differences in risk. If one company has higher risk (i.e., has a higher cost of capital), it would have a lower value and hence a lower price/EBITDA ratio. The corporate valuation model, on the other hand, requires the analyst to estimate the cost of capital for each company, which will reflect investors' perceptions of risk inherent in each.

Although these comparative approaches to valuation are frequently used (particularly by less sophisticated investors), they are clearly flawed, because they do not take into account many important differences between companies, such as the ones described above. Their appeal undoubtedly rests upon their ease of use—our view of that is "easy come, easy go" (value, that is)! While the corporate valuation model is more time consuming, its richness provides many insights about valuation that you simply won't get using the simplistic comparison criterion approaches.

Summary

In this chapter you learned how to calculate the weighted average cost of capital for a simple company. You also saw how to calculate the forecasted free cash flows from given forecasted financial statements. When the growth in free cash flows is not constant throughout the entire forecast period, you must first calculate the value of the firm at the end of the forecast period, which is called the horizon value. To find the current value of the firm, you discount the horizon value and the forecasted free cash flows during the forecast period at the weighted average cost of capital.

The appendix to this chapter provides a more technical discussion of security valuation. The next two chapters focus on developing the skills necessary to forecast financial statements.

Spreadsheet Problems

4-1 ACME Valuation

The current (2003) and projected financial statements for ACME General Corporation are shown in the worksheet in the file ***Prob 04-01.xls***. Fill in the yellow cells with formulas.

a. Start with the FCF calculation. Use the entries in the balance sheets and income statements to calculate the elements of FCF, and the resulting FCF for each year through the forecast period.
b. Use the information given in the WACC section to estimate ACME's costs of debt and equity financing. Using your calculated costs of debt and equity and the target proportions of debt and equity, calculate ACME's WACC.
c. Finally, estimate per share value of ACME stock. This will require calculating the horizon value, then summing the present values of the horizon value and the FCFs during the forecast period. Then the value of nonequity claims must be subtracted, and the residual equity value divided by the number of outstanding shares.

4-2 ET Valuation

The current (2003) and projected financial statements for ET Enterprises are shown in the worksheet in the file ***Prob 04-02.xls***. Fill in the yellow cells with formulas.

a. Start with the FCF calculation. Use the entries in the balance sheets and income statements to calculate the elements of FCF, and the resulting FCF for each year through the forecast period.
b. Use the information given in the WACC section to estimate ET Enterprises's costs of debt and equity financing. Using your calculated costs of debt and equity and the target proportions of debt and equity, calculate ET Enterprises's WACC.
c. Finally, estimate per share value of ET Enterprise stock. This will require calculating the horizon value, then summing the present values of the horizon value and the FCFs during the forecast period. Then the value of nonequity claims must be subtracted, and the residual equity value divided by the number of outstanding shares.

Appendix 4

Security Valuation

The Whole versus the Sum of the Parts

This appendix will cover the most basic securities issued by firms and show how each type of security is valued by investors. We discuss the features and valuation principles developed for these three basic categories of securities.

Fundamentals of Security Valuation

The three most basic security types are debt, preferred stock, and common stock. As we shall see, they are distinguished from one another in terms of three basic features: their places in the legal priority of claims against the firm's cash flows and assets, the characteristics of the associated cash payments to investors, and the rights they convey to investors in governance of the firm. Before discussing valuation of each of the these security types, we will define two terms that will be used in every valuation problem, regardless of the security being analyzed:

- **market value**—the price at which an investor may purchase the security.
- **opportunity rate**—the rate that an investor could earn on another security that the investor feels is a close substitute for the security being valued.

In many situations, the market value at a point in time can be found by consultation with a securities brokerage firm. Sources such as *The Wall Street Journal* and many online sources (we cover some of these later) give daily, or even more frequent, "quotes" on the most current security prices. But there are also many securities, for example, the stock of a closely held firm, that are not traded frequently and for which, therefore, current market quotes are not readily available.

Finding the opportunity rates for a particular security is sometimes rather straightforward and sometimes very difficult and subjective. For example, consider a corporate bond issued by a large company with an Aaa Moody's credit rating. An investor can fairly easily find another bond issued by a similar-size firm, maybe even in the same industry, with the same credit rating and maturity. Such a bond would certainly represent a very close, if not perfect, substitute for the bond in question. On the other hand, there are certainly numerous securities for which close substitutes would be difficult to find—trying to find a perfect substitute for Amazon.com common stock may not be so easy. (This is what makes investments interesting.)

Corporate Debt

Exhibit 4A-1 lists the characteristics of fixed-rate debt financing.

The parameters that influence the value to the investor of an investment in a typical corporate bond are:

- **par value** (face value)—M (usually $1,000) equals the amount carried on the corporation's books as the value of each outstanding bond, before adjustment for any premium or discount. (This will, in general, not be the same as the market value.)
- **coupon rate**—r_c equals the interest rate (stated as an annual rate), which, when multiplied by the par value, gives the annual interest payments on the bond.
- **payment frequency**—p, either semiannually (2) or annually (1).
- $\mathbf{r_c \times M \div p}$—Interest payment.
- **maturity**—a period ranging from 5 to 30 years, or even longer.
- **principal amount**—par value, payable to the investor at the maturity date, along with the final interest payment.

Consider the bonds issued by ACME General Corporation, which are described in a footnote to ACME's financials. The note, excerpted from ACME General's annual report, is shown in Exhibit 4A-2.

ACME's long-term bonds are typical in that they pay semiannual interest until they mature, when both interest and principal are paid. In 1999, ACME issued 1 million of these $1,000 par value bonds, with a maturity date of 2029. These account for the $1,000 million in long-term debt on ACME's balance sheet (see Exhibit 4-1 in the chapter). As of December 31, 2003, these bonds, with semiannual interest payments, have 26 years remaining to maturity. To an investor originally purchasing a $1000 par bond, an 8.0% coupon rate means interest payments of $40 (calculated as (0.08/2) × $1,000) semiannually, for 30 years, and in addition to the interest received in Year 30, the investor also receives a repayment of the par value. These cash flows to the investor for each of the 60 semiannual periods are as depicted in Exhibit 4A-3.

Exhibit 4A-1 Basic Features of Corporate Debt

Priority of Claim	⇒	Before either preferred or common stockholders.
Nature of Cash Flows	⇒	Periodic interest at regular intervals, principal repayment at maturity.
Governance Rights	⇒	Debt contracts may restrict certain actions by the firm; creditors do not participate directly in governance unless the firm is in default, in which event the creditors may exercise certain rights to protect their interests.

Exhibit 4A-2 Notes to Consolidated Financial Statements—Long-Term Debt Agreement

The Company's long-term debt at December 31, 2003 and 2002 is summarized as follows:

	2003	2002
Senior Secured Bonds, 8.0%, due 2029	$1,000	$1,000
Total	$1,000	$1,000

During 1999, the Company issued long-term debt in the form of Senior Secured Bonds, 8.0% due December 31, 2029. Coincident with the issuance of new debt, the Company prepaid the total principal remaining on the previously existing Senior Notes of $500 million.

SENIOR SECURED BONDS

The Senior Secured Bonds were issued for $1,000 million, bearing 8.0% interest due in 2029. The Company's obligations under the Senior Secured Bonds are secured by a first property lien on substantially all existing and future real property and equipment of Acme General, including all of the assets required in connection with the Modernization and Expansion Project.

The Senior Notes contain certain restrictive covenants that limit the Company's ability to incur additional indebtedness, create liens, pay dividends, repurchase capital stock, engage in transactions with affiliates, sell assets, engage in sale or leaseback transactions, and engage in mergers or consolidations.

An important characteristic of the investment in such a bond is that the future cash flows to the investor are fixed by the stated coupon rate (as set in the contract governing the relationship between the investor and the firm, known as the bond **indenture**). So even as interest rates in the economy rise or fall after the bond issue, the cash flows to the investor will not change. Such a security is known as a **fixed income security**.

Suppose Cokie, a typical investor in such bonds, felt that she should earn a return of about 8.4 percent annually on investments similar to the ACME bond. She might have arrived at this opportunity rate by considering the rates she could earn on similar bonds issued by other companies. Other companies' bonds having the same rating and about the same maturity would be considered "similar" for the purpose of determining the appropriate opportunity rate. Since ACME's bond pays interest on a semiannual basis, we need to convert the 8.4% annual rate to a

Exhibit 4A-3 Bond Cash Flows

Period	1	2	3	4	. . .	59	60
Cash flow	$40	$40	$40	$40	. . .	$40	$1,040

semiannual equivalent. We are looking for a semiannual rate such that compounding the rate over a year (two semiannual periods) would result in a net gain of \$0.084 for each dollar invested. If r_D is the semiannual equivalent rate, the mathematics of compound interest dictates that $(1 + r_D)^2 = 1.084$, or $r = 0.0412$, or 4.12%. To find the intrinsic value that represents the amount that Cokie would be willing to pay for the ACME bond, we must solve the following problem for the unknown value, V_B, using our knowledge of her required rate of return.

$$V_{4.12\%} = \frac{40}{(1 + .0412)} + \frac{40}{(1 + .0412)^2} + \frac{40}{(1 + .0412)^3} + \frac{40}{(1 + .0412)^4} + \ldots + \frac{1{,}040}{(1 + .0412)^{60}}$$
$$= \$973.46$$

Of course, the market value of the bond could be higher or lower than Cokie's intrinsic value. If she could buy the bond at a price lower than \$973.46, then she would obviously earn a return greater than 4.12% because she would be receiving the same (fixed) income flows, but on a smaller investment. The return would be less than 4.12% if she had to pay more than \$973.46 for the bond.

Suppose, in fact, that the ACME bond did have a current market price of exactly \$973.46. The fact that the market value of this bond is \$973.46 implies that there is a consensus among investors that that the 4.12% semiannual YTM is a reasonable return for investing in the ACME bonds. The discount rate that gives a DCF value for a bond equal to the market price of the bond with semiannual interest payments is called the semiannual **yield-to-maturity (YTM)** for that bond. Since we have shown that discounting the interest and principle payments on this bond at 4.12% results in a \$973.46 DCF value of the bond, we would say that the semiannual YTM for the ACME bond is 4.12%. If existing bondholders believed that a 4.12% YTM was inadequate, they would want to sell their bonds at the current price, in turn putting downward pressure on market prices. Conversely, if investors felt that 4.12% was more than a reasonable yield for such an investment, then they would want to invest more in the bonds, in the process putting upward pressure on the market price. Suppose Cokie had determined that the semiannual opportunity rate for such a bond is 3.8% instead of 4.12%, that is, she has identified other bonds, which have YTMs of 3.8%, that are good substitutes for ACME's bonds. Then the DCF value (intrinsic value) that she would place on the ACME bond would be \$1,047.02.

It is interesting to note that if an investor paid exactly \$1,000 for this bond, then the semiannual YTM would equal exactly 4%, which is the same as the bond's semiannual coupon rate. As the market price increases above the par value (i.e., the bond is selling at a **premium**), the YTM declines, and as the market price falls below par value (i.e., the bond is selling at a **discount**), the YTM increases. If we think of the YTM as reflecting the consensus of investors' opinions about the appropriate opportunity rate for a given bond, then we see that market values diverge from par values because the consensus opportunity rate diverges from the fixed coupon rate set on the bond when it was issued.

To summarize the mathematics of bond valuation, we will use the following equation:

$$V_B = \sum_{t=1}^{n} \frac{r_c M/p}{(1 + r_D)^t} + \frac{M}{(1 + r_D)^n}. \quad \textbf{(4A-1)}$$

Debt valuation is important from the firm's perspective, since it is one of the determinants of the firm's cost of capital. If a firm already has outstanding debt issues that have equal priority and similar maturity to new debt that the firm might offer, then those outstanding debt issues represent close substitutes for the new debt, and the YTM on the outstanding debt is a reasonable estimate of the firm's cost of borrowing. If a firm has a variety of long-term debt issues outstanding, the average cost of those issues may be used as an estimate of the firm's cost of borrowing. We address this and other issues relating to a firm's cost of capital in Chapter 11.

Floating-rate debt is a form of debt where the interest rate paid by the firm is periodically "reset" to reflect current market interest rates. An example would be bank term loans, which, unlike the bonds and notes described in the previous example, are **amortized**, that is, the principal amount is repaid in installments over the life of the loan. The debt contract specifies the benchmark rate to which the interest rate is "pegged"—usually the contract calls for setting the interest rate on the debt equal to the benchmark rate plus a "markup," called the **spread**, of a fixed number of "basis points" (hundredths of a percent). A common benchmark is LIBOR, or London Interbank Offer Rate. LIBOR is the rate for interbank dollar loans in the Eurodollar market. Since these interbank loans are considered very safe investments, floating rate debt issued by nonbanks will generally be considered riskier, hence the rates for floating rate loans will generally be significantly higher than LIBOR. The market value of floating rate debt will almost always be close to its par value, because, under the provisions in the debt contract, the "floating" rate will automatically adjust to reflect consensus rates.

Preferred Stock

Exhibit 4A-4 summarizes the basic characteristics of preferred stock.

Exhibit 4A-4 Basic Features of Preferred Stock

Priority of Claim	⇒	After debt claims, but ahead of common stockholders; it is usually cumulative, meaning that dividends that are owed (*in arrears*) on preferred stock must be paid before any dividends on common stock can be paid.
Nature of Cash Flows	⇒	Periodic dividends, usually quarterly; either a specified dollar amount or a specified percentage of the par value; no set maturity; sometimes convertible into common stock.
Governance Rights	⇒	As specified in the firm's articles of incorporation, but usually minimal, even if the firm is in arrears on dividends.

The characteristics of a typical preferred stock are:

- **par value** (face value, often $100)—the amount carried on the corporation's books as the value of each outstanding share, before adjustment for any premium or discount. (This will, in general, not be the same as the market value.)
- **dividends**—d_p equals the periodic (usually quarterly) dividend payment per share.
- **payment frequency**—may be quarterly, semiannually, or annually.
- **maturity**—usually infinite.

Like bonds, preferred stock is a fixed income security, since the cash flows to investors do not fluctuate over time, but are fixed in advance by the terms of the issue. It is carried on the firm's accounts at its par value, plus any premium or less any discount at the time it was initially sold to investors.

ACME doesn't have preferred stock, but many companies, especially utilities and financial institutions, do. Consider some hypothetical preferred shares, with a $100 par value, a 5% dividend rate (this is the same as $5 per year, or $1.25 per quarter), and no stated maturity. The cash flows to the investor for each quarter stretch out in perpetuity. Suppose Cokie's husband, Bob, believes that an investment in this preferred stock should yield an annual return of 6%. Since 6% annually is equivalent to 1.467% with quarterly compounding (solve for r such that $(1 + r)^4 = 1.06$, or r = .01467, or 1.467%), we can find the DCF value (intrinsic value) that Bob would be willing to pay for a share of ACME preferred stock by discounting the anticipated dividend flows at 1.467%.

$$P = \frac{1.25}{(1 + .01467)} + \frac{1.25}{(1 + .01467)^2} + \frac{1.25}{(1 + .01467)^3} + \ldots + \frac{1.25}{(1 + .01467)^\infty}$$
$$= 85.21$$

Further suppose that the actual market value of the shares is $84.00. Then the quarterly rate of return to an investor who buys at the market price and holds forever will be the value of r that solves

$$84.00 = \frac{1.25}{(1 + r)^1} + \frac{1.25}{(1 + r)^2} + \frac{1.25}{(1 + r)^3} + \ldots + \frac{1.25}{(1 + r)^\infty}.$$

Fortunately, mathematicians have discovered that the right side of the above equation can be represented simply as $1.25/r, so it is easy to solve for r. In this case r is r = $1.25/$84.00 = 0.01488, or 1.488%. Since the periods are quarters, then the 0.01488 represents a quarterly rate of return, which when converted to an annual rate is 6.09% ($1.01488^4 - 1 = .0609$). From Bob's perspective, the preferred shares would be a reasonable investment, since they have a YTM higher than his required rate of return, or equivalently, the market price at which the preferred shares could be purchased is less than the $85.21 Bob would be willing to pay.

As with the bonds analyzed above, a market price of $84.00 implies that the market's consensus about the appropriate opportunity rate is 1.488% quarterly. From the issuing firm's perspective, the cost of financing with preferred stock is the rate of return that must be offered to investors in order to make the shares attractive, that is, for share P in our example, it is 1.488%.

To summarize the mathematics of preferred stock valuation, we will use the following equation.

$$V_P = \frac{d_P}{r} \tag{4A-2}$$

Common Stock

Often the phrase **common equity** or just **equity** is used to denote the same thing as common stock. Exhibit 4A-5 summarizes the basic characteristics of common stock.

The parameters relating to the characterization of investment in typical common stock are

- **par value** (face value)—the amount carried on the corporation's books as the value of each outstanding share.
- **dividends**—d_t equals the periodic (usually quarterly) dividend payment per share (the "t" subscript denotes that the dividend may change from time to time.
- **payment frequency**—usually quarterly.
- **maturity**—infinite.

Common stock shares are most definitely *not* fixed income securities. Indeed, there is nothing in writing by the company that even provides investors with an estimate of the future dividend stream to which their shares will entitle them. Take ACME General, for example. ACME has 100 million shares of stock outstanding in both 2002 and 2003 and paid dividends of $160.04 million in 2002 and $104.89 million in 2003. This is $1.60 per share in 2002, and $1.05 in 2003. Therefore, it is clear that dividends fluctuate from year to year, sometimes rather dramatically. The obvious question is that if we have difficulty predicting dividends, which are

Exhibit 4A-5 Basic Features of Common Stock

Priority of Claim	⇒	Subordinate to debt claims and preferred stockholders; there is no guarantee or promise of dividend payments.
Nature of Cash Flows	⇒	Companies that pay dividends usually declare those dividends on a quarter-by-quarter basis by informing investors of a specified dollar amount; the dividends are subject to change due to operating performance; the shares have no set maturity.
Governance Rights	⇒	As specified in the firm's articles of incorporation, shareholders have the right to attend annual meetings, vote on candidates for the board of directors and certain other matters, as specified in the articles of incorporation and bylaws. They are the owners of the firm. Some companies have more than one class of shares, where the classes differ according to voting rights and dividend payments.

especially problematic for firms that have no dividend history, how can we value the shares? (As a matter of fact, this dilemma is the source of one of the major attractions of free-cash-flow analysis, since FCF does not require that the analyst know the future dividends to shareholders.)

Whether we discount free cash flow or dividends, we first need to determine an appropriate discount rate. There are two popular methods that investors and analysts use to determine a fair (or in the language of finance, "required") rate of return on their investments in common stock.

- Capital Asset Pricing Model (CAPM)
- Bond-yield-plus-risk-premium approach

Neither requires knowledge of the firm's future dividend stream per se. Rather, a stock's required return should be the risk-free rate, plus a premium related to the risk of the stock. They differ in how they benchmark the risk of a company's stock.

Required Return on Common Stock: The Capital Asset Pricing Model (CAPM) Approach The basic idea of this approach is that investors expect a rate of return commensurate with the risk of the investment. When coupled with the predictions of modern capital market theory, this basic idea leads to a rule of thumb for estimating required rates of return for equity investments. The underlying results of capital market theory include the following:

- Investors will hold well-diversified portfolios.
- Risk should be measured relative to the investor's portfolio.
- A statistical concept known as "beta" represents an estimate of how sensitive the return on the stock in question is to changes in the value of an index of overall stock market value.
- Investors' required returns will be linearly related to the appropriate measure of risk, and "beta" is the right measure.

Following up on the third point, for example, a beta of 2.0 means that, on average, a stock will lose 2% in value for each percentage point loss in the stock market as a whole. Finding the beta value for a particular company involves a statistical procedure called regression. To illustrate, Exhibit 4A-6 is a scatter plot of 60 monthly returns from holding ACME's common stock, and the returns that would have been earned had an investor owned shares in a portfolio containing all the stocks in the S&P 500 stock index. To determine the monthly return for any month, first calculate the gain (or loss) from purchasing one share of ACME's stock, which consists of any dividend received ($d_{ACME,\,t}$) plus appreciation in ACME's stock price during the month ($P_{ACME,\,t} - P_{ACME,\,t-1}$). Express this total gain (or loss, if negative) as a percentage of the amount paid for the stock at the end of the prior month.

$$r_{ACME,\,t} = (d_{ACME,\,t} + P_{ACME,\,t} - P_{ACME,\,t-1})/P_{ACME,\,t-1} \qquad \textbf{(4A-3)}$$

The return on the "market" is a similar measure applied to a well-diversified portfolio of stocks, such as a portfolio of the 500 stocks in the S&P 500 stock index. Such "portfolio" returns are available for a number of broad stock indexes.

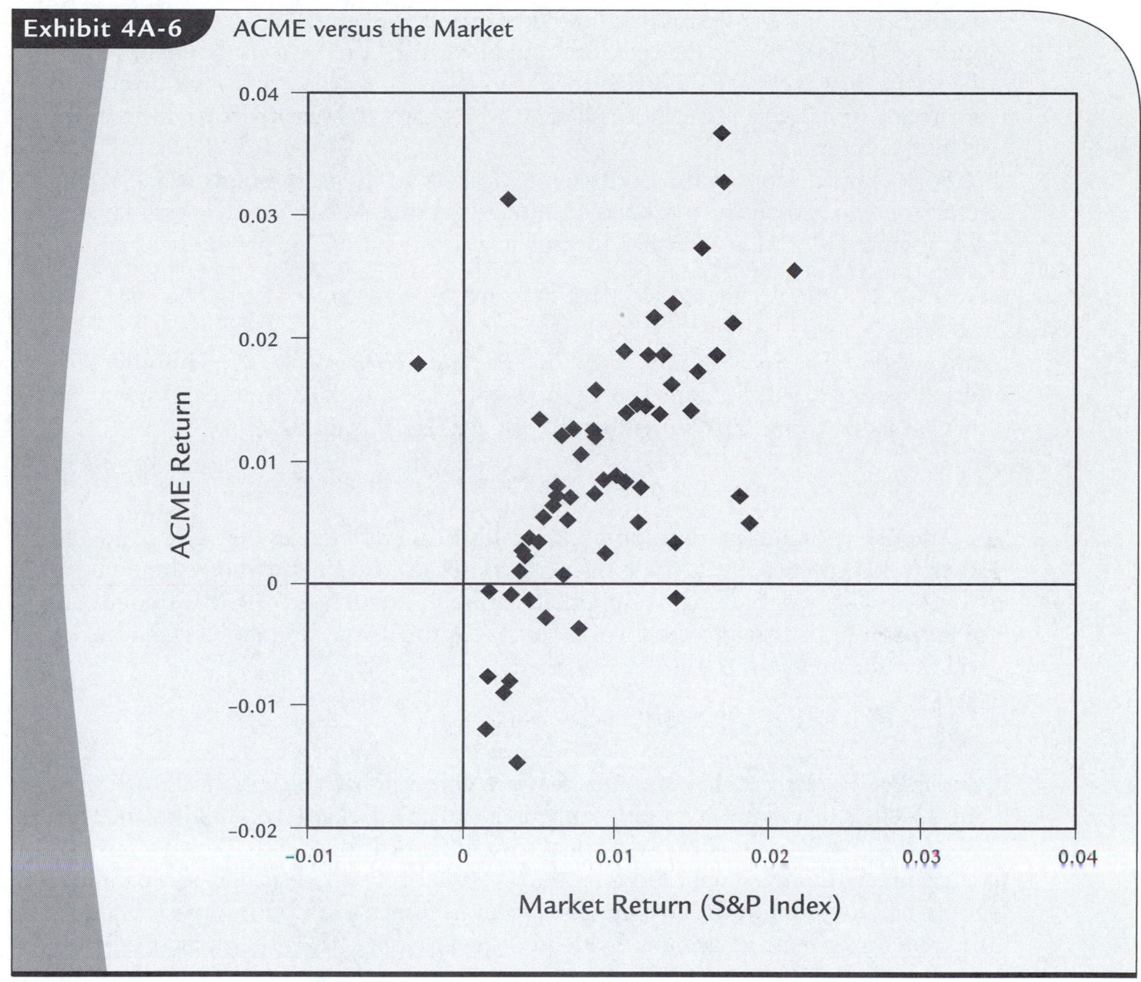

Exhibit 4A-6 ACME versus the Market

Exhibit 4A.6 is a scatter plot of the returns for ACME and the S&P index for the period from January 1999 through December 2003. Note that since these are monthly returns, they will seem small compared to annualized returns.

ACME's beta is estimated by fitting a straight line to the scatter plot, using linear regression. We did this and calculated the slope of the line to be 1.1. The implication is that over the past 60 months the average response of ACME to a 1% change in the return on the market was about 1.1%.

According to the **Capital Asset Pricing Model (CAPM)**, the required rate of return on a stock consists of the rate that an investor would earn on a riskless asset, plus a premium for bearing unavoidable risk. The unavoidable risk (also known as "systematic risk") is measured by the stock's beta. Mathematically, the CAPM says that the return an investor should expect from a stock is related to its beta risk according to a relationship known as the **Security Market Line**:

$$E(r_{ACME}) = r_{RF} + [E(r_M) - r_{RF}]\beta_{ACME} \tag{4A-4}$$

where $E(r_{ACME})$ is the return that should be expected from the stock in question (in our case, ACME), r_{RF} is the rate that could be earned on Treasury bonds, $E(r_M)$ is the return that is expected on the stock market generally (i.e., on a well diversified portfolio), and β_{ACME} is the beta risk of ACME, that is, its sensitivity to fluctuations in market returns.

For example, suppose the risk-free rate on 20-year Treasury bonds is 5.4%. The return anticipated on the market is 11.4%. Given that ACME's beta is estimated at 1.1, then the CAPM argues that a reasonable return on ACME would be

$$E(r_{ACME}) = .054 + 1.1(0.114 - 0.054) = 0.120, \text{ or } 12.0\%.$$

Required Return on Common Stock: Bond-Yield-Plus-Risk-Premium Approach This approach simply asserts that a company's stock should provide a fixed return premium beyond that provided by the firm's own bonds. For ACME, this implies that

$$E(r_{ACME}) = \text{ACME's bond yield} + \text{Risk premium}. \qquad \textbf{(4A-5)}$$

The risk premium is based on observed historical differences between bond and stock yields. There appears to be a general consensus that the premium should be in the 3% to 4% range. If, as we supposed earlier in this chapter, ACME's bonds are selling at a price that provides a YTM of 8.4% to ACME bondholders, and if we feel that the premium should be 3%, then

$$E(r_{ACME}) = 8.4\% + 3\% = 11.4\%.$$

Valuing Common Stock: The Gordon Growth Model One approach to common stock valuation focuses on estimation of the future dividend payments to stockholders and then estimates a DCF value of the stock by discounting those dividends, perhaps at a rate determined through application of the CAPM or bond-yield-plus-risk-premium approach discussed in the two previous sections. Once a discount rate is obtained, the remaining issue in using a dividend discount approach is that we don't know the future dividends with certainty. A frequently used technique is the dividend growth model (or sometimes the Gordon growth model after its inventor, Myron Gordon). Using this model requires that the analyst project future dividends on a period-by-period basis until the firm reaches a point where subsequent dividends will grow at a constant annual rate forever, then forecast that constant rate. While this approach to stock valuation places demands on the analyst that may appear to be heroic, this forecasting of growth rates is in fact a major activity by analysts, as witnessed by the existence of growth estimates by services such as Zacks (**http://www.zacks.com/**).

The table below gives the future dividends per share to the holder of ACME stock, assuming that the projections in the chapter are correct. The dividends are expected to grow at 6% after Year 3.

Period	2003	2004	2005	2006	2007
Cash dividend	1.049	1.351	1.914	2.029	2.151
Growth rate		28.8%	41.7%	6.0%	6.0%

The DCF value of the dividend stream is computed as

$$V_S = \frac{d_1}{(1 + r_S)^1} + \frac{d_2}{(1 + r_S)^2} + \frac{d_3}{(1 + r_S)^3} + \frac{d_4}{(1 + r_S)^4} + \frac{d_5}{(1 + r_S)^5} + \frac{d_6}{(1 + r_S)^6} + \ldots$$

Fortunately, the tedious calculation above can be avoided by using a shortcut formula for what is called a growth perpetuity. Once the growth rate in the future dividends has settled down to a constant growth rate, the following formula can be used to find the present value of all dividends from that point forward.

$$VGP = \frac{d_0(1+g)}{r_S - g} \qquad \textbf{(4A-6)}$$

where VGP is the present value of the growth perpetuity, d_0 is the amount of "base period" dividend, g is the perpetual growth rate, and r_S is the discount rate. The numerator, $d_0(1 + g)$, is the projected next cash flow, equal to the product of the last dividend times one plus the growth rate.

To summarize the mathematics of common stock valuation, the following equation applies.

$$V_S = \sum_{t=1}^{h} \frac{d_t}{(1 + r_S)^t} + \frac{1}{(1 + r_S)^h}\left[\frac{d_h(1 + g)}{r_S - g}\right] \qquad \textbf{(4A-7)}$$

where h is the "horizon" over which dividends are estimated using period-by-period growth rates and after which dividends are expected to grow at a perpetually constant rate, g.

For ACME's stock, the perpetual growth rate is 6%, beginning in period 2, so the period 2 dividend of \$2.029 would be the base-period cash flow. VGP would be the present value as of the end of period 2, of all dividends in period 3, and thereafter.

$$VGP = \frac{\$2.029}{r_S - .06} \qquad \textbf{(4A-6a)}$$

As with both bonds and preferred shares, the investor can use knowledge of an appropriate opportunity rate for the investment in common shares to find the present value of the stream of predicted dividends for ACME shares. For example, suppose the investor has used the CAPM as we did in the previous section to estimate that the appropriate opportunity rate is 12%. Then the present value of future expected dividends under the dividend growth formula is

$$\begin{aligned} V_S &= \frac{\$1.351}{(1.12)^1} + \frac{\$1.914}{(1.12)^2} + \frac{1}{(1.12)^2} VGP \\ &= \frac{\$1.351}{(1.12)^1} + \frac{\$1.914}{(1.12)^2} + \frac{1}{(1.12)^2}\left[\frac{\$2.029}{0.12 - 0.06}\right] \\ &= \$29.69. \end{aligned}$$

Except for rounding differences, this is the same stock price as found in the body of the chapter, using the corporate valuation model. Thus, we can see that for ACME the corporate valuation model produces about the same stock price as the discounted dividend model.

PART 3

Projecting Financial Statements

Chapter 5

Projecting Free Cash Flows

Introduction

Chapter 4 began by assuming that your faithful assistant had already projected a firm's financial statements. We then showed you how to take these projected financial statements, calculate projected free cash flows (FCFs), discount the projected FCFs, estimate the firm's value of operations, and calculate its stock price. Unfortunately, if you are like us, you probably don't have a faithful assistant, and you must project the financial statements yourself.

Creating a model to forecast financial statements is certainly important for valuation—you can't perform the calculations discussed in Chapter 4 without forecasted statements. In addition, going through the process of projecting financial statements has several valuable side effects:

- It forces you to explicitly articulate your assumptions regarding future sales, profitability, and asset utilization.
- It gives you a better understanding of the factors that "drive" the value of the firm.
- The resulting financial statements provide an easy way for you to determine whether your assumptions are economically realistic, and whether your model is "accountingly" correct.
- The resulting financial statements also show how much additional external financing the firm must raise to support its growth plans.

We're not going to kid you; projecting financial statements can be a pretty complicated topic. To make it easier, we're going to break it down into several smaller pieces that build upon one another. First, this chapter will focus on developing a 1-year forecast of the parts of the financial statements necessary to calculate free cash flows. Second, Chapter 6 will start with these projections and then show you how to finish the 1-year forecast by projecting a complete set of financial statements. Third, Chapter 7 will extend this to a multiyear forecast and perform a valuation based on the forecasts. Finally, Chapter 8 will explain some alternative ways to model the projected financial statements.

Requirements for Useful Financial Projections

For the projected statements to be useful in calculating free cash flow and the value of the firm, they must meet two requirements:

- **Economic Plausibility**—the statements must reflect how the firm might realistically be expected to operate in the future, given current information about the firm, its industry, and the economy as a whole.
- **Accounting Consistency**—unless the company is Enron, the projections must satisfy basic accounting rules. For example, the balance sheets must balance, with projected total assets equal to projected total liabilities and owners' equity.

We'll focus on economic plausibility in this chapter and address accounting consistency in the next. Projecting economically plausible statements requires the use of good judgment and a thorough understanding of the firm.[1] But even with the best tools and the best research available, your own judgment as an analyst is required, and the projected financial statements are no better than your judgment about the future. If your judgment is poor and does not reflect all the information that is available, then the ultimate predictions will themselves be poor. The goal is to make the most reasonable predictions possible, utilizing all the information available. As you follow our discussion and analysis, you may be puzzled that we gloss over, or appear to be more casual about some items than others. It's good to keep in mind that we are "estimating" and that we know in advance that our projections are imperfect. Our strategy as analysts should be to concentrate our energies on "consequential" factors, those that would be more likely to significantly alter our conclusion about the value of a firm. Understanding what factors are likely to be consequential comes with experience, and we will provide some guidelines in later chapters.

We'll begin the process by examining the financial statements of Van Leer, Inc., a manufacturer of plastic products.

Van Leer, Inc.

As we discuss Van Leer's financials and the process of making projections, you'll note that we are using some information not reported in the historical financials, but gleaned by our analyst either from very pointed questions directed to the right people in the company, or from our knowledge of developments in the economy at large. The analyst may be a corporate "insider," using the corporate valuation model to help project the financial results from alternative strategies (e.g., a marketing campaign designed to increases sales growth or a re-engineering program designed to cut the cost of goods sold). Alternatively, the analyst might be an "outsider," who will advise investment clients whether Van Leer stock is a good buy. In either case, although the sources of information will be different for inside and outside analysts, the instinct and insights of the analyst in knowing the right questions, and to whom they should be directed, are critical to the forecasting and valuation process.

Van Leer Products, Inc., manufactures a range of extruded plastic products—from Happy Meal® toys, to plastic dinnerware, to lawn furniture. Van Leer's financial statements are reported in Exhibit 5-1. These are a bit more complicated than ACME's from Chapter 3, but this added complexity allows us to project more realistic financial statements.

[1] We have found that such understanding may be facilitated by applying any of a number of strategic management analytical tools: Porter's Five Forces Analysis; SWOT (Strengths, Weaknesses, Opportunities, and Threats); or RiDUCES (Rivals, Downstream, Upstream, Complements, Entrants, and Substitutes).

Exhibit 5-1 Van Leer Products, Inc. (millions of dollars)

Van Leer Products, Inc.

Income Statement	Actual 2001	Actual 2002	Actual 2003
Net sales	$840	$944	$1,000
Cost of goods sold	520	625	640
Selling, general & administrative	200	205	215
Depreciation	41	42	45
Operating profit	$ 79	$ 72	$ 100
Interest income	0	1	0
Interest expense	9	9	10
Earnings before taxes	$ 70	$ 64	$ 90
Taxes	28	25	36
Net income	$ 42	$ 39	$ 54
Dividends	12	11	16
Additions to RE	$ 30	$ 28	$ 38

Balance Sheet	Actual 2001	Actual 2002	Actual 2003
Assets			
Cash	$ 42	$ 47	$ 50
Short-term investments	10	15	25
Inventory	75	85	100
Accounts receivable	65	70	75
Total current assets	$192	$217	$ 250
Net PPE	275	280	300
Total assets	$467	$497	$ 550
Liabilities and Shareholders' Equity			
Accounts payable	$ 80	$ 70	$ 75
Accrued expenses	8	10	10
Short-term debt	50	30	25
Total current liabilities	$138	$110	$ 110
Long-term debt	54	84	99
Total liabilities	$192	$194	$ 209
Common stock	125	125	125
Retained earnings	150	178	216
Total common equity	$275	$303	$ 341
Total liabilities and equity	$467	$497	$ 550

One difference between ACME and Van Leer is that Van Leer sometimes makes short-term investments in nonoperating assets. For example, Van Leer accumulates cash from operations before it makes dividend payments or pays its suppliers. Rather than letting this money sit in a checking account, Van Leer either invests it in a money market account, purchases short-term Treasury securities, or purchases the short-term debt of other companies (this is called **commercial paper**). In either case, Van Leer earns interest on these investments, which appears on its income statement in the "interest income" account. Since these short-term investments are assets for Van Leer, their value appears under the "short-term investments" category in the current assets section of the balance sheet.

If financial statements were prepared by accountants expressly for use in valuation analysis, they would always report the cash needed for operations in the cash account and any extra short-term investments in the short-term investment account. Unfortunately, accountants frequently will combine the accounts into something called "cash and marketable securities." Fortunately, Van Leer's accountants have shown cash and short-term investments separately. In Chapter 12, we'll show you how to handle the situation if the reported statements don't appropriately separate cash and short-term investments.

The only other difference between Van Leer's balance sheet and ACME's is that we have done away with the gross PPE and accumulated depreciation items. Our calculation of investment in operating capital, free cash flow, and return on invested capital depend on net PPE rather than gross PPE, so we don't need accumulated depreciation and gross PPE for valuation purposes. You will see later in this chapter that it also makes more economic sense to project net PPE instead of gross PPE.

Projecting Financial Statements

There are two steps to projecting financial statements. First, you must build a model that captures the important economic relationships that underlie the firm's business. Second, you must make reasonable choices for the input parameters governing the identified relationships. These steps require an understanding of the company's financial history and its plans for the future. They also require considerable judgment on your part, and a combination of art and science. The following sections apply these steps to Van Leer.

Modeling the Financial Statements

The reason we create a model of the financial statements is to reduce the work needed to construct projections; it would be a great deal of work to project each of the items on the income statement and balance sheet separately and independently. Even if you were willing to do this, you would not capture the important relationships among the items. We want to reduce our projections to a limited number of "drivers" and use projections of these drivers to fill in the financial statements. One of the primary drivers is the level of sales, as discussed below.

Operating Accounts that Vary Directly with Sales

Probably the most important driver for changes in financial statements is sales growth. For most companies, cost of goods sold is (more or less) directly proportional to sales, so as sales increase, COGS will also increase. But what about selling, general and administrative expenses? Does it make sense to model SGA as proportional to sales? For most companies, the answer is "yes," especially when considering a long time horizon. Even though SGA may not vary directly with sales every year, over time it does tend to move with sales. For example, if a company's sales are growing, then over time its level of SGA expense will have to increase as the company provides increased administrative support.

Over time, a growing firm must acquire more assets to support its sales growth. Most firms must maintain some minimal level of cash balances in order to function because they cannot predict exactly how much money is going to come in or go out on a given day. This minimum requirement is usually larger for larger firms, so the cash balance will tend to increase with sales. Similarly, accounts receivable are generated when the firm makes credit sales, so its level should be proportional to sales. A growing company must maintain more inventories as sales increase in order to avoid stock-outs, so we might expect inventories to be proportional to sales.[2] Although a company might not make major additions to PPE each and every year, net PPE will also tend to increase with sales over the long term because a growing company will eventually outgrow its facilities.[3]

Just as operating assets must expand as a firm grows, some of its operating liabilities tend to expand spontaneously as it grows. For example, a growing company uses trade credit when it purchases materials from suppliers, so its level of accounts payable will increase with sales. As a growing company's payroll increases, accruals such as accrued taxes and accrued wages will increase as well.

As indicated above, many operating items on the financial statements will be tied directly to sales. This suggests that the first step in modeling financial statements should be to identify those items whose values depend on sales. In our projections we will assume that the following operating items vary directly with sales:

- Cost of goods sold
- Selling, general and administrative expenses
- Cash
- Inventory
- Accounts receivable
- Net PPE
- Accounts payable
- Accrued expenses

Once sales have been forecasted, then projecting these items requires an estimate of their relationship to sales, for example, the ratio of COGS to sales. The projected level of COGS will be projected sales multiplied by the projected COGS/sales ratio. Analysts commonly use this forecasting technique, called the "percent of sales" method.

Operating Accounts that Vary with Other Accounts

Some operating items may not vary with sales. For example, the amount of depreciation charged is really a function of the book values of the assets being depreciated and the assumed lives of the assets. Although we probably won't know the depreciation schedule for all of the assets in a firm, we can estimate an average rate of

---

[2] See Chapter 8 for some alternative ways to model inventory.

[3] Chapter 8 shows other ways to model net PPE.

depreciation using the current year's total depreciation charges as a percentage of the current year's net PPE. A higher ratio means that the firm is depreciating its assets rapidly and therefore they have shorter accounting lives. A lower ratio means the assets are depreciated more slowly and have longer lives.

As you probably have guessed by now, one of the techniques of forecasting is to use current and historical relationships between variables (such as sales and COGS) to estimate future relationships. We explain this in more detail later in the chapter.

Modeling the Financial Statement Items Required to Project Free Cash Flow

Notice that we have specified the relationships for all the items needed to forecast free cash flow, as shown in Exhibit 5-2. In particular, given a forecast of sales, we can forecast COGS and SGA, which allows us to calculate operating profit. With an assumed tax rate, we can then calculate net operating profit after taxes (NOPAT). We can calculate net operating working capital (NOWC) because we have forecasts of operating current assets (cash, accounts receivable, and inventory) and operating current liabilities (accounts payable and accruals). We also have a forecast of net PPE, which allows us to calculate operating capital. With NOPAT and the projected investment in operating capital, we can calculate free cash flow.

If we were only concerned with valuation, we could stop here and not bother to forecast the rest of the financial statements. However, forecasting the complete set of financial statements provides valuable information about the company's future needs for external financing, and so we always forecast the entire set of financial statements, as we shall do for Van Leer in Chapter 6.

Exhibit 5-2 Projecting Free Cash Flows with Partial Financial Statements

Income Statement	Forecast method
Net sales	Forecasted
Cost of goods sold	Percent of sales
Selling, general & administrative	Percent of sales
Depreciation	Percent of net PPE
Operating profit	Calculated from the entries above

Balance Sheet	Forecast method
Operating Assets	
Cash	Percent of sales
Inventory	Percent of sales
Accounts receivable	Percent of sales
Net PPE	Percent of sales
Operating Current Liabilities	
Accounts payable	Percent of sales
Accrued expenses	Percent of sales

Choosing Inputs for the Model

The previous sections described the logic underlying the percent of sales technique for projecting financial statements. The next sections illustrate the model by choosing inputs and projecting the portions of Van Leer's financial statements that we need to calculate free cash flow for the next year. Keep in mind that we will project the complete financial statements in Chapter 6, and we will project more than 1 year in Chapter 7.

Projecting the Sales Growth Rate

The first step in making the actual financial projections is to project sales growth. As an analyst, you should use the recent historical sales growth rates, your knowledge about the company and its industry, and expectations about inflation to guide you. Van Leer's sales were $840, $944, and $1,000 million in the last 3 years. As Exhibit 5-3 shows, the growth rate in 2002 was ($944 – $840)/$840 = 12.4%. The growth rate in 2003 was 5.9%. The average growth rate over the last 2 years has been 9.2%. Because the economy is predicted to recover substantially during 2004, our analyst predicts more rapid growth than either 2003's growth rate or the average growth rate. After speaking with marketing and operations, our analyst predicts that Van Leer's sales will increase by 9% next year due to increased unit sales and by 2% due to anticipated inflation. Dollar sales, therefore, are projected to increase by a total of 11% from $1,000 million to $1,110 million.

Projecting Operating Items on the Income Statement

The following sections show how to project the items required to calculate net operating profit after taxes (NOPAT).

Exhibit 5-3 Historical Ratios Used to Project Free Cash Flows

	2001	2002	2003	Average
Ratios to calculate operating profit				
Sales growth rate	na	12.4%	5.9%	9.2%
COGS/Sales	61.9%	66.2%	64.0%	64.0%
SGA/Sales	23.8%	21.7%	21.5%	22.3%
Depreciation/Net PPE	14.9%	15.0%	15.0%	15.0%
Ratios to calculate operating capital				
Cash/Sales	5.0%	5.0%	5.0%	5.0%
Inventory/Sales	8.9%	9.0%	10.0%	9.3%
Accounts receivable/Sales	7.7%	7.4%	7.5%	7.6%
Net PPE/Sales	32.7%	29.7%	30.0%	30.8%
Accounts payable/Sales	9.5%	7.4%	7.5%	8.1%
Accruals/Sales	0.9%	1.1%	1.0%	1.0%
Ratios to calculate operating taxes				
Tax rate (Taxes/EBT)	40.0%	39.1%	40.0%	39.7%

Cost of Goods Sold The first input to choose is the ratio of COGS/sales. What are the economic forces that affect this ratio? A higher COGS/sales ratio can come from lower sales prices with dollar production costs held constant, or higher production costs with sales prices remaining constant, or a combination of the two. Lower values of COGS as a percentage of sales can come from a reduction in production costs, with sales prices remaining the same, or higher sales prices and stable production costs, or a combination of the two. If we translate these changes into possible business scenarios, then reductions in COGS as a percentage of sales, which increase the gross profit margin, may come from cost containment, quality improvement (and a higher sales price because of the quality improvement), or both. Increases in COGS as a percentage of sales may come from runaway production costs, or from sales price declines, which might result from a decrease in quality or a reduction in demand as the industry contracts or from competition drawing away customers.

Van Leer's marketing department is projecting that, as the economy moves out of recession, increased demand for plastic goods will allow it to raise prices. But, at the same time, increased demand in the world economy for oil, which is the major raw material in plastic, will drive up its raw materials costs. Most of this increased production cost can be passed on to Van Leer's customers so, on balance, Van Leer expects that cost of goods sold as a percentage of sales revenues will decrease slightly from last year's value of 64% to 62.5% in 2004.

Selling, General and Administrative Expenses SGA for Van Leer consists of the general and administrative expenses plus commissions to its sales force. Van Leer does only minimal advertising in its trade magazines *Plastics Monthly* and *Innovations in Extrusion*. This year's SGA was 21.5% of sales, which was lower than the 3-year average of 22.3%. This year was different from the previous years because Van Leer managed to hold the line on salaries and the commission rate, while still achieving a modest sales increase. 2004 is expected to differ, in that the dollar-value of SGA expenses is expected to increase next year due to inflation. Van Leer is still not anticipating adding any staff (other than replacement due to attrition), and salary increases are expected to be only at the rate of inflation. The sales commission rate, which averaged 9% of sales in 2003, will increase in 2004 to 12% of sales as Van Leer implements a more aggressive sales plan. Note that the projected sales figures for 2004 do not reflect much of an increase due to this plan, since the results are expected to become apparent only after 1½ years. With Van Leer holding the line on dollar administrative costs, SGA as a percent of sales should decline even more from 2003's figures if there is sales growth, as we project. However, the increase in the commission rate represents an increase in SGA as a percent of sales. The net result for Van Leer is an overall increase in SGA as a percent of sales from last year's 21.5% to 22.5% in 2004.

Depreciation Expense The depreciation schedule is determined by the prices of the assets that Van Leer purchases, how long the assets are expected to last, and whether straight line or accelerated depreciation is used. Short term assets are depreciated quickly, and the depreciation charge is a large percentage of the initial book value of the asset and also of the net book value of the asset in any given year. Long-term assets are depreciated slowly, and their depreciation charges are a small percentage of both the initial and the remaining book values of the asset. Most assets are now categorized as 3-, 5-, 7-, 10-, or 30-year assets. Under straight-line depreciation, 3-year assets are depreciated 33.33% each year and 10-year assets are depreciated 10% each year. Van Leer's depreciation has averaged 15% of net PPE, reflecting Van Leer's mix of medium and long-term assets. There are no plans to change the type of assets Van Leer uses in production for 2004, so depreciation as a percent of net PPE is expected to remain at 15% for 2004.

Tax Rate Van Leer's average combined federal, state, and local tax rate has been approximately 39.7% in past years. This is not expected to change in 2004.

Projecting Operating Items on the Balance Sheets

As already discussed, Van Leer must acquire operating assets to support its growth. The amount Van Leer must spend on new assets in 2004 depends on whether it plans to change the way it uses its existing assets and whether it must buy more assets to support the additional sales for next year. For example, if Van Leer is planning to implement a just-in-time inventory management system, inventory may not need to increase to support sales growth and may even decline. If Van Leer is currently operating its plants at less than full capacity because of the recession last year, then it can probably increase sales without investing in new PPE. But if Van Leer is running its plants three shifts and bursting at the seams, then it will probably have to make a substantial investment in fixed assets to support any sales increase over the rate of inflation. The analyst's job is to search for all relevant facts related to each category of operating assets.

Van Leer's operations will require operating assets, but it will also generate operating liabilities, such as accounts payable. The following sections explain our choices for the inputs needed to calculate operating assets and operating liabilities.

Cash Van Leer, just like any other company, has to maintain a cash balance so that checks written on its accounts won't bounce. If there is considerable uncertainty about how much money will come into the company on a given day, and how much money must be paid out, then the cash balance must be larger. This level of cash that Van Leer must maintain is really an operating asset; it is not money that is available for distribution to shareholders since it must be sitting in a checking account to make sure checks clear. In recent years the technology for predicting how much cash will come into a company and how much cash will need to be paid out on a given day has improved dramatically. Many companies have point of sales terminals that record receipts and transmit the information to a central computer in real time. The technology for transferring cash into and out of investment accounts has also improved. The combination of these two trends means that the amount of cash a company needs to maintain has dropped from about 5% of sales to less than 1% of sales for many companies.

Cash as a percentage of sales has averaged about 5% of sales during the past 3 years at Van Leer. However, Van Leer has recently hired a new CFO who is working on better information technology, and she predicts that cash balances can be maintained at 3% of sales next year without an increased chance of bounced checks.

Accounts Receivable Van Leer's level of accounts receivable depends first on the volume of sales and second on its credit policies. Accounts receivable as a percent of sales has averaged 7.6% over the last 3 years. The reciprocal of this ratio is popularly known as the receivables turnover ratio. For Van Leer, this is 13, which means that Van Leer generates $13 of sales for every dollar it has tied up in receivables. Another way of looking at Van Leer's accounts receivable management is to estimate how long it takes the company to collect the receivables. We can estimate this by dividing receivables by daily sales (annual sales divided by 365 days). For Van Leer, this has averaged about 28 days. This is pretty good, considering that Van Leer's credit terms are net 30—that is, that customers can pay the purchase price 30 days later without penalty. Reducing accounts receivable would free up cash and increase free cash flow, but doing so would require changing its credit terms from net 30 to something more stringent, say net 20, or offering a discount for cash purchases. Since the industry standard is net 30, Van Leer does not think it can profitably tighten up its credit terms, so it anticipates that accounts receivable will remain at 7.6% of sales in 2004.

Inventory In recent years, inventory has averaged about 9% of sales. The reciprocal of this ratio, popularly known as the inventory turnover ratio, indicates that average sales are 11 times inventory, quite high by industry standards. In other words, Van Leer ties up only 9 cents in inventory for every dollar of sales. This excellent inventory performance came about because Van Leer actively pursued supply chain negotiations with its suppliers and customers, investing in information technology to better predict the products it would have to supply and the lead time required to order raw materials. As a result of the economic downturn in 2003, Van Leer's inventories increased a little to 10% of sales. Van Leer actually anticipates that inventories will increase a little more, to 11% of sales, in 2004, as it stocks up on raw materials in anticipation of a summer recovery in plastics demand. Although Van Leer could drive its inventory levels back down to the historical 9% figure, it is especially concerned about stock-outs in the summer of 2004 and is willing to support this higher level of inventory to make the most of the summer recovery.

Net PPE One of the small blessings for Van Leer during the latter part of 2002 and 2003 was that the company was approaching full capacity. As sales increased, albeit slowly, it did not have to invest in as many operating assets because it was able to use a factory that had excess space and capacity in 2001. This meant that net PPE as a percent of sales declined over the last three years as investment did not have to keep up with sales growth. However, in 2004 Van Leer must bring on line more equipment and build another plant in order to keep pace with growing demand. If Van Leer were able to invest in small fractions of a plant every year, then it would be able to maintain PPE at approximately 30% of sales, but it must build an entire plant at once. This leaves Van Leer with an expected overcapacity in 2004 and PPE of 34% of sales. Of course, as Van Leer grows into its new plant, its ratio of PPE to sales will decline back down to its full capacity level of 30%. We'll revisit this point in Chapter 7, when we get to the multiyear projections.

Accounts Payable and Accruals The level of accounts payable reflects the firm's payment policies and the credit policies of its suppliers. The **payables deferral period** (or **PDP**) is the number of days, on average, that a company takes to pay its bills, and is calculated as

$$\text{Payables deferral period} = \frac{\text{Accounts payable}}{(\text{Cost of goods sold}/365)}. \tag{5-1}$$

To put this in terms of our ratios so far **(5-2)**

$$\text{PDP} = 365\left(\frac{\text{Accounts payable}}{\text{Cost of goods sold}}\right) = 365\left(\frac{\text{Accounts payable}}{\text{Sales}}\right) \div \left(\frac{\text{Cost of goods sold}}{\text{Sales}}\right).$$

Van Leer's accounts payable has averaged about 8% of sales, and because cost of goods sold has been about 64% of sales, PDP = 365(0.08/0.64) = 45.6 days. So Van Leer takes, on average, about 46 days to pay its bills. This is consistent with the industry standard credit policy of net 45. If Van Leer were to increase accounts payable by paying its bills later, it would free up cash and increase free cash flow (remember, an increase in a liability account is a source of cash). However, if Van Leer repeatedly pays its suppliers later than their terms allow, the loss of its best suppliers may reverse the improvements that Van Leer has made in supply chain reorganization and the associated reductions in inventory. On the other hand, since its suppliers typically require net 45 payments, there is no compelling reason to pay them any earlier. So Van Leer plans on maintaining its current payment policy, which results in accounts payable remaining at about 8.1% of sales.

Van Leer's accruals arise because of the lag between reporting payroll taxes due and actually paying the payroll taxes. For the most part, the payment schedule for these taxes is set by the various government entities, and Van Leer is not at liberty to change them, so accrued expenses will remain at 1% of sales.

Exhibit 5-4 includes the historical information in Exhibit 5-3, plus the projected "inputs" suggested by our analysis.

Calculating Free Cash Flow

We now have enough information to forecast the parts of the income statement and balance sheet necessary to calculate free cash flow, as shown in Exhibit 5-5 on page 90. Based on our forecast, we project Van Leer to generate negative $9.9 million of FCF in 2004. We'll have a lot more to say about this in Chapter 7, when we make our multiyear forecast, but for now you should recognize that Van Leer's 15.06% return on invested capital (ROIC) looks pretty good. This suggests that the negative FCF is being caused by profitable growth. When the growth eventually slows, Van Leer's FCF's should become positive and large.

Exhibit 5-4 The Inputs for Calculating Free Cash Flow

	2001	2002	2003	Average	Projected
Ratios to calculate operating profit					
Sales growth rate	na	12.4%	5.9%	9.2%	11.0%
COGS/Sales	61.9%	66.2%	64.0%	64.0%	62.5%
SGA/Sales	23.8%	21.7%	21.5%	22.3%	22.5%
Depreciation/Net PPE	14.9%	15.0%	15.0%	15.0%	15.0%
Ratios to calculate operating capital					
Cash/Sales	5.0%	5.0%	5.0%	5.0%	3.0%
Inventory/Sales	8.9%	9.0%	10.0%	9.3%	11.0%
Accounts receivable/Sales	7.7%	7.4%	7.5%	7.6%	7.6%
Net PPE/Sales	32.7%	29.7%	30.0%	30.8%	34.0%
Accounts payable/Sales	9.5%	7.4%	7.5%	8.1%	8.1%
Accruals/Sales	0.9%	1.1%	1.0%	1.0%	1.0%
Ratios to calculate operating taxes					
Tax rate (Taxes/EBT)	40.0%	39.1%	40.0%	39.7%	39.7%

Summary

In this chapter, we discussed how to project the parts of financial statements needed to calculate free cash flows. The first step is projecting sales growth. As we showed, you should incorporate both past historical performance and knowledge about the company and the industry. The second step is to project the operating items on the financial statements. We project these as a percentage of sales or as a percentage of net PPE. Again, you must combine useful information about past performance with your judgment and knowledge to choose the inputs for the forecast.

Given the projections for the operating portions of the financial statements, you can calculate free cash flow. But as we said at the beginning of this chapter, it's also important to project complete financial statements. We will do this in Chapter 6 by incorporating additional information and assumptions about Van Leer's financial policies.

Spreadsheet Problems

5-1 Projection of Van Leer Operating Results

Open the file ***Prob 05-01.xls***. You will note that it has five worksheets, or "tabs." In this project, you will work only with three. You will not use the *WACC* or *Proj. of Financials and Valuation* worksheets. The actual historical (2001 to 2003) financial statements for Van Leer are shown in the rightmost tab, labeled *Actual*.

Exhibit 5-5 Forecasting Free Cash Flow for Van Leer, Inc. (millions of dollars)

Van Leer Products, Inc.

Income Statement	Actual 2001	Actual 2002	Actual 2003	Projected 2004
Net sales	$840.0	$944.0	$1,000.0	$1,110.0
Cost of goods sold	520.0	625.0	640.0	693.8
Selling, general & administrative	200.0	205.0	215.0	249.8
Depreciation	41.0	42.0	45.0	56.6
Operating profit	$ 79.0	$ 72.0	$ 100.0	$ 109.9
Balance Sheet				
Cash	$ 42.0	$ 47.0	$ 50.0	$ 33.3
Inventory	75.0	85.0	100.0	122.1
Accounts receivable	65.0	70.0	75.0	84.4
Net PPE	275.0	280.0	300.0	377.4
Accounts payable	$ 80.0	$ 70.0	$ 75.0	$ 89.9
Accrued expenses	8.0	10.0	10.0	11.1
Free Cash Flow Calculations				
Operating income	$ 79.0	$ 72.0	$ 100.0	$ 109.9
Tax on operating income	31.6	28.1	40.0	43.6
NOPAT	$ 47.4	$ 43.9	$ 60.0	$ 66.3
Net operating WC	94.0	122.0	140.0	138.8
Net operating long-term assets	275.0	280.0	300.0	377.4
Total net operating assets	$369.0	$402.0	$ 440.0	$ 516.2
Investment in net operating assets	na	33.0	38.0	76.2
Free cash flow	na	$ 10.9	$ 22.0	$ -9.9
ROIC	na	11.89%	14.93%	15.06%

a. Your first task is to calculate the historical ratios as discussed in the text. Click on the *Historical Analysis* tab and fill in the yellow-shaded cells with formulas. Note that many of the cells have comments, indicated by a red triangle in the upper right hand corner. You can view the comments by letting your cursor hover above one of the cells, and they provide hints or instructions for filling in the cell. There are additional instructions in the sheet itself. You will calculate historical ratios and free cash flows in this worksheet.

b. Next, click on the *Inputs* tab to open that worksheet. In the yellow cells, using information in the text of the chapter, fill in the "projected" values for 2004 for the various ratios needed for projecting the operating results. Be careful not to enter anything in other cells. (These values are given in Exhibit 5-4.).

c. Open the worksheet labeled *Projection of FCF* and use the projected ratios to build formulas that complete the 2004 projections (column D) of operating income entries in the income statement and the operating asset and liability entries in the balance sheet by entering appropriate formulas. For example, the estimate of 2004 sales will equal the actual 2003 sales multiplied by one plus the projected growth rate in sales. To enter the formula, click on cell D6, enter an "=" sign, click on the adjacent cell, C6, type "*(1+" then open the *Inputs* worksheet by clicking on the *Inputs* tab and click on the cell containing the 2004 sales growth rate, which is cell C4. Now type a close parentheses, ")", hit the return key, and the formula will be entered as "=C6*(1+Inputs!C4)", with the numerical result 1110.0. For another example, to get the estimate of COGS for 2004, we want to multiply the sales level we just estimated by the COGS to sales ratio. Click on cell E7, enter a "=" sign, then click on cell D6 and then enter the "*" sign. Now go to the *Inputs* worksheet by clicking on the tab, then click on cell C5, and hit return. The formula entered should be "=D6*Inputs!C5", and the numerical result, 693.8.

d. Finally, using the estimates for the operating portions of the balance sheet and income statements, estimate the components of free cash flow in the middle section of the worksheet labeled *Projection of FCF*, again, by entering the appropriate formulas into the cells. (Check your results against the projections in Exhibit 5-5. When your results agree with the Exhibit, you have successfully completed the project.)

5-2 Projection of Powell Products' Operating Results

The historical (2001 to 2003) financial statements for Powell Products are shown in the worksheet in the file ***Prob 05-02.xls***.

a. Start with the *Projected Parameters* section. Calculate the average historical ratios and use these averages for the projected 2004 ratios.

b. Using the projected ratios, project the operating portions of the balance sheet and income statement for 2004.

c. Finally, using the estimates for the operating portions of the balance sheet and income statements, estimate free cash flow and return on invested capital for 2004.

Chapter 6

Projecting Consistent Financial Statements: The Miracle of Accounting

Introduction

In the last chapter, we used key operating drivers to project free cash flows. But for several reasons, it is also important to project complete financial statements. First, it's much easier to spot possible mistakes in modeling or in your choice of inputs if you project the complete financial statements. Second, it's important for managers and investors to know how much additional financing a company will require to implement its operating plans. And third, complete statements are needed to determine whether the projections meet the test of accounting consistency. For example, if projected total assets do not equal projected total liabilities and owners' equity, then either the assets, or the liabilities, or both are incorrect. Errors on either side of the balance sheet may cause the cash flow projections to be incorrect. As we shall see, there are relationships that must be maintained among several of the accounts in a complete set of financial statements, and so these relationships must be maintained in our projections. So, in addition to the operating assets and liabilities we projected for Van Leer, we will also project nonoperating assets and liabilities, including short-term investments, short-term debt, long-term debt, and shareholders' equity.

Financial Policies and Projecting Financial Statements

In the last chapter, our sole objective was to project free cash flow, and so we projected only the portions of Van Leer's Inc.'s financial statements related to operations. However, many analysts and investors focus on a firm's earnings, or earnings per share, which involve "nonoperating" components, such as interest expense. In addition, financial managers must plan how to finance their asset acquisitions, which involve nonoperating liabilities like debt and equity. Fortunately, it doesn't require much additional effort to project these nonoperating components, once we have projected free cash flows. For example, in order to project Van Leer's earnings, we need to project interest income and interest expense, which depend upon the amounts of Van Leer's short-term investments and short- and long-term debt. These amounts are due to explicit choices that management makes about *financing policies*, as opposed to *operations*. One such financing policy is the amount of debt to use. Van Leer needn't use debt to support its operations; instead, Van Leer could secure all of its financing in the form of equity. Similarly, Van Leer's operations don't require any short-term investments, which reflect a temporary "parking place" for any extra cash. However, Van Leer does have debt and short-term investments on its balance sheet, and this is the result of a conscious financial policy choice by the firm's management.

Financial policies relating to nonoperating assets and liabilities fall into three areas: cash management, capital structure, and dividends. Cash management deals with how to maintain the cash balances required for transactions and to provide flexibility for dealing with potential opportunities and contingencies. Capital structure decisions involve the company's relative amounts of debt and equity, while dividend policies reflect the level and stability of dividend payments. For now, we will take the key financial policies as a given and concentrate on showing how coupling these policies with projected operating results enables us to "fill out" the full set of financial statement projections. We defer discussion on evaluating *changes* in financial policies to Chapter 8.

Projecting Long-Term Debt and Dividends

The level of long-term debt and the mix of financing between equity and debt are decisions that are usually made by senior managers, or even by the board of directors. Fortunately for us, many established companies have an amount of long-term debt that is a fairly constant proportion of total assets. This means we can plausibly model long-term debt as a percentage of operating assets, where operating assets are defined as net PPE plus cash, inventory, and accounts receivable.

The level of common stock (i.e., the stock raised directly from investors) is also a major management decision. Issuing common stock is expensive and time consuming, so most companies do it infrequently, relying on retention of profits as the primary means of increasing the equity capital in the firm.[1] Chapter 8 will explain how to incorporate stock issuances and repurchases into projected financial statements, but for now we will assume that Van Leer does not issue or repurchase common stock during our projection period. For most valuations, details of how a company goes about adjusting its dividends, stock issues, and stock repurchases to arrive at its desired debt/equity mix will be secondary to our efforts to project key operating variables like sales growth or the COGS to sales ratio. With this in mind, let's consider some "reasonable" ways to go about making plausible assumptions about corporate dividend policy.

The board of directors sets dividend payments. Within some very broad bounds, management can pay any amount of dividends it chooses, as long it has the cash. For example, some companies, like Cisco, pay no dividends at all, while others have

[1]Stock issuance often sends a negative signal to the market. For example, you would never sell your car to us for a price less than you think it is worth. You know the value of your car better than we do, because you know its mileage, maintenance record, and history of wrecks. Therefore, if you offered to sell the car to us for $10,000, we would immediately think the car is worth $10,000 or less. Investors follow the same thought process when a company issues stock. Investors generally assume that managers know more than they do about the company's future prospects, so if managers are willing to sell stock, the managers must believe the stock is worth no more than the current price. Thus, investors perceive a stock sale by a mature company as a negative signal, and its stock price usually falls.

dividend payments that sometimes exceed their net income. There are a variety of ways that dividend policy can be incorporated into projected financials, but most firms have a pretty simple policy: They want to set dividends at a level that can be sustained over the "long run," and they let dividends grow at a relatively stable rate. At one extreme, some firms may have a constant growth rate of zero, in which case their dividends are constant from year to year. At the other extreme, firms may try to maintain a steadily increasing dividend, with the growth rate equal to the growth rate they have achieved in the past or at the same rate as the anticipated long-term growth rate in sales.

As noted, conventional financial wisdom holds that firms will set dividend levels at a sustainable level to avoid having to announce a dividend cut. We usually assume steady dividend growth when we forecast financial statements. We assume that firms currently not paying dividends will continue not paying dividends throughout the projection period, and that firms that have been paying dividends will increase payments at a rate equal to their historical average rate. We will discuss several alternate dividend policies, and their potential consequences for valuing a company, in Chapter 8.

Making Balance Sheets Balance: The Plug Approach

The projected financial statements must be consistent with accounting conventions, and one accounting rule is that balance sheets must "balance": Total assets must equal total liabilities and stockholders' equity. Accountants require this, but it also serves a practical purpose—the liabilities and owners' equity side of the balance sheet is a cumulative record of the sources of funds used to purchase the assets listed on the assets side. If the projected funds are less than the projected asset purchases, then the company can't purchase the assets, and so cannot implement its operating plans.

We have already made assumptions regarding long-term debt financing and dividend payout. These assumptions will determine how much additional long-term borrowing will be required as operating asset levels grow or shrink and how much of the firm's profit will be retained and reinvested in new operating assets. If our projections don't balance, for example, because we project more assets than total liabilities and equity, even after allowing for increases in long-term debt and earnings retention, then the company won't have enough financing in place to actually purchase the operating assets it needs to support its level of sales. We will force a balance in our projections in one of two possible ways, depending on whether assets are greater than liabilities and stockholders' equity, or vice versa.

First, if assets are too large, then the firm will sell any marketable securities it has, reducing projected assets. Once this source is exhausted, the firm will issue short-term debt (or borrow short-term from a bank), adding to the liabilities section of the balance sheet. In other words, once a company has exhausted its inventory of highly liquid marketable securities, it will use short-term borrowing to cover any shortfall in the capital needed to fund operating assets.[2] Therefore, the firm uses

[2]This short-term borrowing is often accomplished with line-of-credit or revolving credit arrangements between companies and their banks. Other sources of short-term borrowing are commercial paper, receivables financing, and inventory financing, the latter two representing collateralized loans.

short-term debt to "plug" the difference between projected total assets and projected total liabilities and shareholders' equity.

Second, if projected liabilities and equity are greater than projected assets, then the company will raise more cash than it needs to purchase the required operating assets. In such a situation, we will assume that the firm will first reduce short-term debt (i.e., pay off its short-term loans). Next, if there is still too much funding relative to the required operating assets, it will increase short-term investments. This policy is consistent with the observed behavior of many managers, who often "park" funds not necessary for operating assets in income-producing liquid assets.[3] In other words, the firm uses short-term investments to "plug" the difference between total liabilities and shareholders' equity and total assets.

These balancing methods ensure that the forecasted financial statements are consistent with plausible assumptions about corporate financing policies. Given our methods for projecting long-term debt (as a percentage of operating assets) and dividend policy (constant year-on-year growth) and the use of short-term investments and short-term debt as balancing (i.e., "plug") entries, we have a complete forecasting model. This gives us not only projected operating results, but also a set of financing policies that are consistent with achieving those operating results. The result is a complete set of projected financial statements.

Projecting Interest Expense and Interest Income

Neither interest expense nor interest income depends on sales. Interest expense depends on the level of debt and its interest rate, and interest income depends on the level of short-term investments and the yield on these investments. The annual charge for interest is actually equal to the sum of all the daily interest charges, and the daily charges depend on the balance of debt at the beginning of the day. It is impossible for us to build this exact relationship into our model, and so we face a choice. If a company doesn't add any debt until the last day of the year, then the interest expense should equal the interest rate multiplied by the debt at the beginning of the year (which is also equal to the debt shown on the previous year's balance sheet). If the company adds all its debt on the first day of the year, then the interest expense should equal the interest rate multiplied by the debt at the end of the current year (which is shown on the current year's balance sheet). If the company adds debt smoothly throughout the year, then the interest expense should equal the interest rate multiplied by the average amount of debt during the year. The average amount of debt is the average of the debt at the beginning of the year (shown on the previous year's balance sheet) and the debt at the end of the year (shown on the current year's balance sheet).

Of course, none of these situations exactly apply to any company, so any choice we make will be an approximation. Furthermore, any differences between our approximations and the actual interest expenses will tend to average out over a

[3]Examples are short-term certificates of deposit, Treasury securities, or commercial paper issued by other firms. Even though the yields on these investments are low, the firm can use these investment vehicles to meet its liquidity needs, while still earning some return on what would otherwise be idle cash balances.

period of several years.[4] Indeed, this is a good example of a detail that is not "consequential" for most analyses (at least those not involving banking or financial firms). In this chapter, we will explain one approach to projecting interest income and expense, which is to base them on the levels of short-term investments and debt at the beginning of the current year rather than the end. Our experience has shown that this produces fairly accurate forecasts of interest expense and interest income. Chapter 8 explains how to implement the other choices in a spreadsheet, but for the remainder of the book we will base interest expense on the debt at the beginning of the year.

We have now identified methods for projecting all the line items on the income statement and balance sheet. Exhibit 6-1 provides a summary of the way each financial statement item will be projected.

[4]For example, suppose a company had debt of $8 in 2000, $15 in 2001, $10 in 2002, and $6 at the end of 2003, at an interest rate of 10%. Using the beginning-of-year balance approach gives interest payments of $0.80, $1.50, and $1.00, respectively, for 2001 to 2003. Using the average balance approach gives $1.15, $1.25, and $0.80, respectively. The totals differ only by $0.10, or about 3% of the total interest payments made, and over a longer period, the percentage difference would be even smaller.

Exhibit 6-1 How the Financial Statements Are Projected

Income statement	Forecast method
Net sales	Forecasted
Cost of goods sold (COGS)	Percent of sales
Selling, general & administrative (SGA)	Percent of sales
Depreciation	Percent of net PPE
Operating profit	Calculated: Sales - COGS - SGA - Depreciation.
Interest income	Interest rate on short-term investments multiplied by the amount of short-term investments at the beginning of the year.
Interest expense	Interest rate on short-term and long-term debt multiplied by the amount of debt at the beginning of the year.
Earnings before taxes (EBT)	Calculated: Operating profit + Interest income - Interest expense.
Taxes	Calculated: Tax rate(EBT).
Net income	Calculated: EBT - Taxes.
Dividends	Constant growth relative to previous year
Additions to retained earnings	Calculated: Net income - Dividends.

(continued)

Exhibit 6-1 How the Financial Statements Are Projected (continued)

Balance sheet	Forecast method
Assets	
Cash	Percent of sales
Short-term investments	Plug: zero if operating assets are greater than sources of funding; otherwise, it is the amount required to make the sheets balance (i.e., the excess of funding over operating assets).
Inventory	Percent of sales
Accounts receivable (AR)	Percent of sales
Total current assets	Calculated: Cash + Short-term investments + Inventory + AR.
Net PPE	Percent of sales
Total assets	Calculated: Total current assets + Net PPE.
Liabilities & Owner's Equity	
Accounts payable (AP)	Percent of sales
Accrued expenses	Percent of sales
Short-term debt	Plug: zero if sources of funding are greater than operating assets; otherwise, it is the amount required to make the sheets balance (i.e., the excess of operating assets over other funding).
Total current liabilities	Calculated: AP + Accrued expenses + Short-term debt.
Long-term debt	Percent of operating assets
Total liabilities	Calculated: Total current liabilities + Long-term debt.
Common stock	Constant (same as previous year)
Retained earnings	Calculated: Prior year's retained earnings + (Net income - Projected dividends).
Total common equity	Calculated: Common stock + Retained earnings.
Total liabilities and equity	Calculated: Total liabilities + Common equity.

Completing the Projections: Implementing the Financial Policies

The following sections explain how to incorporate Van Leer's financial policies into its income statements and balance sheets.

Projecting a Complete Income Statement

We'll begin with the partially projected financial statements from Exhibit 5-5 in Chapter 5. The remaining items on the income statement are interest income, interest expense, and dividend payments.

Interest Income and Interest Expense

Interest income and expense depend on the rates that are earned or charged in the market and may change annually, or even more frequently. Van Leer's bank charges 9% for the loans that are outstanding, and this rate is expected to stay the same in 2004. Van Leer earns 3% on its money-market account. As we explained earlier, we will apply these rates to the amounts of debt and short-term investments that are outstanding at the beginning of the year, which is the amount reported on the balance sheets at the end of the previous year, 2003.

Using these inputs, Van Leer's 2004 interest income is \$0.8 million.

$$(0.03)(\text{2003 short-term investments}) = 0.03(\$25) = \$0.75 \approx \$0.8$$

Van Leer's 2003 total debt is the sum of its short-term debt and its long-term debt, \$124 million (\$25 + \$99 = \$124). This means its projected interest expense in 2004 is \$11.2 million (0.09(\$124) = \$11.16 ≈ \$11.2).

Dividends

Predicting dividends for Van Leer is difficult. Since 2001 was the first year Van Leer paid dividends, there isn't much of a history to guide us. To compound the problem, Van Leer has been erratic in its dividend payments the last three years, decreasing dividends in 2002 due to some financial difficulties it experienced at year-end and then substantially increasing dividends in 2003. However management recognizes that its shareholders would prefer a more stable dividend policy and has decided that it should be able to increase dividends by 10% a year for the next several years. Because this is a new policy, it is subject to annual evaluation, but management is quite certain that, barring unforeseen financial difficulties, dividends will increase by 10% in 2004. Since Van Leer's dividends were \$16 million in 2003, its 2004 dividends will be \$17.6 million (\$16(1.10) = \$17.6).

Based on these inputs and the partial projections from Exhibit 5-5 in Chapter 5, Exhibit 6-2 shows the projected income statements for Van Leer.

Projecting Complete Balance Sheets

In Chapter 5, we projected all items on the asset side of the balance sheet except short-term investments. We'll set this to zero for now, but we may have to change it to make the balance sheets balance.

Most companies are financed by a combination of common stock, long-term debt, short-term debt, and retained earnings. Firms issue common stock when they are initially founded, and occasionally thereafter when they need to change their capital structures or have an especially large investment requirement. Since common stock is expensive to issue in terms of transactions costs and negative signaling, most firms rarely issue it after the IPO. Van Leer, like most firms, does not intend to issue any additional common stock in 2004, or any time in the near future.

Exhibit 6-2 Projected Income Statements for Van Leer, Inc. (millions of dollars)

	Actual 2001	Actual 2002	Actual 2003	Projected 2004
Income Statement				
Net sales	$840.0	$944.0	$1,000.0	$1,110.0
Cost of goods sold	520.0	625.0	640.0	693.8
Selling, general & administrative	200.0	205.0	215.0	249.8
Depreciation	41.0	42.0	45.0	56.6
Operating profit	$ 79.0	$ 72.0	$ 100.0	$ 109.9
Interest income	0.0	1.0	0.0	0.8
Interest expense	9.0	9.0	10.0	11.2
Earnings before taxes	$ 70.0	$ 64.0	$ 90.0	$ 99.5
Taxes	28.0	25.0	36.0	39.5
Net income	$ 42.0	$ 39.0	$ 54.0	$ 60.0
Dividends	12.0	11.0	16.0	17.6
Additions to RE	$ 30.0	$ 28.0	$ 38.0	$ 42.4

Debt, unlike common stock, is relatively easy and inexpensive to issue. Interest payments are tax deductible while dividend payments are not, so it is cheaper than common stock on a year-to-year basis as well. Debt is not a perfect financing source, though. If a firm suspends dividend payments on common stock, the stockholders may grouse, but they have little recourse other than being unhappy or selling their shares. If a firm defaults on an interest or principal payment on its debt, the debtholders may be legally entitled to take the firm away from the stockholders in order to satisfy the obligation. Even if the missed payment results only in a renegotiation of the debt agreement, this process is costly to the firm. So excessive debt involves some increase in risk to the firm's stockholders that may offset its low interest rate and tax deductibility features.

Van Leer has been very conservative in its use of long-term debt to date. As a percentage of operating assets, long-term debt has recently ranged from 11.8% to 18.9%. The recent increase in debt came about because of Van Leer's dramatic increase in dividends for 2003. Once Van Leer started paying out dividends, it had to either make smaller investments in assets or find another source of investment capital to replace the dividends it paid. Given the decision to hold dividend growth to 10%, which is far lower than the 45.5% increase of 2003, Van Leer's management will likely decrease the amount of debt in the capital structure in 2004 to 15% of total operating assets. Van Leer's projected operating assets in 2004 are the sum of its cash ($33.3), accounts receivable ($81.1), inventories ($122.1), and net PPE ($377.4), which is $617.2 million. Therefore, Van Leer's projected debt is $92.6 million (0.15($617.2) = $92.6).

Retained earnings for 2004 will equal the retained earnings from 2003 ($216 million) plus the addition to retained earnings in 2004 ($42.4 million) for a total of $258.4 million.

The only remaining item is short-term debt. As with short-term investments, we'll set this to zero for now, but we may have to change it to achieve a balance between total assets and liabilities plus owners' equity.

These financial policy choices for our 2004 projections, along with the operating assumptions we made in Chapter 5, are summarized in Exhibit 6-3.

Based on these inputs and financial policy choices, the preliminary projections for Van Leer's balance sheets are shown in Exhibit 6-4. Recall that Exhibit 6-2 shows the projected income statement, including the projected dividends. Given the projected net income and dividends, we know the addition to retained earnings, $258.4 million. As you will notice, we have a problem: The balance sheet doesn't balance! In the projections, total assets are $617.2 million, and total liabilities and shareholders' equity are $577.0 million.

Exhibit 6-3 Inputs for Projecting Van Leer, Inc.'s Financial Statements

	2001	2002	2003	Average	Projected
Ratios to calculate operating profit					
Sales growth rate	na	12.4%	5.9%	9.2%	11.0%
COGS/Sales	61.9%	66.2%	64.0%	64.0%	62.5%
SGA/Sales	23.8%	21.7%	21.5%	22.3%	22.5%
Depreciation/Net PPE	14.9%	15.0%	15.0%	15.0%	15.0%
Ratios to calculate operating capital					
Cash/Sales	5.0%	5.0%	5.0%	5.0%	3.0%
Inventory/Sales	8.9%	9.0%	10.0%	9.3%	11.0%
Accts. receivable/Sales	7.7%	7.4%	7.5%	7.6%	7.6%
Net PPE/Sales	32.7%	29.7%	30.0%	30.8%	34.0%
Accts. payable/Sales	9.5%	7.4%	7.5%	8.1%	8.1%
Accruals/Sales	1.0%	1.1%	1.0%	1.0%	1.0%
Ratios to calculate operating taxes					
Tax rate (Taxes/EBT)	40.0%	39.1%	40.0%	39.7%	39.7%
Dividend and debt ratios					
Dividend policy: growth rate	na	-8.3%	45.5%	18.6%	10.0%
Long-term debt/ operating assets	11.8%	17.4%	18.9%	16.0%	15.0%
Interest rates					
Interest rate on short-term investment	na	10.0%	0.0%	5.0%	3.0%
Interest rate on debt	na	8.7%	8.8%	8.7%	9.0%

Exhibit 6-4 Preliminary Projections for Van Leer, Inc.'s Balance Sheets (millions of dollars)

	Actual 2001	Actual 2002	Actual 2003	Projected 2004
Balance Sheet				
Cash	$ 42.0	$ 47.0	$ 50.0	$ 33.3
Short-term investments	10.0	15.0	25.0	0.0
Inventory	75.0	85.0	100.0	122.1
Accounts receivable	65.0	70.0	75.0	84.4
Total current assets	$192.0	$217.0	$250.0	$239.8
Net PPE	275.0	280.0	300.0	377.4
Total assets	$467.0	$497.0	$550.0	$617.2
Accounts payable	$ 80.0	$ 70.0	$ 75.0	$ 89.9
Accrued expenses	8.0	10.0	10.0	11.1
Short-term debt	50.0	30.0	25.0	0.0
Total current liabilities	$138.0	$110.0	$110.0	$101.0
Long-term debt	54.0	84.0	99.0	92.6
Total liabilities	$192.0	$194.0	$209.0	$193.6
Common stock	125.0	125.0	125.0	125.0
Retained earnings	150.0	178.0	216.0	258.4
Total common equity	$275.0	$303.0	$341.0	$383.4
Total liabilities and equity	$467.0	$497.0	$550.0	$577.0

Notice that all of the projected items on the asset side of the balance sheet are operating assets that are required to support the projected sales. In other words, we have specified a total of $617.2 million in assets we need to support our operating plan. In order to finance these assets, Van Leer must achieve a cumulative total of $617.2 in financing. The liabilities side of the balance sheet shows that Van Leer has already specified certain sources of funding, including accounts payable, accrued expenses, long-term debt, and total common equity. The total of these specified sources of financing is $577.0. With $617.2 in assets that need to be financed and only $577.0 in sources of financing, Van Leer's preliminary projections give a shortfall in financing of $617.2 – $577.0 = $40.2 million. Therefore, Van Leer must either raise an additional $40.2 million or cut back on its assets—which would mean cutting back on its growth plans.

Like most companies, Van Leer does not want to forego profitable growth, and so it will add $40.2 million in short-term debt. Notice that Van Leer began the year with short-term investments. Even after selling those investments, Van Leer must secure an additional $40.2 million in short-term debt financing. If a firm has access to a line of credit, such as the one Van Leer has, it doesn't make sense to hold short-term investments and short-term debt at the same time. It is smarter to liquidate investments in short-term securities before resorting to short-term borrowing, because the interest earned on short-term investments is usually lower than the rate charged on short-term debt.

In 2004, Van Leer projected more specified operating assets than sources of financing, but suppose the opposite had occurred. In particular, suppose the projected specified assets were \$617.2 million and specified sources of financing were \$632.7 million. In this case, Van Leer would have \$632.7 million worth of financing but would only need \$617.2 million. This leaves \$632.7 – \$617.2 = \$15.5 million in excess funds. Van Leer could use these funds in a number of ways: (1) buy more operating assets; (2) pay more dividends; (3) pay off some long-term debt; (4) repurchase some stock; or (5) invest in nonoperating assets such as short-term investments. Option 1 isn't a good choice, since Van Leer is already acquiring all the operating assets it needs to support its growth plans. Options 2 through 4, in which Van Leer returns funds to investors, are definitely viable choices, but all of them represent departures from the set of financial policies we have assumed Van Leer would follow. The board of directors usually makes these decisions, and we discuss them in more detail in Chapter 8. For now, we assume that Van Leer will maintain the financial policies that underlie the projections. This leaves only option 5, in which Van Leer purchases short-term investments such as T-bills and commercial paper.

We can summarize the "rules" we use to balance the financial statements:

1. If specified assets are greater than the specified sources of financing, then:
   Short-term debt = Specified assets – Specified liabilities, and
   Short-term investments = zero.
2. If specified assets are less than the specified sources of financing, then:
   Short-term debt = zero, and
   Short-term investments = Specified liabilities – Specified assets.

In other words, we are using short-term debt and short-term investments as "plug" variables, because they are "plugged" into the balance sheets to make them balance.

Van Leer's completed balance sheet projections, which include the additional \$40.2 million in short-term debt, appear below in Exhibit 6-5.

Checking Your Projections for Plausibility

Now that we have projections that satisfy our assumptions and give us financial statements that are consistent with each other, it is time to take the most important step in the entire projection process: check the projections for plausibility. As our projections are only one year out in this chapter, there is relatively less possibility for the projections to go awry, but we will use these same techniques to analyze our multiperiod projections in Chapter 7. The idea is to see if the actual numbers in the income statement and balance sheet are consistent with what you know about the firm, and if the implied rates of return are reasonable in terms of common sense and experience.

In the completed income statement in Exhibit 6-2, we can see that it looks very much like the income statements from the previous three years. Sales increases are not

Exhibit 6-5 Final Projections for Van Leer, Inc.'s Balance Sheets (millions of dollars)

	Actual 2001	Actual 2002	Actual 2003	Projected 2004
Balance Sheet				
Cash	$ 42.0	$ 47.0	$ 50.0	$ 33.3
Short-term investments	10.0	15.0	25.0	0.0
Inventory	75.0	85.0	100.0	122.1
Accounts receivable	65.0	70.0	75.0	84.4
Total current assets	$192.0	$217.0	$250.0	$239.8
Net PPE	275.0	280.0	300.0	377.4
Total assets	$467.0	$497.0	$550.0	$617.2
Accounts payable	$ 80.0	$ 70.0	$ 75.0	$ 89.9
Accrued expenses	8.0	10.0	10.0	11.1
Short-term debt	50.0	30.0	25.0	40.2
Total current liabilities	$138.0	$110.0	$110.0	$141.2
Long-term debt	54.0	84.0	99.0	92.6
Total liabilities	$192.0	$194.0	$209.0	$233.8
Common stock	125.0	125.0	125.0	125.0
Retained earnings	150.0	178.0	216.0	258.4
Total common equity	$275.0	$303.0	$341.0	$383.4
Total liabilities and equity	$467.0	$497.0	$550.0	$617.2

out of line with historical increases, and cost of goods sold, depreciation, taxes, and dividends are all consistent with historical levels. The only figure that seems a bit out of line is the projected selling, general and administrative expenses. SGA is projected to increase by $34.8 million in 2004 although the largest increase before that was $15 million. However, recall that we explicitly projected a large increase in SGA because a sales incentive plan goes into effect in 2004, raising the cost of commissions.

Exhibit 6-5 shows the final projections for Van Leer's balance sheets. On the assets side of the balance sheet, accounts receivable, inventory, and net PPE are all similar to their 2003 values. Cash balances are predicted to fall significantly, but that is due to our information about the new CFO who is working on better information technology and has predicted that cash balances can be reduced from 5% to 3% of sales.

One of the common problems in projections is smoothly transitioning from one level of asset utilization to another. In the case of net PPE, an increase in net PPE as a percent of sales coupled with a relatively large increase in sales can lead to a very large increase in projected PPE. The increase in net PPE of $77.4 million for 2004 is much larger than any previous increase in net PPE. Again, there is a good reason for this unusually large increase. Recall that Van Leer is bringing a new plant on line during 2004 to deal with its production capacity shortage, and this plant will not be fully utilized for several years. So in this case there are perfectly good reasons to project an unusually large increase in net PPE for 2004.

The one number on the assets side of the balance sheet that is substantially different from the 2003 figure is short-term investments. In 2003 short-term investments were $25 million, and in 2004 they are projected to be zero. What explains this large reduction? First, notice that in 2001, 2002, and 2003, Van Leer maintained both short-term investments and short-term debt. Given that Van Leer's yield on its short-term investments is substantially less than its cost for short-term debt, it is financially unsound to borrow money at a high interest rate, only to invest it in marketable securities with a low rate of return. We have assumed that Van Leer will not do this in our projections; as long as it has short-term debt, it will have no short-term investments. Van Leer must liquidate its short-term investments in order to pay for the assets it is purchasing in 2004.

The liabilities sides of the 2003 and 2004 balance sheets do have some differences. Short-term debt is projected to increase substantially in 2004, in order to finance Van Leer's substantial investments in assets. However, long-term debt is projected to decrease. Does this really make sense? Recall our thinking on this: We assumed that the recent high debt ratio exhibited in Van Leer's 2003 financials was partially the result of its decision to substantially increase dividends during 2004 and that the prior years' levels of debt in relation to operating assets represented a more reasonable level for Van Leer, going forward. Therefore, this is, in fact, a reasonable consequence of Van Leer's stated policies, but it also points out that sometimes reasonable policies can result in large balance sheet changes. For example, if the company has decided to increase or decrease its debt as a percentage of total operating assets in order to take advantage of the changing debt costs, you may see large increases in projected debt in a given year. Certainly companies sometimes increase their debt substantially in a short time period, but often they do it over several years. So if you predict that your company is going to increase its debt ratio substantially, you will find that your projections are likely to be more realistic if you phase in this increase over several years. We will discuss multiyear projections in the next chapter.

Summary

In this chapter, we discussed how to make plausible assumptions about a firm's financial policies and use these assumptions, in conjunction with projected operating results, to project complete financial statements. Long-term debt is projected to be a percentage of total operating assets, dividends are forecasted to grow at a constant rate, and short-term debt and short-term investments are used jointly to balance total assets with liabilities plus owners' equity. In Chapter 7, we will make multiyear projections and use them to estimate the value of Van Leer's stock. In Chapter 8, we will return to the issue of making reasonable financial policy assumptions and discuss possible refinements to the assumptions we made for Van Leer.

Spreadsheet Problems

6-1 Projection of Van Leer Full Financial Results

This project is an extension of Project 5-1, so you will start with the spreadsheet that you developed in completing that project. Recall that the historical (2001 to 2003) financial statements for Van Leer are shown in the last tab, *Actuals* in the file ***Prob 05-01.xls***, and in doing Project 5-1, you entered the operating parameters necessary for projecting the operating components of Van Leer's performance for 2004, enabling a projection of free cash flow for that year in the *Projection of FCF* worksheet. The purpose of this project is to complete a projection of the full financial statements for Van Leer for 2004, so our focus turns to the *Proj. of Financials & Valuation* worksheet tab. This construction will allow short-term debt and short-term investments to jointly make your balance sheet balance.

Start with your solution to the Chapter 5 Excel construction and make the following modifications to your model:

a. Go the *Inputs* tab, scroll to the bottom, and enter the projection for the dividend growth rate, the ratio of long-term debt to operating assets, and the interest rates on short-term investments and debt. (See Exhibit 6-3.)

b. Go to the *Proj. of Financials & Valuation* tab in the spreadsheet. In column C, enter the results from the operating income projections that you already completed (Project 5-1) in the *Projection of FCF* tab of the spreadsheet. For example, in cell C4, for the 2004 net sales projection, you will enter an equal sign (=), then click the *Projection of FCF* tab, and scroll to cell D6. Clicking on D6 and pressing the return key will result in the following formula being entered into C4 on the *Financials* tab: "='Projection of FCF'!D6". This will copy the projected sales from the *Projection of FCF* tab into the appropriate cell in the *Proj. of Financials & Valuation* tab. When this step has been completed for all the *operating* items, the only income statement and balance sheet entries that have not been calculated are the short-term investments and short-term debt items.

   IMPORTANT: For the interest income (C9) and interest expense (C10) cells, recall that we are using the convention that estimates interest income and expense based on the amounts of short-term investment and short-term debt outstanding at the end of the previous year. Also, for the projected balance sheet entries, leave the short-term investments (C20) and short-term debt (C29) cells blank for now, but incorporate these cells into other formulas where appropriate (e.g., current assets and current liabilities)—we'll use short-term investments and short-term debt below to balance the balance sheet. Also recall that, although long term debt is not an "operating liability," we are determining long-term debt as a constant proportion of operating assets.

c. Create a new entry in cell C39, in the row labeled "Specified Assets." The formula in C39 should be the sum of the operating asset accounts: Cash + Inventories + Accounts receivable + Net PPE. This will give you total assets less marketable securities, BUT you can't calculate it as TA – Short-term investments, because short-term investment hasn't been calculated yet!

d. Create another new entry in cell C40, in the row labeled "Specified Liabilities." It will contain the sum: Accounts payable + Accrued expenses + Long-term debt + Total common equity. The resulting number will change after we make some further entries (below), but don't worry about that—it will all turn out right before we are through.
e. In cell C41, calculate the difference between Specified Assets and Specified Liabilities (i.e., enter the formula "=C39-C40"). The row is labeled "Asset-Liability Gap" and this number represents the magnitude of the "plug" we need to balance the balance sheet.
f. Enter another formula in cell C42, in the row labeled "Discrepancy," that calculates the difference between the total assets (C25) and total liabilities plus owners' equity (C36).
g. Now the fun part! We have to make the Accounting Miracle work! Recall the logic: if total assets exceed liabilities plus owners' equity, use short-term debt to plug the gap; if total assets are less than liabilities plus owners' equity, use short-term investments to plug the gap. To operationalize this we use the Asset-Liability Gap calculation in cell C41. If the Gap is positive, set short-term debt equal to the amount of the gap [enter "=IF(C41>0,C41,0)"]; if the Gap is negative, set short-term investments equal to minus the amount of the gap [enter "=IF(C41<0,-C41,0)"—this will give a positive number for short-term investments]. Another formula that works for the short-term investments plug is "=MAX(-C41,0)". Similarly, for the short-term debt plug, we could use "=MAX(C41,0)".
h. If you have entered these formulas correctly then you should get zero for short-term investments and 40.2 for short-term debt.

Now you have a spreadsheet that "articulates." For any change in inputs, short-term debt and short-term investments will change to make your balance sheet balance.

6-2 Sensitivity Analysis

The operating assumptions you made in your projections of Van Leer's financial statements impact Van Leer's accumulation of short-term investments, or the amount of short-term debt it must issue. Fill in the following table with how you expect the resulting short-term investments and debt will be affected by the following changes in your projections for 2004. Use a + to indicate an increase, and – to indicate a decrease. Why are short-term investments and debt affected in this way? Check your work by making the indicated changes in the spreadsheet you developed in Problem 6-1.

Projection item	Change	Impact on short-term investments (+/–)	Impact on short-term debt (+/–)
Sales growth	increase 1%		
CGS/Sales	increase 1%		
SGA/Sales	increase 1%		
Depreciation/ Net PPE	increase 1%		
Cash/Sales	increase 1%		
Inventory/Sales	increase 1%		
Accts. rec./Sales	increase 1%		
Accruals/Sales	increase 1%		
Tax rate	increase 1%		
Dividend growth rate	increase 1%		
Long-term debt/ Operating assets	increase 1%		
Sales growth	1% higher		

Chapter

7

Multiyear Projections and Valuation

Introduction

In Chapter 4 you learned how to value a company if you were given a set of projected financial statements, and in Chapters 5 and 6 you learned how to project financial statements 1 year ahead. Now we will show you how to take your 1-year financial projections and extend them into the multiyear projections needed for valuation purposes.

One-Year versus Multiyear Projections

Van Leer's current market price is $40.12 per share. Given what we know about Van Leer's plans for the future, is this a fair price? Put another way, is the current market price of $40.12 per share consistent with our expectations about Van Leer's future performance? In order to answer this question we must estimate Van Leer's intrinsic value, and this requires that we look considerably further ahead than the 1-year projection we made in the last chapter. The projections for Van Leer Products, Inc., in Exhibits 6-2 and 6-5 were based on historical financial statements and specific information that we had about Van Leer's plans for the coming year. As we extend our projections farther and farther into the future, we will have less specific information about the firm's plans and will have to rely more on long-run industry characteristics, such as prospects for expansion, technological trends, and competitive forces. Ultimately, we will have to project statements far enough into the future so that the company is in a "steady state" by the last year of projections. We'll explain exactly what this means a little later in the chapter, but for now consider the timeline in Exhibit 7-1. The period during which projections are based on specific plans of the firm is the **short-term projection period**. The period beginning with our last explicitly projected year is the **steady state period**. The period between the short-run projection period and the steady state period will be called the **long-term projection period**.

This approach to financial forecasting is driven by three guiding principles. First, extraordinary investment returns result from product or process innovations that create a competitive advantage for the firm. Second, as we project farther into the

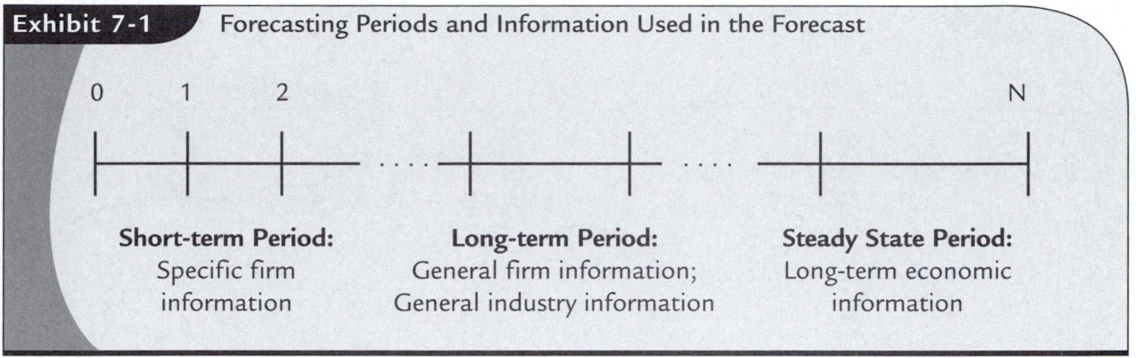

future, our limitations as forecasters will naturally reduce our ability to distinguish an individual firm's performance from that of its industry. Third, every industry experiences a "maturing" process in which the forces of competition will ultimately erode the ability of any firm to generate extraordinary returns to investors. This means that the long-term performance of any individual firm will tend to converge to that of other firms in its industry, and ultimately to the performance of the economy at large. When this happens, we say that the steady state period has been reached. The point at which specific short-run considerations are overwhelmed by long-term industry considerations varies from firm to firm, but most analysts feel comfortable making projections based on information about a firm's specific plans for about 3 to 5 years into the future. After that, the forecast is driven by general characteristics of the firm and of its industry.

Exhibit 7-2 shows the historical growth patterns for some well-known companies. Of the six companies presented, four (Intel, Home Depot, Wal-Mart, and Microsoft) had extraordinary growth, yet show a definite downward trend as the company's growth rate "fades" down to that of the economy at large. Coca-Cola and Ford have some cyclical ups and downs, but the average growth rate reflects the intensely competitive nature of their mature industries.

Competition (including competition from new technology that renders old products obsolete) and market saturation affect our projections in two important ways. First, these forces will ultimately erode every company's growth, causing all companies to eventually reach a level of steady state growth that is consistent with the overall growth rate for the industry and for the economy as a whole. Second, they will ultimately erode a firm's prospects for extraordinary returns. Managers create value for shareholders by creating and maintaining competitive advantages. For example, management might be able to improve internal processes, which lowers production and distribution costs, hence improving profitability relative to the firm's competitors. But these process improvements will ultimately be discovered or emulated by competitors, eliminating the source of above-average profits. Value creation depends critically upon how long any above-average performance can be sustained; that is, how long can managers fend of the inevitable steady state?

In making projections for any firm, it is important to forecast enough years to reach the steady state. This may require many years, as evidenced by Microsoft's

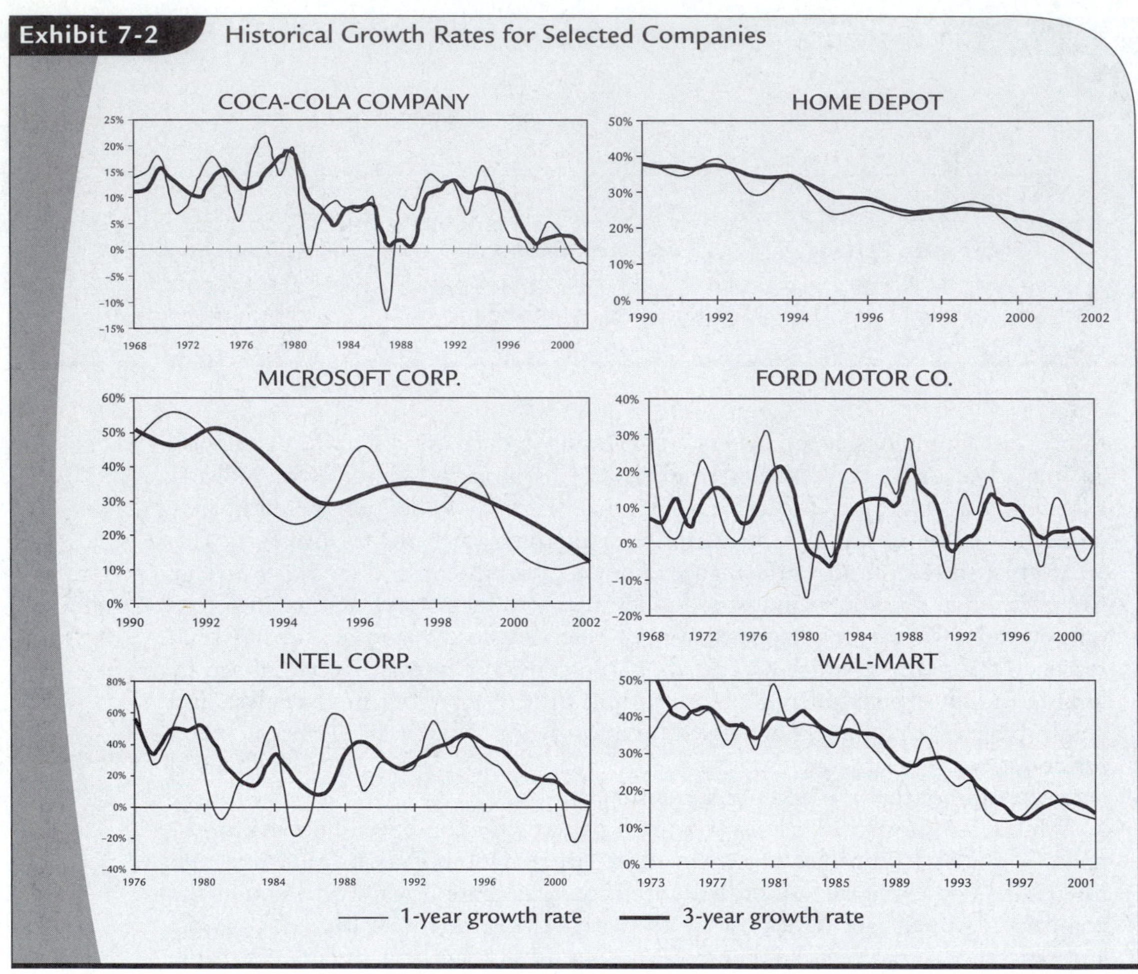

Exhibit 7-2 Historical Growth Rates for Selected Companies

sustained growth during the 1980s and 1990s (Exhibit 7-2). Similarly, both Home Depot and Wal-Mart developed innovative marketing and distribution methods that resulted in enormous growth, but this growth has been eroding at a steady pace due to saturation and competitive pressures, as we can see from Exhibit 7-2. Most firms must face the reality that growth in their existing line of business is limited by the potential size of their industry. Once a firm becomes very large relative to the markets it serves, it becomes more and more difficult to maintain extraordinarily high levels of profitable growth. Ford, Coca-Cola, and even Intel, for example, compete in relatively mature, globally competitive industries, and their recent modest growth rates are a result of this maturity. As the examples illustrate, the length of time until steady state is reached is itself a judgment call that the analyst must make, relying on knowledge of industry trends and global economic fundamentals as well as insight regarding the relative strengths and weaknesses of the firm being analyzed.

In the Short Run Anything Can Happen. In the Long Run. . . .

In the short-run, a firm can plan for rapid growth, efficiency improvements, and new product innovations in its existing lines of business. But a simple numerical exercise in compound growth illustrates why extraordinary growth cannot last forever. Suppose a firm has sales in 2003 of $10 million, and we project 30% growth. In 2004, the firm must first generate $10 million in sales just to stay even with the previous year, and then it must generate $3 million in additional sales—either through new customers or new products. In a growing, vibrant industry this $3 million in new sales may be easy to generate. But imagine now that this firm has grown at a 30% rate for each of the 20 years between 2004 and 2023, and has 2023 sales of $1.9 billion. In order to grow at 30% in its 21st year, the company must first generate $1.9 billion in sales just to stay even with the previous year, and it must find an additional $570 million worth of sales from new customers, or new products, or both. This is almost two hundred times the level of new sales that was required in 2004! If the overall industry is fairly mature, then it can only achieve high growth by taking sales from its competitors, which is quite difficult. And for this growth to add value to the firm, it must maintain a return on these sales that exceeds its cost of capital, something that becomes increasingly difficult as the industry matures. The moral is that for most firms, extraordinary growth rates are probably not sustainable for more than 10 years (notwithstanding the phenomenal records compiled by Wal-Mart and Microsoft, which are truly exceptional).

The same issues are also faced by an industry as a whole. The U.S. and world economies tend to grow at a real rate of about 2% to 3% a year. Factoring in inflation, global growth rates in the range of 4% to 6% per year would appear to be realistic for the foreseeable future. For any particular industry to grow faster than that, it must steal sales from other industries. There are some examples of this transition—notably, the service and technology industries have grown tremendously in the past 20 years in the United States, while blue-collar manufacturing has declined. However, over the long-run, even growing industries and growing firms like Wal-Mart and Microsoft must face the dreary fact that high growth rates cannot persist forever.

This is also true for profitability, especially in industries that do not experience above average revenue growth. When entrepreneurs identify an industry that is quite profitable, they enter the market. Eventually, this influx of competitors occurs in all profitable industries, and the increased competition will drive down profits for everyone in the industry, perhaps even while revenue is increasing.

For now let's focus on projections for Van Leer, using information concerning recent developments within the company, in the plastics industry, and in the economy at large. We'll assume that the information (commonly called "business intelligence") has already been gathered from reputable public and perhaps private sources. For now, we'll concentrate on how to incorporate such information into the process of projecting financial performance. (We'll give examples of useful information sources in Chapters 9–12.)

Considerations for the Long Run

In projecting Van Leer's financial statements, we need to consider some industrywide and economywide conditions. The plastics industry has been in a slump for the last 5 years. Industry sales actually fell by over 4% in recent years, and capital spending declined by 22%. Some of this poor performance was due to the mild recession the U.S. economy experienced in 2001; however, even before the recession, the industry was facing consolidation, especially in commodity plastics. Van Leer is positioned to weather the consolidation because it produces specialty and niche products. It should benefit from declining feedstock prices and increased demand for consumer products as the economy picks up. Using this information about Van Leer and the plastics industry as a whole, we can begin making multiyear projections.

Projecting Operating Profit

The following sections explain how to choose the inputs necessary for projecting multiyear financial statements, beginning with projections for sales.

Long-Run Sales Growth

Long-term and steady state sales growth projections must incorporate the growth rate of the economy, the growth rate of the firm's industry, and the position of the firm within its industry. Over most years, the overall U.S. economy grows at a real rate of around 2% to 3%—at the high of this range when coming out of a recession, and at the low end when heading into a recession. Adding inflation of around 2% to 3% gives an average growth rate of around 4% to 6%, with higher growth rates when inflation is higher. When making sales growth projections, we should consider recent sales growth for the company and industry, and then temper those measures with our understanding of how the company compares with its industry peers. If we project faster growth than the industry as a whole, we need to understand how the company is going to take sales away from its competitors.

Because Van Leer has an expanding market niche, we project sales revenues to increase by 11% in 2004. However this growth rate isn't sustainable for very long in the current market. After the 11% bump in 2004, we expect revenue growth to decline to 8% in 2005.

After 2005, Van Leer expects unit sales to increase by about 3% a year. However, inflation will tend to increase the selling price of these units, and so it is important to understand what inflation rate is anticipated over the next 5 to 10 years. The historical average real risk-free rate of return has been on the order 2% to 3%. The current observable rate on 5- to 10-year Treasury securities is about 6%. Since this is about 3% or 4% higher than the historical real rates, we can estimate that the market expects inflation of around 3% to 4%.[1] Combining a 4% inflation rate with a 3% increase in unit sales results in approximately a 7% increase in the total dollar sales per year. This is the sales increase Van Leer expects through 2007. After 2007,

[1]Under a rule of thumb known as Fisher's equation, the nominal rate of interest (the rate on Treasuries) is the sum of the real rate of interest and the anticipated rate of inflation, so, by deduction, the expected inflation rate equals the nominal interest rate minus the real rate, which is believed to be relatively stable through time.

Van Leer expects sales to increase at the same rate as the economy as a whole, which has averaged about 2% in real terms plus about 4% inflation, for a total of 6%. The predicted sales growth rates from 2004 to 2009 are shown in Exhibit 7-3.

Competition and Cost of Goods Sold (COGS)

Firms whose services or products have many substitutes—whether from direct competitors, close substitutes, or from technological advancements that make their products obsolete—will see their profit margins erode. However, firms with a competitive advantage can maintain or even improve their profit margins. There are many ways to establish and maintain a competitive advantage. For example, firms in the pharmaceutical and technology industries invest in research and development, then patent their inventions, which limits competition. Some firms spend money on advertising to build a brand identity and use this recognition to charge higher prices for their products than are possible on unbranded or off-brand products. Other firms may establish a reputation for outstanding service or quality and are able to charge a corresponding premium. Finally, some firms have a corporate culture (such as Southwest Airlines), existing infrastructure, supply chain, or technological capabilities that make them the best at controlling costs. Even though these firms may not charge a premium price for their products, they earn a premium profit because of their lower cost structure. In many instances, they are able to sustain their profit margin for a number of years because the specific competitive advantage is difficult for rivals to emulate.

In each of these examples, the key to maintaining or improving profit margins over the long run is the ability to establish and defend some form of competitive advantage. To justify projecting an increasing profit margin, we must have reason to believe the firm is going to maintain and improve its competitive position. But if the firm is in a maturing industry without any obvious competitive protection or advantage, then in all likelihood we will see declining profit margins.

Although Van Leer operates in a profitable niche within its industry, the industry itself is stagnant and consolidating, if not actually contracting. The fact that Van Leer's niche is profitable is likely to attract competitors, and with this competition will come price pressures. Van Leer projected that it could raise prices in 2004 as the economy continues to improve. However, competitors are likely to enter, since the plastics fabricating industry has few technological or legal barriers to entry. Thus, Van Leer is likely to see its profit margins erode. Based on an analysis of the competition and the potential entrants into the industry, Van Leer's analysts predict that a dip in COGS/sales to 62.5% can persist for an additional 2 years, but will climb to 63% in 2007, to 64% in 2008, and remain there for the foreseeable future.

Exhibit 7-3 Van Leer Revenue Growth to 2009

Year	2004	2005	2006	2007	2008	2009	Thereafter
Sales Growth	11%	8%	7%	7%	6%	6%	6%

Selling, General and Administrative (SGA) Costs as a Percent of Sales

Many companies' advertising and commission expenses have a consistent relationship with sales. For example, sales growth naturally results in increased commissions, and increased advertising is often required to stimulate increased sales. In addition, all growing companies must invest in administrative infrastructure to support increased sales.

In projecting SGA as a percentage of sales, the analyst needs to be especially aware of how these expenses interact with sales growth. If sales growth is projected to be more rapid than in the past, we should ask whether there will be any increases in advertising or sales commissions to stimulate this sales growth. If there isn't any plan for stimulating the increased sales, then we should investigate further to determine the source of these new sales. If sales growth is projected to level off or decline to a steady state level, we should ask ourselves (or, better yet, the marketing department) whether this decline in growth is accompanied by cutbacks in advertising. The point is that plans for sales growth often are accompanied by changes in expense patterns in SGA, and we should make sure we understand these changes and incorporate them into our projections.

We projected that Van Leer's SGA as a percentage of sales will increase slightly in 2004 to 22.5% of sales. Although we also project that sales growth will decline in 2005 and thereafter, Van Leer must advertise in trade journals just as before and will continue to pay its salespeople the same commission rate as before. This means that SGA is likely to remain at 22.5% of sales for the indefinite future. One point to note, though, is that if competition heats up in the specialty plastics market, then Van Leer will either have to increase its advertising budget or increase its incentives in order to hold the line against encroachment from its competitors.

Depreciation as a Percent of Net PPE

The depreciation rates for assets are set by their expected lives, and the only way a company can change this is to invest in assets with longer or shorter expected lives. Van Leer's technology determines its asset mix and expected asset life, and over the years depreciation has remained constant at 15% of net PPE. We project that it will remain at this level throughout our projections.

A summary of the ratios used for calculating operating profit appears in Exhibit 7-4.

Projecting Operating Capital

Calculating free cash flow (FCF) also requires projecting investments in operating capital. The following sections explain how to estimate the inputs for calculating operating capital, beginning with cash.

Cash

As we discussed in Chapter 5, some minimal amount of cash is required for a company to function. This minimal level of cash is actually an operating asset, just like inventory, accounts receivable, or even machinery. Efficiencies in the financial services industry have reduced the minimal level of required cash from somewhere near 5% of sales to less than 1% of sales for many companies. Van Leer has historically maintained a cash balance of 5% of sales. However, as mentioned in Chapter 5, Van Leer's CFO believes she can reduce the ratio of cash to sales in 2004 to 3%. She believes the ratio will remain at 3% through 2005 and 2006, but she thinks she can reduce it to 2% in 2007 and thereafter. Notice that freeing up this cash is a permanent reduction of investment in the firm. The freed-up cash is available for investing in more productive assets within the firm, paying down debt, or increasing future dividends. For example, if Van Leer is able to reduce its required cash balance from $50 million to $33.3 million, then the $16.7 million can either be paid out to investors or used to purchase the additional PPE that will be required to support projected sales growth.

Inventory

Inventory varies from day to day and year to year because of fluctuations in demand and production. Many firms maintain a base level of inventory to ensure that the chance of a stock-out is minimized, and this minimal level can be reduced if the firm invests in information technology for supply chain management. By carefully tracking sales and projecting demand, a firm can reduce the amount of inventory it must carry, and the dollars freed up from this inventory reduction can be used elsewhere or paid out to the firm's investors. As mentioned in Chapter 5, Van Leer anticipates an 11% ratio of inventory to sales in 2004. Van Leer has no plans to change its inventory management system, and so inventory is projected to remain at 11% of sales thereafter.

Accounts Receivable

Van Leer's accounts receivable policy is the same as the rest of the firms in its industry. Van Leer requests terms of net 30, and is almost always paid within that period. Occasionally a firm will pay earlier, and occasionally a firm will have some cash flow difficulties and request an extension (or just delay payment), but Van Leer has about 28 days of sales outstanding overall.

If Van Leer were to tighten its credit policies by requiring quicker payments or by giving terms of net 20 rather than net 30, it would free up cash. But since the industry standard is net 30, Van Leer would probably lose some customers. On the other hand, Van Leer might lengthen its terms to 60 days to attract new customers. This might increase sales, but the old customers would also take advantage of the longer payment period, so the additional investment in accounts receivable might be substantial. Van Leer has done a cost-benefit analysis of its terms and has decided to keep its current policy. Therefore, it is reasonable to assume that Van Leer will maintain a 7.6% ratio of accounts receivables/sales.

Capacity and PPE as a Percent of Sales

The relationship between PPE and sales varies from industry to industry, and within an industry it varies from company to company. Some industries, such as steel production or automobile manufacturing, are asset-intensive, meaning they require a lot of fixed assets to generate sales. Others, such as service industries (e.g., hotel management, business consulting, and public accounting) or low-tech industries (e.g., farming or textile production) require relatively lower levels of fixed assets. Even within an industry, there may be considerable variation in fixed assets requirements

Exhibit 7-4 Ratios for Calculating Operating Profit (Van Leer)

Projected parameters	Actual 2001	Actual 2002	Actual 2003	Actual Average	Projected 2004	Projected 2005	Projected 2006	Projected 2007	Projected 2008	Projected 2009	Projected Thereafter
Ratios to calculate operating profit											
Sales growth	na	12.4%	5.9%	9.2%	11.0%	8.0%	7.0%	7.0%	6.0%	6.0%	6.0%
COGS % of sales	61.9%	66.2%	64.0%	64.0%	62.5%	62.5%	62.5%	63.0%	64.0%	64.0%	64.0%
SGA % of sales	23.8%	21.7%	21.5%	22.3%	22.5%	22.5%	22.5%	22.5%	22.5%	22.5%	22.5%
Depreciation % of net PPE	14.9%	15.0%	15.0%	15.0%	15.0%	15.0%	15.0%	15.0%	15.0%	15.0%	15.0%

Exhibit 7-5 Ratios for Calculating Operating Capital (Van Leer)

	Actual 2001	Actual 2002	Actual 2003	Actual Average	Projected 2004	Projected 2005	Projected 2006	Projected 2007	Projected 2008	Projected 2009	Projected Thereafter
Ratios to calculate operating profit											
Cash % of sales	5.0%	5.0%	5.0%	5.0%	3.0%	3.0%	3.0%	2.0%	2.0%	2.0%	2.0%
Inventory % of sales	8.9%	9.0%	10.0%	9.3%	11.0%	11.0%	11.0%	11.0%	11.0%	11.0%	11.0%
AR % of sales	7.7%	7.4%	7.5%	7.6%	7.6%	7.6%	7.6%	7.6%	7.6%	7.6%	7.6%
Net PPE % of sales	32.7%	29.7%	30.0%	30.8%	34.0%	31.5%	30.8%	30.8%	30.8%	30.8%	30.8%
AP % of sales	9.5%	7.4%	7.5%	8.1%	8.1%	8.1%	8.1%	8.1%	8.1%	8.1%	8.1%
Accrued exp. % of sales	1.0%	1.1%	1.0%	1.0%	1.0%	1.0%	1.0%	1.0%	1.0%	1.0%	1.0%

among firms, depending on their manufacturing technology, their product mix, or their capacity level.

The capacity level has important implications for net PPE as a percentage of sales, especially over the next 5 years or so. If a firm is operating at full capacity, any increase in sales requires new investments in factories and physical plant. But most firms don't just purchase or construct "1 year's worth" of additional factory at a time. Because plant construction generally entails long lead times and economies of scale, when most firms decide to build a plant, they build enough that the firm will be able to grow into it over several years. This means that even if sales are growing at a steady pace, the firm makes very little investment in some years and large investments in others. This affects our projections of net PPE in two ways. First, we must estimate how much excess capacity the firm has. Second, we must try to estimate the steady state relationship between sales and net PPE. Fortunately, we can use historical data to help us estimate these relationships. Most firms' PPE as a percentage of sales tends to cycle. The percentage is lowest when the firm is at full capacity and highest when the firm has just invested heavily in new plant and equipment.

Van Leer's ratio of net PPE/sales has decreased over the last 3 years from 32.7% to 30.0% as a result of growing into production facilities that were brought on line 4 years ago. Van Leer is currently operating at about 95% capacity, which means that it can increase unit sales by up to 5% with only minimal increases in plant and equipment. We are projecting that Van Leer will increase unit sales by more than this for 2004, so it will have to make immediate investments in plant and equipment if it is to be able to satisfy its sales projections. During the last multiyear cycle of investment, Van Leer's ratio of net PPE/sales has averaged 30.8%. As Van Leer's construction projects come on line in 2004, we project that PPE will increase to 34% of sales. Following 2004, rather than projecting a cyclical increase and decrease in the ratio of PPE to sales, we will simply let the 2004 percentage slowly drop down to 30.8%, the expected long-run rate. Although these are only rough estimates, they capture the essence of Van Leer's capital usage.

Accounts Payable and Accrued Expenses

Van Leer's accounts payable policy, like that of most companies, is largely determined by the terms under which Van Leer purchases its raw materials and equipment. Most of Van Leer's suppliers have credit terms of net 45, which means Van Leer pays the net amount within 45 days. Van Leer could pay earlier, but there is no good reason to pay earlier as long as the supplier doesn't require it—the longer Van Leer waits, the longer it has use of the funds. On the other hand, there are compelling reasons not to pay later than the required 45 days. If Van Leer consistently pays late, then its suppliers may tack on late fees or may simply stop doing business with Van Leer. Van Leer is currently taking almost exactly 45 days to pay its accounts, so there is no reason for Van Leer to change its payment policies. Since Van Leer's payables have averaged 8.1% of sales over the last 3 years, this is what we project for the foreseeable future.

Accrued expenses have consistently been 1% of sales, and there is no reason for this to change. A summary of the ratios used to calculate operating capital appears in Exhibit 7-5.

Projecting Operating Taxes

A firm's effective tax rate changes as its pre-tax income level goes up and down. Our federal tax system has a **progressive tax structure**, which means that the tax on an additional dollar, called the **marginal tax rate**, increases with the overall level of income. For example, if a company's pre-tax income is less than $50,000, then each dollar is taxed at a rate of 15%. If a company's pre-tax income is between $100,000 and $335,000, then each dollar over $100,000 is taxed at a rate of 39%. Actually, the tax structure isn't exactly progressive. It has a "hump" at the $100,000 to $335,000 range and a dip back down to 35% for firms with pre-tax income over $18.3 million. In addition to federal income tax, almost all states impose a tax on corporate income. The end result, though, is that at different income levels the firm will pay different average and marginal tax rates.

The federal and state governments determine the tax rates, so in principal the amount of tax should just be a deterministic function of income. But a variety of accounting details make it more difficult than that for an analyst. Firms can take advantage of various tax credits and they can carry losses forward or backward to offset the losses against future or past profits when calculating the taxes they owe. Even if the firm could predict the timing and amount of opportunities for tax credits, outside analysts typically don't have all of these details. Therefore, we make assumptions about the firm's effective tax rate based on historical data and the existing tax code. In the case of Van Leer, the effective tax rate has been 39.7% of earnings before taxes, and this is expected to be the effective rate for the future as well. Later, we might want to compare this rate with rates paid by similar firms, just to see if it is a reasonable assumption.[2]

Dividend and Debt Ratios

The operating profit and operating capital projections are driven by the sales forecast, but the dividend and debt ratios are chosen by management. Although these financial policies don't affect how much free cash flow is generated, management doesn't choose them arbitrarily.

The tax deductibility of interest makes debt a relatively attractive financing choice, although in the event of financial distress, debt's priority over equity increases the risk exposure of stockholders. All else equal, a firm with more debt has lower taxes, but riskier common stock.

With respect to dividend policy, a firm's dividend history may have attracted a certain investor clientele (i.e., "retirees, widows, and orphans" may choose high-dividend companies, while "growth" investors may choose low-dividend companies), and unexpected variation in dividends will probably not be well received by many stockholders. Additionally, a firm that pays out more in dividends must find greater sources of external capital than a firm paying out less in dividends. We're not going to take you through all of the ins and outs of capital structure and dividend policy decisions; if you are interested in these issues, then look in a finance

[2]State income tax rates range from about 1% to 10% (Delaware's rate is a flat 8.7%). Because federal taxes are usually deductible, state tax is paid only on after-federal-tax income, making the effective top-end federal-plus-state tax rate in the neighborhood of 40%. Van Leer's situation is, therefore, representative of most companies.

textbook.[3] Instead, we will assume that the analyst identifies the company's target dividend growth rate and debt ratio either from historical financial statements or from policies articulated by management.

Dividend Growth Rate

As stated in Chapter 6, a firm can choose from a wide range of dividend strategies. Frequently, we see that firms in the initial stage of development will choose to pay no dividends at all because they have significant reinvestment needs and choosing to retain all of the company's earnings reduces the amount of external capital the firm must obtain. Once a firm's reinvestment needs decrease, either because it has ended its rapid growth period or because it has developed other sources of capital, it may begin to pay dividends. Dividends often start low and increase as the firm becomes more comfortable paying them (because the firm believes that they are sustainable). This pattern may result in a high growth rate in dividends in a firm's initial years of dividend payments, followed by a decline to a level that is sustainable in the long run, which is usually a growth rate similar to the expected long-term growth in earnings (which is, in turn, linked to the long-term growth rate in sales).

Van Leer is still in the phase where dividends are increasing faster than sales. Dividend growth rate has been erratic because Van Leer paid out each year what it felt it could afford to pay, given its reinvestment needs and the other sources of financing it had arranged. Starting last year, Van Leer decided to stabilize its dividend policy. The dividend growth rate was tentatively set at 10% a year through the end of 2007. Although Van Leer did not make any projections for after 2007, given our projections for declining sales growth after 2004, it would appear reasonable that Van Leer's dividend growth will ultimately decline. Therefore, we assume that dividends will grow at 8% in 2008 and only 6% thereafter.

Target Financing

Debt is cheaper than equity, because interest payments are deductible and because debt is less risky than equity. However, Van Leer has avoided using very much debt because it increases the potential for financial distress or even bankruptcy. Over the last 3 years, Van Leer has, on average, financed about 16% of its operating capital with long-term debt. Any additional borrowing that Van Leer needs over and above this 16% of operating capital has been accommodated with its line of credit, which is part of its short-term debt. Even though this level of debt is lower than most of its competitors, Van Leer's CEO and CFO are both very conservative, and they are committed to reducing the level of long-term debt to 15% of operating capital for the foreseeable future.

Interest Expense and Income

We assumed in Chapter 6 that the interest rate earned on short-term investments was 3% and that the cost of short-term and long-term debt was 9% for 2004. There is no reason to change these assumptions for the next several years, so they will be used throughout our projections.

---

[3]For example, see E. Brigham and P. Daves, *Intermediate Financial Management*, 8th Ed., South-Western, 2004.

The Projected Statements

We have chosen all the required inputs for making multiyear projections. First, we should reiterate how we balance the balance sheets, given the operating and financial policies of Van Leer.

Balancing

Recall that we are using short-term debt and short-term investments to balance total assets with liabilities and owners' equity. If the sum of all projected assets (other than short-term investments) is greater than the sum of all projected liabilities and owners' equity (other than short-term debt), then we have projected more assets than we can afford, given the specified sources of financing. This means we need an additional source of financing, and we assume that Van Leer will fill this need with short-term borrowing. On the other hand, if projected liabilities and owners' equity (excluding short-term debt) is greater than projected assets (excluding short-term investments), then we have more sources of funds than we need. In this case, we assume that Van Leer will use the excess funds to purchase highly liquid short-term investments.

For example, we concluded in Chapter 6 that, in 2004, the total specified assets (i.e., assets other than short-term investments) are $617.2 million. The total sources of specified financing on the liabilities side of the balance sheet (liabilities and equity other than short-term debt) are $577.0 million, which is less than the specified assets by $40.2 million. This means Van Leer must find another $40.2 million in financing to fund the assets needed to support its growth plan. We assume that Van Leer will draw $40.2 million on its line of credit, which is a part of its short-term debt.

As shown in Exhibit 7-6, the opposite situation occurs in 2006. Excluding short-term investments, Van Leer needs $672.1 million in assets to support its sales. However, Van Leer has $702.4 million in financing. This means Van Leer has $30.3 million in cash left after all of the assets have been acquired. Rather than increase the cash balance by this amount, we assume that Van Leer will invest this amount in short-term investments such as Treasury bills, commercial paper, or negotiable CDs.

The procedure we just described is only one of many possible ways to balance the statements. We discuss other financial policies and other methods of balancing in Chapter 8.

Also, keep in mind that we used a spreadsheet model to project the financial statements shown in Exhibit 7-6. Although Exhibit 7-6 shows only one digit to the right of the decimal, the spreadsheet used the full numbers in all calculations. Some totals in Exhibit 7-6 may add up exactly, but this is due to the rounded numbers reported in the financial statements.

Checking the Projections

Exhibit 7-6 shows the projected income statements (Panel A) and balance sheets (Panel B) for Van Leer that reflect our operating assumptions and financial policies. After making these projections, the next step is to make sure that the projections are

Exhibit 7-6 Van Leer's Projected Financial Statements (millions of dollars)

Panel A. Van Leer Projected Income Statements

	Actual 2001	Actual 2002	Actual 2003	Projected 2004	Projected 2005	Projected 2006	Projected 2007	Projected 2008	Projected 2009
Net sales	$840.0	$944.0	$1,000.0	$1,110.0	$1,198.8	$1,282.7	$1,372.5	$1,454.9	$1,542.1
Cost of goods sold	520.0	625.0	640.0	693.8	749.3	801.7	864.7	931.1	987.0
SG&A	200.0	205.0	215.0	249.8	269.7	288.6	308.8	327.3	347.0
Depreciation	41.0	42.0	45.0	56.6	56.6	59.3	63.4	67.2	71.2
Operating profit	$ 79.0	$ 72.0	$ 100.0	$ 109.9	$ 123.2	$ 133.1	$ 135.6	$ 129.2	$ 136.9
Interest income	0.0	1.0	0.0	0.8	0.0	0.0	0.9	1.9	2.5
Interest expense	9.0	9.0	10.0	11.2	11.9	8.7	9.1	9.5	10.1
Earnings before taxes	$ 70.0	$ 64.0	$ 90.0	$ 99.5	$ 111.2	$ 124.5	$ 127.4	$ 121.6	$ 129.3
Taxes	28.0	25.0	36.0	39.5	44.2	49.4	50.6	48.3	51.3
Net income	$ 42.0	$ 39.0	$ 54.0	$ 60.0	$ 67.1	$ 75.1	$ 76.8	$ 73.3	$ 78.0
Dividends	$ 12.0	$ 11.0	$ 16.0	$ 17.6	$ 19.4	$ 21.3	$ 23.4	$ 25.3	$ 26.8
Additions to RE	$ 30.0	$ 28.0	$ 38.0	$ 42.4	$ 47.7	$ 53.8	$ 53.4	$ 48.0	$ 51.2

Panel B. Van Leer Balance Sheets

	Actual 2001	Actual 2002	Actual 2003	Projected 2004	Projected 2005	Projected 2006	Projected 2007	Projected 2008	Projected 2009
Cash	$ 42.0	$ 47.0	$ 50.0	$ 33.3	$ 36.0	$ 38.5	$ 27.5	$ 29.1	$ 30.8
Short-term investments	10.0	15.0	25.0	0.0	0.0	30.3	63.5	83.1	104.0
Inventory	75.0	85.0	100.0	122.1	131.9	141.1	151.0	160.0	169.6
Accounts receivable	65.0	70.0	75.0	84.4	91.1	97.5	104.3	110.6	117.2
Total current assets	$192.0	$217.0	$ 250.0	$239.8	$ 258.9	$307.3	$346.3	$382.8	$421.7
Net PPE	275.0	280.0	300.0	377.4	377.6	395.1	422.7	448.1	475.0
Total assets	$467.0	$497.0	$ 550.0	$617.2	$ 636.6	$702.4	$769.0	$830.8	$896.7
Accounts payable	$ 80.0	$ 70.0	$ 75.0	$ 89.9	$ 97.1	$103.9	$111.2	$117.8	$124.9
Accrued expenses	8.0	10.0	10.0	11.1	12.0	12.8	13.7	14.5	15.4
Short-term debt	50.0	30.0	25.0	40.2	0.9	0.0	0.0	0.0	0.0
Total current liabilities	$138.0	$110.0	$ 110.0	$141.2	$ 110.0	$116.7	$124.9	$132.4	$140.3
Long-term debt	54.0	84.0	99.0	92.6	95.5	100.8	105.8	112.2	118.9
Total liabilities	$192.0	$194.0	$ 209.0	$233.8	$ 205.5	$217.5	$230.7	$244.6	$259.2
Common stock	125.0	125.0	125.0	125.0	125.0	125.0	125.0	125.0	125.0
Retained earnings	150.0	178.0	216.0	258.4	306.1	359.9	413.3	461.3	512.5
Total common equity	$275.0	$303.0	$ 341.0	$383.4	$ 431.1	$484.9	$538.3	$586.3	$637.5
Total liabilities & equity	$467.0	$497.0	$ 550.0	$617.2	$ 636.6	$702.4	$769.0	$830.8	$896.7

reasonable and consistent with our understanding about the company. Although we have been careful to choose inputs that reflect economic realities and company-specific information, we must look at the statements themselves to ensure that they do in fact reflect how we expect the company to look during the projection horizon. (It has probably never happened to you, but we sometimes make typos when entering numbers in a spreadsheet, and so we want to make sure none of our projections look peculiar.)

"Debugging" Projections: What Is "Reasonable?"

In evaluating projected financial statements, we always ask ourselves the following questions:

1. Is it reasonable for the company's sales to be as large as predicted at the end of the projection period, or are the sales forecasts just wishful thinking? In answering this question, we should think about growth in the industry and how the company's growth compares to it. If projected growth is much larger than the industry's, are there compelling reasons why the company should be increasing its position within the industry, or is there a compelling plan to accomplish this goal? How big is the company now relative to the industry, and how big will it be relative to the expected size of the industry?
2. What do the asset investments look like from year to year? What about net investment in operating capital? Are increases in net PPE on a dollar basis similar to those in earlier years? If not, are there good reasons for this difference? Is there a large jump or decline in any of the asset categories from the last year of actual data to the first year of projections? If so, are there good reasons for this jump or is it simply due to a large change in the first projected year for one of the asset utilization ratios, such as the inventory to sales ratio? If so, then you should consider phasing the change in over several years.
3. Are the dividend payments sustainable? What is the dividend payout ratio at the beginning of the projection period and at the end of the projection period? Only the most stable and low-growth companies will have dividend payout ratios in excess of 50%. How do the dividend payments compare to free cash flow? If dividend payments exceed free cash flow, then the firm must either borrow more or issue more stock in order to fund the dividends.
4. What is happening to short-term debt? If short-term debt is increasing significantly, then we should reconsider our projections of long-term debt policy and dividend policy, because a long-term debt policy that doesn't include enough borrowing and a too-generous dividend policy will force the firm to issue too much short-term debt. Although short-term debt isn't bad in and of itself, the fact that it is short-term and might not be renewed by the bank makes it a risky source of long-term funding.
5. What is happening to short-term investments? If a firm is accumulating large amounts of short-term investments, then it has probably either chosen a dividend policy that isn't generous enough or has set the long-term debt level too high. Although there are notable exceptions, most firms won't accumulate huge short-term investment balances unless they have strategic reasons for them. If

a firm consistently generates excess cash, it usually increases dividends, or repurchases stock (we'll discuss these financial policy choices in more depth in Chapter 8), or borrows less. But if this increase in cash is accompanied by a reduction in overall company risk as well, then the firm will most likely increase its payout rather than decrease its debt level because less-risky firms are able to carry more debt.

6. What are the growth rates in free cash flow and the ROICs in each of the projected years? Are the ROICs comparable with ROICs from earlier years and the ROICs of comparable companies? If not, then either there should be a good reason for the deviation or the parameters you have chosen aren't consistent with what we really expect the company to do, and we should go back and look over the input parameters.

Are Van Leer's Statements "Reasonable?"

From Exhibit 7-6 we can see that Van Leer's sales are expected to increase from $1 billion in 2003 to $1.542 billion by 2009, a 54% increase. This growth is not unreasonable given what we know about Van Leer. Exhibit 7-7 shows Van Leer's free cash flow calculations and the various growth rates discussed above. The investment in net operating capital from year to year is consistent with the historical investment levels, and from the balance sheet we can see that PPE makes no unusual "jumps."

Van Leer's free cash flows are projected to be positive in every year except 2004. A rapidly growing firm will usually generate negative free cash flows due to large investments in operating assets required to achieve the growth, but we would expect positive free cash flows after the rapid growth rate subsides. This is precisely the case with Van Leer, where the negative free cash flow in 2004 can be traced to the projected large investment ($76.2 million) required to provide assets in support of the anticipated high revenue growth. Comparing Exhibits 7-6 and 7-7 reveals that, except for 2004, dividends are projected to be less than free cash flow in each of the projection years. The fact that Van Leer is paying out less than it could in almost every year is reflected in the accumulation of short-term investments—a total of $104 million by 2009. Unless Van Leer has specific plans for this money, it should consider increasing the dividend growth rate, decreasing the debt level, or engaging in a stock repurchase (we discuss stock repurchases in Chapter 8).[4] In any case, this is a decision that must be made by the board of directors. So we will leave the projections as they are.

Van Leer's return on invested capital is projected to remain in the 13% to 15% range, which is consistent with its historical returns. Had projected ROIC been substantially higher than in the past, we would have had to ask ourselves whether our projections were overly optimistic.

[4]Indeed, this observation indicates just how the free cash flow valuation model and its associated financial projections may be useful in corporate long-term financial planning.

Exhibit 7-7 Van Leer's Free Cash Flow Calculation and ROIC (millions of dollars)

	Actual 2001	Actual 2002	Actual 2003	Projected 2004	Projected 2005	Projected 2006	Projected 2007	Projected 2008	Projected 2009
Operating income	$ 79.0	$ 72.0	$100.0	$109.9	$123.2	$133.1	$135.6	$129.2	$136.9
Tax on operating income	31.6	28.1	40.0	43.6	48.9	52.9	53.8	51.3	54.4
NOPAT	$ 47.4	$ 43.9	$ 60.0	$ 66.3	$ 74.3	$ 80.3	$ 81.8	$ 77.9	$ 82.6
Net operating WC	94.0	122.0	140.0	138.8	149.9	160.3	157.8	167.3	177.3
Net operating long-term assets	275.0	280.0	300.0	377.4	377.6	395.1	422.7	448.1	475.0
Total net operating capital	$369.0	$402.0	$440.0	$516.2	$527.5	$555.4	$580.6	$615.4	$652.3
Investment in net operating capital	na	33.0	38.0	76.2	11.3	27.9	25.2	34.8	36.9
Free cash flow	na	$10.88	$22.00	$ -9.89	$62.95	$52.34	$56.61	$43.07	$45.65
Growth in FCF	na	na	102.3%	-144.9%	na	-16.9%	8.2%	-23.9%	6.0%
ROIC	na	11.89%	14.93%	15.06%	14.39%	15.22%	14.72%	13.42%	13.42%

Note: All calculations were performed in a spreadsheet using full numbers. Therefore, some totals may not sum exactly due to rounding.

Using Projections for Valuation

Since Exhibit 7-7 has the free cash flow calculations, all we need to estimate the value of operations is the weighted average cost of capital and the horizon value. We briefly discussed how to calculate the cost of capital in Chapter 2 and will discuss the topic in greater depth in Chapter 11, but let's assume that we have gathered the necessary information to estimate the cost of capital. Currently, Van Leer has a target of 19.8% debt and 80.2% equity in its capital structure. Let's assume that Van Leer will maintain these weights going forward. Van Leer's beta coefficient is estimated at 1.30, and the market risk premium, RP_M, is estimated at 5%. The risk-free rate is 6%, so the CAPM cost of equity for Van Leer (using Equation 4-3) is

$$r_S = r_{RF} + \text{beta}(RP_M)$$
$$r_S = 6.0\% + 1.4(5.0\%) = 13.0\%. \quad \textbf{(4-3)}$$

We have already estimated the cost of debt to be 9% before tax, and because Van Leer is expected to be in a 39.7% tax bracket, the after-tax cost of debt is 5.4%. Now we are ready to apply Equation 4-1 to get Van Leer's WACC.

$$\text{WACC} = (1 - T)r_D w_D + r_S w_S$$
$$\text{WACC} = (1 - 0.397)(9.0\%)(0.198) + (13.0\%)(0.802) = 11.5\% \quad \textbf{(4-1)}$$

We will use the simplest version of the horizon value for Van Leer (we discuss alternative methods of calculating the horizon value in Chapter 13). Recall from Chapter 4 (Equation 4-5) that the horizon value as of 2009 can be calculated as

$$HV_{2009} = \frac{FCF_{2009}(1 + g)}{\text{WACC} - g}. \quad \textbf{(4-5)}$$

where g is the steady state growth rate in free cash flow. Exhibits 7-4 and 7-5 show that the predicted operating ratios don't change after 2008, so it is predicted to have reached a steady state growth rate by then. Exhibit 7-7 shows that the 2009 growth rate for FCF is 6%, which is also the growth rate in sales. In fact, the growth rate in free cash flow will always equal the growth rate in sales in the steady state.

The horizon value, then, is

$$HV_{2009} = \frac{FCF_{2009}(1 + g)}{\text{WACC} - g} = \frac{\$45.65(1.06)}{0.115 - 0.06} = \$879.80.$$

which is the value of operations as of the end of 2009.

Van Leer's current value of operations is the present value of the horizon value plus the present value of the free cash flows from Exhibit 7-7 when discounted at the weighted average cost of capital, 11.5%. The cash flows are summarized in Exhibit 7-8.

Exhibit 7-8 Summary of Horizon Value and Free Cash Flow for Van Leer, Inc.

	2004	2005	2006	2007	2008	2009
Horizon value	na	na	na	na	na	$879.80
Free cash flow	$(9.89)	$62.95	$52.34	$56.61	$43.07	$ 45.65
FCF + Horizon value	$(9.89)	$62.95	$52.34	$56.61	$43.07	$925.45

The present value of the bottom row, when discounted at 11.5%, is $622.79 million, which is the value of operations as of the end of 2003. According to Exhibit 7-6, at the end of 2003 Van Leer had $25 million in short-term investments and total debt of $124 million. The value of Van Leer's equity is $622.79 + $25 – $124 = $523.79 million. If Van Leer has 10 million shares outstanding, then the value of Van Leer's stock would be $52.38 per share. Comparing this to the current value of $40.12 per share, our analysis suggests that Van Leer is a good investment at this time. Naturally, before calling our broker or advising our client, we would review the key assumptions made in estimating our intrinsic value and do some sensitivity analysis to determine how much the estimated price changes if we make changes in the input parameters.

Summary

In this chapter, we extended our analysis of Van Leer Products, Inc., by projecting Van Leer's financial statements out to 2009. Although the case was hypothetical, it nevertheless illustrated how macroeconomic and industry-level knowledge are combined with specific information about a firm's strategic strengths and weaknesses, as well as current information about operating policies and initiatives, to provide the means of forecasting the firm's future financial performance.

Clearly, the usefulness of the result depends upon the quality of the many judgments we made when choosing input parameters. When conducting a valuation of an actual company, we always do a sensitivity analysis. We try different assumptions regarding demand growth, cost control initiatives, and asset utilization (e.g., inventory and PPE as a percent of sales). This helps identify which assumptions have the biggest impacts on the estimated stock price. If a particular assumption doesn't have a big impact, we move on to the next one. For those assumptions with the biggest impacts, we often do further research, so that we can make the best assumptions possible.

The Van Leer analysis also provided insights for how the projected financial statements may be used by the firm's managers as a tool in long-term financial planning. The firm's financial policies are interrelated with operating results, and the resulting financial statement projections help identify the plausibility of the financial policies. In the next chapter, we will explain how to project financial statements when there are different financial policies.

Spreadsheet Problems

7-1 Multiyear Projection and Valuation of Van Leer

This project builds upon those of the previous two chapters. It extends the projection of Van Leer's free cash flow and financials to 2009, then calculates the corresponding estimate of the per share value of the firm's stock. Follow these instructions.

Start with your solution to the Chapter 6 Excel construction and make the following modifications to your model:

a. In the *Inputs* tab, go to columns E through I, and fill out the projected inputs for the year 2005 to 2009 (these growth and ratio projections can be found in Exhibits 7-4 and 7-5).

b. Now open the *Projection of FCF* tab. Fill out the projection for the Income Statement section through 2009. Just copy the formulas in column D, rows 6 to 12, over into columns E through I. [Use your cursor to highlight the block of cells D6 to D12. Then grab the lower right corner of the block, and drag over to column I. It's as simple as that!]

c. Similarly, repeat the procedure to fill out the Balance Sheet and the Free Cash Flow and ROIC sections of the worksheet.

d. Now go to the *Proj. of Financials & Valuation* tab, and fill out the Financial Statement projections in a similar manner. This will give a full set of pro forma financials for every year from 2004 through 2009.

e. All that remains is to discount the projected free cash flows to get the value of operations. The entries in row 45 just copy the year-by-year free cash flow projections from the *Projection of FCF* tab. The WACC calculation for Van Leer is done in the *WACC* tab, and the resulting cost of capital is entered in cell B47 and used to find the present value of the expected free cash flows in rows 49 and 50. Row 49 uses the horizon value formula to calculate the present value of the constantly growing stream of free cash flow from year 2010 onward. The entries in row 50 give the value, each year, of the cash flow received in that year plus the discounted present value of free cash flows in all subsequent years. The formulas are already entered, but you should satisfy yourself that they are correct.

f. Then row 52 and 53 add in the current level of short-term investments and rows 54 and 55 deduct the outstanding debt obligations, resulting in the aggregate value of equity.

g. Rows 56 and 57 use the number of outstanding shares (from the *WACC* tab) to convert the value to per share amount ($52.37). Notice that this is significantly different from the value in the book due to rounding.

Now you have a spreadsheet that converts the myriad elements of the analyst's efforts into a coherent picture of future cash flows and financial statements, and produces an estimate of intrinsic value.

7-2 Sensitivity Analysis for Van Leer

This project builds and tests the sensitivity of the intrinsic value estimate to changes in some of the assumption made in Chapters 5 to 7.

The value estimate resulting from the analysis of Van Leer is only as good as the assumptions made by the analyst. The precision of estimates of growth rates, cost ratios, cost of capital, and both working capital and long-term capital requirements will vary considerably according the reliability of the analyst's sources and to unforeseen events. Suppose we have an idea of the range of variation from our original estimates for several "parameters" of the valuation model. Start with your solution to the previous project and make the following modifications to your model. After each modification, set the inputs back to their original values before making the next change (i.e., consider only "one-at-time" changes). Construct a table that summarizes the resulting intrinsic values.

a. Reduce the estimated revenue growth rates by 1 percentage point for each year.
b. Increase the COGS/sales ratio by 2 percentage points each year.
c. Increase the Cash/sales ratio to a flat 5% for all years.
d. Increase the market risk premium (*WACC* tab) from 5% to 6%.
e. Increase SGA to 25% of sales in 2004 and thereafter.

Of the four changes, which has the most severe consequences for estimated value?

Think about how you, as the analyst, might use these "sensitivity" results in reaching an ultimate conclusion as to the wisdom of investing in Van Leer.

7-3 Valuation of Pigeon River Brown Ale

The most recent financial statements for Pigeon River Brown Ale are shown in the worksheet in the file ***Prob 07-3.xls***. Follow these instructions.

a. Using the inputs shown in the file, project Pigeon River Brown Ale's financial statements.
b. Calculate the projected free cash flows.
c. Estimate the stock price.

Chapter 8

Technical Issues in Projecting Financial Statements and Forecasting Financing Needs

Introduction

Although the techniques described in Chapter 7 work well for most firms, there may be situations in which different assumptions are more appropriate. We present three modifications and extensions to the forecasting model developed in the previous chapters:

- Extensions to the constant percentage of sales projection method:
  - Linear model with an intercept,
  - Non-linear model,
  - Modeling "lumpy" assets;
- Alternative financing policies:
  - Constant growth, fixed payout, and residual dividend policies,
  - Common equity issuances and repurchases,
  - Maintaining debt as a percentage of market value;
- Projecting interest expense and interest income based on the average debt and short-term investment levels during the year rather than beginning-of-period values.

These extensions should allow you to develop reasonable models for most types of companies and cost structures.

Before diving into the details, think about our primary concern as analysts: we want to make the most accurate estimate possible of intrinsic value. We know we will make mistakes in our projections of some individual components of cash flow, but these should average out to some extent because we are projecting many individual components. In other words, we might be too high on some, but too low on others. As long as we are not systematically overly optimistic or pessimistic, our resulting estimate of intrinsic value should be reliable.

When discounting future free cash flows, a mistake in estimating the near-term free cash flows causes a bigger error in the intrinsic value than a mistake of the same magnitude in more distant cash flows. Therefore, we are generally more concerned about accuracy in the near-term projections and are more willing to accept rougher approximations for the more distant components of free cash flow. As you will see, several of the extensions discussed in this chapter follow this principle—we are more concerned about "getting it right" in the near term than in the far term.

When Projections Aren't a Percentage of Sales

In Chapter 7, we projected most items on Van Leer's financial statements as a percentage of sales.[1] But some firms may have items that require a different approach. For example, the sales, general and administrative expenses (SGA) for some firms, particularly small ones, may have a fixed component (such as the overhead costs of corporate headquarters) and a variable component (such as advertising or sales commissions) that is related to sales. For this situation, a better model for SGA might be

$$\text{SGA} = \text{Fixed expenses} + \text{Sales (Variable SGA expenses as a \% of sales)}. \quad \textbf{(8-1)}$$

Another example is inventory. Researchers have shown that for some companies the optimal level of inventory doesn't increase linearly as sales increase. Rather, the optimal level of inventory increases at a slower rate than sales. So at a sales level of $10 million, the firm might optimally have $1 million in inventory, producing an inventory/sales ratio of 10%. But at a sales level of $20 million, the firm might need $1.8 million in inventory, for an inventory/sales ratio of 9%. At sales of $30 million, the firm might need only $2.55 million in inventory, for an inventory/sales ratio of 8.5%. In this case, a nonlinear projection for inventory as a function of sales might be more appropriate.

The following sections explain the linear and nonlinear models.

Linear Model with Intercept

A natural way to model the case discussed above with SGA consisting of a fixed and a variable component is a linear model

$$\text{SGA} = a + b(\text{Sales}) \quad \textbf{(8-2)}$$

where a and b are coefficients. If you have access to the company's accounting records, you might be able to determine values for a and b by examining all of the individual expenses associated with SGA and characterizing them as fixed or variable. However, an external analyst won't have access to these records, and so we must use historical data to estimate a and b.

Linear regression is the statistical technique of estimating a and b from historical data. It is easy to implement in spreadsheets, statistical software packages, and even on some financial calculators. The idea behind linear regression is to plot the data and find the line that fits it best. For example, below are the sales and SGA data for Van Leer back to 1999 in millions of dollars.

	1999	2000	2001	2002	2003
Sales	$770	$800	$840	$944	$1,000
SGA	171	187	200	205	215

[1]Some exceptions are depreciation (a percentage of net PPE), interest expense (which depends on the debt at the beginning of the year), and "financial policy variables," such as debt and dividends.

The equation for the line that best fits this data can be found using the regression tool in your spreadsheet program. The regression results show that this line, called the **trend line**, has the equation

$$\text{SGA} = 55.4 + 0.1610(\text{Sales}). \qquad \textbf{(8-3)}$$

The interpretation of this equation is that there is a base level of SGA expenses of $55.4 million per year and that these expenses would be incurred even if there were no sales. On top of this fixed expense is a variable expense for SGA that averages 16.1% of sales. The picture of the data in Exhibit 8-1 with the thicker trend line clearly shows how well this trend line fits.

The difference between this way of modeling SGA expense and the Chapter 7 approach also affects the projections. Exhibit 8-1 shows the projected SGA if sales are $1,500 million: SGA = 55.4 + 0.1610 × 1,500 = $296.9 million. On the other hand, if we used the fixed percentage of sales method from Chapter 7, we might be inclined to use the average percentage of sales—in this case the average over the 5 years is 22.52% of sales. If we used this percentage to calculate SGA, we would project SGA = 0.2252($1,500) = $337.8 million. The predicted line based on this fixed percentage is shown as the thin line in Exhibit 8-1. Like the regression line, it has a constant slope, but unlike the regression line, the "intercept" that is implied when using the percentage of sales method is zero.

Which projected level of SGA is correct when sales are $1,500 million? Should it be $296.9 million, or should it be $337.8 million? The answer obviously matters and depends on which is a better model of SGA expenses for your company. Choosing between the two models requires that you know something about the

Exhibit 8-1 Van Leer Sales and SGA (millions of dollars)

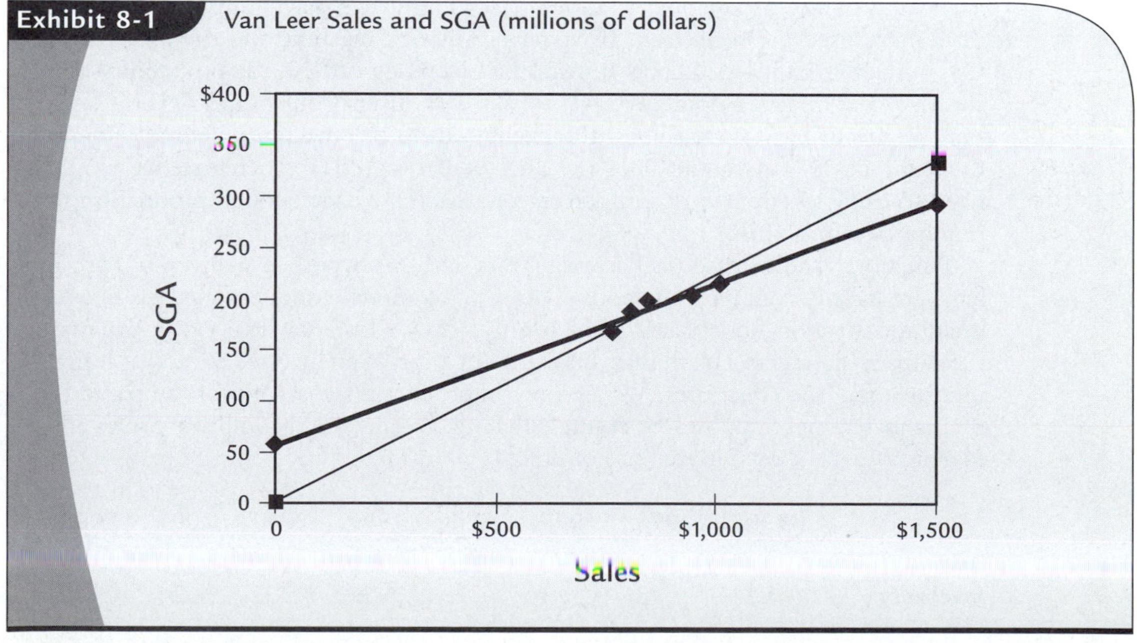

structure of the SGA expenses, and also it would help to look at the data visually, as in the picture above. Some firms have components of SGA expense that are fixed in the short and medium term—say for up to 5 years or so, and other components that are variable, even over the short term. This could happen if a firm is starting a new marketing program where there are fixed start-up costs (e.g., establishing brand-name recognition in a new market through an intensive advertising campaign or extraordinary costs of developing new supplier relationships in a foreign market), which make SGA disproportionate to sales for the first few years. As the program matures, the fixed component goes away. In such cases, the most accurate approach would be to use a model with slope plus intercept for projecting the first 5 years, and then a constant percentage of sales (i.e., with an intercept of zero) thereafter.

Nonlinear Models

Not all items on a firm's financial statements are necessarily linear functions of sales. Inventory is a classic example of a balance sheet item that depends on sales, but may do so in a nonlinear fashion. Under some fairly reasonable assumptions, the optimal level of inventory for many types of companies increases with sales, but does so at a decreasing rate, resulting in a ratio of inventory to sales that is declining as the sales level increases. That is, if your sales are $10 million and you plan to increase sales by $1 million, you might need an additional $100,000 in inventory, or 10% of the incremental sales, in order to support the additional $1 million in sales. But if your sales are already $50 million and you plan on increasing sales by $1 million, you would need only an additional $900,000 in inventory, or 9% of the incremental sales. The logic of this can be seen by considering the reasons for holding work-in-process inventory "just in case" a machine in the manufacturing process malfunctions. As total output of a given product increases and we expand production facilities accordingly, we have duplicates of the machinery used in production. If we have only one machine and the probability that a given machine will break down on a given day is 0.10, the probability of a shutdown if we don't hold any inventory is 10%. But if our output level is such that we are using two machines, the likelihood of *both* machines being down on the same day is only about 0.01 (i.e., $0.1 \times 0.1 = 0.01$). Therefore, we would need to carry less inventory as a percent of sales if we have enough production to require two machines.

Functions that increase at a decreasing rate, like this hypothetical inventory problem, are called "concave" functions. One way to model concave functions is as a quadratic function—one that is of the form $y = ax^2 + bx + c$ where $a < 0$. You may recall from high school math that this is the equation of an inverted parabola; it first increases and then decreases. We are only interested in the section of the parabola that is increasing. Suppose, for example that a company has the following sales and inventory data, shown in millions of dollars:

	1995	1996	1997	1998	1999	2000	2001	2002
Sales	$50	$60	$70	$80	$90	$100	$110	$120
Inventory	11	13	15	18	20	22	24	25

You can fit a parabola to a series of data using the trend function in Excel. It is a little more complicated than the linear trend because you must use both sales and sales^2 as independent variables in the trend function.

Exhibit 8-2 shows the inventory data and the fitted quadratic function for the region of interest. Notice that the fitted parabola reaches a peak and then declines. We are interested only in the increasing region—because it makes no sense for inventory to actually decrease with increasing sales!

A reasonable question is how do these projections differ from the linear trend or the constant percentage of sales? Exhibit 8-3 shows the inventory data, the fitted trend line, and the fitted linear trend and constant percentage of sales for sales levels up to $175 million. The equation for the fitted parabola is

$$\text{Inventory} = -0.00071(\text{Sales}^2) + 0.331(\text{Sales}) - 4.10. \qquad \textbf{(8-4)}$$

The projected inventory at a sales level of $175 million is $31.9 million for the quadratic projection, $37.3 million for the linear trend, and $38.1 million for the constant percentage of sales projection. Clearly the different models give different answers. Which is correct? Certainly you would not use the quadratic projection method for inventory levels above about $225 million, since the projected inventory levels would actually decline, as you can see in Exhibit 8-2. But if your inventory management system is efficient, you will probably experience inventory levels over the short- to medium-term more like the quadratic model than either of the linear models. If you use a linear model when a quadratic model is more appropriate, you will tend to overestimate the required levels of inventory, and this will bias downward your free cash flow projections and your value of operations! The best method

Exhibit 8-2 Fitting a Quadratic Function to Sales and Inventory (millions of dollars)

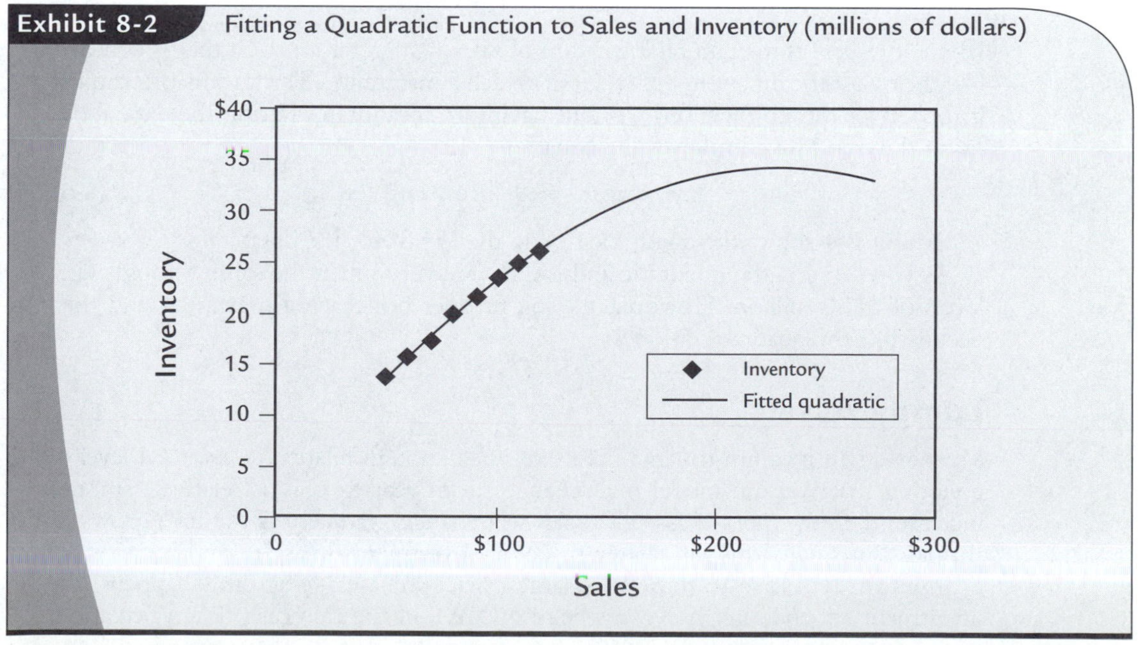

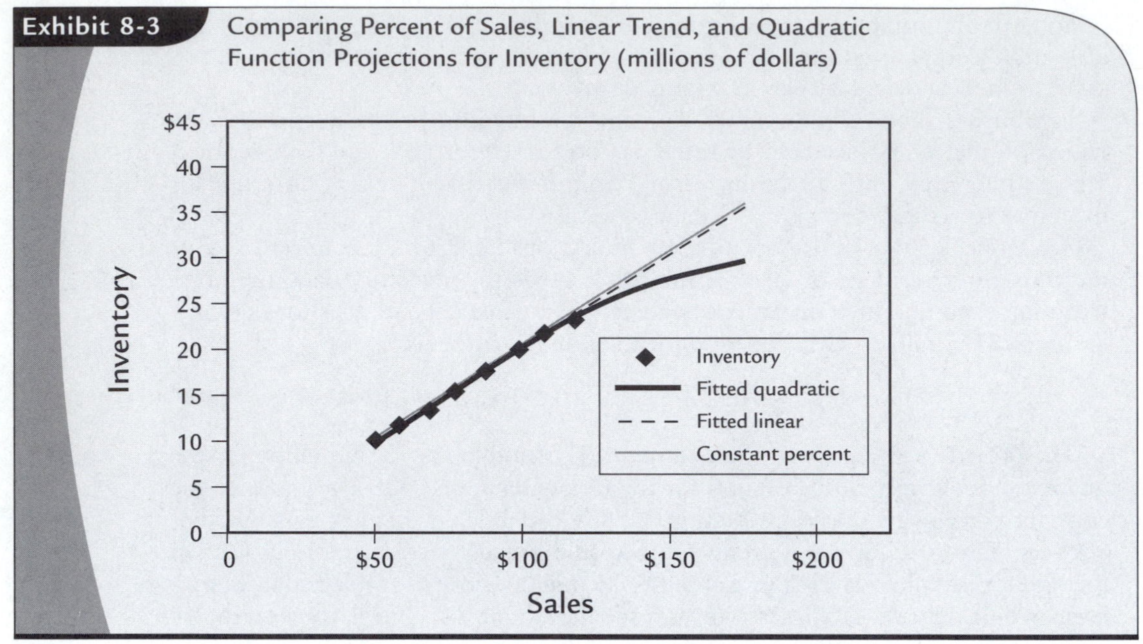

Exhibit 8-3 Comparing Percent of Sales, Linear Trend, and Quadratic Function Projections for Inventory (millions of dollars)

in practice would be to use a quadratic projection for the short- to medium-term, but recalibrate the coefficients a, b, and c, every 3 or 4 years so you don't project into the region where the inventory is decreasing.

Another function that is useful in projections is the natural logarithm function. If you fit the function

$$\text{Inventory} = a + b \ln[\text{Sales}] \quad \textbf{(8-5)}$$

where ln[Sales] is the natural logarithm of sales, you get a function that is concave, like the quadratic function, but it doesn't reach a maximum. This means you can use it for longer-term projections without having to recalibrate. Fitting the data above using the trend function gives the equation

$$\text{Inventory} = -55.8 + 16.9 \ln[\text{Sales}]. \quad \textbf{(8-6)}$$

Exhibit 8-4 shows the quadratic fit and the log fit for the data.

As you can see, the quadratic and log fits are very much the same through sales levels of $200 million. However, the log fit does not reach a maximum and then decline like the quadratic fit does.

Lumpy Assets

Most assets in medium to large firms are small enough relative to the total level of investing that you can model their changes from year to year as relatively smooth increases, i.e., the ratio of assets to sales will change gradually as the firm grows or shrinks. But small firms must often make big investments in assets, and occasionally a large firm will have to make very large asset purchases. When this happens, the investment expenditure may overwhelm NOPAT in the free cash flow calculation,

Exhibit 8-4 Comparing Quadratic and Log Function Projections for Inventory (millions of dollars)

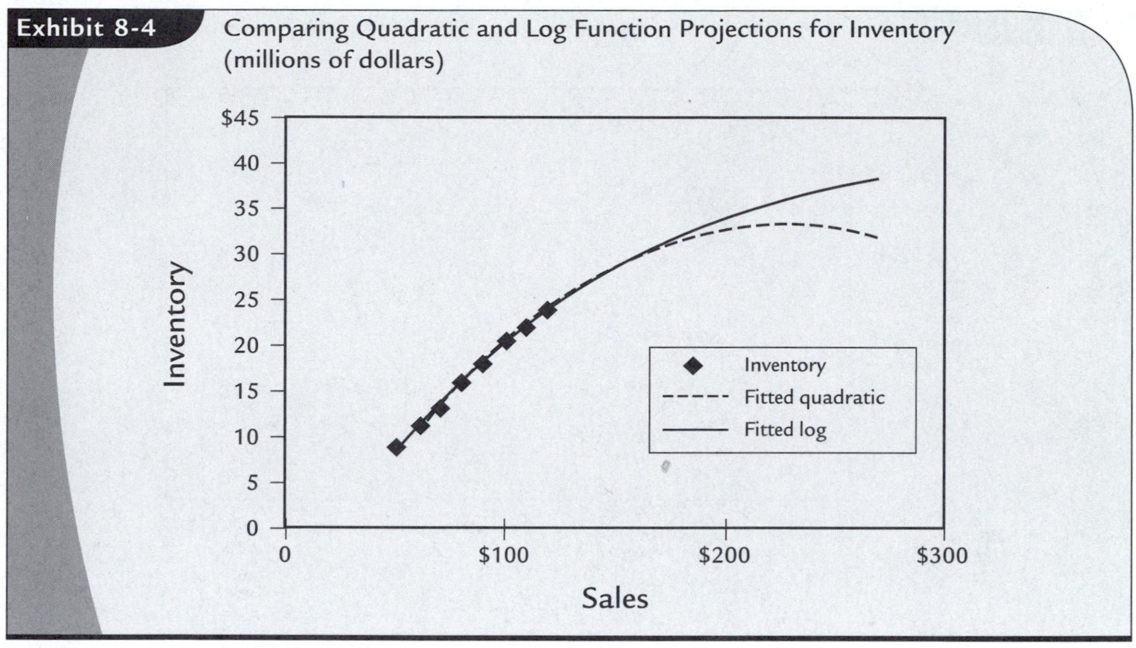

resulting in a large negative free cash flow. This is the situation projected for Van Leer for 2004, when the projected 11% revenue growth called for investment in net operating assets of $76.2 million results in a negative $9.9 million free cash flow. In these cases, where we have specific information concerning capacity utilization, we may improve our estimate of intrinsic value by incorporating this information into our projections for investment in PPE, rather than assuming that PPE remains a constant percentage of sales. It just makes more economic sense to model asset changes as "lumpy." Exhibit 8-5 shows Van Leer's net PPE levels for the last 7 years, revealing that in the past, Van Leer has been able to go 4 to 5 years between major plant expansions, and we could repeat this process of incorporating a major plant expansion every few years. Van Leer made a substantial investment in a manufacturing plant in 2000. During 1998 and 1999, Van Leer was apparently expanding into and using up the capacity at its existing plants, and during 2000, Van Leer was expanding into its new plant. Within about 4 years from 2000, then, we expect Van Leer's continued growth will necessitate another major investment in net PPE.

This cyclical pattern of gradual sales expansion, accompanied by periodic large investments that step-up capacity and followed by a series of smaller investments (mainly in operating working capital) until the new capacity level is reached, is common in growing companies. We want to model this pattern in such a way that it captures what is occurring and ultimately gives us an accurate picture of the firm's value, but is not unnecessarily complicated. In keeping with our emphasis on near-term accuracy in projections, the best way to do this is to explicitly take into account the lumpiness of the firm's investing over the short to medium term, and then assume that it will invest smoothly thereafter. Recall from Chapter 7 that we projected that net PPE will be 34.0% of sales in 2004, 31.5% of sales in 2005,

Exhibit 8-5 Net PPE by Year for Van Leer—1997 to 2003 (millions of dollars)

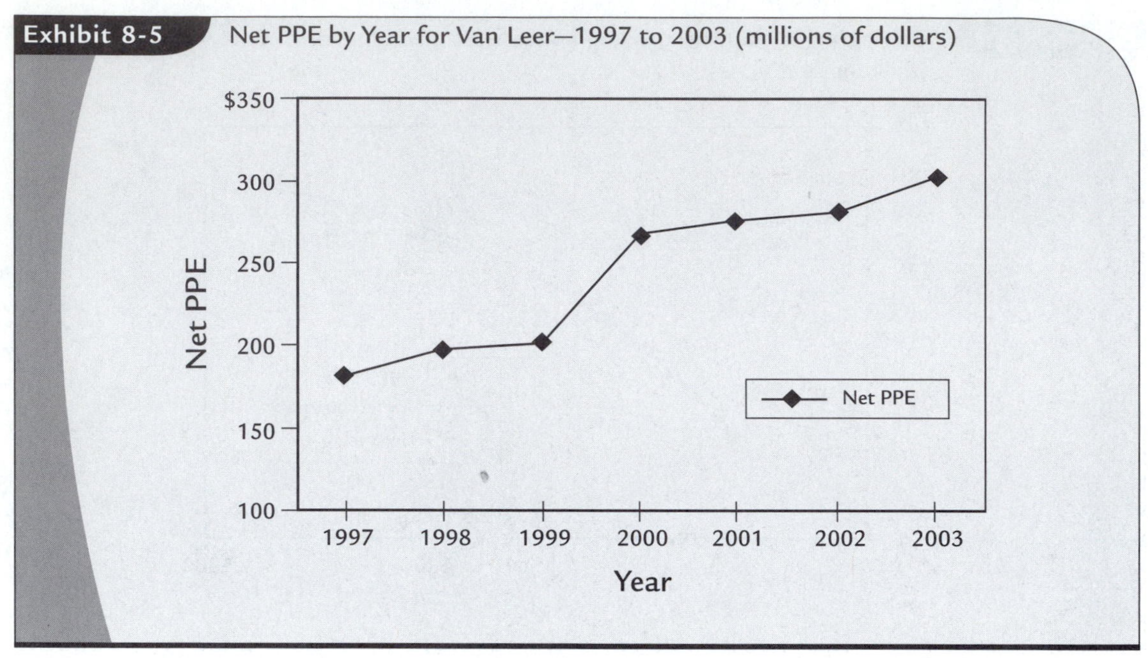

and 30.8% of sales thereafter. This corresponds to net PPE levels of $377.4, $377.6, and $395.1 million in 2004, 2005, and 2006, respectively, as shown in Exhibit 7-6. This projection was based on the historical average of 30.8% of sales and information to the effect that Van Leer was already operating near capacity and would have to make a sizable investment in PPE in 2004. If we dig further, we see that Van Leer will have to make a total net investment of $77.4 million in 2004. Only a $0.2 million investment is required in 2005, and $17.5 million in 2006. Thereafter, we projected that revenue growth would move to about 6% a year, and PPE expenditures "settle down" to the $25 to $28 million range.

Even if the timing of distant (i.e., beyond 5 years) plant expansions could be projected with some precision, it would not appreciably change the estimate of the value of the firm. If we use a constant percentage of sales to estimate future PPE after 2006, when, in fact the PPE additions are "lumpy," it will lead to underestimates of net PPE in some years, followed by overestimates in other years. In other words, the errors tend to cancel each other over a long period. In the process of discounting the future cash flow projections, distant errors that tend to cancel out due to year-to-year variation won't have an appreciable impact on our ultimate value estimate. Rather, when we consider the distant future, it is better to focus our attention on Van Leer's average ratio of PPE to sales. We use 30.8%, which is the historical average of net PPE as a percent of sales over an entire plant acquisition cycle, as the long-term estimate for this ratio. This projection allows for the fact that part of the time Van Leer will be operating at less than full capacity, and part of the time it will be operating at full or close to full capacity.[2]

[2]By the way, after completing the exercises in Chapters 5–7, you can readily test the sensitivity of our intrinsic value estimate to variations in the long-term PPE to sales ratio. For example, raising the long-term PPE/sales ratio to 32% from 2006 onward reduces the intrinsic value estimate by $4.40 per share.

Financial Modeling: Art versus Science

Keep in mind that all models are "wrong" in the sense that they are attempts to represent reality, and no model can perfectly capture all the aspects of the "real world." However, the value of a model lies in its ability produce conclusions that are useful. There is always a trade-off between the desire for additional accuracy and simplicity of use. Often, even imprecise models can give valuable insights regarding the impact of a change in the operating environment or corporate strategy. We have found that the simple percent of sales approach works well for most mature companies, and we use it more often than the other methods described above. However, we want you to know about these alternative approaches, since there are undoubtedly circumstances when you will need them. The book's web site provides illustrative spreadsheets.

Alternative Financing Policies

In our previous projections for Van Leer in Chapter 7, we assumed that dividends would grow at a constant rate, that long-term debt would remain a constant percentage of operating assets, and that no common stock would be sold or repurchased. However, these assumptions may not apply to all firms. For example, not all companies pay dividends, and for those that do, dividends may not grow at a constant rate. Not all companies target debt as a percentage of operating assets—they may target debt as a percentage of total market value, or according to an entirely different rule. And not all companies refrain from selling or buying back their common stock. Although these different financial policies don't affect free cash flow, they do affect the book values of debt or equity, net income, and the ratios calculated from these items. Even more important, they may affect the firm's cost of capital, due to the impact of taxes (interest obligations are deductible) or due to the effect of financial leverage on the risk premium that investors attach to the firm's securities.[3] If we use the valuation model to forecast the firm's funding requirements, then changes in assumptions about these financial policies also affect the amount of external funding the company needs to execute its operating plans. In summary, there are important reasons to model financial policies as accurately as possible. The following sections explain several different financial policies. The book's web site provides illustrative spreadsheets for each policy.

Alternative Dividend Policies

We considered the constant growth rate dividend policy in the Van Leer case in Chapters 6 and 7. In this section, we will consider two additional policies. The first is one in which the company pays out a fixed proportion of its net income, called a **fixed payout ratio policy**. The second is a policy in which the company pays out all funds that are not needed for reinvestment, called the **residual dividend policy**.

[3]For example, debt ratios are an important consideration when rating agencies assign ratings to corporate bonds. Also, finance theory states that increasing a firm's financial leverage will increase its common stock's beta coefficient.

Fixed Payout Ratio

This policy is simple to implement. If net income is positive, then dividends are a fixed percentage, say 20%, of net income. If net income is negative or zero, then dividends are zero. The result is that dividends will tend to grow with net income, but will fluctuate with the business cycle. For example, Exhibit 8-6 shows Van Leer's net income, and its actual and predicted dividends under the original assumption of a constant growth rate of 10% from 2003 through 2007. It also shows its effective payout ratio under this policy. Finally, it shows the dividends it would have paid if its payout ratio were a constant 29%. Keep in mind that changing dividends will change the amount of "internal equity" financing (i.e., it will affect retained earnings), and therefore it will have an effect on the magnitude of short-term investments or short-term debt that is needed to plug the balance sheet.

Notice that Van Leer's constant growth policy produces payout ratios that are fairly stable. However, the fixed payout policy for Van Leer's projections produces dividend growth rates that are fairly volatile, due to the changing operating inputs during the first years of the forecast.

Residual Dividend

In the constant growth dividend policy we discussed in Chapter 6, if projected assets were larger than projected liabilities, then we had not projected enough sources of funds to pay for the assets we needed. We assumed that this funding gap would be filled with short-term debt. If, on the other hand, projected liabilities were greater than the projected assets, that meant we had arranged for more funding than we really needed, so the excess cash was put into short-term investments. This is the **short-term debt/short-term investment** balancing method. Under this policy there will be either a short-term debt balance or a short-term investment balance, but not both, and dividends could be anything management chooses to pay.

Exhibit 8-6 Comparison of Dividends under Constant Dividend Growth and Fixed Dividend Payout Ratio (millions of dollars)

	Actual 2003	Projected 2004	Projected 2005	Projected 2006	Projected 2007
Net income	$54.0	$60.0	$67.1	$75.1	$76.8
Constant growth policy:					
Dividends	$16.0	$17.6	$19.4	$21.3	$23.4
Growth rate in dividends		10.0%	10.0%	10.0%	10.0%
Payout ratio		29.3%	28.9%	28.4%	30.5%
Fixed payout policy @ 29%:					
Projected dividends	$16.0	$17.4	$19.5	$21.8	$22.3
Growth rate in dividends		8.8%	12.1%	11.8%	2.3%
Payout ratio		29.0%	29.0%	29.0%	29.0%

Under the residual dividend policy, when projected assets are bigger than projected liabilities, then we will do almost the same thing as with the short-term debt/short term investment policy. We will make up any funding shortfall with short-term debt, but only after first reducing dividends to zero. This way there is less of a need for short-term debt because we have set the cash "drain" from dividend payments to zero. The big difference between the two policies is when projected liabilities exceed projected assets. In this case, rather than putting the excess cash in short-term investments, we will pay it out as a dividend.[4] This means the steps to identify the amount of a dividend to pay are just like the steps to identify the amount of short-term investments as discussed in Chapter 6:

1. Project sales, the components of operating profit, and the components of operating capital. This leaves us with a completed income statement up to taxes, and a completed balance sheet except for short-term debt and retained earnings. Go ahead and finish the income statement by calculating net interest expense and taxes.
2. Project the completed balance sheets assuming short-term investments, short-term debt, and dividends are all zero. We'll call these the *trial* balance sheets. Calculate trial total assets and trial total liabilities and equity under these assumptions. The balance sheets probably won't balance yet.
3. If trial total assets exceed trial total liabilities and equity, then set dividends to zero and short-term debt equal to this difference: Short-term debt = Trial assets – Trial liabilities and equity.
4. If trial total liabilities and equity exceed trial total assets, then set short-term debt to zero and set dividends to this difference: Dividends = Trial liabilities and equity – Trial total assets.

So under a residual divided policy, we are balancing the projected financial statements using a combination of dividends and short-term debt, instead of using short-term investments and short-term debt, as we did with both the constant growth rate and constant payout ratio policies. Thus, the underlying logic for balancing the financial statements is different under the residual dividend policy than it is under either the constant growth rate policy or constant payout ratio policy.

Notice how this differs from the balancing technique used in Chapter 6. In Chapter 6, if trial liabilities and equity exceeded trial assets, we increased assets by the difference by putting the extra cash in short-term investments. Under the residual dividend policy we instead decrease stockholder's equity by paying a dividend. The reason this decreases stockholder's equity is that the retained earnings balance is last year's retained earnings plus this year's net income, less any dividends paid. If we increase the dividends, we decrease the amount added to last year's retained earnings. By the way, don't be intimidated at the apparent labor involved in working through trial balances, then reworking the spreadsheet to determine final balances. Most spreadsheet software packages are set up to let the computer do all the recalculations. We will provide you with spreadsheets that take advantage of this capability for "iterative" problem solving.

[4]A firm's debt covenants might limit the amount of dividends it can pay. For example, the firm may be prohibited from paying a dividend that would drive cumulative retained earnings to zero. We'll assume the firm can pay any level of dividends it chooses.

Van Leer's 2003 financial statements and its 2004 projected financial statements under the short-term debt/short-term investment and the residual dividend policy are in Exhibit 8-7.

Notice that under the constant dividend growth rate policy, trial assets exceeded trial liabilities by $40.2 million, given a dividend payment of $17.6 million, so short-term debt had to be $40.2 million in order to fund the difference. Under the residual dividend policy, the first source of funding comes from reducing dividends, so trial liabilities are higher. By reducing dividends from $17.6 million to $0, Van Leer frees up enough cash so that the necessary short-term borrowing declines from $40.2 to $22.6 million. Notice that in this case, the constant dividend growth rate policy and the residual dividend policy result in the same level of total assets. This will happen whenever the short-term debt/short-term investments policy projects zero short-term investments. However, any other time the residual dividend policy will project a lower amount of total assets (and hence a lower amount of total liabilities and equity) because there will be no short-term investments.[5]

See the book's web site for an illustrative model.

[5]Short-term investments may be necessary if dividends are restricted. For example, if increasing the dividend beyond a certain level would result in negative retained earnings, such a situation might violate the firm's debt covenants.

Exhibit 8-7 Panel A: Van Leer Income Statement under Alternative Dividend Policies (millions of dollars)

	Actual 2003	Projected constant growth dividend policy[a] 2004	Projected residual dividend policy[b] 2004
Income Statement			
Net sales	$1,000.0	$1,110.0	$1,110.0
Cost of goods sold	640.0	693.8	693.8
Selling, general & administrative	215.0	249.8	249.8
Depreciation	45.0	56.6	56.6
Operating profit	$ 100.0	$ 109.9	$ 109.9
Interest income	0.0	0.8	0.8
Interest expense	10.0	11.2	11.2
Earnings before taxes	$ 90.0	$ 99.5	$ 99.5
Taxes	36.0	39.5	39.5
Net income	$ 54.0	$ 60.0	$ 60.0
Dividends	16.0	17.6	0.0
Additions to RE	$ 38.0	$ 42.4	$ 60.0

Notes:

[a]Balancing with short-term debt and short-term investments

[b]Balancing with residual dividends and short-term debt

Exhibit 8-7 Panel B: Van Leer Balance Sheet under Alternative Dividend Policies (millions of dollars)

	Actual 2003	Projected constant growth dividend policy[a] 2004	Projected residual dividend policy[b] 2004
Cash	$ 50.0	$ 33.3	$ 33.3
Short-term investments	25.0	0.0	0.0
Inventory	100.0	122.1	122.1
Accounts receivable	75.0	84.4	84.4
Total current assets	$250.0	$239.8	$239.8
Net PPE	300.0	377.4	377.4
Total assets	$550.0	$617.2	$617.2
Accounts payable	$ 75.0	$ 89.9	$ 89.9
Accrued expenses	10.0	11.1	11.1
Short-term debt	25.0	40.2	22.6
Total current liabilities	$110.0	$141.2	$123.6
Long-term debt	99.0	92.6	92.6
Total liabilities	209.0	233.8	216.2
Common stock	125.0	125.0	125.0
Retained earnings	216.0	258.4	276.0
Total common equity	$341.0	$383.4	$401.0
Total liabilities and equity	$550.0	$617.2	$617.2
Trial assets		$617.2	$617.2
Trial liabilities and equity		$577.0	$594.6

Notes:
[a]Balancing with short-term debt and short-term investments
[b]Balancing with residual dividends and short-term debt

Dividend Policies in Practice

Within bounds, management plans the amount of dividends it pays each year or each quarter. In principle, dividends can be more or less than the dividends paid the earlier year. They can be omitted or increased. They can even be more than the total net income for the year. We have described three methods for setting dividends: the constant growth policy, the fixed payout ratio policy, and the residual dividend policy. Notice that the fixed payout ratio and residual dividend policies can result in very volatile dividend growth rates from year to year.

Managers and board members ("insiders") of a company have better information about future earnings and cash flow than ordinary investors ("outsiders"). Therefore changes in dividends may be interpreted as a signal of future prospects—dividend increases are "good news," decreases are "bad news." In practice, management usually tries to avoid "negative surprises" by maintaining consistent increases in dividends, which appears to make stockholders happier than when dividends are volatile. Therefore, in our projections we usually have constant growth in dividends.[6]

Alternative Common Stock Policies

In all of the financial policies that we have discussed, we assumed that firms do not issue or repurchase common stock. In reality, companies frequently use common stock repurchases ("buybacks") as a complement to, or a substitute for, dividend payments. The reasons for repurchasing common stock rather than paying a dividend are

1. Common stock repurchases are usually seen as "special," and so investors don't assume that they will happen on a regular basis or that the size of the repurchase will be consistent over time. This means that distributions to stockholders in the form of share buybacks do not necessarily create an expectation that they will continue. This gives the company more flexibility in distributing cash than if it had to stick to a fixed or constant growth dividend policy. In effect, a company can couple a fixed or constant growth dividend policy with occasional stock repurchases to achieve almost the same results as the residual dividend policy.
2. Until 2003, investors had to pay taxes on dividends at the ordinary income rate. This meant that investors who sold their shares in a repurchase may have been able to pay taxes on their profits at the lower capital gains rate, provided the shares were held long enough. So historically, distributing cash via a repurchase saved investors taxes vis-à-vis a dividend. As of 2003, Congress has cut the top rate on dividends and capital gains to 15%. Since dividends and capital gains will be taxed at the same rate, the current tax provisions will eliminate the preference for stock repurchases over dividend payments. Note, though, that this provision is set to expire in 2008 if Congress doesn't extend it before then.
3. If top managers and directors feel that the market price of their firm's stock is below its intrinsic, or fundamental value, it makes sense for them to use corporate cash to buy back some of their outstanding stock. Many firms give this as the reason for buybacks. On average, announcements of stock buybacks are associated with stock price increases for the announcing company.

Mature firms rarely issue common stock. One reason stock issues are infrequent is that the transaction costs for issuing new common stock are high relative to the costs of borrowing—investment banking fees are substantially higher for stock than for debt financing, and the company essentially pays these fees out of the proceeds of the stock issue. For small stock issues, these costs can run as high as 18% of the amount of stock issued! To the extent that firms' earnings permit them to accumulate equity financing gradually via their dividend policy (i.e., low or no dividends), they tend to prefer this "internal" source of equity capital relatively to "external" equity financing (issuing new shares) because they can avoid the transaction costs of new issues.

[6]We will occasionally let dividends grow at the same rate as sales. Keep in mind that sales growth must eventually level off to a constant rate, so dividend growth is ultimately constrained.

Nevertheless, there are situations when companies decide to issue stock. Reasons for issuing common stock rather than debt are

1. The company already has more debt than it can safely bear and must retire some of the debt with the proceeds from the stock sale to avoid the financial problems associated with not being able to make interest payments.
2. The company's cash needs are so great that if it used debt to fund them, its level of debt would be too high, and so stock is the only alternative.
3. The company's managers feel that the stock price is relatively high, or even overpriced, and so want to take advantage of this high price by selling stock. Of course, investors often suspect this is management's motive for selling stock, even if it isn't the true reason, and will bid down the stock price accordingly. In fact, many studies document price declines when companies announce that they are going to issue more stock.

Note that issuing or repurchasing common stock changes the number of shares outstanding. This affects all of the per-share measures, such as dividends per share and earnings per share. The challenge in making projections where the amount of common stock changes is estimating the price at which stock is issued or repurchased. Although this information is not necessary for projecting the income statement or balance sheet, it is necessary for determining the number of shares outstanding and hence important figures like price per share or earnings per share.

As we show later with examples, changing the assumptions about a firm's financing policies will not necessarily change the current estimate of the firm's value or of the current per share value of its stock, unless the changes affect the cost of capital. For example, we show that future stock issues or repurchases will not affect the current estimate of intrinsic share value as long as the cost of capital doesn't change and the stock is sold or repurchased at its intrinsic value.

Stock Repurchase

As far as our financial statement projections are concerned, using a repurchase is a lot like paying a dividend. Both reduce the potential amount of common equity: a dividend payment reduces stockholders' equity by reducing retained earnings, relative to what it would be without the dividend. A stock repurchase reduces stockholders' equity by reducing the subaccounts of shareholders' equity called **common stock at par value and paid in capital**, or by increasing **treasury stock**.[7] Collectively, these accounts keep track of the amount of money contributed by investors through their stock purchases and the amount of money distributed to investors through stock repurchases.

The key point in evaluating how repurchases affect financial projections is that the repurchase of stock in and of itself does not create or destroy any value, rather it simply distributes some of the firm's value to its shareholders as cash, so that they may invest it elsewhere. Although the number of shares outstanding is reduced

[7]The terminology may vary somewhat from one company to another. When companies repurchase stock, they may retire it (as if it never existed), or they may hold it. If the stock is retired, the sum of the reductions in the common stock at par and capital surplus accounts will equal the amount paid out to selling shareholders. If the company holds the stock, it will be reported in an account called treasury stock, which is an offset (a contra-account) to the other equity subaccounts in calculation of total shareholders' equity.

through a repurchase transaction, the cash distribution represents a corresponding reduction in the value of the firm's equity.[8] So the pre-repurchase value of the firm's stock should equal the cash distributed to shareholders via the repurchase plus the post-repurchase value of the remaining stock. Let N_{pre} be the number of shares outstanding before the repurchase and let N_{post} be the number of shares outstanding after the repurchase. Let P_{pre} be the market price of the equity before the repurchase, and P_{post} be the market price of the equity after (calculated as in Chapter 4 as the value of operations less the value of debt) and let R be the total amount of money the company wants to distribute in the repurchase. Then the number of shares repurchased is $N_{pre} - N_{post}$, and setting the pre-repurchase value of the equity equal to the sum of the cash distributed to shareholders via the repurchase and the post-repurchase value of the remaining stock gives

$$N_{post}P_{post} + P_{post}(N_{pre} - N_{post}) = P_{pre}N_{pre}. \quad \textbf{(8-7)}$$

Most repurchases by firms follow a public announcement of a policy of buying back their own stock, which will be carried out simply by purchasing the shares through brokers at market prices. The purchases will be spread out over time to avoid driving up the market price, so investors will generally not be aware that the firm is buying shares on any particular day. Under these circumstances it seems reasonable to assume that the price per share paid in the repurchase will be a "fair" price, in the sense that it is neither higher nor lower than the pre-repurchase value per share, P_{pre}. You can see why this should be by imagining what would happen if the price were expected to change once the repurchase was completed. Suppose investors thought the post-repurchase price of the stock would be higher than the current price. Then they would refuse to sell at the current price (since they could wait and get a higher price), and the repurchase could not go forward until the current price rose to the price expected after the repurchase. On the other hand, if investors thought the post-repurchase price would be lower than the current price, they would sell their shares before the repurchase went through, driving down the price before the repurchase to the level expected after the repurchase. The upshot is that rational behavior by investors should ensure that the expected pre- and post-repurchase date stock prices are the same. So setting P_{post} equal to P_{pre} in the above equation, and solving for N_{post}, gives

$$N_{post}P_{pre} = P_{pre}N_{pre} - R \quad \textbf{(8-8)}$$

$$N_{post} = N_{pre} - \frac{R}{P_{pre}}. \quad \textbf{(8-9)}$$

This is the number of shares that should be outstanding after the repurchase and is the number of shares to use in calculating all of the per-share values after the repurchase.

To use Equation 8-9, you must first calculate the price per share that would have been observed prior to the repurchase. This is not particularly cumbersome if you only want to analyze a stock repurchase in a single year, but it requires too much

[8]Recall in our valuation calculations (Chapter 7) that, in determining the value of the firm's equity, the value of short-term investments is added to the value of operations before deducting nonequity claims. In a repurchase, the cash for repurchasing stock would come from either liquidation of these short-term investments or from new borrowing. The combination would reduce the calculated value of equity by precisely the amount of the repurchase.

"user intervention" when making repurchases in more than one year. Fortunately, there is a simplification that lends itself to multiyear projections. First, recall that the value of operations is the present value of the projected free cash flows and horizon value, discounted at the weighted average cost of capital. Second, the estimated value of equity is equal to the value of operations plus short-term investments minus debt. Notice that if the repurchase had not been made, the cash used for the repurchase would have been added to short-term investments. Therefore, the estimated value of equity before the repurchase, VE_{pre}, is equal to the value of equity after the repurchase, VE_{post}, plus the cash that will be used to repurchase stock, R:

$$VE_{pre} = VE_{post} + R. \tag{8-10}$$

The stock price before the repurchase is equal to the value of equity before the repurchase divided by the number of shares before the repurchase:

$$P_{pre} = \frac{VE_{pre}}{N_{pre}}. \tag{8-11}$$

Substituting 8-11 and 8-10 into 8-9 gives a simple expression for the number of shares of outstanding after the repurchase:

$$N_{post} = N_{pre}\left(\frac{VE_{post}}{VE_{post} + R}\right). \tag{8-12}$$

See the book's web site for a spreadsheet model illustrating stock repurchases.

Finally, notice that stock repurchases as an alternative to dividends for distributing cash to shareholders are, aside from the personal tax implications for shareholders, **wealth neutral**. This means that the choice of how to distribute cash to shareholders—either as a dividend or a share repurchase—will not influence the current intrinsic value. In other words, in valuing a firm's common stock today, we need not concern ourselves with which of the two methods, future stock repurchases or future higher cash dividends, the firm will choose to distribute cash.

Issuing New Common Equity

Issuing new equity is just the reverse of repurchasing stock. If the company issues new equity instead of debt, then the sum of the common stock (at par value) plus paid-in-capital accounts increases by the amount of funds raised. A similar argument to that used above for the case of stock repurchases shows that the per-share stock price immediately before the equity issue should be the same as the per-share price immediately after the equity issue. Otherwise the transaction would not be acceptable to investors before and after the transaction. The immediate use of the cash from the new shares issued will be a combination of an increase in marketable securities and/or a decrease in outstanding debt. The number of shares outstanding increases through share sales, and the cash proceeds represent a corresponding increase in the value of the firm's equity because it is new capital that has been contributed. So the post-repurchase value of the firm's stock should equal the sum of the pre-repurchase value of the stock and the cash received from new shareholders via the sale:

$$N_{post}P_{post} = P_{pre}N_{pre} + P_{post}(N_{post} - N_{pre}). \tag{8-13}$$

Let $N_{post} - N_{pre}$ be the number of shares issued. This means that if R is the amount of money the company raises with its equity offering, then $R = P_{post}(N_{post} - N_{pre})$. Substituting R into the above equation, setting P_{post} equal to P_{pre}, and solving for N_{post}, gives

$$N_{post}P_{post} = P_{pre}N_{pre} + R \tag{8-14}$$

$$N_{post} = N_{pre} + \frac{R}{P_{pre}}. \tag{8-15}$$

For projections where a company might issue equity in more than one year, Equation 8-16 provides an easier way to calculate the number of shares after the stock issuance:

$$N_{post} = N_{pre} = \left(\frac{VE_{post}}{VE_{post} - R}\right). \tag{8-16}$$

See the book's web site for a spreadsheet model illustrating stock issuances.

At this point we should note that many market observers will tell you that issuing new stock causes a company's stock price to drop. This conclusion is supported by many studies showing that when firms *announce* that they are going to sell stock, the announcement is accompanied immediately by a fall in the price of the company's stock. As we explained earlier, this announcement-related price drop may occur because the market realizes that the motives described above for issuing new stock don't bode well for the stock. The price will drop if investors believe the announcement of a new issue reveals that managers think the stock is currently overpriced or if the announcement reveals that managers believe the company can't handle the level of debt that it has without raising more cash through a stock offering. This price drop is a big negative incentive (in addition to the transaction costs mentioned earlier) to issuing new stock!

Therefore, in a stock repurchase or a stock issuance, there are really three separate events. First, there are the circumstances leading up to the decision to repurchase or issue stock, such as an improvement in free cash flow, a great new investment opportunity, or a change in capital structure. Such situations can certainly affect the stock price. Second, there is the announcement of the upcoming repurchase or issuance. This announcement may send a signal to the market, and this too can affect the stock price. Third, there is the actual transaction, either a repurchase or an issuance, and this affects neither the stock price nor the wealth of the equity investors.

Projecting Debt as a Proportion of Market Value

Finance theory tells us that companies ought to decide on the level of debt based on the market values of the debt and equity rather than on the book value of its operating assets. In operation, this is a pretty straightforward principle: If your company is publicly traded, then take the number of shares, multiply it by the share price, and that gives you the market value of equity. If your market value of equity is \$100 million and your target debt/(debt + equity) ratio is 30%, then solving for D gives you

$$\begin{aligned} 0.30 &= D/(D + \$100) \\ \$30 &= 0.70\ D \\ \$42.9 &= D. \end{aligned}$$

You would want to have $42.9 million in debt. The practice of using market values in your target debt level becomes dicier if the company isn't publicly traded because you have to use a valuation model such as the one in this book to determine the value of equity. Using market-value debt ratios to project debt balances makes the process of projecting financial statements more difficult because determining the amount of debt in a given projection year requires determining the projected value of the firm in that year.

The steps for using market value weights for debt are

1. Decide on the target percentage ratio for debt to the value of operations. This is the same as determining the target w_D when estimating the weighted average cost of capital in Chapter 2.
2. Project all of the items required for calculating operating profit, operating capital, and operating taxes for each year. You don't need to make your balance sheets balance yet, but this is enough information to calculate free cash flow and the value of operations. Note that we are assuming that you can calculate taxes on operating income without knowing the debt level and interest payments. This is a reasonable assumption if you are inside the company and have access to both the financial statements prepared for tax purposes and those prepared under GAAP accounting for financial reporting purposes.
3. Project NOPAT, net investment in operating capital, free cash flow, and the horizon value. From this information, calculate a value of operations for each year as the present value of all of the projected future free cash flows from that year forward.
4. Set the long-term debt level in each year to be the specified percentage of the value of operations, and then use whatever technique you choose to make the financial statements balance—the short-term debt/short-term investments method, the residual dividend method, or some other combination of financing methods discussed above.

This will ensure a constant ratio of long-term debt to market value. If the projected balance of short-term debt builds up, then the company should increase its projected target w_D. See the book's web site for a spreadsheet illustrating this type of model.

Projecting Interest Expense Based on the Average Debt during the Year

Recall from previous chapters, and so far throughout this chapter, that we have based interest expense on the debt at the beginning of the year, which was the previous year's end-of-year debt. If we had instead based interest expense on the current year's debt level, then we would have had the following interdependencies in a single year:

net income depends on interest expense;
interest expense depends on short-term debt;
short-term debt depends on the amount of required financing;
the amount of required financing depends on retained earnings;
the addition to retained earnings depends on net income;
net income depends on interest expense;
. . . . and we repeat the circular process indefinitely.

Basically, the point is that interest expense depends on other items that ultimately depend on interest expense.[9]

This type of interdependence between items on the financial statements is called "circularity." Although there is nothing wrong in principle with having a circular relationship in our model of a firm's financial statements, circularity does introduce some complications in programming a spreadsheet. Even more importantly, it makes it more difficult to explain the process and logic of projecting statements. Of course, our goal is to produce an accurate model of the financial statements, and interest expense and income projections will be more accurate if they are based on the average level of debt and short-term investments during the year, rather than the end-of-prior period values. In a company with growing debt levels, using end-of-prior year debt when calculating interest expense will understate annual interest expense.

Algebraic Solution to Circularity

The circularity above means that there is really a pair of **simultaneous equations** that describe interest expense and short-term debt. You can see this in even the simplest example. Suppose a company pays no dividends, has no short-term investments, and interest expense is based on the average value of debt during the year. Then

$$NI = [EBIT - I(D_t + D_{t-1})/2](1 - T). \quad \textbf{(8-17)}$$

Here NI is net income, I is the interest rate on the debt, T is the tax rate, D_t is this year's debt (at year-end), and D_{t-1} is last year's debt (also at year-end). But D_t is used to make the balance sheet balance, so

$$D_t = TA - (\text{Specified liabilities} + RE_{t-1} + NI).$$

Here TA is total assets, specified liabilities are all of the liabilities except for debt, and RE_{t-1} is last year's retained earnings, so that this year's retained earnings are RE_{t-1} + NI. Notice that D_t depends on NI, but NI depends on D_t, which is circular. We can actually solve this little system of two equations in two unknowns for D_t by substituting the equation for NI into the equation for D_t, collecting the D_t terms together and solving for D_t.

$$D_t = TA - \text{Specified liabilities} - RE_{t-1} - [EBIT - I(D_t + D_{t-1})/2](1 - T) \quad \textbf{(8-18)}$$

$$D_t - ID_t(1 - T)/2 = TA - \text{Specified liabilities} - RE_{t-1} - [EBIT - ID_{t-1}/2](1 - T) \quad \textbf{(8-19)}$$

Or,

$$D_t = \{TA - \text{Specified liabilities} - RE_{t-1} - [EBIT - ID_{t-1}/2](1 - T)\}/[1 - I(1 - T)/2]. \quad \textbf{(8-20)}$$

Spreadsheet Solution to Circularity

Even though we can, in principle, algebraically solve for D_t, that doesn't mean we should! Instead, we can let Excel solve the equations. Before entering the circular formulas, we need to ensure that Excel is set for "Iterations." To do this, select Tools from the Excel menu, and then select Options. Choose the Calculation tab and make sure the box for Iteration is checked. Then when we enter the circular formulas,

[9]The same holds true for interest income if we base interest income on the current level of short-term investments.

Exhibit 8-8 Interest Expense and Income Calculation—Beginning-of-Year versus Average Values of Debt and Short-Term Investments (millions of dollars)

	Actual 2003	Projected 2004	Projected 2005	Projected 2006	Projected 2007	Projected 2008	Projected 2009
Based on beginning-of-year values							
Interest income	$ 0.0	$ 0.8	$ 0.0	$ 0.0	$ 0.9	$ 1.9	$ 2.5
Interest expense	$10.0	$11.2	$11.9	$ 8.7	$ 9.1	$ 9.5	$10.1
Net income	$54.0	$60.0	$ 67.1	$75.1	$76.8	$73.3	$78.0

	Actual 2003	Projected 2004	Projected 2005	Projected 2006	Projected 2007	Projected 2008	Projected 2009
Based on average values							
Interest income	$ 0.0	$ 0.4	$ 0.0	$ 0.5	$ 1.4	$ 2.2	$ 2.8
Interest expense	$10.0	$11.6	$10.3	$ 8.9	$ 9.3	$ 9.8	$10.4
Net income	$54.0	$59.5	$68.1	$75.2	$77.0	$73.3	$78.0

Excel will iterate until each change in values is too small to be noticed. In other words, it will find the same solution as the algebraic equation, but with a lot less effort on our part. Therefore, our solution to the "problem" of circularity is to allow it to remain and let Excel find the solution.

An Illustration Using Van Leer

As discussed above, basing interest expense on the average level of debt rather than the beginning of period level tends to be more accurate. Using the average level of debt avoids underestimating interest expense when debt is growing and beginning of period values are used, and it avoids overestimating interest expense when debt is declining. Exhibit 8-8 shows Van Leer's projected interest expense, net income, and debt levels under the two methods for calculating interest.

The first section of Exhibit 8-8 shows the projections that we made in Chapter 7 when interest income and expense were based on beginning of year values. The second section of Exhibit 8-8 shows how the projections would look if interest expense and income were instead based on average values and Excel iterates to find the solution.

Although all of this appears to be complicated, it isn't when you set up the spreadsheet. Just make interest expense depend on the average debt level, and the spreadsheet will iterate to find the solution!

Summary

This chapter showed you how to modify your projections to incorporate several refinements and several different financial policies. We discussed linear and nonlinear projections and how to deal with lumpy asset purchases. We extended the types of dividend policies to include a constant payout policy and a residual dividend policy. We extended the number of financing policies to include stock repurchases, stock issuance, and debt as a percentage of the value of operations.

Some financial policy choices, such as whether to pay cash dividends or buy back stock, are wealth neutral because they have no direct effect on value (ignoring possible signaling effects). On the other hand, policies that result in significant changes in financial leverage may have an impact on value via their effect on the cost of capital. Therefore, we usually don't worry about the details of dividend policy, stock issuance, or stock repurchases, unless they influence the cost of capital.

Finally, we discussed the technical details associated with circular calculations and showed how to base interest income and expense on average balance sheet values rather than beginning of period balance sheet values. These refinements make the free cash flow framework quite versatile. Analysts can tailor the model to fit different industries, different life cycle circumstances, and different economic environments. Insiders with financial responsibilities can use the framework in a financial planning context to project the additional financing requirements that result from anticipated operating results and the firm's financial policies. Sensitivity tests are easily performed to gauge the impact of changing financial policies.

Spreadsheet Problems

8-1 Incorporating Nonproportional Projections

This problem is based on the Excel spreadsheet ***Prob 08-01.xls***. The spreadsheet contains 5 years of historical data for Van Leer, and is set up to balance using debt and short-term investments as the plug figures. Rather than using a constant proportion of sales, you are to create new projections for the line items based on the following functions.

Line item	Function
Income Statement	
Net sales	Same percentage growth rate as in Chapter 7
Cost of goods sold	a + b(Sales)
Selling, general & administrative	a + b(Sales)
Depreciation	Same percentage of Net PPE as in Chapter 7
Interest income	Same percentage of short-term investments as in Chapter 7
Interest expense	Same percentage of debt as in Chapter 7
Taxes	Same percentage of EBT as in Chapter 7
Dividends	Same growth rate as in Chapter 7
Balance Sheet	
Cash	a + b ln(Sales)
Short-term investments	plug
Inventory	a + b ln(Sales)

Accounts receivable	a + b ln(Sales)
Net PP&E	a + b ln(Sales)
Accounts payable	a + b ln(Sales)
Accrued expenses	a + b ln(Sales)
Short-term debt	plug
Long-term debt	Same percentage of operating assets as in Chapter 7
Common stock	Constant, as in Chapter 7

Note that you will need to estimate two parameters for each line item—an a coefficient and a b coefficient. Although the table above shows the same letters a and b in each line item, you really will calculate a different a and a different b coefficient for each line item, based on the historical data for that line item. In the steps below, we'll show you how to estimate the parameters and incorporate them in your forecast.

a. First, you will need a column to hold your two parameters. Insert two columns before the first year's worth of historical data in the problem's spreadsheet.
b. Next, notice that some of the functions are functions of the log of sales. To use this in your estimation, you'll need to create a row that has ln(Sales) in it. The simplest, although probably not the neatest looking, solution is to insert a row above the years near the top of the spreadsheet. Label this row "ln (Sales)" and use the formula =log() (where you put the cell reference for sales for that year inside the parentheses!) to calculate ln(Sales) for each year.
c. We are going to use the Excel function *=intercept()* to calculate the a coefficients and the Excel function *=slope()* to calculate the b coefficients. In this example, we'll do it for cost of goods sold, which is supposed to be of the form COGS = a + b(Sales). In the first (leftmost) of your two new columns, in the COGS row, use the function wizard to enter the intercept function. You'll find it in the statistical section. When the dialog box comes up, the first fill-in box will ask you for the "known y's." Click there, and highlight the 5 years' worth of COGS for the y-values. The second fill-in box asks for the "known x's," and you should highlight the 5 years' worth of sales figures for this. Click "OK," and your cell will show the intercept. Do the same thing in the next column, except select the slope formula instead of the intercept formula from the function wizard, highlighting the same x and y values. This will calculate the b coefficient.
d. Once the sales figures have been projected (recall, we are assuming the same sales growth rates as in Chapter 7), COGS is easy to calculate; it is simply a + b(Sales) where a and b are the values you just calculated in step (c), and sales is the projected sales for the year.
e. The balance sheet uses the functional form: Cash = a + b ln(Sales). You will calculate the a and b coefficients just as you did in step (c), except, of course, you will use the 5 years' worth of cash balances for the y-variables, and you

will use the values of ln(Sales) you calculated in step (b) as the x-variables, instead of just sales.

f. The projections on the balance sheet using the a + b ln(Sales) formula are just the same as you did in part (d), except you will multiply b by the row that has ln(Sales) in it instead of just sales.

PART 4

Valuing Actual Companies with the Corporate Valuation Spreadsheet

Chapter 9

The Starting Point for Corporate Valuation: Historical Financial Statements

Introduction

So far you have learned all the basic concepts of valuation, including: (1) forecasting financial statements, (2) calculating free cash flows, (3) estimating the weighted average cost of capital, (4) estimating the value of operations (even when the free cash flows initially grow at a nonconstant rate), and (5) estimating the stock's price per share. Looking at this list, you can see that you have mastered quite a few concepts and have developed a formidable arsenal of financial skills and techniques! Now we're going to show you how to apply those skills to an actual company using our spreadsheet model. We'll illustrate the approach by taking you on a step-by-step valuation of Home Depot.

An Overview of the Corporate Valuation Spreadsheet

Before we begin the analysis, here is a brief overview of the spreadsheet and the process. The overview will be easier to understand if you open the file ***Home Depot.xls*** and follow along as we describe it. The spreadsheet is similar in many respects to the one we developed for Van Leer. For example, it has a several worksheets, which you can select using the Tab bar at the bottom of Excel window; this is shown Exhibit 9-1.

Starting from left to right, these tabs are *Proj & Val* (short for Projections and Valuation), *Inputs*, *WACC*, *Hist Analys* (short for Historical Analysis), *Condensed*, *Comprehensive*, and *Actual*. We will explain each of these worksheets in more detail later in this and subsequent chapters, but here's a quick overview of the valuation process.

1. Put actual historical financial statements into the *Actual* worksheet (preferably from an electronic source so that all you have to do is cut and paste).
2. Enter formulas in the *Comprehensive* sheet so that every item in the *Actual* sheet is linked to an item in the *Comprehensive* sheet.

Exhibit 9-1 Worksheet Tabs in the Valuation File

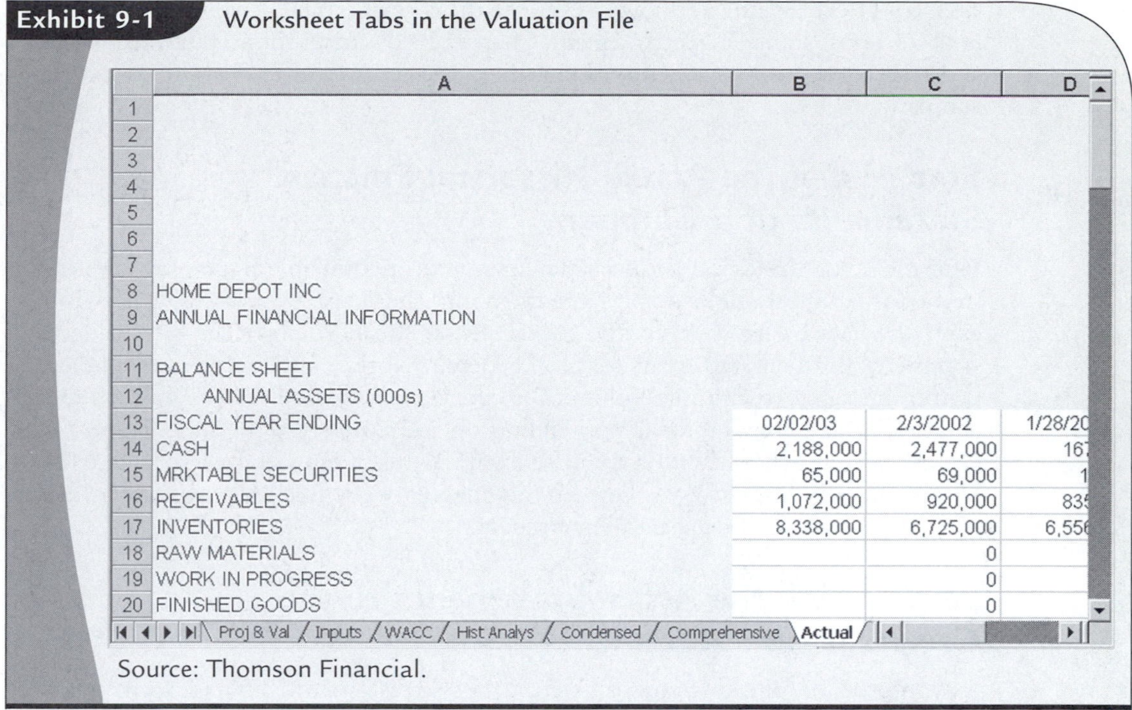

	A	B	C	D
1				
2				
3				
4				
5				
6				
7				
8	HOME DEPOT INC			
9	ANNUAL FINANCIAL INFORMATION			
10				
11	BALANCE SHEET			
12	ANNUAL ASSETS (000s)			
13	FISCAL YEAR ENDING	02/02/03	2/3/2002	1/28/20
14	CASH	2,188,000	2,477,000	167
15	MRKTABLE SECURITIES	65,000	69,000	1
16	RECEIVABLES	1,072,000	920,000	835
17	INVENTORIES	8,338,000	6,725,000	6,556
18	RAW MATERIALS		0	
19	WORK IN PROGRESS		0	
20	FINISHED GOODS		0	

Proj & Val / Inputs / WACC / Hist Analys / Condensed / Comprehensive / **Actual** /

Source: Thomson Financial.

3. Let the valuation model in the *Condensed* worksheet condense the financial statements into the simplest statements that are still realistic enough to accurately value a company. (This does all the really heavy lifting for you with respect to accounting manipulations!)
4. Analyze the current and historical position of the company using the *Hist Analys* worksheet. You should find that the graphical interface in this worksheet really makes it easy to see what has been happening to a company.
5. Estimate the weighted average cost of capital in the *WACC* worksheet, using its structured approach.
6. Choose inputs (in the cleverly named *Inputs* worksheet) for projecting the financial statements. Again, the graphical interface makes it easy to *see* whether your projected inputs are reasonable.
7. Let the *Proj & Val* worksheet project the financial statements, calculate free cash flows, and then estimate the value of the company. All you have to do is check the output, and then go back to steps 5 and 6 if you want to perform sensitivity analysis (which we always recommend).

The following sections explain each of these steps in a little more detail. Then the remainder of the chapter focuses upon steps 1 and 2 (i.e., finding financial statements on the Internet, pasting them into the *Actual* sheet, and then linking these actual financial statements to the *Comprehensive* sheet). Chapter 10 provides a detailed discussion of steps 3 and 4, with an emphasis on how to analyze a company's current and historical position from the perspective of corporate valuation.

Chapter 11 explains step 5, how to estimate the cost of capital. Chapter 12 explains how to choose inputs in step 6. Finally, Chapter 13 discusses some additional issues and techniques associated with valuing the projected free cash flows of an actual company.

Step 1: Get the Actual Historical Financial Statements of a Company

Find the actual historical financial statements for a company. If they are in electronic form, you should cut and paste them into the *Actual* worksheet; otherwise, enter the data by hand. If you go to the *Actual* sheet, you will see the financial statements for the last 10 years for Home Depot. Notice that the most recent data is in column B. For example, column B in the *Actual* sheet of ***Home Depot.xls*** has data for Home Depot's fiscal year ending on 2/2/2003. We used the Thomson ONE-Business School Edition database from Thomson Financial as the source for Home Depot's financial data. Later in this chapter, we will describe this and other Internet sources for financial statement data.

Step 2: Link the *Actual* Statements to the *Comprehensive* Statements

As you probably already know, different data sources provide different formats for the financial statements of a company. Rather than reinvent the wheel for each company, we want to put the actual financial statements into a standardized format based specifically on the data required for valuing a company with the FCF approach. There are two stages to standardizing the data: (1) "map" the *Actual* data to the *Comprehensive* worksheet, and (2) let the spreadsheet itself condense the *Comprehensive* statements into the simplest statements that are still realistic enough to accurately value a company. Notice that we didn't need to do this with Van Leer's simple financial statements, but we definitely need to standardize data from actual companies.

We'll explain mapping in more detail later in this chapter, but the basic idea is to create a link from each item in the financial statements of the *Actual* worksheet to an item in the *Comprehensive* worksheet. Click on the *Comprehensive* tab of ***Home Depot.xls***, and you can see that the *Comprehensive* sheet is in fact very comprehensive, with entries for virtually all of the items that you may encounter on any actual financial statement. These entries are shown in Exhibit 9-2. The good news is that we won't make projections or perform valuation analyses with such complicated financial statements. Then why include them, you might be asking? Because flexibility in GAAP accounting rules and terminology allows different companies to name similar items in slightly different ways. For example, we know that one of the items needed for calculating free cash flow is the amount of operating current assets. For Van Leer, this includes cash, inventory, and accounts receivable. However, real companies often have many other short-term assets that are required by the firms' operations, such as tax refund receivable, progress payments, prepaid expenses, and

Exhibit 9-2 The Comprehensive Financial Statements

Part 1—Income Statement

Total net revenues
Cost of goods sold expense
Cost of services or operations expense
Depreciation expense (for tangible assets, if reported separately)
Amortization expense (for goodwill and intangible, if reported separately)
Depreciation and amortization expense (if reported combined)
Research & development expense
Sales & marketing expenses (if not included in SGA)
General & administrative expenses (if not included in SGA)
Selling, general & administrative expense (if reported as a single item)
Minority interest expense (if shown as pre-tax operating expense)
Merger and restructuring costs
Asset impairment losses or write-downs
Extraordinary charges or expenses (if shown on pre-tax basis)
Extraordinary credit or income (if shown on pre-tax basis)
Other operating expenses (income)
Interest expense (income)
Interest capitalized
Interest income
Reserve expense (income) (increase in reserves is expense, decrease is income)
Investment income (expense) (if shown on pre-tax basis)
Gain (loss) on sale of assets or discontinued operation (if shown on pre-tax basis)
Remitted income (expense) or equity earnings (losses) in affiliates
Unremitted income (expense) or equity earnings (losses) in affiliates
Minority interest expense (if shown as pre-tax nonoperating expense)
Losses on equity investees and other (if shown on pre-tax basis)
Other nonoperating income (expense) (if shown on pre-tax basis)
Special nonrecurring items income (expense) (if shown on pre-tax basis)
Provision for income tax expense (rebate)
Minority interest expense (if shown on after-tax basis)
Equity in earnings (if shown on after-tax basis)
Extraordinary items (if shown on after-tax basis)
Discontinued operations (if shown on after-tax basis)
Extraordinary items and discontinued operations (if shown on after-tax basis)
Investment gains (losses) (if shown on after-tax basis)
All other income (losses) (if shown on after-tax basis)
Cumulative effect of accounting changes
Net income

other operating current assets.[1] We included each of these by name in the comprehensive balance sheet so that if your actual statements have any of these items, it will be easy for you to link them to the *Comprehensive* statements.

In our experience, the *Comprehensive* worksheet has just about all the entries needed to capture variations in most companies' financial statements. Although it might seem unlikely to you right now, starting with these complicated financial statements will actually make your task easier if you intend to apply the model to

[1]The Disclosure and Thomson Financial formats have already been standardized; for example, they have already collapsed the items mentioned into the line item for other current assets. If you use another source for the historical data, you may see these items listed separately.

Exhibit 9-2 The Comprehensive Financial Statements (continued)

Part 2a—Balance Sheets (Assets)

Cash and equivalents
Marketable securities
Notes receivable
Short-term investments or investment securities
Accounts receivable
Tax refund receivable
Progress payments
Prepaid expenses
Current deferred tax asset
Inventories
Other nonoperating current assets
Other operating current assets
Total current assets

Long-term receivables
Investments in unconsolidated subsidiaries
Other investments
Net property, plant, & equipment (PPE)
Goodwill (if shown separately)
Intangibles (if shown separately)
Cost in excess of fair value of net assets acquired (also called goodwill)
Goodwill and intangibles (if shown combined)
Deferred tax asset (long-term)
Long-term notes receivable
Other operating long-term assets
Deferred charges
Deposits
Investments & advances to subsidiaries
Other nonoperating long-term assets
Total assets

Exhibit 9-2 The Comprehensive Financial Statements (continued)

Part 2b—Balance Sheets (Current Liabililties)

Notes payable
Current portion of long-term debt
Current portion of capitalized leases
All other short-term debt
Accounts payable
Short-term unearned revenue
Interest payable (or accrued interest)
Dividends payable
Short-term deferred taxes
Taxes payable or accrued taxes
Accrued wages or salary
Other accrued expenses or accruals
Other nonoperating current liabilities
Other operating current liabilities
Total current liabilities

many different companies with data from many sources, because just about any accounting entry you encounter will already be included in the *Comprehensive* sheet. This means you won't have to spend a lot of time figuring out how to accommodate slight variations in accounting formats.

Our task is to map the items from the *Actual* sheet into the appropriate items of the *Comprehensive* sheet. For example, if we click on cell B5 in the *Comprehensive* sheet, which is for total net revenues, we will see a formula, =Actual!B63. This formula sets the value for total net revenues in the *Comprehensive* sheet equal to Home Depot's sales, shown in cell B63 of the *Actual* sheet. We'll give detailed instructions for mapping the *Actual* historical financial statements into the *Comprehensive* financial statements later in this chapter, but the basic idea is to link each item in the *Actual* sheet to its corresponding entry in the *Comprehensive* sheet. (It's okay if many of the *Comprehensive* items are left at their default values of zero, as long as each item in the *Actual* sheet is linked to the *Comprehensive* sheet.) Although this may seem like an unnecessary step, it sets the stage for letting the valuation model condense the financial statements into a format that facilitates projections and valuation analysis.

Here is the really good news: if you use the historical financial statements provided in spreadsheet form by Thomson Financial (you have access to this service with the purchase of this book—see the book's web site for details), you can simply cut and paste the data directly into the *Actual* sheet—you don't need to map anything! One of the spreadsheet valuation models that comes with this book already has mapping for the Thomson data, as we describe later in this chapter. In fact, the Home Depot data you see in the *Actual* sheet was pasted from the Thomson Financial web site.

Exhibit 9-2 The Comprehensive Financial Statements (continued)

Part 2c—Balance Sheets (Liabililties and Equity)

Noncurrent portion of long-term debt
Mortgages
Noncurrent portion of capitalized leases
Convertible debt
Any other long-term debt
Provision for risks and charges
Reserve accounts
Deferred tax liability in untaxed reserves
Deferred income taxes (long-term)
Deferred income
Long-term unearned revenue
Restructuring obligations
Commitments and contingencies
Other long-term liabilities
Retirement, pension, and health insurance-related liabilities
Minority interest
Nonequity reserves
Preferred stock
Common stock (at par)
Common stock capital surplus or paid-in-capital
Revaluation of reserves
Other appropriate reserves
Unappropriated (free) reserves
Retained earnings
Equity in untaxed reserves
ESOP guarantees
Treasury stock
Common stock warrants and stock options
Other equity
Unrealized gain (loss) on marketable securities
Accumulated other comprehensive income or cumulative other adjustments
Unrealized gain (loss) on foreign exchange
Cumulative foreign currency translations
Total shareholder equity
Total liabilities and equity

Step 3: Condensing the Comprehensive Statements

The *Comprehensive* sheet has much more detail than needed to perform a valuation. For example, there are five different categories for long-term debt and four categories for short-term debt. Instead of trying to project all of these separate items, we have combined them in ways that simplify the job of making projections but are economically meaningful. These simplified financial statements are on the *Condensed* tab.[2] For example, suppose your source for historical financials includes prepaid expenses, which, as we indicated in the previous section, is really an operating current asset. The mapping from the *Comprehensive* to the *Condensed* format will automatically combine this item with other operating current assets, so only the total will be displayed in the *Condensed* format.

Look at the *Condensed* sheet; a copy of its financial statement items is shown in Exhibit 9-3. The *Condensed* statements are a little more complicated than the financial statements you used for Van Leer, but not nearly as complicated as the *Comprehensive* financial statements and probably not as complicated as the *Actual* financial statements.

As we describe in Chapter 10, you may find that net income on the *Condensed* statements may not be exactly equal to the net income on the *Comprehensive* statements; total assets on the *Condensed* statements may not be exactly equal to total assets on the *Comprehensive* statements. This is because the simplifications underlying the *Condensed* statements are consistent with economic reality, not necessarily with accounting rules. We explain this in more detail later, but we don't want you to panic (or, even worse, to think that we had made mistakes!) if you noticed any differences.

The Chapter 9 appendix gives a simple example illustrating the nature of the condensing process, and the Chapter 10 appendix describes the underlying accounting and economic rationales for condensing the statements in excruciating, tedious detail.

[2]A caveat is in order at this point. The mapping from the *Comprehensive* to the *Condensed* formats is based on our experience with many companies, and it works well for the vast majority of them. However, it is not possible for any particular mapping to work flawlessly for all companies. There may well be situations in which you might want to modify the mapping. The book's web site describes these in more detail.

Exhibit 9-3 The Condensed Financial Statements

Part 1—Income Statement

Sales
Costs of goods sold
Sales, general and administrative
Depreciation
Operating profit
Interest expense
Interest income
Nonoperating income (expense)
Earnings before taxes
Taxes
Net income before extraordinary items
After-tax extraordinary income (expense)
Net Income

Dividends—preferred
Dividends—common
Additions to RE

Exhibit 9-3 The Condensed Financial Statements (continued)

Part 2—Balance Sheet

Assets
Cash
Inventory
Accounts receivable
Other short-term operating assets
Short-term investments
Total current assets

Net plant, property and equipment (PPE)
Other long-term operating assets
Long-term investments
Total assets

Liabilities and Equity
Accounts payable (AP)
Accruals
Other operating current liabilities
All short-term debt
Total current liabilities

Long-term debt
Deferred taxes
Preferred stock
Other long-term liabilities
Total liabilities

Par plus PIC less treasury (and other adjustments)
Retained earnings (RE)
Total common equity
Total liabilities and equity

But the bottom line is that you don't need to make any changes in the *Condensed* worksheet: it picks up all the data you need from the *Comprehensive* sheet and does the condensing for you.

Step 4: Analyzing the Current and Historical Financial Position of the Company

Before projecting a company's financial statements, it's a good idea to understand its current and historical financial situation. In our experience, most companies, especially large ones, don't turn on a dime, and their historical performances are a good starting point for predicting their future performances. The *Hist Analys* worksheet structures this analysis for you in a way that best facilitates performing a corporate valuation. The graphical interface in this worksheet makes it easy to see, literally, how a company has performed in the past for a wide range of performance measures. For example, in predicting future sales growth, it is helpful to see a graph of past growth rates. Chapter 10 explains this in more detail, including how to access Internet data sources with information about a company's past, current, and expected future performance.

Step 5: Estimating the Weighted Average Cost of Capital

To perform a valuation, you will need an estimate of the weighted average cost of capital (WACC) for your company. The *WACC* worksheet is structured to lead you through this calculation, which we explain in detail in Chapter 11. We also show you how to access Internet data that will be helpful in making the calculation.

Step 6: Choose the Inputs for Your Projections

To perform a valuation, you must project the financial statements, and to project financial statements you must choose your inputs, such as the growth rate in sales, the ratio of costs/sales, the interest rates, etc. In our experience, this is truly the hardest part of valuation analysis and requires some familiarity with such specifics as economywide and industry conditions that may affect the firm being analyzed, as well as recent company-specific news, such as changes in managers or management philosophy, and announced or likely restructuring plans. If you combine thorough research with an understanding of the firm's historical data, then you should be able to create plausible estimates of the key input ratios that drive cash flows and the resulting valuation.

The *Inputs* worksheet is where you specify input choices. The required inputs are similar to those that you used Chapters 5–7, but there are some features we have added to make the process easier for you. In Chapter 12, we will explain the features of the *Inputs* worksheet in detail, using Home Depot as an example.

Step 7: Completing the Valuation

The *Proj & Val* worksheet has three sections: projected financial statements, free cash flow, and valuation. In most ways, these projected financial statements are similar to the ones you did in Chapters 5–7. There are a couple of key differences, however. First, the data for the current year, such as Cells C7:C19, have formulas that refer back to the *Condensed* worksheet. Second, if you click on any of the projected items, such as projected sales in cell D7, you will see that the formula uses the input from the *Inputs* worksheet. Third, the Valuation section has a few modifications that incorporate the correct valuation techniques for actual companies; these are described in detail in Chapter 13.

The bottom line is that you don't need to make any changes in the *Proj & Val* worksheet. It picks up all the data you need from the other worksheets. This allows you to focus on outcomes.

Getting Financial Statements from the Internet

The *Actual* worksheet will contain the actual historical financial statements for the company that you are analyzing. In the old days (just a few years ago), the most common way to get this data was to get a printed copy of the company's financial statements. You would go to a library and copy the statements from its annual report, or you might call the company and request that it send a copy of its annual report to you. Your library might possibly have had copies of the 10-K reports that the company had to file with the Securities and Exchange Commission (SEC), and you might have made a copy of the 10-K report instead of the annual report. You still can do this, but it means that you must enter the data by hand in the *Actual* worksheet.

Fortunately, now there are many electronic data sources for financial information. Following is an explanation of some of the most useful sources. We have concentrated the discussion on sources that are either free or readily accessible through many municipal or university libraries' networks.[3] Since web sites change frequently, you might want to check the book's web site for an updated list. As you look through some of these sites, notice that most sources report historical data with the most recent year occurring in the column closest to the labels. For example, most show the labels in column A and the most recent year in column B, with earlier years occurring in column C, column D, etc. In the example shown in the file ***Home Depot.xls***, we have 2003 shown in column B, 2002 in column C, 2001 in column D, etc. We have 10 years of data, which is ideal. No matter how many years of data you enter, make sure that the most recent year is in column B.

Following are descriptions of some sources of data from the Internet.

1. Thomson Financial and Thomson ONE-Business School Edition

Most university libraries have a data source called Thomson Research, provided by Thomson Financial. Also, as a purchaser of this book, you have access to a portion of this data, the Thomson ONE-Business School Edition; see the book's web site for instructions to access this data. The Thomson data is by far the best source that we have seen, because it provides 10 years of standardized financial statements in Excel files. A major advantage of this source is that Thomson has already incorporated some adjustments to the company's statements that facilitate intercompany and interyear comparisons. The Thomson data actually comes in two flavors. The first is called SEC data, and the second is called Worldscope data. Both sources provide 10 years of financial statements. Both are excellent, and this book's web site provides separate valuation templates that allow you to cut and paste data from either source into the *Actual* sheet. In fact, the data you see for Home Depot was cut and pasted from Thomson's SEC data source into our spreadsheet. We do have to offer one caveat when using the Thomson data. It reports some data as not available and shows NA in the cell rather than zero. Before cutting and pasting the data into the *Actual* worksheet, you should use Excel's Edit, Replace feature to replace NA with 0.

---

[3]This means we have not included some very good fee-for-service data sources that may be available to some readers. Obviously, readers that have access to such data providers may find it advantageous to use them.

2. Edgar

Under federal securities law, public companies are required to file a number of reports with the Securities and Exchange Commission (SEC). The 10-K report contains annual financial statements, and the 10-Q report contains quarterly financial statements. If you go to the SEC's web page at **http://www.sec.gov**, you will see a section called Filings and Forms (EDGAR). One of the sub-sections allows you to search for company filings. The instructions are pretty clear, so it's easy to get electronic copies of the filings, including the 10-K reports. Unfortunately, the reports come formatted as either text or HTML, neither of which is easy to put into a spreadsheet. It is possible to download these reports as text documents, then cut and paste the data into a spreadsheet, but this is tedious work because each 10-K will cover only the current year and the prior year's financial results. However, the SEC web site is often useful for gathering other information about a company, such as the Management's Discussion and Analysis section of the 10-K or compensation plans for its key executives from the proxy statement.

3. EdgarScan

PricewaterhouseCoopers supports a web page called EdgarScan, located at **http://www.edgarscan.pwcglobal.com**. From there you can enter EdgarScan, which extracts financial data from SEC filings, such as 10-K reports, and puts the extracted data into Excel spreadsheets. You can then download these Excel files. Then you simply cut the data out of the EdgarScan files that you downloaded and paste it into the *Actual* sheet of our spreadsheet. Unfortunately, these files contain only a couple of years of data each, and so you will have to retrieve older files as well to create *Actual* financial statements with 5 to 10 years of data. And we've got to warn you, the process is not always flawless. Sometimes companies restate their older financial statements, so data that is retrieved in a piecemeal fashion from several different filings may not always match up.

4. Yahoo!

Yahoo! provides an incredible amount of very useful data. In fact, we believe Yahoo!Finance is one of the most useful of the "free" web sites. You can go directly to its financial web site at **http://finance.yahoo.com**. Once there, you enter the ticker symbol for a company, and it brings up a page containing the current stock price and other data. If you select the link Profile, it will bring up a page that provides an overview of the company. If you scroll down the page, you will see a section on the left side of the page labeled More From Multex. Below it is a link labeled Ratio Comparisons. Click on this link, and it will bring up a page containing data from Multex Investor. This is a great source of data for ratio analysis, and we'll use it in Chapter 10 when we analyze the condensed statements of Home Depot. For now, though, you should take a look at the left side of the screen, which shows headings for the three parts of a financial statement: Income Stmt, Balance Sheet, and Cash Flow. If you select one of these, it will bring up the financial statements. Unfortunately, these are in an HTML format and are difficult to put into Excel.

5. Company Web Pages

Many companies provide financial statements on their own web pages, usually in an Investor Relations section. Most companies will provide their financial statements in either text or HTML format, and a few will provide some statements in Excel files. But very few companies actually provide multiple years of all financial statements in Excel files.

Mapping Your Financial Statements from the *Actual* Worksheet into the *Comprehensive* Worksheet

Let's assume that you have put data for the financial statements of your company into the *Actual* sheet. Unfortunately, different data sources use slightly different formats for their financial statements, and different companies use different names for many of the items on their financial statements. Also, when a company doesn't have a particular item, such as noncurrent portion of capitalized leases, it simply doesn't include that item in its financial statements. The result is that it is extremely rare for any two financial statements to have identical formats.

After we began using the free cash flow valuation approach, we realized that, due to the variation in format and nomenclature we found among firms' financial statements, it would be much easier to use a standardized format. In other words, instead of changing our spreadsheet model for each company we wished to value, we would change the format of the company's financial statements to fit the *Condensed* financial statements format that we described earlier in this chapter.

It occurred to us that we always should start our analysis with a *Comprehensive* sheet that would include just about any accounting entry that a company might have (hence, "comprehensive"). As we explained earlier in the chapter, we then created formulas that automatically condense the financial statements in our *Comprehensive* sheet into the financial statements of our *Condensed* sheet, which has enough detail to do the free cash flow valuation. The result is that the only "accounting" work we now have to do is to link each item from the *Actual* financial statements to a corresponding item on the *Comprehensive* statements. (It's okay if many of the items on the *Comprehensive* statements are left at their default value of zero; this is expected, since the *Comprehensive* statements have more categories than the typical *Actual* statements.) We refer to this as mapping the *Actual* financials into the *Comprehensive* financials.[4]

Following are explanations for the three sections of the *Comprehensive* sheet: income statement, balance sheet, and special items.

Before proceeding, however, you might want to check the book's web site. We have several "video" files that illustrate the mapping process, and these are probably more interesting than the written discussion in the remainder of this section. In fact, you might want to skip the remainder of this section until you actually need to map

[4]One always takes some risk when taking a firm's financial statements at face value, and assuming that the firm is following flawless GAAP accounting. Enron is a painful example (and not the only one!) of how blind acceptance of audited financial reports may lead investors astray. At a minimum, we recommend reading the footnotes to a firm's financials and the section of the 10-K that provides management's own assessment of its recent performance and strategies.

some actual financial statements for a company that you are analyzing. To be honest, unless you are actually working on a problem that requires you to map data, you'll find the rest of this section pretty dry. Also, if you are using data from Thomson ONE-Business School Edition, then you won't have to do the mapping, since our spreadsheets are designed to map the Thomson data for you.

Income Statement

Exhibit 9-4 shows the items for the income statement in the *Comprehensive* sheet. It also shows the comments in the *Comprehensive* sheet. Notice that when we say to map an item into the *Comprehensive* sheet, we mean to enter a formula that refers to the appropriate item in the *Actual* sheet. For example, the formula for total net revenues in cell B5 in the *Comprehensive* sheet has this formula: =Actual!B63, where B63 in the *Actual* sheet has the net revenues for the company in the *Actual* statements.

There are several points to notice about this section. First, you only have to enter formulas for column B; you can copy the formulas from column B into the other columns. Second, all cells on the *Comprehensive* income statement will be either a zero or a formula referring to the *Actual* income statement; you will not enter any

Exhibit 9-4 The Comprehensive Income Statement

Item	Comment
Total net revenues	Enter all operating revenues and income, net of any returns, from the actual income statement.
Cost of goods sold expense	Enter costs of goods as shown on the actual income statement. Note that most income statements include deprecation and amortization in the cost of goods, instead of reporting depreciation and amortization as separate lines on the income statement.
Cost of services or operations expense	Enter cost of services or operations expense if it is shown as a separate item instead of costs of goods sold or in addition to cost of goods sold.
Depreciation expense (for tangible assets, reported separately)	Enter a value here only if depreciation is shown as a separate line on the actual income statement. If it is not shown as a separate line, enter a zero. Note: Even if you enter a zero for depreciation here, you will enter the actual depreciation figure further down in this worksheet. See the row for depreciation in the special items section that follows the balance sheets for details.
Amortization expense (for goodwill and tangible, if reported separately)	Enter a value here only if amortization is shown as a separate line on the actual income statement. If it is not shown as a separate line, enter a zero. Note: Even if you enter a zero for amortization here, you will enter the actual amortization figure further down in this worksheet. See the row for amortization in the section for special items that follows the balance sheets.

Exhibit 9-4 The Comprehensive Income Statement (continued)

Item	Comment
Depreciation and amortization expense (if reported combined)	Enter a value here only if depreciation and amortization is shown as a combined line on the actual income statement. If it is not shown as a combined line, enter a zero. Be careful not to double count; enter a zero here if you have entered depreciation and amortization separately above. Note: Even if you enter a zero for depreciation here, you will enter the actual depreciation and amortization figure further down in this worksheet in the section for special items. See the row for depreciation in the special items section that follows the balance sheets for details.
Research & development expense	Enter the R&D expense if it is shown on the actual statements as a separate line item.
Sales & marketing expenses (if not included in SGA)	Show any sales & marketing that are reported as a separate line item in the *Actual* sheet. Note that many companies combine sales & marketing with general & administrative expenses. If this is the case, simply report the combined value as shown below.
General & administrative expenses (if not included in SGA)	Show any general & administrative expenses that are reported as a separate line item in the *Actual* sheet. Note that many companies combine sales & marketing with general & administrative expenses. If this is the case, simply report the combined value as shown below.
Selling, general & administrative expense (if reported as a single item)	Enter the total reported SG&A from the actual income statements if they are shown as a single item. Note: Some sources include depreciation and amortization with SG&A and don't show depreciation and amortization as separate lines on the income statement.
Minority interest expense (if shown as pre-tax operating expense)	Show any minority interest expense that is shown as a pre-tax operating item on the *Actual* sheet. Note: Some companies report minority interest expense in several places (as a pre-tax operating expense, a pre-tax nonoperating expense, or an after-tax expense). Be sure to report it as shown on the *Actual* sheet, and be sure not to report it more than once on the *Comprehensive* sheet if it is shown only once on the *Actual* sheet.
Merger and restructuring costs	Show any merger and restructuring costs here, provided they are reported on a pre-tax basis.
Asset impairment losses or write-downs	This is a special charge for amortization and goodwill.
Extraordinary charges or expenses (if shown on pre-tax basis)	Companies usually report extraordinary items like discontinued operations on an after-tax basis below, but if the company reports extraordinary expenses on a pre-tax basis, enter it here.
Extraordinary credit or income (if shown on a pre-tax basis)	Companies may report one-time or nonrecurring sources of income here on a pre-tax basis.

Exhibit 9-4 The Comprehensive Income Statement (continued)

Item	Comment
Other operating expenses (income)	Enter any operating costs that don't fit in any other categories. Since expenses are shown as a positive number, be sure to show any other operating income as a negative number.
Interest expense (income)	If the actual income statements report interest expense and interest income separately, then report them here separately. But many income statements only report net interest expense. If this is the case, then report net interest expense in the row here for interest expense, and enter a zero in the row below for interest income. Note: Some companies only report a single item for net interest expense. If they report a negative number for net interest expense, it really means that the company has more interest income than expense. If this is the case, make sure your entry is also negative.
Interest capitalized	This is the portion of interest expense that is capitalized rather than expensed. If shown as a positive number, it reduces the interest expense.
Interest income	If the actual income statements report interest expense and interest income separately, then report them here separately. But many income statements only report net interest expense. If this is the case, then report net interest expense in the row above for interest expense, and enter a zero in the this row for interest income.
Reserve expense (income) (increase in reserves is expense, decrease is income)	In a perfect world this is an operating expense, but many companies use it to manage earnings, and so we classify it as an extraordinary expense.
Investment income (expense) (if shown on pre-tax basis)	Show any investment income that is shown as a separate line item in the *Actual* sheet. Be sure to report any investment expense as a negative number.
Gain (loss) on sale of assets or discontinued operation (if shown) on pre-tax basis)	Sometimes companies report this as pre-tax item. Be sure to report a loss as a negative number. Be sure not to report this twice; if it is reported on an after-tax basis, report it below, not here.
Remitted income (expense) or equity earnings (losses) in affiliates	Show any remitted income as a positive number and expense as a negative number.
Unremitted income (expense) or equity earnings (losses) in affiliates	Show any unremitted income as a positive number, and any expense as a negative number.

Exhibit 9-4 The Comprehensive Income Statement (continued)

Item	Comment
Minority interest expense (if shown as pre-tax non-operating expense)	Show any minority interest expense that is shown as a pre-tax non-operating item on the *Actual* sheet. Note: Some companies report minority interest expense in several places (as a pre-tax operating expense, a pre-tax nonoperating expense, or an after-tax expense). Be sure to report it as shown on the *Actual* sheet, and be sure not to report it more than once on the *Comprehensive* sheet if it is shown only once on the *Actual* sheet.
Losses on equity investees and other (if shown on pre-tax basis)	Report any losses on equity investees (as a positive number) if shown on the *Actual* sheet on a pre-tax basis.
Other nonoperating income (expense) (if shown on pre-tax basis)	Sometimes statements show a pre-tax nonoperating income or expense. If it is income, show it as a positive number. If expense, show it as a negative number.
Special nonrecurring items income (expense) (if shown on pre-tax basis)	Sometimes statements will show a nonrecurring pre-tax item. If it is a source of income, show it as a positive number. If it is a loss, show it as a negative number.
Provision for income tax expense (rebate)	This should come from the actual statements. Since this is a provision-for income taxes expense, it should be positive if the company is paying the taxes, and negative if it is a rebate from previous years' tax payments.
Minority interest expense (if shown on after-tax basis)	Most companies show minority interest as an after-tax item. If that is the case, report minority interest here. However, some companies show minority interest as a pre-tax item. If so, then show a zero here, and report it in the pre-tax line above here.
Equity in earnings (if shown on after-tax basis)	See the comment on minority interest.
Extraordinary items (if shown on after-tax basis)	Sometimes companies show extraordinary items separately on an after-tax basis. Enter those items here. If they are income, enter them as positive numbers; if they are losses, enter them as negative numbers. If they are combined with discontinued operations, then enter them in the combined row below. Be careful not to enter them twice.
Discontinued operations (if shown on after-tax basis)	Sometimes companies show discontinued operations separately on an after-tax basis. Enter those items here. If they are income, enter them as positive numbers; if they are losses, enter them as negative numbers. If they are combined with extraordinary items, then enter them in the combined row below. Be careful not to enter them twice.

HOW DO I GET STARTED?

START

Follow these easy steps to gain access to Thomson ONE – *Business School Edition* for Corporate Valuation: A Guide for Managers and Investors!

Daves, Ehrhardt, and Shrieves

STEP 1:

Visit the Thomson ONE for Corporate Valuation Web site by going to **http://daves.swlearning.com** and clicking on the link for Thomson ONE – *Business School Edition*.

STEP 2:

Click on "register" to enter your serial number.

STEP 3:

Enter your serial number exactly as it appears on this card and select a User ID.

STEP 4:

When prompted, select a password and submit the necessary information. Record your User ID and password in a secure location.

STEP 5:

You are now registered. Return to the above URL, follow the Thomson ONE link, and click on "enter" to access Thomson ONE – *Business School Edition*.

STEP 6:

Use the Thomson ONE – *Business School Edition* online database to work either assigned problems and projects from the textbook or additional instructor assigned problems, cases and projects.

SERIAL #: SC-0000GD0I-TABV

If you need technical assistance in registering, contact our Technical Support Team at 1-800-423-0563 or support@thomsonlearning.com.

Thomson ONE *Business School Edition*

ISBN 0-324-29076-4

DON'T THROW THIS CARD AWAY!

THIS MAY BE REQUIRED FOR YOUR COURSE!

Bring Wall Street to the Classroom with Thomson ONE!

Thomson ONE – *Business School Edition* is a Web-based portal product that provides integrated access to Thomson Financial content for the purpose of financial analysis. This is an educational version of the same financial resources used by Wall Street analysts on a daily basis!

For 500 companies, this online resource provides seamless access to:

- **Current and Past Company Data:** Worldscope which includes company profiles, financials and accounting results, market per-share data, annual information, and monthly prices going back to 1980.
- **Financial Analyst Data and Forecasts:** I/B/E/S Consensus Estimates which provides consensus estimates, analyst-by-analyst earnings coverage, and analysts' forecasts.
- **SEC Disclosure Statements:** Disclosure SEC Database which includes company profiles, annual and quarterly company financials, pricing information, and earnings.
- *And More!*

Thomson ONE *Business School Edition*

Exhibit 9-4 The Comprehensive Income Statement (continued)

Item	Comment
Extraordinary items and discontinued operations (if shown on after-tax basis)	Sometimes companies show extraordinary items and discontinued operations combined on an after-tax basis. Enter those items here. If they are income, enter them as positive numbers; if they are losses, enter them as negative numbers. If they are reported separately (not combined), enter them separately in the rows above; be careful not to enter them twice.
Investment gains (losses) (if shown on after-tax basis)	Sometimes companies show investment gains or losses on an after-tax basis. Report those figures here.
All other income (losses) (if shown on after-tax basis)	Report all other income on an after-tax basis here. If it is a loss, be sure to show it as a negative number.
Cumulative effect of accounting changes	Sometimes firms have to make accounting changes, perhaps because of accounting irregularities. When this happens, accountants put in this line item to make the current financial statements consistent with the corrected past statements.
Net income from *Actual* sheet	This should come directly from the income statements on the *Actual* worksheet, not calculated from the rows above.
Calculated net income from *Comprehensive* sheet	This is net income calculated from the line items above. We use it to check whether the *Comprehensive* income statement is consistent with the *Actual* income statement.
See if calculated net income is consistent with *Comprehensive* sheet	Don't enter anything here. The calculation from this formula should be the same as the net income reported one row above. If it is not the same as the row above, then you probably have omitted an item or given an item the wrong sign. See the comments above for help in tracking down your mistake. The book's web site also provides guidance in trouble-shooting errors.

actual numbers in the *Comprehensive* sheet. Third, for most companies, many items on the *Comprehensive* income statement will be zero or blank, since it includes more items than are typically found on an income statement.

Balance Sheets

Exhibit 9-5 shows the items that are on the *Comprehensive* balance sheets. Note that all cells in the *Comprehensive* balance sheet will either have a zero or a formula referring to the *Actual* balance sheet. Also note that for most companies, many items on the *Comprehensive* balance sheet will be zero, since it includes more items than are typically found on a balance sheet.

Exhibit 9-5 The Comprehensive Balance Sheet

Part 1—Assets

Item	Comment
Cash and equivalents	Report only the row in the *Actual* sheets shown as cash.
Marketable securities	Report any excess marketable securities.
Notes receivable	Report any notes receivable.
Short-term investments or investment securities	Report any other items that are short-term investments or investment securities.
Accounts receivable	Report any accounts receivable.
Tax refund receivable	Report any tax refund receivable.
Progress payments	This is like a prepaid expense.
Prepaid expenses	Enter any prepaid expenses.
Current deferred tax asset	Enter any current deferred tax asset.
Inventories	Some balance sheets show subcategories for raw materials, work-in-process, or finished goods. Be sure to report only the total inventory.
Other nonoperating current assets	Enter any other current assets not listed that are obviously not related to operations.
Other operating current assets	Report the total for any other current assets that are shown on the actual statements but are not already reported in the rows above.
Total current assets	Don't enter anything here (we already have a formula), but check to make sure this subtotal is the same as the total current assets on the actual financial statements.
Long-term receivables	This is a long-term investment.
Investments in unconsolidated subsidiaries	This is a long-term investment.
Other investments	This is a long-term investment.
Net property, plant, & equip. (PPE)	Report the net property, plant, & equipment, which is sometimes called net fixed assets. Some balance sheets show the gross PPE (or gross fixed assets) and the accumulated depreciation. Be sure you report only the net figure here.
Goodwill (if shown separately)	Enter any goodwill shown as a separate item on the *Actual* balance sheets. If it is combined into a single account, goodwill and intangibles, then show it below.
Intangibles (if shown separately)	Enter any intangibles shown as a separate item on the *Actual* balance sheets. If it is combined into a single account, goodwill and intangibles, then show it below.
Cost in excess of fair value of net assets acquired (also called goodwill)	This is just another way of categorizing goodwill.

Exhibit 9-5 The Comprehensive Balance Sheet (continued)

Part 1—Assets

Item	Comment
Goodwill and intangibles (if shown combined)	Report any goodwill and intangible assets if shown combined. If they are shown separately, then enter each above. Be careful not to double count.
Deferred tax asset (long term)	Report any long-term deferred tax asset shown on the *Actual* sheet.
Long-term notes receivable	Report any notes receivable.
Other operating long-term assets	Include any other operating assets that are not included in one of the items shown on the *Comprehensive* sheet. If it is a nonoperating asset, be sure to include it in the other nonoperating assets shown below.
Deferred charges	Report any deferred charges.
Deposits	Report any deposits.
Investments & advances to subsidiaries	Report any investments & advances. Sometimes these are shown in two different categories (one for investments & advances—equity method, and one for investments & advances—other method). Be sure to report only the total here.
Other non-operating long-term assets	Report any other nonoperating assets that are not included in the items above.
Total assets from *Actual* sheet	This should come directly from the income statements on the *Actual* worksheet, not calculated from the rows above.
Calculated total assets from *Comprehensive* Sheet	Don't enter anything here (we already have a formula).
Check to see if total assets consistent with *Actual* sheet	Don't enter anything here (we already have a formula). But this figure should be the same as the total assets on the row above. If not, then you have probably left out an item or have double counted an item.

Part 2—Liability and Equity

Item	Comment
Notes payable	Report any notes payable (this may also be called bank debt).
Current portion of long-term debt	Report any current portion of long-term debt.
Current portion of capitalized leases	Report any current portion of capitalized leases.
All other short-term debt	Report any other interest-bearing debt shown in the current assets, but not already reported in the three rows above.

Exhibit 9-5 The Comprehensive Balance Sheet (continued)
Part 2—Liability and Equity

Item	Comment
Accounts payable	Report any accounts payable (sometimes it is called trade credit).
Short-term unearned revenue	Report any short-term unearned revenue.
Interest payable (or accrued interest)	Report any interest payable.
Dividends payable	Report any dividends payable.
Short-term deferred taxes	Report any short-term deferred taxes.
Taxes payable or accrued taxes	Report any taxes payable.
Accrued wages or salary	Report any accrued wages.
Other accrued expenses or accruals	Report any accruals not included in the lines above.
Other nonoperating current liabilities	Report any other current liabilities that you think are not related to operations here.
Other operating current liabilities	Report the sum of all items not included in the rows above. If in doubt about an account on the current liability section of the *Actual* sheet, you should classify it as an other operating current liability.
Total current liabilities	Don't enter anything here (we have already entered the formula), but this figure should be the same as the total current liabilities shown on the *Actual* statements. If not, then you probably have omitted an item or have double counted an item.
Noncurrent portion of long-term debt	Enter any noncurrent portion of long-term debt.
Mortgages	Enter any mortgages. This might also be called secured debt.
Noncurrent portion of capitalized leases	Enter any noncurrent portion of capitalized leases.
Convertible debt	Enter any convertible debt.
Any other long-term debt	Report any other debt that charges interest.
Provision for risks and charges	Enter any provision for risks.
Reserve accounts	Enter any reserves.
Deferred tax liability in untaxed reserves	Enter deferred tax liability.
Deferred income taxes (long-term)	Enter any deferred income taxes.
Deferred income	Enter any deferred income.

Exhibit 9-5 The Comprehensive Balance Sheet (continued)
Part 2—Liability and Equity

Item	Comment
Long-term unearned revenue	Enter any long-term unearned revenue.
Restructuring obligations	Enter any restructuring obligations.
Commitments and contingencies	Enter any contingencies.
Other long-term liabilities	Record any other long-term liabilities that do not charge interest.
Retirement, pension, and health insurance-related liabilities	Report any liabilities shown for retirement, pension, or health insurance.
Minority interest	Report any minority interest.
Nonequity reserves	Report any nonequity reserves.
Preferred stock	Report any preferred stock.
Common stock (at par)	This is the common stock at par. If there is more than one class of common stock, add them all together here. Note: Some companies report common stock at par and paid-in-capital in a single entry. If so, be sure to include it either here or in the row below, but not in both rows.
Common stock capital surplus or paid-in-capital	This is the common stock capital surplus or paid-in-capital. If there are multiple classes of stock, be sure to add all capital surplus accounts here. Note: Some companies report common stock at par and capital surplus as a single line. If that is the case, report the combined amount either here or above, but not in both places.
Revaluation of reserves	Report any revaluation of reserves.
Other appropriated reserves	Report any appropriated reserves.
Unappropriated (free) reserves	Report any unappropriated reserves.
Retained earnings	Report any retained earnings here.
Equity in untaxed reserves	Report any equity on untaxed reserves.
ESOP guarantees	This should be entered as a negative number, if it is not shown as a negative number on the *Actual* sheet.
Treasury stock	This should be entered as a negative number because it represents the dollar value of all stock that the company has repurchased.
Common stock warrants and stock options	If common stock warrants and stock options are shown as a separate account on the *Actual* balance sheet, then show them here. If they are not shown as a separate account, just put a zero here. If you want to make a special accounting adjustment, see the section below.

Exhibit 9-5 The Comprehensive Balance Sheet (continued)
Part 2—Liability and Equity

Item	Comment
Other equity	Report any other equity.
Unrealized gain (loss) on marketable securities	Report any unrealized gain as a positive number; report a loss as a negative number.
Accumulated other comprehensive income or cumulative other adjustments	Report any accumulated other comprehensive income or cumulative other adjustments.
Unrealized gain (loss) on foreign exchange	Report any unrealized gain on foreign exchange as a positive number, any loss as a negative number.
Cumulative foreign currency translations	Report cumulative foreign currency translations.
Total shareholder equity from *Actual* Sheet	This should come directly from the income statements on the *Actual* worksheet, not calculated from the rows above. Note: It should include preferred stock and common equity.
Calculated total shareholder equity from *Comprehensive* Sheet	This is calculated from the balance sheet in the *Comprehensive* sheet.
Check to see if total shareholder equity is consistent with *Actual* sheets	Don't enter anything here (we already entered the formula), but make sure this figure is the same as the total common equity shown in the row above. Note: Most actual statements include preferred stock as a part of total shareholder equity, and so we also include it. But you should verify that your source of data for the actual statement does in fact include preferred stock as a part of total shareholder equity.
Total liabilities and Equity from *Actual* Sheet	This should come directly from the income statements on the *Actual* worksheet, not calculated from the rows above.
Calculated total liabilities and equity from *Comprehensive* sheet	Enter the figure for total liabilities and equity from the actual statements.
Check to see if total liability & equity consistent with *Comprehensive* sheet	Don't enter anything (we have already entered the formula), but check to make sure the figure shown here is the same as the figure in the row above. If not, then you probably have omitted an item, double counted an item, or have the wrong sign on an item.
Check for balancing of statements	This checks to see if the calculated total assets is actually equal to the total liabilities and equity. If it shows "Error", then the sheets do not balance and there is a mistake in the way the items were entered.

Required Special Items

There are some other items (i.e., those that come from some other source than the *Actual* income statement and *Actual* balance sheets) that you will need in your analysis. These are shown in the *Comprehensive* sheet in the section called "Required Special Items." Exhibit 9-6 shows the special items. These may be entered either as a number or a formula referring to the *Actual* sheet.

Exhibit 9-6 Required Special Items on the Comprehensive Statements

Item	Comment
From Statement of Cash Flows	
Preferred dividends paid	This usually can be found in the statement of cash flows. This usually is shown as a negative number because it is a payment, so show it as a negative number here. If instead it is shown as a positive number on the *Actual* statement of cash flows, show it as a negative number here.
Common dividends paid	This usually can be found in the statement of cash flows. This usually is shown as a negative number because it is a payment, so show it as a negative number here. If instead it is shown as a positive number on the *Actual* statement of cash flows, show it as a negative number here.
Depreciation and amortization of PPE and tangible assets	This usually can be found in the *Actual* statement of cash flows or in footnotes. Report the number here even if you reported a value for depreciation in the income statement. Don't worry if the two values are not equal. Sometimes the income statement will report only the portion of depreciation not due to costs of goods sold, while the statement of cash flows will always report the true total depreciation. If depreciation and amortization are combined on the *Actual* statement of cash flows, then report the combined value as depreciation, unless you know how to identify the portion due to depreciation and the portion due to amortization.
Amortization of goodwill and intangibles	This usually can be found in the *Actual* statement of cash flow's or in footnotes. Report the number here even if you reported a value for amortization in the income statement. Don't worry if the two values are not equal. Sometimes the income statement will report only the portion of amortization due to costs of goods sold, while the statement of cash flows will always report the true total amortization. If depreciation and amortization are combined on the *Actual* statement of cash flows, then report the combined value as depreciation, unless you know how to identify the portion due to depreciation and the portion due to amortization.

Exhibit 9-6 Required Special Items on the Comprehensive Statements (continued)

From Footnotes or Annual Report

Number of shares outstanding	This can usually be found in the row heading for common equity shown in the balance sheet. If not there, it usually can be found in the annual report. Make sure it is in the same units (e.g., millions, thousands, etc.) as the items on the financial statements.
Assumed marginal tax rate	This is the tax rate that the company will pay on any additional income. For most companies, the federal rate is about 34%. With state and local taxes included, the rate usually is about 38%. Therefore, you should enter a rate of about 38%, unless you have additional information. The default value is the average tax rate, based on the taxes reported in the income statement.[5]

[5]Of course, historical tax rates calculated from prior years can be extrapolated. Many firms provide a summary of taxes paid in the last several years as a footnote to their financial statements. The following was part of footnote 3 to Home Depot's 10-K for 2001: "The Company's combined federal, state and foreign effective tax rates for fiscal years 2000, 1999, and 1998, net of offsets generated by federal, state and foreign tax incentive credits, were approximately 38.8%, 39.0% and 39.2%," respectively.

Optional Special Items

There are some other items (i.e., those that come from some other source than the *Actual* income statement and *Actual* balance sheets) that you might choose to incorporate in your analysis. These are shown in the *Comprehensive* sheet in the section called "Optional Special Items." Exhibit 9-7 shows these special items. These may be entered as a number. The appendix to Chapter 10 explains these in detail.

Exhibit 9-7 Optional Special Items on the Comprehensive Statements

Item	Comment
LIFO reserve (from footnotes of annual report)	LIFO reserve can be found in the footnotes. Be sure to set the LIFO reserve in the year prior to the beginning of data to the same value as the last year of data. However, you may decide to not worry about the LIFO reserve (see the discussion in Chapter 10 Appendix). If this is the case, enter zero here.
Interest rate on pension liabilities	You will need this item only if your company has non-zero values for retirement, pension, and health-related liabilities. If these are zero, then just enter a zero here. Otherwise, enter your estimate for the company's pre-tax cost of debt. See the *WACC* sheet for more details.

Exhibit 9-7 Optional Special Items on the Comprehensive Statements (continued)

Item	Comment
Interest rate on operating leases	You will only need this item if your company has substantial operating lease obligations that are not already capitalized; see the comment in the next line for more details. If your company does not have substantial operating lease obligations, then just enter a zero here. Otherwise, enter your estimate for the company's pre-tax cost of debt. See the *WACC* sheet for more details.
Capitalized value of operating leases	Sometimes companies have substantial operating lease obligations, as shown in the footnotes. If your company does not have large lease obligations, then enter a zero here. Otherwise, calculate the capitalized value of operating leases as shown in the appendix to Chapter 10.
Stock options (warrants)	If warrants and stock options are not shown in the *Actual* balance sheets but you know the value from the footnotes (or some other source), you can enter that value here. If they are shown in the *Actual* balance sheets but you believe the reported value is not accurate, then enter the reported value in the balance sheet account above and enter your corrected value here. The default value is the value shown on the balance sheet, which might be zero.
Capitalized operating costs	Sometimes companies will capitalize operating costs. This usually shows up in the investing section of the statement of cash flows. For example, a company might show an investment called "Cost of additions to internal use software." This is actually money the company spent on developing internal software, and so should be reported as an expense, not as additional assets. If your company has such a situation, report the amount here. Show the sign as it is shown on the statement of cash flows.
Special goodwill impairment	Companies can no longer amortize goodwill on an annual basis, but can only write down goodwill if the market value of the acquisition has fallen. These special write-downs, called impairments, do not affect free cash flow, but they do affect the NOPAT/sales and capital/sales ratios. If you want to incorporate these special write-downs into the historical values of capital, then enter the amount of the write-down here.

At this point, you should be able to map the items from the *Actual* sheet into the *Comprehensive* sheet. This book's web site also has some additional tips and instruction for mapping actual data into the *Comprehensive* worksheet. For now, take a look at our spreadsheet, ***Home Depot.xls***, to see how we mapped Home Depot's *Actual* financial statements into the *Comprehensive* statements.

Summary

This chapter introduced the spreadsheet valuation model and began the process of applying valuation concepts and principles to an actual company. The valuation spreadsheet has six interrelated worksheets: (1) *Proj & Val*, (2) *Inputs*, (3) *WACC*, (3) *Hist Analys*, (4) *Condensed*, (5) *Comprehensive*, and (6) *Actual*. We showed some useful Internet sources for financial statement data and illustrated the valuation using the statements of Home Depot. Following are the steps in a valuation analysis.

Step 1: The first step is to find the actual historical financial statements for a company, and to insert them into the *Actual* worksheet. Be sure to have the financial statement labels in Column A and the most recent year of data in Column B.

Step 2: Since different sources of data provide slightly different formats for the financial statements of a company, the second step is to put the actual financial statements into a standardized format using our *Comprehensive* worksheet. The standardized comprehensive format we have developed has just about all the entries needed to capture variations in the formats of most companies' financial statements, so all you need to do is take an item on the *Actual* statement and insert a link from it to the corresponding item on the *Comprehensive* statement.

Step 3: Once the financials are in the standardized format on the *Comprehensive* worksheet, the spreadsheet will condense them into statements on the *Condensed* sheet. These sheets have enough detail to accurately value a firm but do not have so much detail that the analysis becomes overly complicated. Chapter 10 and its appendix describe the *Condensed* statements.

Step 4: Before projecting a company's future financial statements, it is important to understand a company's current and past financial position. The *Hist Analys* worksheet begins this analysis by calculating the historical free cash flows and key ratios. The worksheet also provides an interactive graphing feature that allows you to see the historical performance of each key variable. Chapter 10 describes this process in detail.

Step 5: The *WACC* worksheet, explained in detail in Chapter 11, is structured to lead you through the calculation of the firm's cost of capital. Chapter 11 will also include some useful Internet resources for cost-of-capital calculations.

Step 6: To perform a valuation, you must project the financial statements by choosing key inputs, such as the growth rate in sales, the ratio of costs/sales, interest rates, etc. and enter your choices for key inputs on the *Inputs* worksheet, which is explained in Chapter 12.

Step 7: The *Proj & Val* worksheet takes your chosen inputs for the key ratios and projects the financial statements. Using these projections, it calculates free cash flows and performs a valuation analysis. Chapter 13 explains this in detail.

Spreadsheet Problems

9-1 Finding and Entering Actual Financial Data into the FCF Valuation Spreadsheet—Lowe's Companies

For this project, find historical financial statements for Lowe's (ticker LOW), and enter the financial data into the FCF valuation spreadsheet. We recommend using Thomson ONE-Business School Edition as the source of data for this project, although it not absolutely necessary.

a. The very first thing to do is start with a blank valuation spreadsheet from the book's web site. Save it as ***Lowe's.xls***, where Lowe's is the name of the company. Then we can start entering data without fear of corrupting the original blank version of the FCF valuation spreadsheet.

b. Use the Thomson ONE-Business School Edition database to obtain the 10-year history of financials for Lowe's. Of course, if fewer years are all that's available, then just obtain as much as possible. If you are using another source of data, you may have to piece together several documents in order to get a 10-year history. This should be put into a spreadsheet document with the last year first, as illustrated in the file ***Home Depot.xls***. This may take a while if the format of the company's financial statements changes slightly from year to year, as is often the case.

c. Paste the 10-year history into the *Actual* tab of the ***Lowe's.xls*** spreadsheet. If using Thomson data, be sure to first replace all cells showing NA with 0.

d. The next step is to map data from the *Actual* sheet to the *Comprehensive* sheet. If you are using the Thomson data, the mappings already provided will probably work fine, but it's a good idea to think about how Lowe's may be unusual in ways that call for a change in the mapping. For example, if it has a large amount of other assets on its balance sheet, you will have to decide whether they should be classified as operating assets or nonoperating assets. You will have to know something about the company in order to do this. You may have read parts of the firm's 10-K. If your data is from a source other than Thomson, you *must* check each entry and you *must* enter appropriate formulas. This is not difficult, but it will take a while; see the book's web site for a video demonstrating the process of mapping *Acutal* statements to the *Comprehensive* sheet.

e. Now look at the *Hist Analys* tab to see if all the ratios have been computed, which should happen automatically if the data has been entered properly into the *Actual* tab. If so, then you are finished with Lowe's for now, but you will return to this valuation problem as we work through the next four chapters of the book.

9-2 Finding and Entering Actual Financial Data into the FCF Valuation Spreadsheet—Another Company

For this project, repeat Project 9-1 using data for another company chosen by you or your instructor.

Appendix

9

Why We Condense the Financials

When we first began doing valuation analysis, we would create a custom spreadsheet for each job, using the particular financial statements of the company in question. Because no two sets of statements had exactly the same items, we would reinvent the wheel for each analysis. It finally occurred to us that we should base our analysis on a standardized set of financial statements. As long as our standardized statements had enough detail to handle any company's valuation, we could use exactly the same approach for projecting the statements, calculating free cash flows, and estimating the company's value. Therefore, we began putting each company's financial statements into our standardized financial format before we began our analysis. We called these the *Condensed* statements.

But we still had a problem because we had to take a company's *Actual* financial statements and condense them into our standardized format. This was hard! Every time we did this, we would have to relearn a lot of complex accounting and then make decisions that would allow us to compress the *Actual* financial statements in an economically meaningful manner. It finally occurred to us that we could add a step between the *Actual* statement of a company and the *Condensed* statements we wanted to use in our analysis. This step was the *Comprehensive* sheet. We found that it was pretty easy to put the *Actual* financial statements into the *Comprehensive* financial statements because we didn't have to make any difficult accounting decisions. All we had to do was take an item on the *Actual* statements and find one that matched on the *Comprehensive* financial statements. Because the *Comprehensive* statements were comprehensive, it was easy to find the match.

Once the *Actual* statements were in the *Comprehensive* statements, we could condense them into the *Condensed* statements using the same approach for all companies. The Chapter 10 appendix describes in excruciating, tedious detail how we condensed the statements, but here's an example to give you a flavor of the process.

Notice that the financial statements in the *Condensed* sheet have only one entry for short-term debt, called all current debt. On the other hand, the financial statements in the *Comprehensive* sheet have four categories of short-term debt: notes payable, current portion of long-term debt, current portion of capitalized leases, and all other short–term debt. If you look at the formula for all short-term debt in cell D42 of the *Condensed* sheet, you will see that it is the sum of all the short-term debt from the *Comprehensive* sheet.

=Comprehensive!B83+Comprehensive!B84+Comprehensive!B85+Comprehensive!B86

Having four categories of short-term debt will not provide any additional accuracy in determining the value of a company, but it definitely adds additional complexity. Because most companies will have short-term obligations in some combination of these four categories, once we have reformatted a particular firm's statements from the *Actual* to the *Comprehensive* format, the same formula for conversion into the *Condensed* format can be used. You might say we have automated this detail of the valuation process once the financials are translated into the *Comprehensive* format.

This logic for simplifying the valuation process works well for many items that might appear on actual statements, and so we let the trade-off between accuracy and complexity guide us when we set up the spreadsheet formulas for translating from the *Comprehensive* to the *Condensed* sheet. In other words, the *Condensed* statements are a simplified version of the *Comprehensive* statements, but are still rich enough to provide the basis for an accurate valuation. The key is to correctly map the complicated items from the *Comprehensive* statements into the *Condensed* statements in a way that captures the economic realities of the company. The *Condensed* sheet already has formulas that do this for you. For those of you with a keen interest in accounting, the appendix to Chapter 10 explains the rationale behind these formulas in detail.

Notice that if our spreadsheet required you to map the *Actual* statements for a complicated company directly into the *Condensed* statements, you would need a very strong background in accounting to do this correctly. Most people don't have (or want) such a detailed knowledge of accounting, and this is why we have the multistage procedure. In the first stage, you map the *Actual* statements into the *Comprehensive* statements. This should be fairly easy because the *Comprehensive* statements have a line for virtually any item that might be on an *Actual* statement. You don't have to make many decisions, you simply find the row in the *Comprehensive* statement that has the same name as the row in the *Actual* statement. It's okay if many rows in the *Comprehensive* statements are equal to zero; we would expect this because there are more lines in the *Comprehensive* financial statements than in the typical *Actual* statements. The spreadsheet does the second stage for you when it automatically maps the *Comprehensive* statements into the *Condensed* sheet.

Chapter 10

The Condensed Financial Statements and Historical Analysis

Introduction

The last chapter described how to put historical financial statements for an actual company into the ***Home Depot.xls*** corporate valuation spreadsheet. We also explained how to map the *Actual* financial statements into the *Comprehensive* worksheet. In terms of data preparation, our work is over. The spreadsheet will take the *Comprehensive* statements and automatically condense them into the *Condensed* sheet. It's not critical that you understand all of the accounting intricacies that provide the logic for the condensing of the *Comprehensive* statements, but if you are curious, see the appendix to this chapter, which explains the logic in detail.

This chapter will focus on the *Condensed* statements and how they are used, not how they were created. We'll explain the ways in which they differ from the statements used in the Van Leer example in Chapters 4–8. We'll also explain how to analyze a company's current and historical position as a prelude to a valuation analysis. In addition, we will show you how to find current financial and economic information that will be helpful when you project the financial statements in the next chapter.

The Condensed Statements

In our years of looking at the actual financial statements that companies submit to the Securities and Exchange Commission or publish in their annual reports, we have never seen any two companies with exactly the same names for the items they report or exactly the same number of reported items. Even worse, they sometimes report items in excruciating detail, such as listing several different types of short-term debt. While the distinction among types of short-term debt might be important for the creditors that provided the short-term financing, it isn't important when conducting a corporate valuation from the shareholders' point of view. Therefore, we have put the financial statements into a standardized format by consolidating those items that are redundant or that don't really require a separate line item. We call the resulting set of statements the condensed financial statements. They are a little more complicated than Van Leer's statements in Chapters 4–8 because we have added several items. In particular, we added items that (1) provide more detail and accuracy in reporting operating performance, (2) account for nonoperating performance, and (3) allow us to convert GAAP-based statements into free cash flows. To illustrate, let's take a look at the *Condensed* statements for an actual company, Home Depot.

Five years of historical data for Home Depot appear in Exhibit 10-1; you can also see this data and the 5 previous years in the file ***Home Depot.xls***. Notice that these financial statements have some items, which we have highlighted, that did not appear in Van Leer's financial statements. We added these items because they often appear in actual financial statements and because they affect valuation. In particular, we added the following items to the income statement: nonoperating income (expense), net income before extraordinary items, after-tax extraordinary income (expense), and preferred dividends. We added the following items to the balance sheet: other short-term operating assets, other long-term operating assets, long-term investments, other operating current liabilities, all short-term debt, deferred taxes, preferred stock, other long-term liabilities, and par plus paid-in-capital less treasury (and other adjustments). The following sections explain these items.

Additional Detail on Operating Performance

Only three new items on the balance sheet are related to operating performance. These are shown as other short-term operating assets, other long-term operating assets, and other operating current liabilities, as explained below.

Other Short-Term and Long-Term Operating Assets

Some firms have short-term operating assets that do not fit neatly into the cash, inventory, or accounts receivable categories. For example, some companies will make payroll advances to their employees. This would be like a short-term loan to the employee and might appear as a short-term term asset under either a separate advances to employees category, or more likely, in an other current assets category. We include a line item called other short-term operating assets to provide a catchall for such items.[1] Similarly, some firms have long-term operating assets that are not categorized as plant, property, and equipment. For example, goodwill and intangibles are often separately listed, as are deposits held by suppliers or deferred charges. We include the line item other long-term operating assets as a catchall line item for assets of these types.

Other Operating Current Liabilities

Just as on the asset side of the balance sheet, some firms have short-term operating liabilities that are not classified as accounts payable or accruals. We include a category called other operating current liabilities on the balance sheet to accommodate these types of liabilities.

---

[1]Often, the analyst's judgment is required in classifying some items as operating or nonoperating assets. For example, whereas payroll advances may be a routine and ongoing aspect of firms' operating policies, a large loan to a CEO would probably not be properly regarded as an operating asset.

Exhibit 10-1 Home Depot Inc.

Part 1—Condensed Income Statements (thousands of dollars)

	02/02/03 2003	02/03/02 2002	01/28/01 2001	01/30/00 2000	01/31/99 1999
Income Statement					
Sales	$58,247,000	$53,553,000	$45,738,000	$38,434,000	$30,219,000
Cost of goods sold (COGS)	39,236,000	36,642,000	31,456,000	26,560,000	21,241,000
Sales, general & administrative expense (SGA)	12,278,000	11,215,000	9,490,000	7,603,000	5,935,000
Depreciation	903,000	764,000	601,000	463,000	373,000
Operating profit	$ 5,830,000	$ 4,932,000	$ 4,191,000	$ 3,808,000	$ 2,670,000
Interest expense	37,000	28,000	21,000	41,000	46,000
Interest income	0	0	0	0	0
Nonoperating income (expense)	79,000	53,000	47,000	37,000	30,000
Earnings before taxes (EBT)	$ 5,872,000	$ 4,957,000	$ 4,217,000	$ 3,804,000	$ 2,654,000
Tax expense	2,208,000	1,913,000	1,636,000	1,484,000	1,040,000
Net income before extraordinary items	$ 3,664,000	$ 3,044,000	$ 2,581,000	$ 2,320,000	$ 1,614,000
After-tax extraordinary income (expense)	0	0	0	0	0
Net income (NI)	$ 3,664,000	$ 3,044,000	$ 2,581,000	$ 2,320,000	$ 1,614,000
Dividends—preferred	$ 0	$ 0	$ 0	$ 0	$ 0
Dividends—common	$ 492,000	$ 396,000	$ 371,000	$ 255,000	$ 168,000
Additions to RE	$ 3,172,000	$ 2,648,000	$ 2,210,000	$ 2,065,000	$ 1,446,000

Exhibit 10-1 Home Depot Inc. (continued)
Part 2—Condensed Balance Sheets (thousands of dollars)

	02/02/03 2003	02/03/02 2002	01/28/01 2001	01/30/00 2000	01/31/99 1999
Balance Sheet					
Assets					
Cash	$ 2,188,000	$ 2,477,000	$ 167,000	$ 168,000	$ 62,000
Inventory	8,338,000	6,725,000	6,556,000	5,489,000	4,293,000
Accounts receivable	1,072,000	920,000	835,000	587,000	469,000
Other short-term operating assets	254,000	170,000	209,000	144,000	109,000
Short-term investments	65,000	69,000	10,000	2,000	0
Total current assets	$11,917,000	$10,361,000	$ 7,777,000	$ 6,390,000	$ 4,933,000
Net plant, property, & equipment (PPE)	17,168,000	15,375,000	13,068,000	10,227,000	8,160,000
Other long-term operating assets	926,000	658,000	540,000	449,000	357,000
Long-term investments	0	0	0	15,000	15,000
Total assets	$30,011,000	$26,394,000	$21,385,000	$17,081,000	$13,465,000
Liabilities and Equity					
Accounts payable (AP)	$ 4,560,000	$ 3,436,000	$ 1,976,000	$ 1,993,000	$ 1,586,000
Accruals	2,477,000	2,209,000	1,755,000	1,634,000	1,257,000
Other operating current liabilities	998,000	851,000	650,000	0	0
All short-term debt	0	5,000	4,000	29,000	14,000
Total current liabilities	$ 8,035,000	$ 6,501,000	$ 4,385,000	$ 3,656,000	$ 2,857,000
Long-term debt	1,321,000	1,250,000	1,545,000	750,000	1,566,000
Deferred taxes	362,000	189,000	195,000	87,000	85,000
Preferred stock	0	0	0	0	0
Other long-term liabilities	491,000	372,000	256,000	247,000	217,000
Total liabilities	$10,209,000	$ 8,312,000	$ 6,381,000	$ 4,740,000	$ 4,725,000
Par plus PIC less treasury (and other adjustments)	3,832,716	5,284,716	4,854,716	4,401,716	2,865,716
Retained earnings (RE)	15,969,284	12,797,284	10,149,284	7,939,284	5,874,284
Total common equity	$19,802,000	$18,082,000	$15,004,000	$12,341,000	$ 8,740,000
Total liabilities and equity	$30,011,000	$26,394,000	$21,385,000	$17,081,000	$13,465,000

Additional Detail on Nonoperating Performance

The new items describing nonoperating performance are long-term investments, nonoperating income, after-tax extraordinary income, all short-term debt, other long-term liabilities, and preferred stock.

Long-Term Investments and Nonoperating Income

Thus far we have assumed that all of the firm's activities are related to operations, with the exception of short-term investments. However, many firms engage in activities that are not operating activities in the sense that they are not related to core operations. For example, many firms make small noncontrolling investments in other firms, particularly if these other firms have related products. For example, Microsoft has numerous small investments in other software firms. Because Microsoft doesn't control these firms, such investments are not directly related to Microsoft's operations. Since such investments are expected to be held for more than a year, they are classified as long-term investments. Many firms also have investments in real estate or other stocks and bonds, and these are also called long-term investments. The income from these investments is reported in the nonoperating income account.[2]

After-Tax Extraordinary Income

As the name suggests, this item represents the impact of activities or events that are not related to the firm's continuing operations. It includes such items as profits or losses from one-time events that firms would classify as extraordinary items, such as the settlement of a lawsuit, casualty losses due to flood, fire, or tornado, and gains or losses on the extinguishment of debt. These are examples of items that are not part of the firm's ordinary income-generating process. We also include in this account items that relate to a firm's decision to discontinue a segment of its operations, for example, the sale or closure of a subsidiary, division, or major segment of its business. These items aren't part of normal continuing operations, so they must be projected separately from operations. Because of these items, firms usually report net income before extraordinary items and then add after-tax extraordinary income (expense) to calculate net income. Notice that firms report these items on an after-tax basis.

All Short-Term Debt

Firms view long-term debt as different from short-term debt. Levels of short-term debt vary from year to year based on the short-term cash needs of the firm, and the levels are not always targeted in the same way that levels of long-term debt are

[2]As with short-term operating assets, the analyst's judgment is often required to make appropriate distinctions. For example, Coca-Cola Co. lists Investments and Other Assets as a category of assets. It includes its investments in numerous bottling companies in this category. The analyst must determine whether these are operating or nonoperating assets, which requires that the analyst have some understanding of the core competencies and long-term strategy of Coca-Cola. In our opinion, these investments are properly regarded as operating assets because Coca-Cola includes its share of the income from these companies in its net income and follows a strategy of creating shareholder wealth via purchase of these companies, improvement of their operating performance, and sale of its investment at a profit.

targeted. For this reason, when we get to Chapter 12 where we discuss the firm's financial policies, we will make projections based on the assumption that the firm wants to maintain, or achieve, a target level of long-term debt and that the firm uses short-term debt to meet any excess or unanticipated cash needs. Most firms also have many different types of short-term debt, but it is only the total amount that is relevant to our valuation. Therefore, the all short-term debt category includes all short-term debt and also the portion of the long-term debt that will come due within a year.

Other Long-Term Liabilities

Some firms have liabilities other than the ones we have already described. Remember, a liability is a claim that some investor other than a shareholder has on the assets owned by the firm. One example is minority interest. Suppose the company being valued owns a majority, but less than 100%, of a subsidiary firm. GAAP accounting requires that the financial statements of the subsidiary firm be consolidated: The income, assets, and liabilities of the subsidiary company are aggregated into the parent company's financial statements. The minority interest item that is reported as a liability of the parent represents that portion of the subsidiary's assets that belong to the minority shareholders in the subsidiary. If you're really interested in accounting, then check out the appendix to this chapter, where we explain this in detail. Because the exact nature of the claims usually is relatively unimportant when it comes to corporate valuation, we simply report a single line item called other long-term liabilities.

Par Plus PIC Less Treasury

In previous chapters we assumed that the firm was not going to issue additional stock or repurchase stock, so that its equity accounts only changed when retained earnings changed. However, with increasing frequency, firms are using stock repurchases as an alternative way of distributing cash to shareholders. The shares that have been repurchased by the firm, but not retired, are called treasury stock. Additionally, although firms do not issue large blocks of shares very frequently, it does happen occasionally. The cash received for selling this additional stock is often divided between two accounts, one account called Par and the other PIC, where PIC stands for paid-in-capital (or, alternately, capital surplus).[3] In addition, many firms now also raise new equity through dividend reinvestment plans (DRIPs) in which shareholders request that their dividends be reinvested in the company's stock. Because only the net effect of equity accounts is important for estimating intrinsic value, we simply have one account called par plus PIC less treasury.

[3]When firms issue stock, they divide the issue price into two pieces, par and paid-in-capital. For example, a firm might sell 1 million shares of stock for $20, raising a total of $20 million. It would probably declare a par value of $1 and add $1 million to the account called par (1 million shares of stock at a par value of $1 per share.) It would add the remaining $19 million to an account called paid-in-capital. Some firms have dropped this practice and simply show a single account for all cash raised by selling stock.

Preferred Stock

In previous chapters we made the simplifying assumption that the only sources of long-term capital for the firm were debt and equity. Preferred stock is another source of capital that is sometimes used, and we must explicitly include it in our projections when it is present. Preferred stockholders are preferred in the sense that they receive their dividends before the common stockholders (i.e., they have priority over common stockholders), but they typically do not have the right to vote. See the Chapter 4 appendix for a more detailed explanation of preferred stock.

Adjustments Due to GAAP

Our *Condensed* balance sheet shows an account called deferred taxes. Here is a quick and dirty explanation. Most firms have two sets of books, one for stockholders and one for the IRS. Firms typically make accounting choices to minimize taxable income for the IRS statements, but they are required to follow GAAP for reporting income to investors. This means that the taxes reported on the stockholder statements may be either more or less than the taxes the company actually pays, based on its IRS statements. For example, GAAP accounting suggests that firms use straight-line depreciation for calculating depreciation expense. Straight-line is simple—it merely assumes that an equal fraction of the purchase price of the asset should be used to amortize the initial cost of the asset over its economic life. GAAP also requires that the taxes shown on the firm's income statement reflect the taxes that the firm *would* pay if it used straight-line depreciation when it filed its tax returns. But when estimating taxable income, the IRS allows firms to use accelerated depreciation, which allows firms to claim a higher percentage of the asset's cost in the early part of the asset's life and a smaller percentage in the latter part of the asset's life. Of course, no matter which method is used, only 100% of the cost of the asset is ultimately depreciated, but under accelerated depreciation, the company has more depreciation expense early in the life of the asset, less later. As a result, in any given year, there is a difference between the taxes that a company reports on its GAAP income statement (which is the one that we see) and the taxes that the company actually pays (determined by the income statement prepared for the IRS).[4]

You and I could probably come up with a simple way to handle this (such as modifying GAAP to make it consistent with tax accounting, as is done in some countries), but in the United States, GAAP creates a new liability account called deferred taxes, which is the cumulative difference between the taxes the company has reported paying and the taxes it actually paid.[5] Almost all companies have a deferred taxes account, and the difference between taxes reported under GAAP and

[4]Naturally, you may ask yourself why the Congress would have conjured up the idea of anything other than straight-line depreciation. The purpose was to spur investment by allowing firms to accelerate the tax savings that result from the depreciation expense (often referred to as depreciation tax shield). Remember the adage "timing is everything"!

[5]The logic (if there really is any) behind this is that the company will eventually have to pay the taxes it has reported but not yet paid, and so the IRS has a claim against the company. In some companies, the payments reported are less than the taxes actually paid, in which case the difference is recorded as a deferred tax asset, instead of a liability. In addition to depreciation-related differences between reported and actual taxes paid, any difference in timing of reporting revenue or expense under GAAP accounting versus reporting under the tax law will result in a difference between reported taxes and taxes actually paid, hence, in changes to the deferred tax account.

taxes actually paid matters when we estimate the company's free cash flow, as we show in the next section. Therefore, we include it on our *Condensed* statements.

Calculating Free Cash Flow

Recall that the rationale for including the new items in the condensed financial statements was to (1) provide more detail and accuracy in reporting operating performance, (2) account for nonoperating performance, and (3) allow us to convert GAAP-based statements into free cash flows. Obviously, the changes in the reporting format have implications for the calculation of net operating profit after taxes (NOPAT), total operating capital, and free cash flow for each year. This section describes these changes. All calculations are shown in the *Hist Analys* worksheet (short for Historical Analysis).

NOPAT Calculation

The NOPAT calculation for an actual company is a bit more complicated than we discussed in Chapter 4. The simplest way to calculate NOPAT is EBIT(1 – T), where EBIT is earnings before interest and taxes and T is the corporate tax rate. However, for a variety of reasons that we will describe below, this doesn't always work well for actual companies. Instead, the more appropriate approach is to calculate operating profits and then remove the taxes that should be attributed to operating profits, hence the all-so-clever name net operating profit after taxes. (I suppose you have already figured out that one of the gifts that finance specialists have is coming up with clever names for calculations.)

Operating profits are sales less cost of goods sold, SGA, and depreciation. This isn't exactly EBIT, because most companies include some nonoperating income items when calculating EBIT. However, our previous efforts in translating the actual reported financials into the condensed financials will now pay off by making it pretty easy to calculate pre-tax operating profits. Three factors that complicate the calculation of the taxes on operating income are explained below.

Marginal Tax Rates

First, in the United States, there isn't really a single tax rate, T. Corporations and individuals face a progressive tax structure where the rate paid on an additional dollar of income is often higher than the average rate. This rate on the additional dollar of income is called the marginal tax rate. For example, a corporation earning between $100,000 and $335,000 will pay $22,250 plus 39% of the difference between the pre-tax income and $100,000. Every dollar over $100,000 is taxed at a marginal rate of 39%, but the average tax rate on income of $250,000, for example, is 32.3% = ($22,250 + 0.39 × ($250,000 – $100,000))/$250,000 = $80,750/$250,000. For large companies, those with pre-tax incomes over $18,333,333, the marginal federal tax rate is equal to the average federal tax rate of 35%. For Home Depot, the average tax rate (which includes any additional state taxes) has been about 38.6%, as shown in the *Hist Analys* worksheet.

Differences in Reported Taxes and Actual Taxes

Second, for a real company, the taxes reported are not equal to the taxes paid, as we explained earlier in this chapter. The difference between these two numbers—the cash taxes paid and the fictitious taxes reported to shareholders—is accumulated in the deferred taxes account on the balance sheet. For growing companies, the difference usually results in deferred tax liabilities. Doesn't this sound confusing? And especially, wouldn't you as a shareholder really like to know the actual amount of income earned and taxes paid, not a made-up amount? Well, that's GAAP accounting! It may be confusing and misleading (for non-accountants), but at least it is consistently so! The good news is that you can easily get a fairly accurate estimate of the amount of taxes actually paid by the company. First, subtract the previous year's deferred tax liability from this year's deferred tax liability. If this is positive (deferred taxes increased), then the company actually paid less than it reported. If the difference is negative (i.e., deferred taxes fell from the previous year's level), then the company actually paid more than it reported. To find the actual taxes that were paid, start with the reported taxes and subtract the change in the deferred tax account. In formula form this is

$$\text{Actual taxes paid} = \text{Reported taxes} - \text{Change in deferred tax liability from the previous year.} \quad \textbf{(10-1)}$$

Taxes on Nonoperating Income

Third, these reported and actual taxes include taxes paid on interest income, tax savings due to interest expenses, and taxes paid on other nonoperating income. In calculating NOPAT, we only want to know the taxes paid on operating income. To correct for these nonoperating items, we calculate taxes on operations as

$$\text{Tax on operating income} = \text{Actual taxes} + \text{Taxes saved because of interest deductions} - \text{Taxes paid on interest income} - \text{Taxes paid on nonoperating income.} \quad \textbf{(10-2)}$$

The taxes saved because of interest deductions are equal to interest expense multiplied by the marginal tax rate, the taxes paid on interest income are equal to interest income multiplied by the marginal tax rate, and taxes paid on non-operating income are equal to the nonoperating income (or expense) multiplied by the marginal tax rate.

After calculating the tax on operating income, we define NOPAT as

$$\text{NOPAT} = \text{Operating profit} - \text{Tax on operating income.} \quad \textbf{(10-3)}$$

In addition, we will also explicitly include extraordinary income in a second measure we call NOPAT adjusted for extraordinary income. The reason we need to add extraordinary income to NOPAT before calculating free cash flow is that even though extraordinary income does not result from ongoing operations and may not be expected to continue, it is available to shareholders and bondholders (after taxes have been paid on it) in any year in which it appears and so contributes to the value of the firm.[6]

[6]However, as the name suggests, extraordinary income is by nature very difficult to forecast, and we will often reasonably project it to be zero for future periods. Exceptions would be items that we have some reasonable basis for projecting, such as planned dispositions of subsidiaries or major assets and litigation claims settlements.

Free Cash Flow Calculations

Recall that free cash flow is NOPAT (for our company, adjusted for extraordinary income) less investment in total operating capital. From the condensed financials format, total operating capital is easy to calculate.

Total operating capital = Net operating working capital + Operating long-term capital

From the condensed balance sheet line items in Exhibit 10-1, operating current assets consist of all current assets except short-term investments. Operating liabilities are all current liabilities except short-term debt, and operating long-term capital is the rest of the long-term assets (net PPE and other long-term operating assets) except long-term investments.

Exhibit 10-2 shows the free cash flow calculations for Home Depot for the last 5 years; these and the previous 5 years are also shown in the file ***Home Depot.xls*** (see the *Hist Analys* sheet). The calculations show the levels of NOPAT adjusted for extraordinary income, the components of total operating capital and the investment in total operating capital in each year, and the free cash flow calculation. In addition, we show the resulting return on invested capital (ROIC), which is NOPAT divided by the beginning of period operating capital, as well as the past economic profits.

Notice that Home Depot has had negative FCFs up until 2002, which is not at all unusual for a rapidly growing company. In fact, most companies have negative or very low free cash flows when they are growing rapidly because of the large capital requirements needed to fund the increasing asset base. Once sales and asset growth decline, we would expect Home Depot's profitability to be enough to generate positive free cash flows, which is what happened in 2002 and 2003.

Take a look at Home Depot's past return on invested capital. Notice that ROIC has been substantially greater than its weighted average cost of capital (around 19% ROIC versus a WACC of around 8% to 10%). Thus, despite the negative free cash flows, growth is actually adding value to the firm. Home Depot's economic profit, which you will recall is calculated as NOPAT – WACC(Capital at the beginning of the year), also shows this additional value. Economic profit measures the amount of value the year's operations have added to the company, considering the fact that investors require a return of WACC on the capital invested in the firm. Economic profit is positive whenever ROIC is greater than WACC, and Home Depot's economic profit ranged from $750 million to over $2 billion during the 5 years shown in Exhibit 10-2.

For many firms—especially those in mature or declining industries—ROIC is less than WACC and growth is not profitable. The paradox for these firms is that even though they may be earning positive accounting profits, positive NOPAT, and generating positive free cash flows, they are not generating enough NOPAT to compensate investors for the use of their capital. For these firms, growth actually destroys firm value, and they would be better off returning the NOPAT that they generate to shareholders and bondholders in the form of debt repayments, dividends, and share repurchases, rather than reinvesting it in the company. Kmart is an example of a company that tried to grow out of its problems throughout the 1990s. With the exception of 1993, Kmart generated positive free cash flows and managed very

Exhibit 10-2 Historical Free Cash Flows for Home Depot (thousands of dollars)

	2003	2002	2001	2000	1999
Historical Free Cash Flow (FCF)					
Assumed marginal tax rate	37.6%	38.6%	38.8%	39.0%	39.2%
Reported income tax expense	2,208,000	1,913,000	1,636,000	1,484,000	1,040,000
Taxes reported but not paid	173,000	(6,000)	108,000	2,000	7,000
Actual taxes paid	2,035,000	1,919,000	1,528,000	1,482,000	1,033,000
Plus tax saved due to net interest expenses	13,913	10,806	8,147	15,995	18,026
Minus tax paid on nonoperating income	29,706	20,454	18,234	14,434	11,756
Tax on operating income	2,019,207	1,909,352	1,517,913	1,483,560	1,039,270
Net operating profit after taxes (NOPAT)	3,810,793	3,022,648	2,673,087	2,324,440	1,630,730
NOPAT/sales	6.5%	5.6%	5.8%	6.0%	5.4%
NOPAT adjusted for extraordinary income	3,810,793	3,022,648	2,673,087	2,324,440	1,630,730
Operating current assets	11,852,000	10,292,000	7,767,000	6,388,000	4,933,000
Operating current liabilities	8,035,000	6,496,000	4,381,000	3,627,000	2,843,000
Net operating working capital	3,817,000	3,796,000	3,386,000	2,761,000	2,090,000
Operating long-term capital	18,094,000	16,033,000	13,608,000	10,676,000	8,517,000
Operating capital	21,911,000	19,829,000	16,994,000	13,437,000	10,607,000
Operating capital/sales	37.6%	37.0%	37.2%	35.0%	35.1%
Investment in operating capital	2,082,000	2,835,000	3,557,000	2,830,000	1,843,000
Free cash flow from ongoing operations	1,728,793	187,648	(883,913)	(505,560)	(212,270)
Free cash flow (including extraordinary income)	$ 1,728,793	$ 187,648	$ (883,913)	$ (505,560)	$ (212,270)
Historical Return on Invested Capital					
ROIC (NOPAT/Beginning capital)	19.2%	17.8%	19.9%	21.9%	18.6%
Historical Economic Profit					
Historical weighted average costs of capital	8%	9%	10%	10%	10%
Economic profit	**$ 2,224,473**	**$ 1,493,188**	**$ 1,329,387**	**$ 1,263,740**	**$ 754,330**

Note: All calculations were performed in a spreadsheet model, so some reported sums in the exhibit may not total exactly due to rounding.

modest sales growth rates of 2% or 3% per year. But its ROIC during that period never exceeded its weighted average cost of capital. In the process, the shareholder wealth that existed at the beginning of that decade was lost.

Analyzing Home Depot's Past and Present Condition

Exhibit 10-1 showed the last 5 years' financial statements for Home Depot, and Exhibit 10-2 showed free cash flow, ROIC, and economic profit for the last 5 years. Sometimes it is much more efficient to analyze a company by looking at a graph of ratios over time, rather than looking at the numbers themselves. For example, the calculations in Exhibit 10-2 represent a great deal of data, and it is helpful to view these in charts. We have made it easy for you to select the number of years you want to view and to quickly view a chart of the data you are analyzing. See Exhibit 10-3, which shows the first several rows in the *Hist Analys* worksheet.

First, notice that cell B6 provides a place for you to enter the number of years of data that you want to view (cells in the spreadsheet are coded by color: yellow is for cells in which you must either enter data or accept the default data, green is for cells in which the spreadsheet performs an intermediate calculation, and tan is for results). We usually use all 10 years of available data, unless there are unusual circumstances. For example, if a company made a major change (such as a major acquisition) 6 years ago, then we might choose to use only the last 6 years instead of the full 10 years.

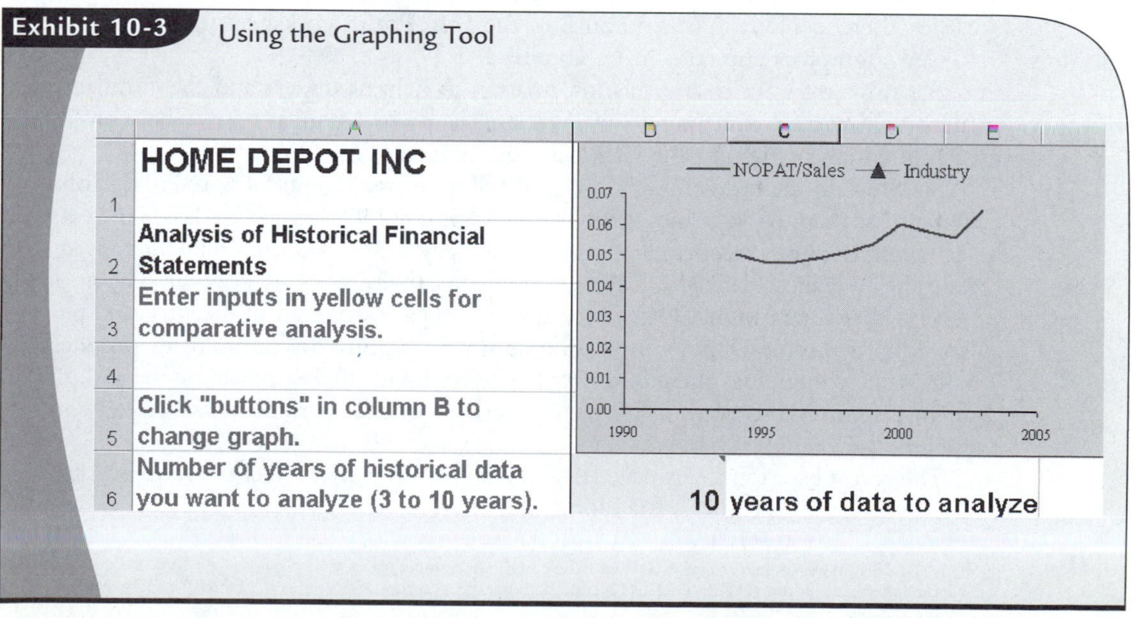

Exhibit 10-3 Using the Graphing Tool

Second, notice the graph in Exhibit 10-3. It shows the ratio of NOPAT to sales for Home Depot for the number of years you specified in cell B6; the chart also shows the industry average for the ratio, if it is available. For Home Depot, there is no available industry average ratio for NOPAT/sales, but Home Depot's own ratio has been increasing, indicating that Home Depot has been steadily improving its operating profitability. To see a chart for another ratio, scroll down the *Hist Analys* worksheet and look in column B. We have placed "radio buttons" next to certain data that you may want to view in a graph; pointing at one of the buttons and clicking on it causes the corresponding graph of the historical measures to appear at the top of the spreadsheet.

In Chapter 12 you will have to choose inputs for key ratios when projecting Home Depot's financial statements. Later in this chapter we will analyze some of the traditional ratios you may have encountered in other finance books, but for now we want to focus upon the ratios required to project Home Depot's financial statements.

Analysis of Ratios Required to Project Financial Statements

Exhibit 10-4 reports 5 years of historical values for the ratios that we will use to project the *Condensed* statements in Chapter 12; 10 years of historical values are shown in ***Home Depot.xls***. In addition to the ratios for each year, Exhibit 10-4 also has columns labeled Average and Trend. For example, Home Depot's sales growth in each of the years 1999 through 2002 has been 25.1%, 27.2%, 19.0%, and 17.1%. In the most recent year, 2003, sales grew 8.8%. The average growth rate during the full 10-year period is 22.9%.[7] The Trend column gives the predicted sales growth if the current trend continues, based on a trend line.[8] Exhibit 10-5 shows the actual sales growth rates for 1999 through 2003, the trend line, and the predicted values based on this trend line for the years 2004 and 2005. As indicated earlier, there is a button in column B of the *Hist Analys* worksheet that allows you to view a graph of any ratio in Exhibit 10-4.

For now, we want to use this information to help us understand the company's current situation. In Chapter 12, we will use the insights gained here to help project each line item on the income statement and balance sheet.

So what do the ratios in Exhibit 10-4 tell us about Home Depot? First, Home Depot has had strong sales growth, averaging 22.9% over the last 10 years. However, the most recent year's growth was only 8.8%, and the Trend value is less than the Average (11.5% vs. 22.9%), indicating that growth is slowing. The good news is that the ratio of COGS/sales appears to have declined in recent years, perhaps due to Home Depot's increasing ability to capture discounts from suppliers as its sales volume has increased. On the other hand, there appears to be a slight upward trend in the ratio of SGA/sales, perhaps due to extra costs associated with opening new stores.

The second section in Exhibit 10-4 shows the ratios that affect operating capital. The two biggest categories for Home Depot are inventory and net PPE. The ratio

---

[7]This is the arithmetic average, calculated using Excel's AVERAGE function.

[8]We used the Excel function, TREND. This function fits a linear regression, with year as the x variable and growth rate as the y variable.

Exhibit 10-4 Historical Ratios

	Historical Values for Ratios Used to Project Financial Statements						
			2003	2002	2001	2000	1999
Ratios to calculate operating profit	**Average**	**Trend**	**Most Recent**				
Sales growth rate	22.9%	11.5%	8.8%	17.1%	19.0%	27.2%	25.1%
COGS/sales	69.9%	67.5%	67.4%	68.4%	68.8%	69.1%	70.3%
SGA/sales	20.2%	20.8%	21.1%	20.9%	20.7%	19.8%	19.6%
Depreciation/net PPE	4.4%	5.3%	5.3%	5.0%	4.6%	4.5%	4.6%
Ratios to calculate operating capital	**Average**	**Trend**	**Most Recent**				
Cash/sales	1.2%	3.1%	3.8%	4.6%	0.4%	0.4%	0.2%
Inventory/sales	14.1%	13.9%	14.3%	12.6%	14.3%	14.3%	14.2%
Accts. rec./sales	1.9%	1.6%	1.8%	1.7%	1.8%	1.5%	1.6%
Other short-term operating assets/sales	0.3%	0.4%	0.4%	0.3%	0.4%	0.3%	0.3%
Net PPE/sales	27.7%	29.0%	29.5%	28.7%	28.6%	26.6%	27.0%
Other long-term op. A./sales	1.2%	1.4%	1.6%	1.2%	1.2%	1.2%	1.2%
Accts. pay./sales	5.7%	6.3%	7.8%	6.4%	4.3%	5.2%	5.2%
Accruals/sales	4.2%	4.0%	4.3%	4.1%	3.8%	4.3%	4.2%
Other current liabilities/sales	0.5%	1.6%	1.7%	1.6%	1.4%	0.0%	0.0%
Ratios to calculate operating taxes	**Average**	**Trend**	**Most Recent**				
Deferred taxes/net PPE	1.2%	1.7%	2.1%	1.2%	1.5%	0.9%	1.0%
Average tax rate (taxes/EBT)	38.6%	38.6%	37.6%	38.6%	38.8%	39.0%	39.2%
Marginal tax rate	38.6%	38.6%	37.6%	38.6%	38.8%	39.0%	39.2%
Dividend growth ratio	**Average**	**Trend**	**Most Recent**				
Dividend policy: growth rate	29.5%	25.5%	24.2%	6.7%	45.5%	51.8%	20.9%
Ratios to calculate rest of income statement and balance sheet	**Average**	**Trend**	**Most Recent**				
Nonop. inc./sales	0.1%	0.0%	0.1%	0.1%	0.1%	0.1%	0.1%
Extr. inc./sales	0.0%	0.0%	0.0%	0.0%	0.0%	0.0%	0.0%
Long-term investments/sales	0.4%	-0.7%	0.0%	0.0%	0.0%	0.0%	0.0%
Other long-term liab./sales	0.8%	0.8%	0.8%	0.7%	0.6%	0.6%	0.7%

Exhibit 10-5 The Trend Line for Home Depot's Sales Growth Rates

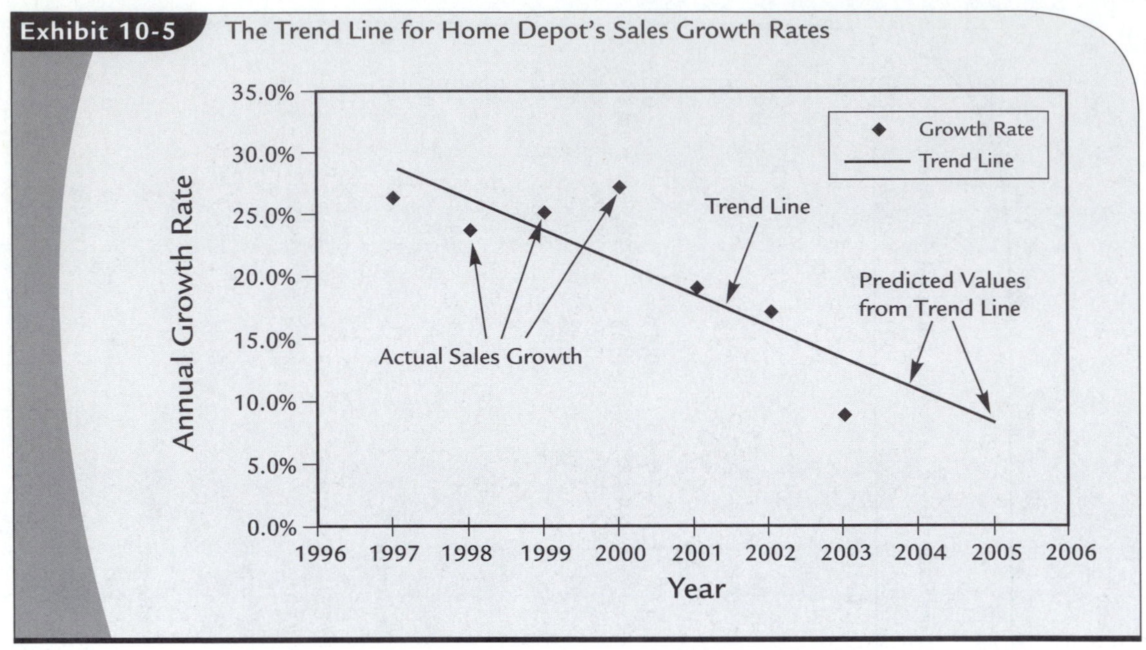

of inventory/sales appears to be quite stable, while the ratio of net PPE/sales has been slightly increasing, possibly due to opening new stores that do not immediately reach full capacity sales.

The third section of Exhibit 10-4 shows ratios related to taxes. Home Depot's tax rate has been very stable, at about 38.6%. This seems a little high; a more detailed analysis of a company's financial statement footnotes often provides additional information about its tax situation.[9]

The fourth section of Exhibit 10-4 shows the dividend growth rate. Home Depot's dividends have been growing rapidly, averaging a 29.5% growth rate during this 10-year period.

The fifth section of Exhibit 10-4 shows the historical ratios related to nonoperating items. These are very small, and so will not have a large impact on Home Depot's projected financial statements.

In summary, these ratios show that Home Depot has been growing rapidly, with a slightly favorable trend in COGS. The trends for SGA and net PPE have been slightly unfavorable, but this could be temporary, due to the rapid expansion. Exhibit 10-2 showed that Home Depot's ROIC has been quite large, around 19% in 2003, indicating that Home Depot's growth adds value to the company. The rapid growth prior to 2002 had caused negative free cash flows. However, the decline in the rate of sales growth, which reduced the need for investment in operating capital, along with the improvement in COGS/sales over the last 2 years, has resulted in positive free cash flows.

[9]Many firms have a detailed breakdown of their taxes as a footnote to their financials. For 2001, Home Depot's footnote on its taxes reveals a 35% average tax rate for its federal taxes, 3.5% for state income taxes, and 0.3% for other taxes.

Analysis of Traditional Ratios as Compared to Competitors

In the previous section we analyzed the historical ratios that will be needed to project Home Depot's financial statements in Chapter 12. However, it is also important to examine Home Depot's position relative to other firms in its industry. Ideally, we would like to see industry ratios for the same ratios needed to project financial statements. Unfortunately, most sources don't report these, but instead report industry ratios in a "traditional" form, such as you may have encountered in other finance books. However, this traditional ratio analysis does provide additional information to help us understand Home Depot's current position.

The first step is to obtain industry ratios. An easy way to do this is through **http://finance.yahoo.com**. If you go to this web site, you will see a dialog box that allows you to enter a ticker symbol and get quotes. If you enter Home Depot's ticker symbol (HD), you will get a page with the current stock price. When we did this, we got a box with the information shown in Exhibit 10-6.

Web pages change frequently, so you may not get a box that is identical to this one, but you should still see links to the same information. All of these links provide valuable information, but we especially encourage you to check out the links for News, Profile, and Research. As you might expect from their names, these links provide current information about Home Depot, including analysts' forecasts of earnings.

If you select the link for Profile, you will get a very informative web page. It has a nice business summary, a listing of the company's officers, and a very helpful section called Statistics at a Glance, as shown in Exhibit 10-7.

These statistics provide a nice snapshot of the company's current condition, including a number of ratios. However, we really need to compare these ratios with other firm's ratios in its industry, and Yahoo! provides a way for us to do this. If you go to the Profile web page, you will see a number of links on the left side. These links are shown in Exhibit 10-8.

Two of these are especially useful. The first is Historical Quote Data. If you select this link, you will get a dialog box that allows you to obtain past stock prices. In addition to actual prices, you will see a column for Adjusted Price. This column automatically adjusts the price for stock splits and dividend payments. For example, suppose

Exhibit 10-6 Yahoo! Financial Stock Quotes Box

Symbol	Last Trade		Change		Volume
HD	2:13pm	**32.35**	-0.73	-2.21%	4,486,800

Chart, Financials, Historical Prices, Industry, Insider, Messages, News
Options, Profile, Reports, Research, SEC Filings, **more...**

Exhibit 10-7 Statistics at a Glance

Statistics at a Glance – NYSE:HD As of 6-June-2003

Price and Volume	
52-Week Low on 29-Jan.-2003	$20.10
Recent Price	$32.86
52-Week High on 11-June-2002	$40.90
Beta	1.36
Daily Volume (3-month avg)	10.8M
Daily Volume (10-day avg)	9.13M
Stock Performance	
52-Week Change	–15.4%
52-Week Change relative to S&P 500	–12.0%
Share-Related Items	
Market Capitalization	$75.4B
Shares Outstanding	2.29B
Float	2.20B
Dividends & Splits	
Account Dividend (indicated)	$0.24
Dividend Yield	0.73%
Last Split factor 1.5 on 31-Dec-1999	

Per-Share Data	
Book Value (mrq*)	$9.02
Earnings (ttm)	$1.59
Earnings (mrq)	$0.40
Sales (ttm)	$25.37
Cash (mrq*)	$1.89
Valuation Ratios	
Price/Book (mrq*)	3.64
Price/Earnings (ttm)	20.63
Price/Sales (ttm)	1.29
Income Statements	
Sales (ttm)	$59.1B
EBITDA (ttm*)	$5.92B
Income available to common (ttm)	$3.71B
Profitability	
Profit Margin (ttm)	6.3%
Operating Margin (ttm)	10.0%
Fiscal Year	
Fiscal Year Ends	Feb 2
Most recent quarter (fully updated)	4-May-2003
Most recent quarter (flash earnings)	30-Apr-2003

Management Effectiveness	
Return on Assets (ttm)	11.83%
Return on Equity (ttm)	18.59%
Financial Strength	
Current Ratio (mrq*)	1.40
Debt/Equity (mrq*)	0.06
Total Cash (mrq*)	$4.34B
Short Interest As of 8-May-2003	
Shares Short	30.2K
Percent of Float	1.4%
Shares Short (Prior Month)	28.7K
Short Ratio	3.07
Daily Volume	9.82K

See Profile Help for a description of each item above; K = thousands; M = millions; B = billions; mrq = most recent quarter; ttm = trading twelve months; (as of 30-Apr.-2003, except mrq*/ttm* items as of 4-May-3003)

Reproduced with permission of Yahoo! Inc. © 2003 by Yahoo! Inc. YAHOO! and the YAHOO! logo are trademarks of Yahoo! Inc.

the actual price for a company at the end of June had been $10 per share and the actual price at the end of May had been $18 per share, but there had been a two-for-one stock split in mid-June. This stock split means that there were twice as many shares of stock in June as there were in May. Rather than report the actual price in May, the adjusted price for May is the price that would have been reported in May if there had been the same number of shares in May as in June. Since there were twice as many shares in June, the adjusted price for May is the actual price divided by 2, or $9 = $18/2. This makes it easy to calculate the rate of return for June. Using the adjusted price of $9 in May, the return in June was 11.11% = 0.1111 = ($10 – $9)/$9. Notice that for the most recent month, the adjusted price and actual price are the same.

A similar adjustment is made for dividends. For example, suppose the actual price for a company at the end of June had been $10 per share, a $1 dividend had been paid in July, and the actual price at the end of July had been $12 per share. The total return for July would be 30% = 0.30 = ($12 + $1 – $10)/$10. The adjusted price for June would be reported as $9.231 = $12/(1.30).[10] Notice that

[10]All adjusted prices in previous months would also be adjusted to reflect the new adjusted price in June.

the percentage change in the adjusted price is 30% = 0.30 = ($12 – $9.231)/$9.231. To summarize, you can always find the rate of return by calculating the percentage change in adjusted prices, even if there has been a stock split or a dividend payment.

The second really useful link is Ratio Comparisons. Selecting this link will take you to a web page sponsored by Multex Investor. This page has some links to news and research reports on the company, but most importantly, it has a section of ratios for the company, the company's industry, the company's business sector, and the S&P 500. This makes it very easy to compare your company with other companies. Exhibit 10-9 shows some selected ratios from this page for Home Depot.

TTM indicates the ratio is for the "trailing twelve months," while MRQ stands for "most recent quarter." Home Depot's dividend payout ratio is

Payout ratio = Dividends/Net income **(10-4)**

and is slightly higher than the industry average, but much less than the typical firm in the S&P 500. Sales growth has been low in comparison to its industry, but comparable to the S&P 500.

Exhibit 10-8 Yahoo! Profile Links

Financial Links

- Top Institutional Holders
- Top Mutual Fund Holders
- Analyst Upgrade/Downgrade History
- Historical Quote Data
- Raw SEC Filings at sec.gov

Competitors:

- Sector: Services
- Industry: Retail (Home Improvement)

Company Websites

- Home Page
- Yahoo! Category
- Search Yahoo! for related links...

Index Membership

- Dow Industrials
- S&P 500

Ownership

- **Insider and 5%+ Owners:** 5%
- Over the last 6 months:
  - 3 insider buys; 4,000 shares
  - 3 insider sells; 343.0K shares (0.3% of insider shares)
- **Institutional:** 60% (63% of float) (2,782 institutions)
- **Net Inst. Buying:** 42.5M shares (+2.95%) (prior quarter to last quarter)

More From Multex

- Highlights
- Performance
- Ratio Comparisons

Reproduced with permission of Yahoo! Inc. © 2003 by Yahoo! Inc. YAHOO! and the YAHOO! logo are trademarks of Yahoo! Inc.

The current ratio is

Current ratio = Total current assets/Total current liabilities. **(10-5)**

The quick ratio is

Quick ratio = (Total current assets – Inventory)/(Total current liabilities). **(10-6)**

Both are measures of liquidity, in the sense that they measure the amount of short-term assets that could be quickly converted to cash relative to the short-term obligations. Home Depot's ratios are comparable to its industry peers, although the quick ratio is significantly less than the S&P 500's. This could pose greater risk to a lender if Home Depot's inventory is not easy to sell. But since construction supplies don't tend to spoil or become technologically obsolete, it is likely that a creditor could easily sell Home Depot's inventory. Thus, Home Depot does not appear to have a problem with liquidity.

Home Depot's debt ratios are very low, both with respect to its industry and the S&P 500. Its ratio of total debt to equity is only 6 percent compared to the industry average of 19 percent and the S&P 500's ratio of 108 percent. Its interest coverage ratio is defined as

$$\text{Interest coverage ratio} = \text{Operating profit/Net interest expense} \quad \textbf{(10-7)}$$

and is quite high at over 123. This means that Home Depot has $123 of operating profit to cover each dollar of interest expense, confirming our conclusion that Home Depot doesn't have very much debt.[11]

Five profit margin ratios are reported in Exhibit 10-9, starting with the gross profit margin.

$$\text{Gross margin} = (\text{Sales} - \text{COGS})/\text{Sales} \quad \textbf{(10-8)}$$

Home Depot's gross margin is comparable to its industry average. EBITD is earnings before interest, taxes, and depreciation. The EBITD margin is

$$\text{EBITD margin} = (\text{Sales} - \text{COGS} - \text{SGA})/\text{Sales} \quad \textbf{(10-9)}$$

and is comparable to the industry. The operating margin is

$$\text{Operating margin} = \text{Operating profit/Sales} \quad \textbf{(10-10)}$$

and is slightly higher than the industry average (10.02% vs. 9.67%). The pre-tax margin is

$$\text{Pre-tax margin} = \text{Earnings before taxes/Sales} \quad \textbf{(10-11)}$$

[11]We can often get help in assessing the financial market's view of debt risk by using ratings for corporate bonds. In Home Depot's case, Moody's currently rates its two publicly traded bond issues as Aa3, and Standard & Poor's rates them as AA, which is roughly equivalent—both ratings imply high grade, high quality bonds. Of course, these ratings may change as market conditions change. Check out **http://www.moodys.com** for the latest ratings.

Exhibit 10-9 Selected Ratio Comparisons for Home Depot

	Company	Industry	Sector	S&P 500
Payout ratio (TTM)	13.77	11.49	16.76	26.85
Sales (TTM) vs. TTM 1 yr. ago	6.17	9.46	12.06	7.26
Sales—5 yr. growth rate	19.25	18.48	18.70	9.98
Quick ratio (MRQ)	0.52	0.48	0.92	1.24
Current ratio (MRQ)	1.40	1.42	1.47	1.75
LT debt to equity (MRQ)	0.06	0.19	0.80	0.73
Total debt to equity (MRQ)	0.06	0.19	0.93	1.08
Interest coverage (TTM)	123.25	14.35	7.01	11.60
Gross margin (TTM)	31.45	31.66	42.03	47.12
EBITD margin (TTM)	10.02	10.71	22.76	20.22
Operating margin (TTM)	10.02	9.67	13.41	18.40
Pre-tax margin (TTM)	10.06	9.69	11.09	16.56
Net profit margin (TTM)	6.29	6.06	7.90	11.95
Return on assets (TTM)	11.83	11.01	5.86	6.26
Receivable turnover (TTM)	48.96	46.73	16.80	9.70
Inventory turnover (TTM)	5.00	4.80	16.66	9.95
Asset turnover (TTM)	1.88	1.82	1.14	0.94

Source: Yahoo! Finance/Multex Investor (***http://yahoo.multexinvestor.com***)

and is again slightly higher than the industry average (10.06% vs. 9.69%). Finally, the net profit margin is

$$\text{Net profit margin} = \text{Net income/Sales} \qquad \textbf{(10-12)}$$

and is slightly higher for Home Depot than the industry average (6.29% vs. 6.06%).

The final four ratios tell us how efficiently Home Depot uses its assets. The return on assets is defined as

$$\text{Return on assets} = \text{Net income/Total assets} \qquad \textbf{(10-13)}$$

and is almost a full percentage point higher for Home Depot than the industry average (11.83% vs. 11.01%). The receivable turnover ratio is

$$\text{Receivable turnover} = \text{Sales/Accounts receivable} \qquad \textbf{(10-14)}$$

and is comparable to the industry. The inventory turnover ratio is

$$\text{Inventory turnover} = \text{COGS/Inventory} \qquad \textbf{(10-15)}$$

and is a little better than the industry average (5.0% vs. 4.8%). Finally, the asset turnover ratio is

$$\text{Asset turnover} = \text{Sales/Total assets} \qquad \textbf{(10-16)}$$

and is slightly higher than the industry average (1.88% vs. 1.82%).

In summary, the comparative ratio analysis reveals that Home Depot is a little more profitable than its industry peers, utilizes its assets a little better than its peers, and has much less debt than its peers.

Exhibit 10-10 Graphing Buttons for Industry Comparisons in the *Hist Analys* Worksheet

Traditional Ratio Analysis: Fill in yellow cells with ratios for industry or for closest competitor for most recent year.	Graph	Most Recent Industry or Competitor	Company's Historical Average	Trend	Most Recent
Payout ratio	Payout Ratio	11.49%	12.0%	13.4%	13.4%
Annual sales growth rate	Sales g	9.46%	22.9%	11.5%	8.8%
Quick ratio	Quick Ratio	0.48	0.40	0.34	0.45
Current ratio	Current Ratio	1.42	1.78	1.53	1.48
LT debt to equity	L-TD/E	0.19	0.16	0.02	0.07
Total debt to equity	Tot D/E	0.19	0.16	0.02	0.07
Interest coverage (Times-interest-earned)	Int. Cov.	14.35	117.27	176.52	157.57
Gross margin	Gross Margin	31.66%	30.1%	32.5%	32.6%
EBITD margin	EBITD Margin	10.71%	9.9%	11.7%	11.6%
Operating margin	Op. Margin	9.67%	8.6%	10.1%	10.0%
Pre-tax margin	Pre-Tax Mgn.	9.69%	8.7%	10.1%	10.1%
Net profit margin	Net Profit Mgn.	6.06%	5.3%	6.2%	6.3%
Return on assets	ROA	11.01%	11.2%	12.9%	12.2%
Receivable turnover	Rec. TO	46.73	53.10	61.73	54.33
Inventory turnover	Inv. TO	4.80	4.98	4.89	4.71
Asset turnover	Asset TO	1.82	2.11	2.09	1.94

Note: the Most Recent ratios are for the most recent fiscal year and may differ from the ratios in Exhibit 10-9, which are for the most recent quarter or trailing twelve months.

As we mentioned earlier, sometimes it is much more efficient to analyze a company by looking at a graph of ratios over time, rather than looking at the numbers themselves. See Exhibit 10-10 for a screen showing some of the graphing possibilities. If you type the industry ratios from Yahoo! Finance, shown in Exhibit 10-9, into the indicated yellow cells in column C of the *Hist Analys* worksheet, you can graph the company's historical ratios along with the most recent industry ratios. For example, clicking on the button in column B for the historical annual sales growth rates causes the graph shown in Exhibit 10-11 to appear at the top of the *Hist Analysis* worksheet for Home Depot.

Notice that Home Depot's annual sales growth rate along with the most recent industry sales growth rate appear on the same chart. As this shows, Home Depot's sales have been slowing, but are still growing as fast as the industry.

Industry data is very useful, but sometimes you might disagree with the firms that Multex Investor includes in the industry. In these situations, you might choose to enter data in column C for your company's closest competitor rather than for the industry average. For example, when analyzing Home Depot, you might choose to enter Lowe's data rather than the industry average.

Summary

In this chapter, we showed you how to use the *Condensed* and *Hist Analys* worksheets in our valuation spreadsheet. We showed you how to analyze the historical free cash flows, ROICs, and ratios. In addition, we showed you some great Internet sources for current information, including a ratio comparison with industry peers.

Exhibit 10-11 Graph of Home Depot's Sales Growth Rates

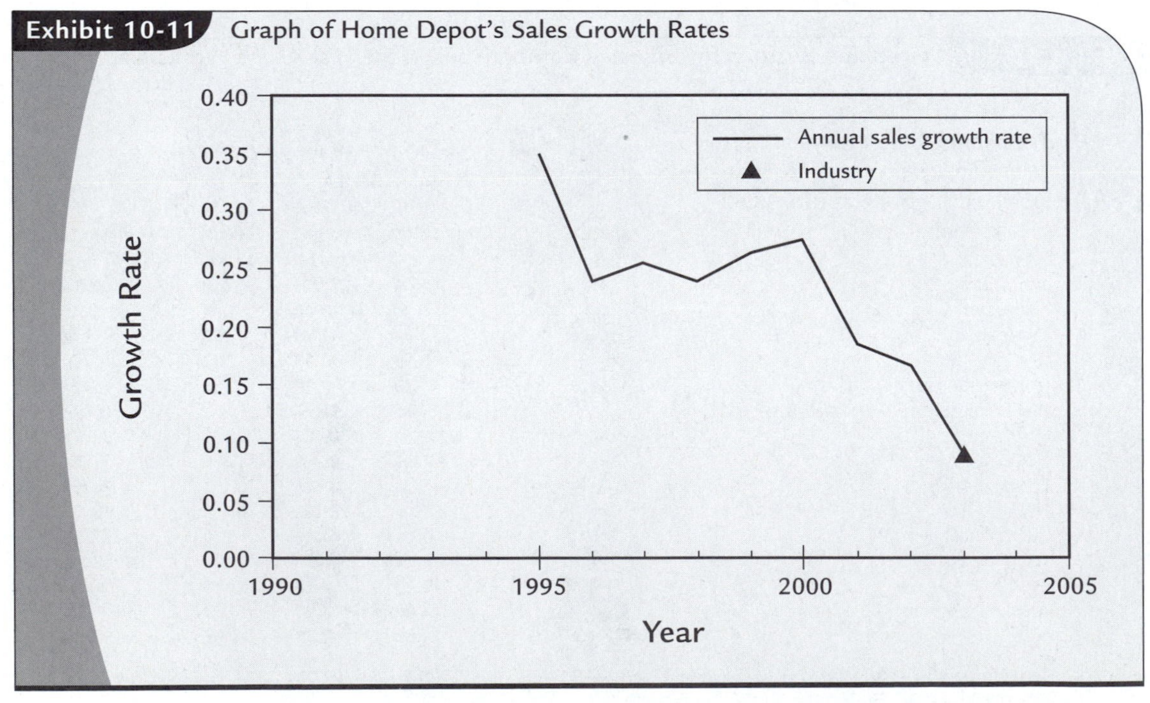

The appendix to this chapter explains in detail the logic and accounting theory underlying the way we simplified the complex *Comprehensive* statements into the *Condensed* statements. Chapter 11 explains how to estimate the cost of capital, Chapter 12 explains how to project the *Condensed* statements, and Chapter 13 explains how to find the value of the company, based on the projected statements.

Spreadsheet Problems

10-1 Lowe's Historical Analysis

Start with the spreadsheet you created for Chapter 9's Problem 9-11.

a. Go to Yahoo! and get the industry ratios for Lowe's as described in the chapter. Type the ratios into the appropriate yellow cells in Column C of the section titled "**Traditional Ratio Analysis**."

b. Analyze Lowe's historical performance as we did for Home Depot in the chapter. How has Lowe's done? How has its sales growth been? Its profitability? Its ROIC? What is your opinion of Lowe's in comparison to its industry?

10-2 Historical Analysis of Another Company

Repeat Problem 10-1, using another company, chosen either by you or your instructor.

Appendix 10

Mapping the Comprehensive Statements to the Condensed Statements: Advanced Issues in Measuring Free Cash Flows

Introduction

Condensing the *Comprehensive* statements into more concise financial statements will simplify the analysis, but it may lead to errors in valuation if the simplification is not done correctly. In other words, the simplification must still represent the economic reality of the company. Simplifying the financial statements of a complicated company requires a fairly extensive knowledge of many different complex accounting issues. However, it's not critical that you understand all of these accounting issues in order to use the valuation spreadsheet, because we have automated that procedure for you. But you might be curious how we mapped the various accounting line items into our *Condensed* sheet, and so this appendix explains the mapping. We'll start with a brief overview. After the overview, we'll discuss some of the more technical issues, such as goodwill, minority interests, investments and advances, operating leases, pension-related liabilities, LIFO reserves, foreign currency translations, and stock options.

Overview of Financial Statement Adjustments and Condensing

The income statements on the *Comprehensive* worksheet have over 35 items, while the *Condensed* income statements have only 13 items. The *Comprehensive* balance sheets have over 75 items, whereas the *Condensed* balance sheets have only 24 items. In total, we are reducing over 110 items from the *Comprehensive* sheets into only 37 items on the *Condensed* sheets. Following is a brief overview of the guiding principles underlying the condensing. Many of the adjustments were simply to combine similar accounts, while some were to put the statements into a format that was more consistent with the economic realities underlying free cash flow.

Income Statements

1. We combined the *Comprehensive* income statement's line items for cost of goods sold and cost of services into a single line item on the *Condensed* sheet, cost of goods sold.
2. We combined several *Comprehensive* line items, such as research and development and sales and marketing, into a single line item on the *Condensed* statements, sales, general and administrative expenses.
3. We put all depreciation, as reported on the *Comprehensive* statement of cash flows, into a single line item on the *Condensed* income statement, depreciation. We also reduced the *Condensed* cost of goods sold so that it does not include any deprecation; in other words, we assumed all depreciation was originally reported in the *Comprehensive* cost of goods sold rather than in the *Comprehensive* sales, general and administrative expenses. This might cause the *Condensed* cost of goods sold to be slightly underestimated and the sales, general, and administrative expenses to be slightly overestimated, but the total operating expenses are unchanged. We believe this sacrifice in possible accuracy is worth the trade-off for a more simplified statement. Also, we were careful not to double count depreciation, so that this adjustment will always result in the same net income on the *Comprehensive* and *Condensed* sheets.
4. We did not include any amortization or other noncash expenses (with an exception for depreciation) in the *Condensed* income statements. We discuss this in much more detail in the following sections, but the short explanation is that when a physical asset wears out (i.e., depreciates), it must ultimately be replaced. Hence, depreciation really is an operating expense.[1] However, when amortization is reported for an intangible asset, there is no reason to believe that the company will ever actually replace the "amount" of the intangible asset that is amortized. Rather than include amortization on the *Condensed* sheets and then go through complicated gyrations when calculating free cash flow (FCF) to reflect the economic reality of amortization, we simply leave it off the *Condensed* income statement. Notice that this will cause the reported net income on the *Condensed* sheet to differ from that on the *Comprehensive* sheet. It also requires some adjustments to the balance sheets, as we explain briefly in the following section on balance sheet adjustments. Also, we discuss these issues in much more detail later in this appendix.
5. The *Comprehensive* sheets have several items for nonoperating income, such as minority interest expense and investment gains, that are shown after the line for provision for income tax expenses.[2] We want to show all nonoperating income on the *Condensed* statements as a pre-tax item. To do this, we moved the after-tax nonoperating items from the *Comprehensive* sheet to the *Condensed* sheet's

---

[1]Depreciation doesn't affect cash flows, hence our definition of net operating profit after taxes (NOPAT) is not actually a cash flow. However, our definition of free cash flow (FCF) is FCF = NOPAT – Net investment in capital. This net investment in capital slightly understates the true cash flow of gross investment because it ignores the depreciation during the year. In other words, NOPAT understates cash flow, net investment in capital overstates cash flow, but FCF is in fact a cash flow. We use these definitions because depreciation really is an operating cost and including it in NOPAT makes the definition of return on invested capital (ROIC = NOPAT/Beginning capital) economically meaningful.

[2]We explain minority interest in much more detail later in this appendix.

pre-tax line for nonoperating income (expense). Because this means reporting an after-tax item as a pre-tax item, we had to increase the reported nonoperating income by the amount of tax owed on the income (and we reduced any nonoperating expense by the amount of tax saved by the deduction). We also adjusted the *Condensed* provision for income tax expenses by the same amount.

For example, if our assumed marginal tax rate is 35% and $65 is reported on the *Comprehensive* sheet as after-tax nonoperating income, we report $100 = $65/(1 – 0.35) as pre-tax nonoperating income on the *Condensed* sheet. We also increase the *Condensed* provision for income tax expense by $35 = $65(0.35/[1 – 0.35]). Notice that these adjustments cancel one another, so they will always result in the same net income on the *Comprehensive* and *Condensed* sheets.

6. The *Comprehensive* sheet has several extraordinary items such as merger and restructuring costs, shown as possible pre-tax items. Because these are not a part of a company's regular operations, we moved them to the *Condensed* sheet's after-tax extraordinary income. As with the nonoperating items described above, we had to make an adjustment for taxes. In this case, we want to report a pre-tax item from the *Comprehensive* worksheet as an after-tax item on the *Condensed* sheet.

   For example, if the *Comprehensive* sheet reports $100 for merger and restructuring expenses as a pre-tax item, then we subtract $65 = $100 (1 – 0.35) from the after-tax extraordinary income on the *Condensed* sheet (because expenses are negative income). We also add back $35 to the *Condensed* provision for income tax expense, because the tax saved by deducting the merger and restructuring costs is not really an operating tax. In other words, we improve the *Condensed* taxable income by $100 because we don't subtract the merger and restructuring costs. We charge the *Condensed* tax provision $35 more, and we reduce the *Condensed* net income by the additional $65 due to the reduction in after-tax extraordinary income. The net effect is zero: these adjustments will always result in the same net income on the *Comprehensive* and *Condensed* sheets.

Balance Sheets: Current Assets

1. We combined several items from the *Comprehensive* balance sheet, such as tax refund receivable and progress payments, into a single line item on the *Condensed* sheet, other short-term operating assets. Notice that this adjustment will always result in the same total assets on the *Comprehensive* and *Condensed* sheets.
2. We combined several items from the *Comprehensive* balance sheet, such as marketable securities and notes receivable, into a single line item on the *Condensed* sheet, short-term investments. Notice that this adjustment will always result in the same total assets on the *Comprehensive* and *Condensed* sheets.
3. The *Comprehensive* sheet has a line item for current deferred tax asset. Instead of showing multiple deferred tax accounts on the *Condensed* sheet (such as deferred tax asset and deferred tax liability), we combined them into a single liability account. Therefore, we subtracted the current deferred tax asset from the *Condensed* liability account for deferred taxes. Notice that this adjustment will

always cause the total assets and total liabilities and equity on the *Condensed* worksheet to differ from those on the *Comprehensive* sheet.

Balance Sheets: Long-Term Assets

1. We combined several items from the *Comprehensive* balance sheet, such as deferred charges and deposits, into a single line item on the *Condensed* sheet, other long-term operating assets. Notice that this adjustment will always result in the same total assets on the *Comprehensive* and *Condensed* sheets.
2. We combined several items from the *Comprehensive* balance sheet, such as long-term receivables and investments in unconsolidated subsidiaries, into a single line item on the *Condensed* sheet, long-term investments. Notice that this adjustment will always result in the same total assets on the *Comprehensive* and *Condensed* sheets.
3. The *Comprehensive* sheet shows a line item for long-term deferred tax asset. Just as we did for the current deferred tax asset, we subtracted this from the *Condensed* liability account for deferred taxes. Again, this adjustment will always cause the total assets and total liabilities and equity on the *Condensed* worksheet to differ from those on the *Comprehensive* sheet.
4. The *Condensed* line item for other long-term operating assets includes several *Comprehensive* items, including goodwill and intangibles. As explained earlier, we don't subtract amortization when finding net income on the *Condensed* statements. We explain this in more detail later in this appendix, but the amount of amortization that we don't subtract from the *Condensed* income statement is added back to the *Condensed* other long-term operating assets and the *Condensed* retained earnings. These adjustments will cause the total assets and total liabilities and equity on the *Condensed* worksheet to differ from those on the *Comprehensive* sheet.

Balance Sheets: Current Liabilities

1. We combined several items from the *Comprehensive* balance sheet, such as short-term unearned revenue and taxes payable, into a single line item on the *Condensed* sheet, accruals. Notice that this adjustment will always result in the same total liabilities and equity on the *Comprehensive* and *Condensed* sheets.
2. We combined the several items from the *Comprehensive* balance sheet, such as notes payable and current portion of long-term debt, into a single line item on the *Condensed* sheet, all short-term debt. Notice that this adjustment will always result in the same total liabilities and equity on the *Comprehensive* and *Condensed* sheets.
3. The *Comprehensive* sheet shows a line item for short-term deferred taxes. We added this to the *Condensed* liability account for deferred taxes, which is shown as a long-term liability. This adjustment will always result in the same total liabilities and equity on the *Comprehensive* and *Condensed* sheets, although current liabilities will differ.
4. The only nonoperating current liability shown on the *Condensed* balance sheet is all short-term debt. Any other nonoperating current liabilities on the *Comprehensive*

sheet that do not explicitly charge interest are shown in the *Condensed* sheet as other long-term liabilities. This adjustment will always result in the same total liabilities and equity on the *Comprehensive* and *Condensed* sheets, although current liabilities will differ.

Balance Sheets: Long-Term Liabilities and Equity

1. We combined several items from the *Comprehensive* balance sheet, such as noncurrent portion of long-term debt and mortgages, into a single line item on the *Condensed* sheet, long-term debt. Notice that this adjustment will always result in the same total liabilities and equity on the *Comprehensive* and *Condensed* sheets.
2. On the *Condensed* sheet, the deferred taxes account includes short-term deferred taxes from the *Comprehensive* sheet. The *Comprehensive* sheet's current deferred tax asset and long-term deferred tax asset are subtracted from the *Condensed* sheet's deferred tax account. These adjustments will cause the total assets and total liabilities and equity on the *Condensed* sheet to differ from those on the *Comprehensive* sheet.
3. When we value the company, we will first find the total value of the company, and then subtract the claims held by debtholders and others. Therefore, the *Condensed* sheet's other long-term liabilities is a catchall for many contingency accounts on the *Comprehensive* sheet, which are claims against the company's value. It also includes any claims by other than current equity holders, such the claims by holders of stock options; this is explained in more detail later in this appendix. These adjustments will always result in the same total liabilities and equity on the *Comprehensive* and *Condensed* sheets.
4. The *Comprehensive* sheet has several different reserve accounts, and these are combined with the *Condensed* sheet's other long-term liabilities. This adjustment will always result in the same total liabilities and equity on the *Comprehensive* and *Condensed* sheets.

An Explanation of Complicated Accounting and the Impact on FCF

Most of the adjustments covered in the previous section are simply to combine similar accounts. However, some of the adjustments are more complex, and we need to explain them in more detail. These complex adjustments involve goodwill, minority interests, investments and advances, operating leases, pension-related liabilities, LIFO reserves, foreign currency translations, and employee stock options. The following sections address each of these issues. Also, the book's web site has spreadsheet models illustrating each of these adjustments.

Goodwill

Goodwill is a line item to account for the difference between the purchase price of some assets and their book values. For example, suppose a company, RPM, decides to acquire a company called Target for $140 million. The current value of Target's assets is $100 million. RPM raises $140 million (to keep the discussion simple, let's assume RPM either borrows or issues equity). At this moment, RPM's financial statements would show an additional $140 million in liabilities (i.e., new debt or equity) and $140 million in new assets (i.e., cash or short-term investments, due to the money that was raised by issuing new debt or equity).

RPM must pay $140 million to acquire Target. This $40 million premium of market price over book price could be because many of Target's assets are fully depreciated but are still usable (so its book value is too low) or because Target has growth opportunities (perhaps due to brand identity, patents, etc.). At any rate, how will accountants show the acquisition on RPM's statements? RPM's liabilities won't change: they still show the extra $140 million in debt or equity. On the asset side of the balance sheet, RPM's cash or short-term investments will go down to reflect the $140 million payment. Here is where it gets tricky. Instead of adding $140 million worth of new operating assets, such as inventory or PPE, to RPM's existing assets, the accountants will add only $100 million of new operating assets—the book value of the assets when they were with Target. They then create a new asset category called goodwill, and add the extra $40 million to this category.

Now things start to get really tricky! Prior to 2002, just as accountants allowed the depreciation of PPE, accountants allowed the amortization of goodwill. In particular, they allowed goodwill to be amortized over a 40-year period on a straight-line basis. So for RPM, there would be an amortization expense of $1 million at the end of the year. This amortization charge would be subtracted from the existing goodwill, so the balance sheet at the end of the year would show goodwill of $39 million. The amortization charge is also considered an expense on the income statement (although it is not a tax-deductible expense on the reported financial statements). This amortization expense on the income statement would reduce net income by $1 million, which in turn would reduce retained earnings on the balance sheet by $1 million.

However, starting in 2002, GAAP accounting rules changed. Goodwill generated through an acquisition such as with RPM is no longer subject to regular amortization.[3] Instead, every year the company must look at the assets that generated the goodwill and estimate their market value (using a valuation model similar to the one in this book). If the company determines that the purchased assets' values have declined, then goodwill is reduced by the amount of the decline. This reduction is treated like the previously described amortization, so it reduces net income. This is called the **impairment test**. In any case, whether through regular amortization or through a write-down as a result of impairment, the impact is to reduce goodwill from year to year.

What impact has all of this had on FCF? When RPM acquired Target, there was definitely an investment in operating capital of $140 million. The increase of $100 million of operating assets presents no problems because the way we calculate FCF will pick this up. However, how can we make sure that our calculation correctly shows the additional investment in capital of $40 million? Also, how much capital

[3]Other types of intangible assets may still be amortized.

does RPM *truly* have invested at the end of the year due to the goodwill, $39 million or $40 million?

Let's tackle the second question first. If a company acquires $100 million in machinery and depreciates it over 10 years using straight-line depreciation, then the depreciation charge for the first year is $10 million and the book value of the machine at the end of the year is $90 million. The reasoning behind this is that the machine is being worn out as it is being used. This might not be a particularly accurate estimate of the true value of the machine because it might be wearing out at either a faster or lower rate. But accountants have tried hard to match up the rate of depreciation and the actual rate of wear and tear. So we usually are content to follow the accountants' rules that reduce the value of the capital by $10 million and accept the value of capital as being the $90 million.

But we are much less confident that the $40 million premium paid during the acquisition is "wearing out" at a rate of $1 million per year. In fact, the value of growth opportunities or brand identities might actually be increasing over time. In many ways, the $40 million premium is like an investment in land: You can't depreciate land for tax purposes (and amortization of goodwill is not deductible for tax purposes), and the value of land might go up or down. Therefore, we believe it is probably more reasonable to assume that the $40 million premium is a permanent investment, like an investment in land. In other words, if we want to reflect the economic reality of the situation, goodwill should not be amortized, just as land is not depreciated. Also, our primary objective is to forecast future free cash flows. The real question is, "How much capital is needed to support sales and sales growth?" If a company needs to pay the premium to acquire the assets to support sales growth, then the projections of future free cash flow should reflect the unamortized value of the acquisitions. This is one of many examples where GAAP accounting just doesn't make good financial and economic sense.

How can we make the *Condensed* statements conform to this? First, each year we combine the goodwill shown on the *Comprehensive* statements with other operating long-term assets on the *Condensed* statements. Second, to correct for all of the past amortization of goodwill we also add to the other operating long-term assets the cumulative total of all the current and previous amortization of goodwill shown on the *Comprehensive* statements. This means that if a company did not make any more acquisitions during the period shown on the *Comprehensive* statements, the correction to other operating long-term assets due to goodwill on the *Comprehensive* statements would be the same from year to year; it would not decrease each year due to amortization. With these corrections, the only way that other operating long-term assets would change due to goodwill is if the company actually increased goodwill by making another acquisition or reduced goodwill by selling some of the acquired assets. In this case, the change in goodwill is an actual cash flow. However, goodwill would not change again until another acquisition or disposition.

Of course, making these adjustments to the balance sheet for one year is like pulling on a thread sticking out of your sweater. If you aren't careful, the whole thing will unravel! To keep the balance sheets in balance, we need to undo the impact that amortization of goodwill had on the retained earnings. After the adjustments, assets will be higher because we don't reduce goodwill due to amortization and net income will be higher because the amortization isn't charged to net income. Therefore, retained earnings should also be higher. We accomplish this by taking the cumulative amortization that we added back to goodwill and also adding it back into retained earnings. Finally, we ignore amortization of goodwill when we construct the *Condensed* income statements.

This treatment is complicated by the new accounting rules regarding goodwill impairment. Financial statements after 2002 will not have regular reductions in acquisition-generated goodwill due to amortization—so our corrections that undo it will have no incremental effect on statements after 2002, other than to add back in the accumulated goodwill amortization prior to 2002. (Other forms of goodwill may still be amortized, and our corrections will still undo the accounting treatment of that amortization.)

However, what is the impact now if a firm takes the impairment test and then writes down its goodwill because it has determined that the value of goodwill has been impaired? For example, AOL Time Warner took a $100 billion charge in 2002, reducing goodwill (and net income and retained earnings) to reflect the reduced value of AOL's operations. In such a case, the firm itself has determined that the cash flows expected to be generated by the assets underlying the goodwill are much lower than at the time of the acquisition. Hence, the value of the assets and of the capital supplied by investors is lower than at the time of the acquisition. This implies that the firm will not have to make similar investments to support its future sales. In such a situation it might make economic sense to reduce operating capital by the amount of the write-down.

To allow you to accommodate this treatment if you so choose, we have included a line item in the *Comprehensive* sheet in the section Optional Items for Special Accounting Adjustments called special goodwill impairment. If you want to incorporate the write-down, then you should input the amount of goodwill to be deducted from capital in the year the write-down occurs; if you choose not to incorporate the write-down, then simply leave the special goodwill impairment at its default value of zero.

For example, suppose RPM takes a $10 million write-down in goodwill because of impairment, and we want to incorporate it in the valuation analysis by entering $10 million in the line for special goodwill impairment. First, the charge will be ignored when the *Condensed* income statement is constructed. It won't be included as a special charge, nor will it be included in amortization or depreciation. However, long-term operating assets will be reduced by the amount of the write-down. To make the balance sheet balance, retained earnings will be reduced by the amount of the charge. To make sure that the write-down has no impact on free cash flows, the charge will be deducted from NOPAT. The net result is that both assets and liabilities will be reduced by the amount of the charge, and free cash flow will be calculated as if there were no write-down. The net result is that the historical ratios of capital/sales that we use to help us choose the future projected ratios will not be upwardly biased by overvalued assets. Thus, we should be able to forecast future free cash flows more accurately.

You may have noticed that the net income on the *Condensed* statements is not always equal to the net income on the *Comprehensive* (and *Actual*) statements.

Similarly, total assets on the *Condensed* statements is not always exactly equal to total assets on the *Comprehensive* statements. One reason for these differences is our treatment of goodwill. In fact, the net effect of our treatment of regular amortization of goodwill is that our condensed net income will be higher than the *Comprehensive* net income by the amount of the amortization of goodwill. Also, our *Condensed* balance sheets will show a higher total assets (and higher total liabilities and owners equity) than the *Comprehensive* balance sheets by the amount of the cumulative current and past amortization of goodwill. In the case of an impairment write-down, the reduction in total assets and total liabilities and equity will be the same on the *Condensed* and *Comprehensive* balance sheets, but net income on the *Condensed* sheet will be higher than net income on the *Comprehensive* sheet by the amount of the write-down.

In summary, our treatment of goodwill should produce more economically reasonable financial statements and lead to more accurate projections of free cash flows.

Minority Interests

This, too, is a complicated topic, and it probably is easiest to start with an example. RPM is a company with operating assets of $500 million, debt of $200 million, equity of $300 million, and net income of $50 million. SUB is a smaller company with operating assets of $50 million, debt of $20 million, equity of $30 million, and net income of $5 million. Suppose RPM decides to buy all of the stock in SUB. To keep it simple, we assume that the market value of SUB's stock is the same as the book value of its equity (if the purchase price were greater than the book value of equity, then there would be goodwill involved, and we would make the adjustments for goodwill that we described earlier). To make this purchase, RPM issues $30 million in debt. Immediately after the issue, RPM will have an additional $30 million in debt shown as a liability, and a total debt of $230 million ($230 = $200 + $30). RPM also will have a new asset account for cash in the amount of the $30 million it raises in debt. Here are some key data immediately prior to the acquisition:

RPM		SUB	
Operating assets	$500	Operating assets	$50
Cash	$30		
Debt	$200 + $30	Debt	$20
Equity	$300	Equity	$30
Net income	$50	Net income	$5

If RPM then uses the cash it raised to buy shares of stock in SUB, how should we show it on the asset side of the balance sheet? First, we definitely reduce the cash account to zero, since RPM pays $30 million for the stock of SUB. But how do we show the stock of SUB? One option would be to create a new category of assets called stock in other companies. But there might be a better way to account for the purchase of SUB's stock.

Because RPM purchased 100% of the stock in SUB, RPM has complete control of SUB (i.e., RPM could elect the entire board of directors) and, therefore, its assets. So it might make sense to consolidate the financial statements of RPM and SUB into a single set of statements. To do this, first add all of SUB's assets to RPM's assets and eliminate the account called stock in other companies. This results in $550 million in operating assets (the sum of RPM's $500 million in operating assets and SUB's $50 million in operating assets). Because we eliminated the account for stock in other companies, there are no other assets, and the total assets are $550 million. Notice that this is equal to the combined total assets of the two companies prior to RPM raising debt for the purchase.

Second, add all of SUB's liabilities to the liabilities of RPM. This gives a total of $250 million in debt, the sum of RPM's debt of $230 million (which reflects the new $30 million in debt that RPM raised to purchase SUB) and the $20 million of SUB's debt. We make no change to RPM's equity, which is still $300 million. So the consolidated sum of liabilities and equity is $550 million ($250 million in debt and $300 million in equity). This is equal to the $550 million in consolidated assets, so the consolidated balance sheets do in fact balance.

Third, add all of SUB's revenues, costs, and so on to the income statement of RPM. In other words, the consolidated income statements looks just like the sum of the various entries in both SUB's and RPM's income statements. Therefore, the consolidated net income is $55 million (the sum of RPM's $50 million in net income and SUB's $5 million). Given these consolidated statements, calculate the FCF in exactly the same manner as we have done throughout the book. The key data reflecting this treatment is shown below.

Purchase 100% and Consolidate	
RPM	
Operating assets	$500 + $50 = $550
Debt	$200 + $30 + $20 = $250
Equity	$300
Net income	$50 + $5 = $ 55

But what happens if RPM doesn't acquire 100% of SUB's stock, but instead acquires only 80% of the stock? Here's where minority interest comes in. With 80% ownership, RPM still has effective control of SUB. Accountants have decided that we should still consolidate the statements of RPM and SUB in almost exactly the same way as when RPM owned 100% of the stock. First, even though RPM doesn't own all of SUB's assets, consolidate the assets as though it did. Therefore, the total consolidated assets still would be $550 million. Consolidate the liabilities as well.

Because RPM is purchasing only 80% of SUB's stock, RPM would need to raise only $24 million: $24 = 0.80($30). RPM's total debt would now be $224 million (the original $200 million plus the new $24 million). SUB's debt is unchanged at $20 million, and so the consolidated debt is $244 million ($244 = $224 + $20). The consolidated equity still is equal to RPM's equity of $300 million. If we were to stop now, the consolidated balance sheets would not balance:

the assets are $550 million and the liabilities and equity are just $544 million ($244 million in debt and $300 million in equity). The reason this doesn't balance is because we have added all of SUB's assets, even though RPM doesn't really own all of them—they own only 80% of them.

The accounting solution is to create a new liability account, minority interest, in the amount of $6 million, which represents the portion of SUB's assets that really belongs to the minority owners of SUB. Now the total liabilities are $250 million ($244 million in debt and $6 million in minority interest), and the total liabilities and equity are equal to $550 million, which is the same as for total assets. In other words, the balance sheets now balance.

In consolidating the income statements, we still add all of the individual items on SUB's income statement to the individual items on RPM's income statements. If we stopped here, the consolidated net income still would be $55 million (the $50 million from RPM and the $5 million from SUB). But because RPM only owns 80% of SUB, RPM's shareholders aren't really entitled to all of SUB's net income. So we now add a new item on RPM's income statement, minority interest or minority interest expense. This usually is shown as an after-tax item, and it is equal to 20% of SUB's net income, which is $1 million: $1 = 0.20($5). So the consolidated net income would be $54 million ($54 = $55 – $1). In other words, we are going to show RPM's income statement as though it owns 100% of SUB, but we are then going to deduct an item called minority interest that is equal the portion of SUB's income that does not belong to RPM.

Here is another way to conceptualize this consolidation. It is as though RPM put up $24 million of it's own money, borrowed $6 from SUB's shareholders, and then bought all of SUB's stock. The amount RPM borrowed shows up on the balance sheet as a liability (just like any other money RPM borrows) called minority interest. The payment on this borrowed money is not a fixed amount, however, but is a percentage of SUB's net income. This payment shows up on RPM's income statements as an after-tax item called minority interest expense. Here is the key data reflecting the 80% purchase.

Purchase 80% and Establish Minority Interest	
RPM	
Operating assets	$500 + $50 = $550
Debt	$200 + $24 + $20 = $244
Equity	$300
Minority interest	$6
Net income	$50 + $5 = $55
Minority interest	(This is an after-tax expense.) 0.20($5) = $1
Net income	$49

So how should we treat this situation when calculating FCF? We treat it just like any other borrowed money. In particular, we do not include the minority interest expense when we calculate NOPAT, just as we don't include other interest expense. In our condensed statements, we include minority interest expense as a part of nonoperating income (note that we include it as a negative amount because it is an expense; notice also that we have to show what the minority interest would have been on a pre-tax basis because we show nonoperating income as a pre-tax item). We show the balance sheet minority interest as a part of other long-term liabilities. Notice that when we find the total value of the firm, we will subtract other long-term liabilities when we find the value of equity, just as we subtract debt.

Investments and Advances

Suppose RPM were to acquire a much smaller percentage of SUB's stock, such a small percentage that RPM did not actually have control over SUB's assets. In this case, the stock of SUB that RPM owns is called investments and advances, and it is shown as an item on the asset side of the *Comprehensive* balance sheets. In the *Condensed* financial statements, this is a part of long-term investments. If SUB pays any dividends, the value of the dividends that are due to RPM are shown as nonoperating income on RPM's income statements.

So with respect to our calculation of FCF, the dividends from SUB are not included as a part of NOPAT because they are a part of nonoperating income. The investments and advances are not shown as a part of operating capital because they are a part of long-term investments. But they do affect the value of the company because we will add the value of long-term investments to the value of operations when we find the total value of the company. (Implicit is the assumption that the present value of the stream of cash flows in nonoperating income is equal to the book value of long-term investments.)

Operating Leases

Suppose a company borrows $100,000 at 10% interest and buys a machine. The machine will last 10 years and will have a zero salvage value at the end of 10 years. The company's balance sheets will show an additional $100,000 of plant, property,

ACCOUNTING ALERT!

In theory, part of minority interest expense represents the NOPAT from the portion of the subsidiary that the parent does not own. Also, part of the minority interest (from the balance sheet) represents operating capital of the subsidiary that the parent does not own. Therefore, in a perfect world it would be best to simply calculate NOPAT and capital for the parent and then subtract the portions of NOPAT and capital that are due to the portion of the subsidiary that is not owned by the parent. Unfortunately, usually we have no way of knowing how much of the minority interest expense of the subsidiary is NOPAT and how much is due to nonoperating income (or nonoperating expenses) of the subsidiary. Similarly, we have no way of knowing how much of the minority interest shown on the balance sheet is due to operating capital and to nonoperating capital. Therefore, most analysts choose to treat minority interest in the way we described.

and equipment (PPE) on the asset side, and an additional $100,000 of debt on the liability side. Each year, the company is obligated to make interest and principal payments of $16,275.

Now suppose that another company, instead of buying the machine, leases the same machine under an arrangement known as an operating lease. The lease payments are $16,275 per year. The company doesn't add the value of the machine to its PPE because it doesn't own the machine. Nor does any liability show up on the balance sheets. But the fact is, the company gets to use the machine for 10 years, and it is obligated to make the lease payments in much the same way as it is obligated to make the scheduled interest and principal payments (i.e., if the company misses a lease payment, then the company may be forced into bankruptcy in much the same way as if it missed a scheduled interest and principal payment). In other words, the company actually "owns" the machine and owes "debt" to the lessor, but it doesn't look like it if we only look at the financial statements.

It doesn't seem fair that the two companies facing the same economic reality (both get to use a machine and both have the same obligated payments) will have very different financial statements simply because a choice is made to lease rather than borrow. Accountants have long recognized this and have stated that companies must "capitalize" leases if they meet certain criteria. At the risk of over-simplification (at least from an accountant's perspective), here is how a capital lease works. Suppose a lease payment is for $23,000 per year for 10 years, payable at the end of each year. First, the portion of the lease payment that is due to insurance, maintenance, and property taxes is reported as an expense. Suppose this portion is equal to $3,000 per year. The company finds the present value of the remaining portion of the lease payments, discounted at the cost of debt. If the cost of debt is 10%, then the present value of 10 payments of $20,000 is equal to $122,891. It then adds this amount to the PPE (or to an asset account called leased equipment under capital leases), and it adds an equal amount to debt (or to a liability account called obligation under capital leases). The interest portion of the lease payment is shown as an interest expense. In the first year, this is equal to $12,289 ($12,289 is equal to the interest rate of 10% multiplied by the beginning balance of $122,891). The remaining portion of the payment is $20,000 – $12,289 = $7,711. So in the first year, the lease liability would be reduced by $7,711, just as debt would be reduced by a principal payment. Also, the company depreciates the asset value of the lease (i.e., the $122,891) each year, just as it would any other piece of equipment. In other words, the accountants do their best to convert a capital lease into the equivalent of purchasing an asset with borrowed money.

Many leases don't meet the accounting definition for a capital lease; these are called operating leases. However, for all practical purposes, many operating leases should be treated as though they are capital leases. Fortunately, the footnotes of most financial statements provide enough information to find the capitalized value of an operating lease. So if your company has lots of operating lease obligations, you should find the capitalized value and include it on the section of special items on the *Comprehensive* worksheet. You should also enter the interest rate on debt.

The *Condensed* statements will add the capitalized value of the operating lease to other operating assets and will add the same amount to long-term debt. In addition, the implied interest payment (the product of the interest rate and the value of the capitalized operating lease) is subtracted from SGA and added to interest expense.

What impact does this have on FCF? NOPAT is improved, since the interest portion of the lease payment is treated as a financing cost and not an operating expense. But capital is increased because the capitalized value of the lease is added to other operating assets.

Pension-Related Liabilities

Many companies sponsor retirement or post-employment health insurance programs for their employees. We are going to use the term pension as a catchall for both retirement plans and post-employment health plans, even though there are some minor differences in the accounting treatment of the two. As you might expect, the accounting treatment of pension plans is quite complicated. Here is a simplified explanation of how these plans work and how they affect the value of the company.

Given the demographics of a company's employees (such as age, gender, smoking habits, etc.), actuaries can quite accurately calculate the future cash flows due to pension plan obligations that the company will pay to these employees after the employees retire. Given a reasonable discount rate, the present value of these obligations can be calculated. This is called the projected benefit obligation. For example, suppose a company uses a discount rate of 10% and calculates a $200 million present value of its expected future pension obligations. Therefore, the company has a $200 million projected benefit obligation.

To meet the obligation, each year the company invests money in a portfolio of stocks and bonds. This portfolio is called the plan assets. Notice that the value of the plan assets will depend on the cumulative amount of money that the company contributes to the plan and the actual return that the stocks and bonds in the portfolio have experienced. If the value of the plan assets is exactly equal to $200 million, then the plan is called fully funded. In such a case, neither the plan assets nor the projected benefit obligation are shown on the balance sheet. However, most plans typically are underfunded, usually because the company has not invested enough money in the plan. For example, suppose the value of the plan assets is only $175 million. In this case, a $25 million liability is shown on the balance sheets, because the employees have a $25 million claim against the value of the company. This is often called pension liability or even unfunded pension liability.

Each year the company will report on its income statement an item called pension expense. On most financial statements, this is shown as a part of SGA and is not shown as a separate line item. The accounting rules for this pension expense are fairly complicated, and we won't cover them all here. However, one component of the pension expense is called the interest cost, and one component of the interest cost is an amount equal to the pension liability multiplied by the discount rate. In our example, this would be $2.5 million: $2.5 = 0.10($25). Note that this component of pension expense is shown on the income statements as a part of pension expense in SGA and is not shown as an interest expense. The pension expense, including this component of interest cost, is tax deductible.

In many ways, it is as though the employees have loaned the company $25 million and charged the company $2.5 million in interest. Therefore, the liability for pension and health insurance should be treated much like debt. We map the retirement, pension, and health insurance related liabilities from the *Comprehensive* balance sheets into long-term debt on the *Condensed* statements. In addition, we show the implied interest expense (the product of the interest rate for the retirement, pension, and health insurance related liabilities multiplied by the amount of retirement, pension, and health insurance related liabilities) as a part of interest expense on the *Condensed* statements. We also deduct this amount from the SGA in the *Condensed* statements.

LIFO Reserves

Part of the COGS is the cost of the materials that are in the products that are sold. How is that cost calculated? Consider the following example. Suppose a company has 100 units of inventory at the beginning of the period and the value of the inventory is $100. This means each unit of existing inventory is worth $1. Suppose the company purchases 100 new units at a cost of $2 per unit. The company uses 100 units in production during the year. At the end of the year, there are still 100 units of inventory, because the company started with 100, added 100, and used 100. But what is the cost of materials that were used in production and what is the value of the inventory at the end of the year?

It depends. Perhaps surprisingly, the answer doesn't depend on whether the company actually used the old inventory or whether it used the new units that it purchased. Instead, it depends on which inventory valuation method the company chooses.

One method is called First-In, First-Out (FIFO). In this method, the inventory is valued as though the first units that were purchased (which is the existing inventory at the start of the period in this example) are the first units that are used. So the cost of materials would be $100, based on using the oldest inventory, which has a cost of $1 per unit. The remaining 100 units are valued as though they are the new units, which cost $2 per unit. So the remaining inventory has a value of $200.[4]

A second method is called Last-In, First-Out (LIFO). In this method, the inventory is valued as though the last units purchased are the first units that are used. So the cost of materials would be $200, based on using the newest units, which have a price of $2 per unit. The remaining 100 units are valued as though they are the old units, which are $1 per unit. So the remaining inventory has a value of $100.

In comparing the methods, when prices are increasing, FIFO has lower reported cost of materials and a higher value of inventory. LIFO has a higher reported cost of materials and a lower value of inventory. Most companies choose LIFO because the higher reported cost will help lower taxes. (Keep in mind that except for taxes,

[4]For example, the following quote from footnote 1 of Home Depot's 2001 10-K reveals that they use FIFO: "MERCHANDISE INVENTORIES. Inventories are stated at the lower of cost (first-in, first-out) or market, as determined by the retail inventory method."

the actual cash flows of the company are the same either way: it paid $200 for the new units of inventory.) But FIFO probably more closely represents the true economic reality of the firm. Therefore, most companies actually report a figure in their footnotes called the LIFO reserve. If you take this LIFO reserve and add it to the reported inventory value (which is based on LIFO), the result will be the value of the inventory as though it had been valued using FIFO.

Suppose a firm uses LIFO, which most firms do use, and you calculated NOPAT, investment in capital, and FCF, but you believe that FIFO more closely represents the economic reality of the firm. Here is how the *Condensed* sheet will adjust the entries from the *Comprehensive* sheet so that the calculated FCF is consistent with FIFO accounting. First, you must specify the value of LIFO reserves in row 158 of the section for special items in the *Comprehensive* sheet. You usually can find this in the footnotes of the company's financial statements. The *Condensed* sheet will add the LIFO reserve to the value of inventory. If we stopped here, the balance sheets would no longer balance, since we have added something to assets, but we haven't added anything to the other side of the balance sheet. Notice that because the company has been overstating its costs by using LIFO, its net income has been understated. If net income has been understated, so has retained earnings. So the *Condensed* sheet will add the LIFO reserve into retained earnings, and the balance sheets will now balance.

Suppose the LIFO reserve is $200 this year and was $150 last year. This means that we have overstated our costs this year by the amount of $50 ($50 = $200 – $150). So to correctly estimate our true costs, the *Condensed* sheet will reduce COGS by this $50. The net effect is to bump up NOPAT by $50. (Note that we will not change taxes because these are the taxes that the company paid.)

Will these adjustments change our calculated FCF? No. The adjustment will increase NOPAT, but it will also increase our investment in capital (due to a higher inventory) by the same amount. Then why go through this trouble? Actually, although it does not change NOPAT, it will change ROIC. This is because it increases NOPAT, which is the numerator of NOPAT, by the same dollar amount that it increases Capital, which is the denominator. If ROIC just happens to be exactly 100%, this change won't affect things. But if ROIC is less than 100% (as you would usually expect), then ROIC adjusted for LIFO reserves will be higher than the unadjusted ROIC.

Foreign Currency Translations

Many firms have foreign subsidiaries whose financial statements are consolidated. But before consolidation, the subsidiaries' statements must be converted into dollars. All of the asset and liability accounts are converted at the current exchange rate. However, the common stock accounts for par, paid-in-capital, and treasury stock are converted at the historical exchange rate based on the day the account was created. To add even more confusion, items on the income statement are converted at the average exchange rate during the year. With all of these different exchange rates, it would be a miracle if the converted balance sheets actually balanced. To make these balance sheets balance (and to correctly reflect the gain or loss that the parent has experienced due to changes in the exchange rates), a new account is created in the equity portion of the balance sheet. This is called cumulative translation gain (loss). The change in this account from one year to the next would reflect the gain or loss that the company experienced that year due to changes in foreign exchange rates.

In summary, many firms own assets and liabilities that are denominated in a currency other than U.S. dollars. When exchange rates change, the company experiences gains or losses. Most financial statements report only the net gain or loss, and call it a foreign currency translation effect. Usually the annual foreign currency translation effect is not shown on the income statement. Sometimes, but not always, the annual translation effect is shown on a statement of retained earnings. Even if the annual translation effect is not shown on the income statement of the statement of retained earnings, the cumulative translation effect always is shown a separate line in the balance sheet in the stockholder's equity section called cumulative translation adjustments.

These net changes do in fact represent a change in the accounting book value of the firm. How does this affect FCF? In particular, the currency translation changes in recorded values of operating assets and operating liabilities would affect operating capital and thus affect historical FCF calculations, even though these translation adjustments are not really cash flows. But we almost never have this level of detail about the components of the foreign currency translation effect. Therefore, we map the cumulative foreign currency translation from the *Comprehensive* sheet into the par plus paid-in-capital (less Treasury stock and other adjustments) in the *Condensed* sheet.

Employee Stock Options

Many companies have granted large numbers of stock options to employees. These options represent a claim against the value of the company that is held by someone other than a current shareholder. Therefore, to determine the market value of equity, these claims by option grantees should be subtracted from the company's total value in exactly the same way that debt is subtracted. If you are analyzing a company with a relatively small number of options, then you may want to ignore them. However, if the company has a large number of these options, then it might be important for you to incorporate them into your analysis. To do this, you may want to include their value in the *Comprehensive* worksheet in the section called optional items for special accounting adjustments. For more on valuing these options see a working paper that is posted to the book's web site.[5]

Summary

This appendix explains much of the accounting rationale for the manner in which the *Comprehensive* financial statements are simplified to the *Condensed* statements. If you want even more discussion of these accounting issues and the method of condensing financial statements, see the book's web site, where there are line-by-line explanations of the *Comprehensive* and *Condensed* statements.

[5]See the paper by M. Ehrhardt, 2003, "Employee Incentive Stock Options: To Be Expensed or Not to Be, That Is Not the Question," working paper, University of Tennessee.

Chapter 11

Estimating the Weighted Average Cost of Capital

Introduction

In Chapters 4 and 7, we showed you how to calculate the weighted average cost of capital (WACC) for hypothetical companies, ACME General and Van Leer Products. In this chapter, we will show you how to calculate the cost of capital for an actual company, Home Depot. The increased realism means considerably more complexity, but we show how to handle this by making maximum use of Internet resources. You should open up the file ***Home Depot.xls*** and go to the *WACC* worksheet because this shows the calculations.

As we estimate Home Depot's cost of capital, note that we are setting the current date to be May 21, 2003 (the date we actually collected the information used in our analysis). Most firms update their WACC estimates at least once each year, and more frequently when significant macroeconomic or firm-specific events occur.

We'll start by estimating the weights in the target capital structure, which are the percentages of the firm's financing that are expected to come from each source of investor capital. Given the sources of financing, we will then estimate each source's cost. Finally, we will estimate the overall weighted average cost of capital.

Estimating the Target Weights

To calculate the WACC, we need to estimate the target percentages of the firm that we think will be financed in the future with long-term debt (w_{LTD}), short-term debt (w_{STD}), preferred stock (w_P), and common stock (w_S). Although Home Depot's actual financing may fluctuate, the target weights are the ones that Home Depot will shoot for in the future. Since our objective is to discount future free cash flows, target weights should be used in our forward-looking valuation analysis.

In Chapter 10, the *Condensed* version of Home Depot's balance sheet for the year ending on February 2, 2003, showed that Home Depot had \$1,321 million in long-term debt. It also showed that Home Depot had \$19,802 million in total common equity. The balance sheet also showed no short-term debt or preferred stock. It's very tempting, but wrong, to calculate w_{LTD}, the percent financed with long-term debt, from these book values:

$$w_{LTD} = \frac{\text{LT debt}}{\text{LT debt + ST debt + Preferred stock + Common stock}} \quad \textbf{(11-1)}$$

$$= \frac{\$1{,}321}{(\$1{,}321 + \$19{,}802)}$$

$$= 0.063 = 6.3\%.$$

However, this would be wrong on two counts. First, the target weights should be based on market values, not book values from the financial statements. This is because investors expect a return on the values of their investments, which are equal to the values as shown in the marketplace, not the amounts shown on the financial statements. Second, they should reflect the firm's target weights for the future, not necessarily the current weights, because the resulting WACC will be used to discount *future* free cash flows.

Estimating the Values of the Financing Components

As a first step in finding the targets, let's calculate the current weights based on market values. In theory, we need the market values of short-term debt, long-term debt, preferred stock, and common stock. The *WACC* worksheet provides cells to enter this data, if it is available. In practice, however, much of this data is not available. For example, in a perfect world, we would find the market value of Home Depot's long-term debt by multiplying the number of bonds by the price per bond. (The number of bonds is usually reported in the footnotes to the financial statements; we'll show you where to find a bond's price in the next section.) We would repeat this for each different bond issue and then sum them to find the total market value of debt. However, market data for long-term debt is often not available because many corporate debt obligations (e.g., long-term bank debt, privately placed bond issues) are often not actively traded. So unless we have reasons to believe that the market values of long-term debt are *significantly* different than the reported book values, we use the value of long-term debt shown on its financial statements as an estimate of the market value of its long-term debt.[1] In summary, if you know the actual total market value of long-term debt, enter it in the *WACC* worksheet. Otherwise, just accept the default value for long-term debt as shown in the *WACC* worksheet, which is the book value of long-term debt taken from the *Condensed* worksheet.

There are two reasons why short-term debt usually has a market value that is close to its reported book value. First, short-term debt often has a floating interest

[1]Generally speaking, market values of debt securities do not fluctuate as much as equity market values; hence the book value for debt is often a reasonable approximation for its market value. Indeed, Home Depot included estimates of the market values of its long-term debt obligations in the footnotes to its February 2003 10-K: "The market values of the publicly traded 6 1/2% and 5 3/8% Senior Notes were approximately $537 million and $538 million, respectively. The estimated fair value of all other long-term borrowings, excluding capital lease obligations, approximated the carrying value of $51 million. These fair values were estimated using a discounted cash flow analysis based on the Company's incremental borrowing rate for similar liabilities." These estimated market values of debt total $1,126 million, which is fairly close to their reported book value of $1,321.

rate, which means its market value is virtually equal to its maturity (or par) value as reported on the balance sheets. Second, even if the interest rate on short-term debt is different than the current market interest rate, the market value of the debt is close to its maturity value because the time until maturity is relatively short. In summary, if you know the actual total market value of short-term debt, enter it in the *WACC* worksheet. Otherwise, just accept the default value for short-term debt as shown in the *WACC* worksheet, which is the book value of short-term debt taken from the *Condensed* worksheet.

Home Depot, like most companies, doesn't have any preferred stock. However, some companies do issue preferred stock, particularly utilities.[2] If you are analyzing a company with preferred stock, then in a perfect world you would enter the market value of the preferred stock in the *WACC* worksheet, found by multiplying the number of preferred shares by the price per share. (The number of shares is usually reported in the footnotes to the financial statements; we'll show you where to find the price of preferred stock in the next section.) However, preferred stock usually makes up only a small part of a firm's financing, so we usually just accept the default value in the *WACC* worksheet, which is the book value of preferred stock as reported on the *Condensed* balanced sheets.[3]

Thus, we are usually willing to use the reported book values for long-term debt, short-term debt, and preferred stock as estimates of their market values. ***However, we never use reported book values for common equity!*** We always use an estimate of the current market value of equity, also known as market capitalization, or just market cap. The *WACC* worksheet has a place for you to enter the current price per share and the current number of shares (the default value for the number of shares is the number reported for the end of the last fiscal year, obtained from the *Comprehensive* worksheet). Home Depot has about 2,336 million outstanding shares (as of February 2, 2003) and a stock price of $30.62 (as of May 21, 2003). Thus, its market value of common equity is calculated in the *WACC* sheet as $30.62(2,336 million) = $71,528 million.

Notice that the actual market value of Home Depot's equity (the current stock price multiplied by the number of shares) is $71.5 billion, but the book value of common equity as reported on its balance sheets is only about $19.8 billion. Therefore, using the book value instead of the market value of equity often leads to large errors. For this reason, we always use the actual market value of equity when the firm is publicly traded.

The total market value of Home Depot is the sum of the values of long-term debt, short-term debt, preferred stock, and common equity.

$$
\begin{aligned}
\text{Total market value} &= \text{LT debt} + \text{ST debt} + \text{Preferred stock} + \text{Common equity} \\
&= \$1{,}321 + \$0 + \$0 + \$71{,}528 \qquad \textbf{(11-2)} \\
&= \$72{,}849 \text{ million}
\end{aligned}
$$

---

[2]We provide a detailed discussion of preferred stock in the Chapter 4 appendix.

[3]For example, Alcoa has preferred stock, but it makes up only a small percentage of its financing. With 557,740 shares of preferred stock selling for $67 per share, the market value of Alcoa's preferred stock is about $37.4 million. Alcoa overall has about $6.6 billion in debt, and about $30.3 billion in common stock (based on its market value). Thus, preferred stock makes up less than 1% of its current financing.

Estimating the Target Weight for Long-Term Debt

The percentage of Home Depot that is currently financed with long-term debt, w_{LTD}, is

$$\begin{aligned} w_{LTD} &= \frac{\text{LT debt}}{\text{LT debt + ST debt + Preferred stock + Common equity}} \\ &= \frac{\$1{,}321}{(\$1{,}321 + \$0 + \$0 + \$71{,}528)} \\ &= 0.018 = 1.8\%. \end{aligned} \tag{11-3}$$

Now comes the part that requires your judgment. We just found the percentage of Home Depot's financing that is currently provided by long-term debt, but we need the target percentage for the future. If you worked at Home Depot, you could ask someone in the CFO's office what proportion of debt and equity would be used in the future. As outsiders, we must use our own judgment. Even though Home Depot currently has a very small amount of long-term debt, we think it will have more long-term debt in the future. First, Chapter 10 showed that it has a times-interest-earned ratio, defined as its earnings before interest divided by its interest payments, of over 123. This is much higher than the industry ratio of 14.35 (see the *Hist Analys* worksheet). Furthermore, most firms don't become financially distressed until this ratio drops to around 3 to 4. Therefore, Home Depot can certainly afford more debt. Second, Home Depot is still growing rapidly and will probably finance this growth by reinvesting earnings and issuing new debt rather than by issuing new equity. Third, finance theory shows that modest levels of debt are valuable because firms can deduct interest expenses when calculating taxable income.

These factors suggest to us that Home Depot will probably increase its utilization of debt financing in the future, so we have assumed a target w_{LTD} of about 22% in market value terms, even though its current w_{LTD} is much lower. When we examine the projected financial statements in Chapter 13, we'll make sure that Home Depot's projected times-interest-earned ratio doesn't drop to a dangerous level based on this assumption. If the times-interest-earned ratio does drop too low, we'll come back and reduce our estimated target w_{LTD}. This illustrates the iterative nature of valuation analysis: You must make many judgment calls, and you will often revisit many of your decisions before you complete your analysis. In summary, unless we have information from the CFO, we usually assume a company will have a future target w_{LTD} in the range of 15% to 30%, depending on its financial strength.

Estimating the Target Weight for Short-Term Debt

The percentage of Home Depot that is currently financed with short-term debt, w_{STD}, is

$$\begin{aligned} w_{STD} &= \frac{\text{ST debt}}{\text{LT debt + ST debt + Preferred stock + Common equity}} \\ &= \frac{\$0}{(\$1{,}321 + \$0 + \$0 + \$71{,}528)} \\ &= 0.0 = 0\%. \end{aligned} \tag{11-4}$$

Home Depot currently has no short-term debt, so we assume that its target future capital structure will also have no short-term debt: $w_{STD} = 0$.

However, some firms do have short-term debt and have had it each year in their historical financial statements. Because annual financial statements are reported only once a year, it could be that a firm has short-term debt only at that particular time of the year. For example, a retailer might have large inventories and finance them with short-term debt during the Christmas season, but pay off the short-term debt during the spring and summer. In this case, we would not consider the short-term debt to be a permanent source of capital, so we would set the target w_{STD} to zero. On the other hand, some companies do have short-term debt throughout the year, and so it is a permanent source of financing. For these situations, we would choose a target w_{STD} that is above zero. We would use the same reasoning as we used for long-term debt. First, we start with the w_{STD} based on the current situation. We usually leave it at this level, unless we have additional information from the CFO. However, after completing our projections, we always verify that the projected times-interest-earned ratio is high enough (above 4) so that the firm isn't likely to become financially distressed. If the ratio is too low, then we come back and reduce the total debt, by reducing w_{STD} and/or w_{LTD}.

Estimating the Target Weight for Preferred Stock

The percentage of Home Depot that is currently financed with preferred stock, w_{PS}, is

$$
\begin{aligned}
w_{PS} &= \frac{\text{Preferred stock}}{\text{LT debt} + \text{ST debt} + \text{Preferred stock} + \text{Common equity}} \\
&= \frac{\$0}{(\$1{,}321 + \$0 + \$0 + \$71{,}528)} \qquad \text{(11-5)} \\
&= 0.0 = 0\%.
\end{aligned}
$$

Home Depot currently has no preferred stock, so we assume that its target future capital structure will also have no preferred stock: $w_{PS} = 0$.

However, some firms do have preferred stock. In these cases, we typically assume the future target weight will be the same as the current weight, unless we have other information from the CFO.

Estimating the Target Weight for Common Equity

We have already estimated the target weights for the other components of financing: long-term debt, short-term debt, and preferred stock. The weights must sum to 100%, so the target percentage of Home Depot that will be financed with common stock, w_S, is

$$
\begin{aligned}
w_S &= 1.0 - (w_{LTD} + w_{STD} + w_{PS}) \\
&= 1.0 - (0.22 + 0 + 0) \qquad \text{(11-6)} \\
&= 0.78 = 78\%.
\end{aligned}
$$

Now that we have estimated the target weights, we must estimate the costs of each source of capital.

Estimating the Cost of Long-Term Debt

Because we're going to use the WACC to find the present value of the company's future free cash flows, we want to know the rate the company would pay if it issued long-term debt today, not the historical rate it has paid on its existing debt. In other words, the pre-tax cost of long-term debt, r_{LTD}, is the rate at which a company could issue new debt in the current investment climate. If you work for a company, its treasurer might know this (or could possibly find the answer by calling the company's banks or investment bankers). But if you don't work at the company you're analyzing, then you must use one of the following methods: (1) calculate the yield on the company's existing debt using the techniques discussed in Chapter 4 (or observe this from a published source, as we describe later), or (2) find other companies' yields on debt with similar features, including risk and maturity, and use that as a proxy for your company's yield.

Some companies have publicly traded bonds for which there is an active market, with the yields reported along with the bond prices. For example, Home Depot's footnotes to its February 2, 2003, financial statements show two outstanding bond issues; one is a 6.5% coupon bond maturing on September 15, 2004; the other is a 5.375% coupon bond maturing April 1, 2006. We'll first see whether these bonds are actively traded and if we can find the yields (yield to maturity, or YTM) on either of those two issues.

If you go to a web site for a company called Bonds Online Group, at **http://www.bondsonline.com**, you will find a wealth of useful information about bonds. If the issues are actively traded, we can find information about individual corporate bond issues, including current market prices and yield calculations. On the right side of the Bonds Online web page is a section called Bond Search/Quote Center. One of the sub-items is Corporate Bonds. Clicking on this, we get a screen with a dialog box asking us to log on. Log on, or if you have never used the web site before, you will have to register (it was free at the time of this writing). Another dialogue box lets us search for bonds. We can enter the name of the company in the box called Issue and search for all bonds issued by the company for which there is an active market.[4] Searching for Home Depot, we obtained a table with all available market data for its bonds. Within that table, clicking on the company name within each bond issue row gives additional detail, including the date the bond was originally issued (called the Dated Date). Exhibit 11–1 contains selected data relating to outstanding offers to sell Home Depot bonds.

We'll discuss the rating a bit later, but notice that both offers are for the same bond issue, namely Home Depot's 5.375% coupon bonds maturing in April 2006. One offer is for 300 bonds, and the other for 500. We don't report the asking prices, but the reported yields are based on the asking prices and were calculated according to the method we discussed in Chapter 4, saving us the time and trouble of calculating the yields ourselves. Apparently, there was no market activity in Home

[4]If we know the CUSIP (which is a unique identifier), then we can enter it and search for a particular bond. We will show you how to find the CUSIP later in this chapter when we use the Moody's web site to find a company's bond ratings.

Exhibit 11-1 Selected Information on Home Depot Bonds

Rating	Dated date	Offer quantity	Coupon rate	Maturity date	Yield (%)
Aa3	04-12-2001	315	5.375	04-01-2006	1.786
Aa3	04-12-2001	500	5.375	04-01-2006	1.628

*Source:: **http://www.bondsonline.com/**, May 21, 2003.*

Depot's 6.5% coupon bond, hence no current quotes. Be careful when navigating its web site—you don't want to accidentally enter a purchase order!

One way of estimating Home Depot's cost of new debt financing is to use the yields on its existing bonds, which implies that Home Depot could issue bonds maturing in about 3 years with a coupon rate in the 1.6% to 1.8% range. This result would be satisfactory, except that is probably unrealistic to assume that Home Depot will issue long-term debt with a maturity of only 3 years. What should we do if we think the long-term debt will have a longer maturity? This brings us to the second approach for estimating Home Depot's cost of debt, which is the same approach we would use if a company had no publicly traded debt.

There are literally thousands of outstanding corporate bond issues, creating demand among investors and issuing firms for up-to-date information about the bond market. One key piece of information is the default risk of a particular company's bonds. Several firms are in the business of providing **bond ratings** that reflect the default risk on specific bonds. The major firms providing such ratings are: Duff & Phelps Credit Rating Co., Fitch Investors Service, Moody's Investor Services, and Standard & Poor's Corporation. For example, Moody's has 21 rating categories, ranging from Aaa, indicating maximum safety, all the way down to C, indicating that the issuer may be in default. When investors want to determine the yield to expect from investing in a given bond or when firms want to know the interest rate they will have to offer to be competitive, they often use bond ratings.

Some sources (the ratings agencies, some investment banking firms, and bond brokers) calculate yields on individual bonds that are publicly traded and provide average yields for all bonds of a given maturity and rating. The data is usually presented in terms of the **spread**, defined as the difference between the yield on bonds of a given rating category and yields on U.S. Treasury securities with the same maturity.

If a firm has bonds outstanding, then the bonds are probably rated by one of the rating agencies, and any new bonds issued will likely have the same rating, unless they are subordinated to the already outstanding bonds (i.e., given a lower payment priority in the event of bankruptcy). Here is the basic approach. First, find the risk-free interest rate. Second, measure the firm's risk, using the rating of its existing bonds, if possible. If the firm does not have rated bonds, use the rating of another firm in the same industry, having similar size and leverage. Third, given this rating, determine the spread. Fourth, add the spread to the risk-free rate. The following discussion applies this approach to Home Depot.

We start with an estimate of the risk-free rate. Since the WACC will be used to discount all future free cash flows, the appropriate risk-free rate is the rate on a long-term U.S. Treasury bond. Our favorite source for this data is Yahoo! Finance, at **http://bonds.yahoo.com/rates.html**. Then navigate to Composite Bond Rates, where we find the risk-free rate data we need, which is reproduced in Exhibit 11-2.

Another good source of Treasury yields is the Federal Reserve, whose web page is **http://www.federalreserve.gov**. When you get to this page, select Economic Research and Data from the panel on the left. When this page comes up, select Statistics: Releases and Historical Data. Finally, select the Daily update for H.15 Selected Interest Rates.[5] After this page comes up, scroll down and find the section on Treasury constant maturities. We found the Federal Reserve web site data was a bit stale, since its most recent quotes were two days old, for May 19, 2003. As it happened, comparing the second and fourth columns of Exhibit 11-2, we observe that yields on long-term Treasury securities dropped about 20 basis points in the week prior to May 21! This illustrates why getting current data may make a difference and why in this case we use the data from the Yahoo! web site.

Of the long-term rates in Exhibit 11-2, which maturity should we pick as the "correct" risk-free rate? To be honest, experts disagree. We usually pick a risk-free rate that is somewhere between the 10-year and 30-year rates, depending on the maturities the company has typically chosen in the past for its debt. As we can see from the information in Exhibit 11-1 on Home Depot's existing bonds, they were issued in April 2001, with only a 5-year maturity. From this limited amount of historical information, it appears that Home Depot has used debt with a relatively short maturity. Let's assume that future debt issues by Home Depot will have longer maturities than those shown in Exhibit 11-1 and that the average maturity

[5]Although we are going to use Fed data only from this source, you might want to look around at the other data items. One especially nice feature is the ability to download historical data.

Exhibit 11-2 Yields on Treasury Bonds for May 21, 2003

	U.S. Treasury Bonds			
Maturity	Yield	Yesterday	Last week	Last month
3 Month	0.93	0.92	0.93	1.06
6 Month	0.98	0.96	1.02	1.13
2 Year	1.29	1.25	1.37	1.66
5 Year	2.29	2.29	2.47	2.95
10 Year	3.32	3.35	3.51	3.98
30 Year	4.28	4.35	4.50	4.89

*Source: **http://bonds.yahoo.com/rates.html**, May 21, 2003.*

of future outstanding bond issues will be 10 years. Given the Treasury yield data in Exhibit 11-2 and this choice of debt maturity, 3.32% is a reasonable estimate of the risk-free rate (but we wouldn't argue if you chose a rate as low as 3.0% or as high as 4.0%, which could be easily justified by different assumptions about average maturity).

Our next step is to estimate the risk of Home Depot's bonds. Fortunately, many bonds have ratings that classify the bond's risk. To find the rating for Home Depot, we could go to any of several web sites, such as Bonds Online or Moody's, **http://www.moodys.com**. Because we've already looked at the Bonds Online, let's try the Moody's site.[6] In the upper right corner of its home page is a box that allows you to search for bond ratings. We find it easier to search by ticker, and so we enter Home Depot's ticker, HD, and then search. The search found Home Depot, and so we click on it, which brings up a page with recent rating reports for two bond issues. Consistent with the information we got from Bonds Online, these reports show that Home Depot's debt has a rating of Aa3.[7]

Now that we have the measure of bond-risk, we need to find the spread, which is the difference between the interest rate on a risky bond and the risk-free rate. To do this, we go to the web site **http://www.bondsonline.com**. On the right side of this screen is a section called Corporate Bonds. Choose the sub-item called Industrial Spreads. This will bring up a table similar to the one shown in Exhibit 11-3.

This table shows the spreads for bonds with various ratings and maturities. Notice that the rows are sorted from least risky (Moody's gives these bonds an Aaa rating, while Standard & Poor's gives them a rating of AAA) to most risky. Notice also that the spreads get bigger as the risk increases. Finally, notice that the spreads for bonds with the same ratings get bigger as the maturity increases because long-term bonds are riskier than short-term bonds.

Home Depot has an Aa3 rating, which, according to the data in Exhibit 11-3, has a spread of 67 basis points (100 basis points equal 1 percentage point). To estimate the rate Home Depot would pay on its long-term debt, we add 0.67% to our estimate of the risk-free rate.

$$\begin{aligned} r_{LTD} &= r_{RF} + \text{Spread} \\ &= 3.32\% + 0.67\% = 3.99\% \end{aligned} \tag{11-7}$$

We can check the consistency of this risk-free rate plus yield spread approach by comparison with the actual yields that we observed for Home Depot's existing bond issues. If we were to assume that Home Depot will always have debt with average maturity of about 3 years, then we should estimate r_{LTD} using a risk-free rate and yield spread for a 3-year maturity. Referring to the data from the shown in Exhibit 11-2 and interpolating between the 2-year and 5-year yields, it looks like the 3-year risk-free rate is about 1.62%. Looking back at the yield-spread data in Exhibit 11-3, the 3-year spread would be about 37 basis points for an Aa3 bond.

[6]You will have to register, but it was free at the time we wrote this.

[7]Sometimes scrolling down the page will show that Moody's has provided data for particular bond issues. If you want to track down the yield on a particular debt issue, click on the debt issue, which will bring up a screen providing more information on the bond. Be sure to write down the CUSIP number because it will be helpful in locating the bond's yield, as we show later in this chapter.

Exhibit 11-3 Bond Yield Spreads for Industrial Bonds

Rating	1 yr	2 yr	3 yr	5 yr	7 yr	10 yr	30 yr
Aaa/AAA	10	15	17	20	30	37	52
Aa1/AA+	15	20	26	30	40	47	60
Aa2/AA	20	30	32	35	48	57	65
Aa3/AA−	25	35	37	43	58	67	72
A1/A+	35	45	51	62	76	85	99
A2/A	45	55	65	78	90	105	122
A3/A−	55	70	81	88	109	120	143
Baa1/BBB+	77	92	106	116	129	147	168
Baa2/BBB	97	112	120	132	145	160	183
Baa3/BBB−	117	125	133	145	157	172	215
Ba1/BB+	375	400	355	350	325	300	325
Ba2/BB	400	525	530	470	425	400	375
Ba3/BB−	475	575	580	525	475	450	525
B1/B+	575	650	725	575	525	475	575
B2/B	600	675	725	600	550	550	850
B3/B−	825	925	880	870	825	900	925
Caa/CCC	1650	1725	1680	1530	1425	1500	1650

Source: ***http://www.bondsonline.com/****, May 21, 2003.*

Therefore, we estimate Home Depot's cost of debt, assuming a 3-year average maturity, to be

$$\begin{aligned} r_{LTD} &= r_{RF} + \text{Spread} \\ &= 1.62\% + 0.37\% = 1.99\%. \end{aligned} \qquad \textbf{(11-7a)}$$

Notice that this is reasonably close to the yields on the outstanding Home Depot bonds, as shown in Exhibit 11-1.

However, as we indicated earlier, few firms use permanent debt financing with such short maturities. Therefore, we believe it is more likely that Home Depot's cost of debt in the future will be closer to our estimate of 4%, based on an assumed 10-year average maturity.

Finally, what if a company's long-term debt isn't listed with Moody's or Bonds Online? Our best bet is to find one or more similar companies (with respect to industry, size, and leverage) that are listed and assume our company would have the same bond rating. Then follow the same procedures as outlined above. For example, Home Depot's closest competitor is Lowe's Companies. As of May 21, 2003, Lowe's has an outstanding 6.375% coupon bond issue maturing in December 2005 that has a quoted yield of about 1.8%. The Lowe's bonds only have an A3 rating, however, and this should be taken into account when using the comparison. Lowe's also has some bonds with longer maturities outstanding, and these corroborate the conclusion we reached earlier when we assumed that Home Depot would use longer maturity in its future debt financing.

Home Depot will deduct its interest expenses when calculating its tax liabilities. Therefore, the after-tax cost to Home Depot of providing a 4% return to its bondholders is 4%(1 − T), where T is its tax rate. The *Hist Analys* worksheet shows that Home Depot's average tax rate has been between 38% and 39%, so we'll use a tax rate of 38.6%. This means Home Depot's after-tax cost of debt is 4%(1 − 0.386) = 2.45%.

In summary, it will cost Home Depot about 2.45%, on an after-tax basis, to provide a 4% return to its bondholders.

Estimating the Cost of Short-Term Debt

For most companies, the rate on short-term debt is a floating rate, that is, the debt contract calls for resetting the interest rate periodically relative to the prime rate or to the London Interbank Offer Rate (LIBOR). You can easily get the current level of the prime rate from the Federal Reserve's web site, following the same procedure we showed earlier for finding the rates on Treasury bonds, and current LIBOR rates are available from a number of sources, including Bloomberg (**http://www.bloomberg.com/markets/rates/index.html**) and Bankrate.com (**http://www.bankrate.com/brm/ratehm.asp**). For example, the prime rate was 4.25% when we obtained the Treasury bond data; the 3-month LIBOR rate was 1.28%. A strong company like Home Depot can probably borrow at the prime rate, or less. As a company's risk increases, the rate on short-term debt will be 1 to 2 percentage points higher than the prime.[8]

Therefore, if Home Depot used short-term debt as a permanent source of financing, we would estimate its pre-tax cost to be about 4.25%. Using the tax rate of 38.6%, Home Depot's after-tax cost of debt is about 4.25%(1 − 0.386) = 2.61%.

Estimating the Cost of Preferred Stock

Home Depot, like most companies, doesn't have preferred stock. However, if a company has preferred stock, the quickest way to estimate its cost is to look at a current quote from the market. For example, Alcoa has preferred stock with a $3.75 dividend payment. Using its Yahoo symbol, AA_p and getting a Detailed Quote, the stock has a yield of 5.6%.[9] If Alcoa were to issue any new preferred stock, then it would have a coupon rate of about 5.6%. Thus, Alcoa's cost of preferred stock, r_{PS}, is about 5.6%.

Estimating the Cost of Common Stock

Our approach to estimating the cost of common stock is similar to that for debt: Find the risk-free rate, and then adjust it for the risk of the stock. Recall from Chapter 4 that the Capital Asset Pricing Model (CAPM) defines the relationship

[8]Banks refuse to lend to very risky companies, and so most of their loans are less than 2% points above the prime.
[9]The detailed quote shows a price of $67.00, so the yield is 5.6% = 0.056 = $3.75/$67.00. Refer back to Chapter 4 and the appendix for details.

between risk and return for stocks. In particular, a stock's risk is measured by beta. Recall that the market risk premium, RP_M, is the extra rate of return that the market (that is, common stocks generally) is expected to provide above and beyond the rate on a risk-free security. Here is the equation for the CAPM.

$$r_s = r_{RF} + \text{Beta}(RP_M) \tag{11-8}$$

To estimate the cost of equity for Home Depot, we need an estimate of beta. We could always download stock prices from Yahoo, calculate historical stock returns, and then use regression analysis to estimate beta, as we described in the appendix to Chapter 4. However, this requires considerable time and effort, so we usually get estimates of betas from Internet sources. Our favorite source is Thomson Financial, at **http://www.thomsonfn.com**. Enter HD in the Stock Quote field (at the top left of the web page), and search. When the next page comes up, select TipSheet (shown on the left column) and then Go. Scroll down and find the beta, which was 1.38 on May 21, 2003.

Another useful source is MultexInvestor, **http://www.multexinvestor.com**. Going to the MultexInvestor web site on May 21, 2003, we entered Home Depot's ticker symbol (HD) in the box at the top of the page and got a new page with lots of information about Home Depot's stock. One section, called Figures At-A-Glance, gives an estimate of beta. For Home Depot, this was 1.38. In other words, Home Depot had a beta greater than 1.0, so it was somewhat riskier than the average stock (which has a beta of 1.0).

Beta is also easily obtainable from **http://www.zacks.com** (after selecting The Whole Enchilada), which reports a beta of 1.30.

Keep in mind that a stock's beta will change as time and conditions change, just as interest rates change, so always get current values. For the remainder of our analysis, we will use the Thomson beta of 1.38.

The difference between the expected return on the stock market (i.e., on a well-diversified portfolio such as the S&P 500 stock portfolio) and the risk-free rate is called the market risk premium (RP_M). Although analysts differ in their opinions about the magnitude of the market risk premium, most think it is fairly stable and is somewhere around 4% to 7%. The risk premium is driven primarily by investors' attitudes towards risk. When investors are feeling cautious, their required risk premium is high, which tends to cause stock prices to be relatively low. On the other hand, when investors are feeling confident, their required premium is low, and stock prices are relatively high. Therefore, when the market is relatively high, we estimate a risk premium that is at the low end of the range; when the market is relatively low, we use a risk premium at the high end of the range. Given the current (May 2003) situation in the equity markets, we are using an estimated risk premium of 5%.

What's the cost of equity for Home Depot as based on the CAPM? Given a beta of 1.38 and a market risk premium of 5%, all we need is an estimate of the risk-free rate. Just as when we found the cost of debt, the risk-free rate should be the rate on a long-term government bond, which on May 21, 2003, for a 10-year Treasury bond was around 3.32%. Note we are using the 10-year rate, consistent with the rate we used for estimating the cost of Home Depot's long-term debt. We use the information we have gathered along with the logic of the CAPM to estimate Home Depot's cost of equity.

$$r_s = r_{RF} + \text{Beta}(RP_M)$$
$$r_s = 3.32\% + 1.38(5\%) = 10.2\% \quad \textbf{(11-8a)}$$

This means that Home Depot's shareholders must get a return of around 10.2% in order to compensate them from the risk they bear.[10]

Putting the Pieces Together: Calculating the WACC

Now that we've done the hard part, it's pretty easy to actually calculate the WACC. Recall from Chapter 2 that even though investors receive their required return on debt, it doesn't cost the company the full amount because the company can deduct the interest payments when calculating its taxes. This means the cost of debt is actually the after-tax required return.

$$\text{WACC} = w_s r_s + w_{LTD}(1 - T)r_{LTD} + w_{STD}(1 - T)r_{STD} + w_{PS}r_{PS} \quad \textbf{(11-9)}$$

As shown in Home Depot's financial statements in Chapter 9, its tax rate is about 38.6%. Using the other values we estimated earlier in this chapter, Home Depot's WACC is approximately

$$\text{WACC} = 0.78(10.2\%) + 0.22(1 - 0.386)(4.0\%) + 0.0(1 - 0.386)(4.25\%) + 0.0(0\%)$$
$$= 8.5\%. \quad \textbf{(11-9a)}$$

Complications and Advanced Issues

The procedure just described for calculating the WACC works well for most companies, but there are some occasions when you might have to address some of the following issues: (1) convertible securities and (2) privately held firms or divisions within a firm.

Convertible Securities

Some debt and preferred stocks are convertible into equity. For example, suppose a nonconvertible bond, often called a straight bond, has a coupon rate of 8% and is selling for $1,000. Suppose instead the company is considering issuing some new convertible debt with a coupon rate of 7% and a maturity of 10 years. Each bond can be exchanged for 20 shares of stock. The new convertible debt will be issued at a price of $1,000 per bond (bonds are normally issued at par, which is a price of

[10]The reader may get the impression that we are overly casual in saying that a particular rate is "about" the rate we give. This is because, in truth, the formulas used to estimate the required return on equity are based on formulas that might best be regarded as rules-of-thumb. Furthermore, the inputs to those formulas, especially the beta coefficient, are estimates that may be subject to considerable estimation error. In our opinion, cost of capital estimates are, at best, only accurate to a couple of tenths of a percentage point and in many cases may be far less accurate. We recommend that when confidence in the estimate of the cost of capital is low, the valuation process should include sensitivity analysis with respect to the estimated discount rate.

\$1,000). Suppose also that the current stock price is \$45 per share. Therefore, the new bond would be worth \$1,000 if kept as a bond, but would be worth only \$900 if it were exchanged for stock (\$900 is equal to 20 shares multiplied by the current stock price of \$45). However, there is some chance that the stock price will climb in the future, which might make the bond more valuable if it is exchanged for stock.

For example, if the stock price climbs to \$60 over the next few months, then the bond would be worth \$1,200 if it were exchanged for 20 shares of stock. Because there is the chance for this future profit, this convertible bond is clearly more valuable than straight debt with the same coupon rate. Because of this extra value, the company can sell the bond for \$1,000 even though it has a coupon rate less than the 8% rate on the straight debt. The yield to maturity is 7%, because the bond is sold at par. But the yield to maturity (at the time the bond is sold and at future dates when market interest rates may have changed) understates the true cost of convertible bond financing to the issuing firm because its shareholders will end up giving the bondholder a "bonus" if conversion occurs. So what is the exact cost of the convertible debt?

If you want an exact answer, you'll have to hire a highly priced consultant. (Hint: Our e-mail addresses are shown at the beginning of the book.) But if you're willing to live with an approximation, which we recommend, then here is how to handle a convertible. First, find the lower bound for the cost of capital by ignoring the conversion feature. Second, find an approximate upper bound for the cost of capital by assuming the convertible bond is replaced with an equivalent amount of straight debt and new equity. Third, pick a WACC somewhere between the upper and lower bounds, depending on the likelihood that the bond will be converted.

To find the lower bound for the WACC, let's naively ignore the conversion feature. For example, suppose the company we considered above has 2 million shares of stock trading at \$45 per share. Its cost of equity is 12%. Let's suppose the company has 30,000 convertible bonds with a 7% coupon rate trading at a par value of \$1,000 per bond. This means the current value of the firm is \$45(2 million) + \$1,000 (30,000) = \$120 million. The current w_s is 0.75 = \$90/\$120, and the current w_{LTD} is 0.25 = \$30/\$120. With a tax rate of 40%, the lower bound for the cost of capital, $WACC_L$, is

$$WACC_L = 12\%(0.75) + 7\%(1 - 0.4)(0.25) = 10.05\%.$$

Of course, we know this is too low, since it doesn't reflect the cost of the conversion feature. In essence, it assumes there is no probability of ever converting the bonds.

To find the approximate upper bound, suppose the firm had instead issued straight bonds and equity. Since the straight bond portion of the convertible bond is equal to \$886.88, the firm essentially raised \$886.88(30,000) = \$26.6 million in straight debt when it issued the convertible debt.[11] Let's suppose it raised the other \$3.4 million by issuing equity. Ignoring flotation costs, the new market value of equity is equal to the old value of \$90 million plus the \$3.4 million in new equity,

[11]To find the value of equivalent straight debt, we discount the convertible bond's payments at the straight debt rate of 8%. If the convertible bond matures in 30 years and has semiannual payments of \$35, then its value is \$886.88.

for a total of \$93.4 million. This results in a new w_s of 0.778 = \$93.4/\$120 and a new w_{LTD} of 0.222 = \$26.6/\$120. Using the 8% cost of debt on the straight debt, the upper bound for the cost of capital, $WACC_U$, is

$$WACC_U = 12\%(0.778) + 8\%(1 - 0.4)(0.222) = 10.40\%.$$

Of course, this is too high, since it assumes a 100 percent probability of immediate conversion.[12]

If there is a very low probability that the bond will be converted, we would use a WACC close to the lower bound of 10.05%. If there were a high probability of conversion, we would use a WACC closer to the upper bound of 10.40%. For this example, the stock price would have to climb to \$50 before it would be profitable to convert. Because the stock price is already at \$45 and there is a long time until the bonds mature, the likelihood of conversion is probably high. Therefore, we would use a cost of capital around 10.3%. This isn't an exact solution, but we have found that it works very well in practice, and it sure beats hiring a high-priced consultant.

Privately Held Firms and Divisions

Much of the data we use for evaluating a publicly held firm is not available for a privately held firm. For example, the market values of debt and equity are not available, nor is the beta. In this situation, you must approximate the beta and cost of debt by using the values for similar publicly traded firms. The target capital structure weights must be obtained from the CFO or may be approximated by the capital structure weights of similar firms.

One appealing feature of the corporate valuation model is that it can be applied to divisions of companies. However, the beta is not available for a division. In this case, use either the beta for the company or the beta for a company that competes in the same line of business as the division. Unless you have some reason to believe differently, use the company's target capital structure weights.

Summary

This chapter showed you how to estimate the weighted average cost of capital for an actual company, Home Depot. The process requires using information from the firm's balance sheets, information from the financial markets (e.g., interest rates, default risk spreads, common stock betas, and the market risk premium), and plenty of judgment. The framework of the *WACC* worksheet is structured to organize the required data and facilitate your judgment calls.

The next chapter will extend the tools from Chapters 6 and 7, showing how to forecast Home Depot's financial statements for several years into the future. Chapter 13 will finish with a valuation of Home Depot's common stock.

[12]It is also too high because the cost of equity will likely be lower if there is less debt in the capital structure. See the Chapter 13 appendix for more on this.

Spreadsheet Problems

11-1 Computing Lowe's Cost of Capital

This project builds upon your expertise in using financial resources on the Internet. Start with the valuation spreadsheet for Lowe's that you created in Chapters 9 and 10.

a. Use Lowe's own web site or the Securities and Exchange Commission's web site (**http://www.sec.gov**) to look at the most recent 10-K (annual report). Confirm that the firm has long-term debt, and if it has a footnote explaining its debt composition, copy that information into a word processing document.

b. Use the MultexInvestor site (**http://www.multexinvestor.com**) to obtain the following data for Lowe's:
   1. A chart, covering the last 2 years, of stock price movements for Lowe's in comparison to the S&P 500 Stock Index. Copy the chart to a word processing document, and print it. (Hint: Try right-clicking on the chart—you will get a dialogue box giving several options on what you can do with the chart image.)
   2. Current stock price, number of shares outstanding, market capitalization, and beta coefficient. (Hint: Try the Snapshot link.) How does this compare with the beta from the Thomson Financial web site (**http://www.thomsonfin.com**)?
   3. Debt/equity ratio for Lowe's and for its industry. (Hint: Try the Ratios link.)
   4. Operating margin and effective tax rates for Lowe's and for its industry. (Hint: Try the Ratios link.)
   5. Identify three firms that you believe are close competitors with Lowe's. (Hint: Where MultexInvestor has identified the sector and industry for Lowe's, click on Industry, and using your own judgment, pick close competitors from the resulting list.)

c. Use the Bonds Online site (**http://www.bondsonline.com**) to obtain the following for Lowe's:
   1. A list of bonds for which there are quotes, including issue date, coupon rate, maturity date, and calculated yield to maturity.
   2. Now do the same for one of the close competitors you selected above. Choose the competitor with size and leverage closest to Lowe's, and check for bond data on the competitor.
   3. Now get the spreads on corporate bonds, and be sure to use the correct set of spreads—probably Industrials, but it depends on the sector/industry that Lowe's is in. (A reminder: Copy the relevant set of spreads, i.e., the ones appropriate to the bond rating category for Lowe's, into a spreadsheet.)

d. Use the Yahoo! Finance site (**http://bonds.yahoo.com/rates.html**) to obtain yields on Treasury securities of varying maturities.

e. Now estimate the current values of Lowe's sources of financing:
   1. Long-term debt.
   2. Short-term debt.
   3. Preferred stock (if any).
   4. Common equity.
f. Now estimate the target values of Lowe's sources of financing, using your own judgment:
   1. Long-term debt.
   2. Short-term debt.
   3. Preferred stock (if any).
   4. Common equity.
g. Now estimate Lowe's component costs of capital:
   1. Cost of long-term debt using the risk–free rate plus yield spread method.
   2. Cost of short-term debt.
   3. Cost of preferred stock (if any).
   4. Cost of equity by the CAPM method (this will require you to assume a value for the market risk premium).
h. Calculate Lowe's WACC.

11-2 Computing a Cost of Capital

Pick another company (or one that your professor assigns) and repeat the analysis in Problem 11-1.

Chapter 12

Projecting Cash Flows for an Actual Company: Home Depot

Introduction

The steps in applying our valuation model to a real company, Home Depot, are similar to those we applied in valuing hypothetical companies in previous chapters. First, we examined Home Depot's competitive environment and its current and historical financial statements in Chapter 10. As before, our analysis focused upon the information required when choosing *inputs* to project Home Depot's financial statements. Second, we estimated its weighted average cost of capital (WACC) in Chapter 11. Third, in this chapter we will use the insights gained from our analysis of Home Depot to help us project its financial statements. We'll also examine the projections to make sure they are economically reasonable. Fourth, in Chapter 13 we will use the projected financial statements to estimate the expected future free cash flows (FCF). We will then discount these projected free cash flows to find the value of Home Depot's operations and its intrinsic price per share.

In this chapter we focus on the mechanics of projection and the insights gained from explicitly linking the competitive analysis to the financial statements. As you will see, an important benefit of linking financial projections to underlying economic factors and operating policies is that it reveals the firm's **leverage points**—those activities, decisions, or policy choices that have the greatest impact on the firm's value. In particular, we will be able to identify the relationship between specific corporate operating policy choices and their financial consequences.

A Useful Perspective on Projections

We need to be candid; no one (at least, no one we know) has a crystal ball or any other device that gives him or her perfect foresight. So *no* projections will ever be 100% correct. As evidence that analysts' forecasts are always wrong, just consider the day-to-fluctuations in stock prices. These fluctuations, which are sometimes quite dramatic, occur because analysts and investors are continually reassessing their prior forecasts as new information arrives. Although projections will not be perfect, they are still extremely useful to investors in estimating the current value of a company, given the current information. They are also very useful to managers because they provide insight about the impact of different operating strategies.

The best way to deal with uncertainty in projections is to acknowledge that forecasts of financial performance are educated guesses and to apply the twin criteria that we discussed in Chapter 5, which bear repeating here:

- **Economic Plausibility.** The projected financial performance must reflect how the firm might realistically be expected to operate in the future given the information you have about the firm, its industry, and the economy as a whole.
- **Accounting Consistency.** The projections must satisfy basic accounting rules. For example, projected total assets must equal the projected total liabilities and owners' equity.

Because there are many combinations of specific assumptions that might meet these criteria, we use a valuation framework that allows us to test our valuation results for various combinations of assumptions. This allows us to identify which inputs are the most critical and gives us a better understanding of the specific operating factors that drive the value of the firm. Each set of assumptions is a scenario, so a **scenario analysis** is when we estimate a firm's value under different assumptions about sales, profitability, and asset utilization. In fact, a key advantage of FCF valuation is that it lends itself to scenario analysis.

The structure of the model, as described in previous chapters, requires us to make assumptions about key operating parameters: revenue growth, profit margins, working capital utilization, and fixed asset utilization. Estimates of key financial policies, such as capital structure and dividend policies, are also necessary for estimating the WACC and projecting financial statements. Not only are there many different types of inputs, but inputs must be chosen for each projected year, and our model projects 20 years.

It may seem that choosing values for such as large number of inputs is a daunting assignment. However, as we'll soon see with Home Depot, we have structured the valuation model to simplify this process. One key feature in our model is the use of **fade rates**, which allow us to make 20-year projections by choosing only a few inputs; we'll explain this in detail later in the chapter. In addition, we'll see that each firm has certain leverage points, and so we can focus our attention on a relatively small number of critical value drivers.

Let's start with the mechanics of projecting the condensed statements.

The Mechanics of Projecting the Condensed Statements

Home Depot's condensed statements are a little more complicated than Van Leer's in Chapters 5–7, but we will use the same basic approach for projecting its financial statements. In particular, we will project all operating assets and operating liabilities as a percentage of sales. We have found that many of the nonoperating items, such as nonoperating income, after-tax extraordinary income, and other long-term liabilities, also tend to vary with sales, and so we will also project them as a percentage of sales. In this chapter, we will develop what we consider to be the most plausible set of estimates, and we'll refer to this as our **base case scenario**. Scenario analysis, simply put, assesses the change in Home Depot's estimated value that results from changing one or more of the assumptions underlying the base case scenario. Scenario analysis is useful for investigating the effect that changes in our estimates of the input parameters—particularly ones that we feel are difficult to accurately predict—have on our estimate of value.

The various interest expense and interest income line items on the income statement depend on the respective debt and short-term investment balances on the balance sheet. Since short-term and long-term interest rates usually differ, we will allow for both a long-term and a short-term interest rate. The interest expense due to short-term debt will be projected as the short-term interest rate multiplied by the balance of debt at the beginning of the year. The interest expense on long-term debt will be projected in a similar manner, and the total interest expense will simply be the sum of long-term and short-term interest expenses.

For the condensed projections, interest income will be the rate of interest earned on any cash deposits multiplied by the cash balance at the beginning of the year, plus the rate of return earned on short-term investments multiplied by the beginning of period level of short-term investments.

Finance theory states that the level of long-term debt should be proportional to the market value of the firm. Therefore, we project long-term debt as a percentage of the value of operations, as described in Chapter 8. Exhibit 12-1 shows how we project each of the items on the condensed statements. The highlighted rows are the line items that are new to this chapter.

The following sections explain how to choose the inputs required to forecast the financial statements, beginning with the projected growth rates in sales.

Using Fade Rates to Input Forecasted Growth Rates

Recall that our method of valuing a company assumes that growth in forecasted sales and FCFs must eventually level off to a constant growth rate. When this happens, we say that the firm has entered its steady state period. For FCF growth to be constant, sales growth must level off. It may take many years before FCF grows at a constant rate, but it is reasonable to assume that this will eventually happen for all companies due to maturation of the businesses in which they operate.

In Chapter 7, we looked at some examples of very successful companies, and in every case, growth eventually leveled off and started declining. Chapter 10 showed that Home Depot grew at an average rate of over 22% during the last 10 years and, as the examples in Chapter 7 illustrate, it is not possible for any company to grow this fast forever. To see why this must be true, consider the two determinants of growth. A company's growth occurs when its markets are growing or when it steals market share from competitors. In the short-term, a company may grow by taking market share from competitors. For example, part of Wal-Mart's extraordinary growth came at the expense of Kmart, and part of Old Navy's growth came from other retailers, such as Gap, Inc. and The Limited. However, Old Navy's success attracted other competitors, such as Kohl's, whose rapid growth hurt Old Navy's sales. By the time this is published, there probably will be a new competitor eating into the sales of Kohl's. Ultimately, these companies will end up competing on price and/or brand identity. In such a mature market, it is very difficult to take market

Exhibit 12-1 Projecting the Condensed Statements

Part 1—Income statement item	**Projecting method**
Sales	Assumed growth rate multiplied by previous year's sales
Cost of goods sold (COGS)	Percentage of sales
Sales, general and administrative (SGA)	Percentage of sales
Depreciation	Percentage of net PPE
Operating profit (OP)	Calculated: Sales - COGS - SGA - Depreciation
Interest expense	(Rate on all current debt)(All current debt at beginning of period) + (Rate on long-term debt)(Long-term debt at beginning of period)
Interest income	(Rate on cash)(Cash at beginning of period) + (Rate on short-term investments)(Short-term investments at beginning of period)
Nonoperating income (expense)	Percentage of sales
Earnings before taxes (EBT)	Calculated: OP - Interest expense + Interest income + Nonoperating income
Taxes	(Tax rate)(Earnings before taxes)
Net income before extraordinary items	Calculated: EBT - Taxes
After-tax extraordinary income (expense)	Percentage of sales
Net income	Calculated: NI before extraordinary items + After-tax extraordinary income
Preferred dividends	(Coupon rate on preferred stock)(Preferred stock at beginning of period)
Common dividends	Growth rate multiplied by previous dividends
Additions to retained earnings	Calculated: Net income - Preferred dividends - Common dividends

(continued on next page)

share from competitors and still remain profitable. The markets for beer and small televisions are good examples of mature, low-profit markets. Therefore, in the long term, growth can occur only when the market itself is growing.

What causes a market to grow? Sometimes changing demographics create market growth, such as the rapidly growing market for home health care that is being fueled by the growing proportion of the elderly. The entry into a new geographic area is another source of growth. Some companies create new markets by producing

Exhibit 12-1 Projecting the Condensed Statements (continued)

Part 2—Balance sheet items (Assets)	**Projection method**
Cash	Percentage of sales
Inventory	Percentage of sales
Accounts receivable	Percentage of sales
Other short-term operating assets	Percentage of sales
Short-term investments	Plug: Chosen to make statements balance
Total current assets	Calculated: Cash + Inventory + AR + Other ST operating assets
Net PPE	Percentage of sales
Other long-term operating assets	Percentage of sales
Long-term investments	Percentage of sales
Total assets	Calculated: Total CA + Net PPE + Other LT operating assets + LT investments

Part 3— Balance sheet items (Liabilities)	**Projection method**
Accounts payable	Percentage of sales
Accruals	Percentage of sales
Other current liabilities	Percentage of sales
All short-term debt	Chosen to make statements balance
Total current liabilities	Calculated: AP + Accruals + Other CL + All ST debt
Long-term debt	Percentage of value of operations
Deferred taxes	Percentage of net PPE
Preferred stock	Percentage of operating assets
Other long-term liabilities	Percentage of sales
Total liabilities[a]	Calculated: Total CL + LT debt + Deferred taxes + Preferred stock + Other LT liabilities
Par plus paid-in-capital (PIC) less treasury (and other adjustments)	Same as previous year
Retained earnings	Previous year's retained earnings plus current addition to retained earnings from income statement
Total common equity	Calculated: Par plus PIC + Retained earnings
Total liabilities and equity	Calculated: Total liabilities + Total common equity

[a] We include preferred stock with liabilities because preferred stock is a claim against the firm's value that has a higher priority than common stock, and our focus is upon valuing the firm's common stock.

products that consumers didn't know they wanted, such as 3M's market for Post-It® notes. Sometimes a new marketing concept or channel of distribution can create a "new" market. For example, Home Depot provided one-stop shopping for a variety of products that were formerly sold at many different specialty stores. Add low prices due to volume purchasing, throw in a demographic trend to do-it-yourself, and it is easy to understand Home Depot's phenomenal growth.

As we noted before, such growth sows its own seeds of destruction. Because Home Depot's growth is profitable, other competitors are entering the market. For example, Lowe's often builds new stores within shouting distance of Home Depot's stores. Such competition increases the rate at which a market becomes saturated, and makes it difficult for any store to continuously increase market share. In other words, success breeds competition.

Therefore, the only source of revenue growth in the long term is the growth in the market itself, which is determined by growth in the quantity of products that are sold and growth in the prices at which the products are sold. Growth in quantity is ultimately limited by the long-term population growth, which most economists estimate at around 2.5% to 3.5%. The dollar value of sales is the product of quantity and price, so another source of growth in sales revenues is inflation. Historically, inflation has averaged about 2% to 3%. Therefore, the long-term sustainable growth rate in sales revenues is about 4.5% to 6.5%.

This means that even a high growth company's sales growth will eventually slow down until it reaches a rate of around 4.5% to 6.5%. Therefore, in our valuation model, we might forecast a high growth rate in the short term, and a rate of about 4.5% to 6.5% in the long term. But how long does it take to reach the long term, and how fast will a company's growth fade from its current level to the long-term growth rate? This is where an analyst's judgment becomes important.

You should always apply the following common sense test: Is there something about the company's strategy or products that is hard for a competitor to replicate? For example, Coca-Cola and Disney have brand identities that are hard to replicate, Merck has drug patents that are illegal to replicate, and Microsoft has such a large base of existing users that it is costly for any user to switch (i.e., it becomes very inconvenient not to use Microsoft products if you work with people who use them). So we might expect these companies to have high growth rates for many years before they eventually fall to the range of 4.5% to 6.5%. On the other hand, some companies are relatively easy to replicate. Blockbuster Videos had very rapid growth in the 1980s, but it was extremely easy for competitors to enter this market. As a result, Blockbuster's growth slowed quite quickly.

For some companies, you might decide that the growth should fade rapidly to 5% within 5 years. For other companies, you might decide that sales growth should slowly fall to 6% within 18 years. FCF valuation requires that the analyst estimate revenue growth for each year through the short-run and long-run projection periods. Thinking about each year in isolation from the others is one approach that an analyst might take, but this approach risks overlooking the long-term trends that must eventually occur. Furthermore, no two analysts (or even the same analyst on different days) will agree on the pattern of growth for a given firm. Given the importance of the growth rate assumptions and given the uncertainty (yes, guesswork) involved in a given set of growth rate estimates, it is imperative that our valuation model be adept at evaluating and comparing alternative growth scenarios. To this end, our spreadsheet model incorporates, at the analyst's discretion, the use of a technique that lends itself to scenario analysis. We call this technique the "fade rate function."

Open the file ***Home Depot.xls***, and look in the *Inputs* worksheet. A portion of this sheet appears in Exhibit 12-2, shown below. We'll explain how to choose the inputs for Home Depot later, but for now let's just look at the capabilities of the fade rate function.

Look in the row for projected sales growth rates (Row 12 in the *Inputs* worksheet of ***Home Depot.xls***). The Average, Trend, and Most Recent data are repeated (in cells B12, C12, and D12) from the *Condensed* worksheet, as described in the Chapter 10. If you are looking at the spreadsheet, you will notice that these cells are shaded green, which indicates that they are a result of a previous calculation. But the subsequent columns show four new required inputs (cells E12, F12, G12, and H12): Starting Rate, Long-Term Rate, Time Until Long-Term, and Fade Rate. Again, if you are looking at the spreadsheet, you will see that these columns are shaded yellow. The yellow shading indicates a portion of the spreadsheet where you, the user, must choose an input, unless you want to accept the default values. The following paragraphs explain these inputs.

Chapter 10 described how to use the *Condensed* worksheet and various Internet sources to analyze the historical growth rates, the current situation for the company, and the expectations of analysts. Based on this information and your judgment, you must enter a growth rate for the first year of the forecast and a sustainable long-term growth rate. We'll discuss Home Depot's particulars later, but for now let's just assume that the analyst has chosen 20% as the starting growth rate, a steady state growth rate of 6%, and that it will take 6 years to reach the steady state. So we now have a scenario for what's going to happen in the short run (1 year), in the long run, and how long it will take to get from the short run to a steady state, but we still have to estimate what the pattern of changes in growth will look like during the 6-year **projection period**.

Exhibit 12-2 The Fade Rate Function

Part 1
Inputs

Ratios for Pro Forma Analysis	Average	Trend	Most recent
Year of analysis			
Ratios to calculate operating profit			
Sales growth rate	22.9%	11.5%	8.8%

Will growth fade quickly or slowly to the 6% long-term rate? The input for the fade rate (cell H12 in ***Home Depot.xls***) allows you to implement different assumptions. If you think the sales growth rate will fade from the short-term rate to the long-term rate by an equal amount each year, you should enter "0" as the fade rate. This will automatically create a series of equal year-over-year changes in growth rates.

For example, suppose we had chosen a starting rate of 20%, a long-term rate of 6%, 6 years until the long term, and a fade rate of 0. Exhibit 12-3 shows how this scenario would look.

If you believe that growth rates will fall more rapidly in the early portion of the long-run projection period and more slowly in the later portion, enter a positive fade rate. For example, Exhibit 12-4 shows the growth rates for a fade rate of +0.3.

If you believe sales growth will fall even more rapidly, enter a higher fade rate, such as +0.6. These results are shown in Exhibit 12-5.

If you believe that growth rates will fall more slowly in the early portion of the long-run projection period and more rapidly in the later portion, enter a negative value for the fade rate. For example, Exhibit 12-6 shows the growth rates for a fade rate of –0.3.

If you believe sales growth will fall even more slowly in the early part of the projection period, enter a smaller fade rate, such as –1.0. These results are shown in Exhibit 12-7.

One aspect of fade rates you may have noticed in the above examples is that positive fade rates give "soft landings," in the sense that change is slowing as the firm enters the steady state. In contrast, with negative values for the fade rate, the firm experiences "hard landings" as it enters the steady state, that is, the most dramatic changes occur immediately prior to entering the steady state. This may be more appropriate for firms that depend upon factors such as patents or regulation for protection from competition and where we can forecast when the protection will end. Since the soft landings associated with positive fade rates seem more plausible in most situations, we will often prefer positive fade rates. When we do use a negative fade rate, it will usually have a small magnitude, say on the order of –0.10 to –0.20.

Starting rate	Long-term rate	Time until long term (years)	Fade rate
?	?	?	?

Exhibit 12-3 An Example of Fade Rates (Fade Rate = 0)

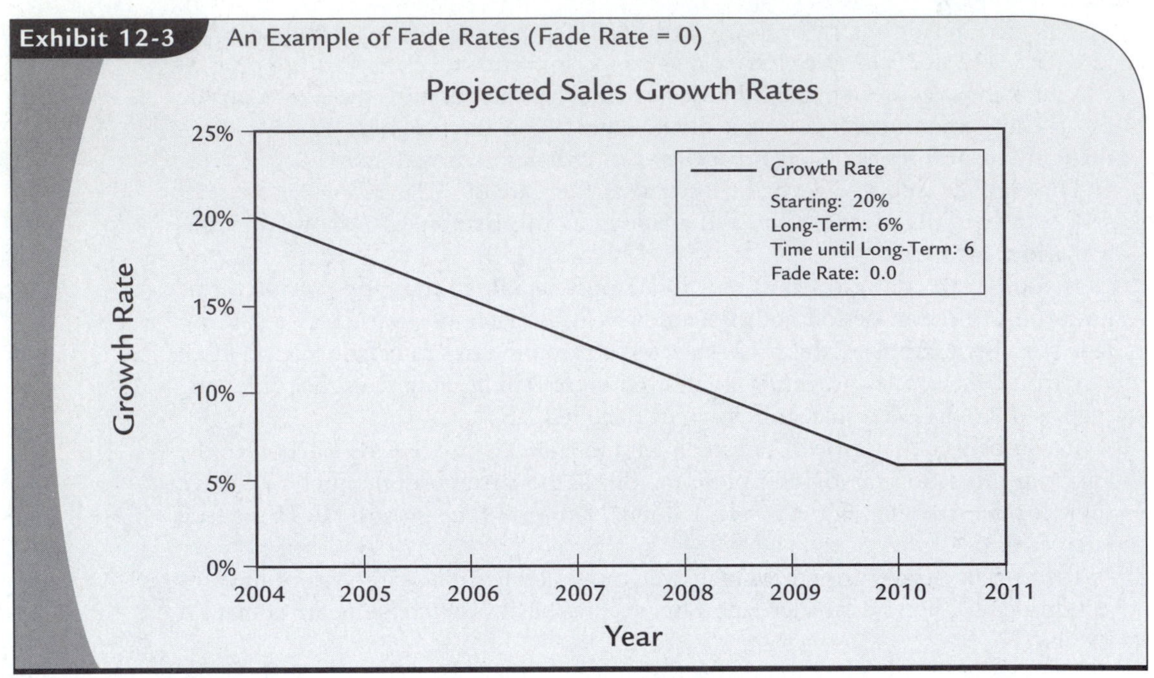

Exhibit 12-4 An Example of Fade Rates (Fade Rate = +0.3)

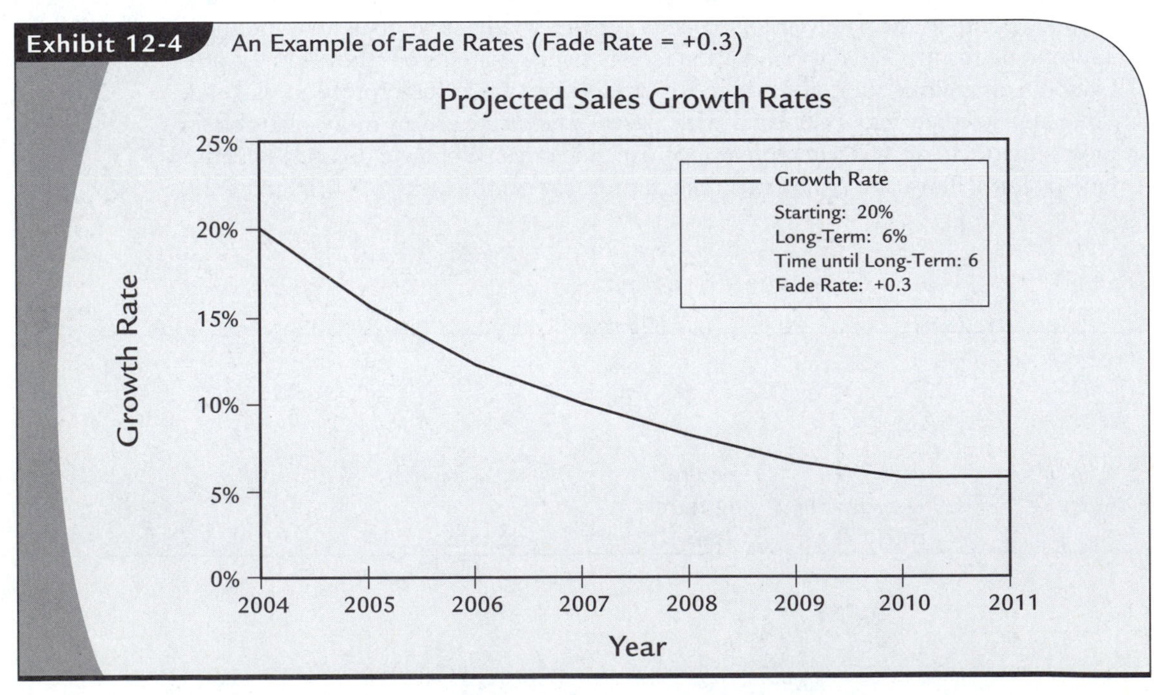

Exhibit 12-5 An Example of Fade Rates (Fade Rate = +0.6)

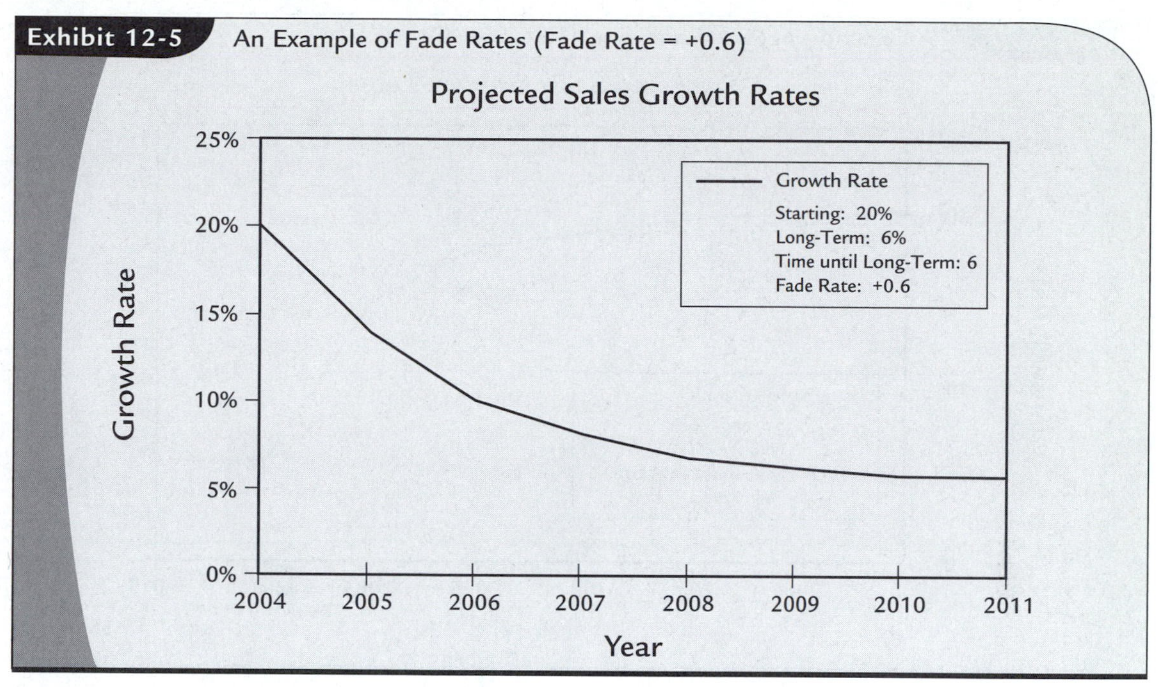

Exhibit 12-6 An Example of Fade Rates (Fade Rate = –0.3)

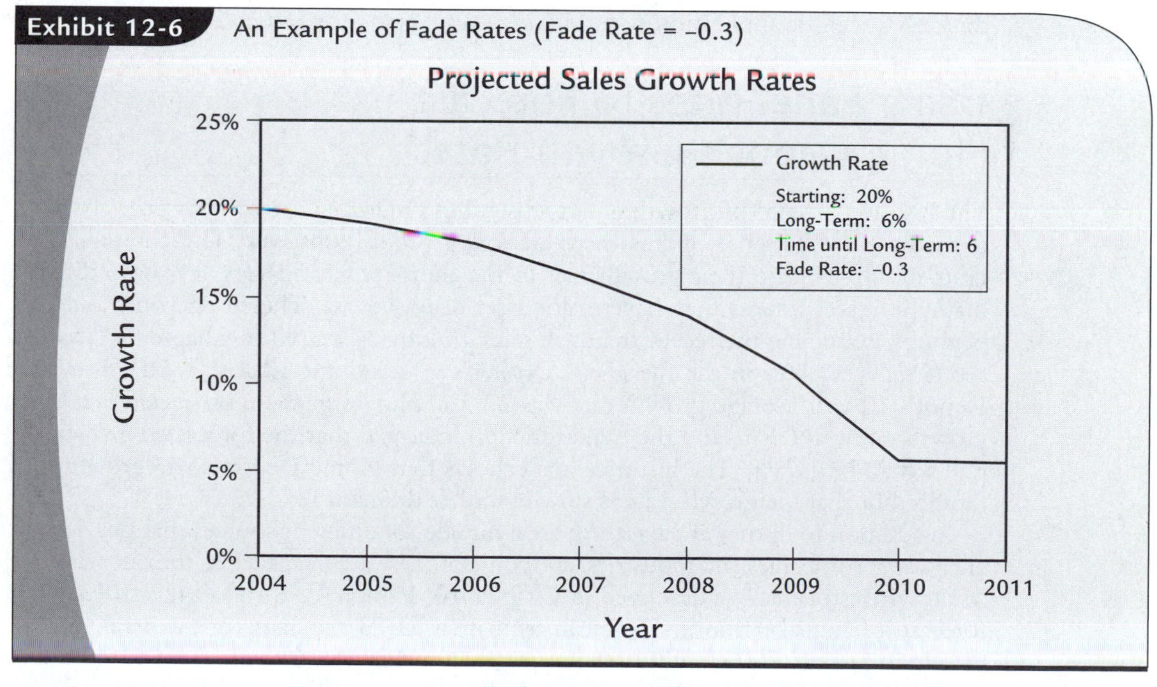

Exhibit 12-7 An Example of Fade Rates (Fade Rate = –1.0)

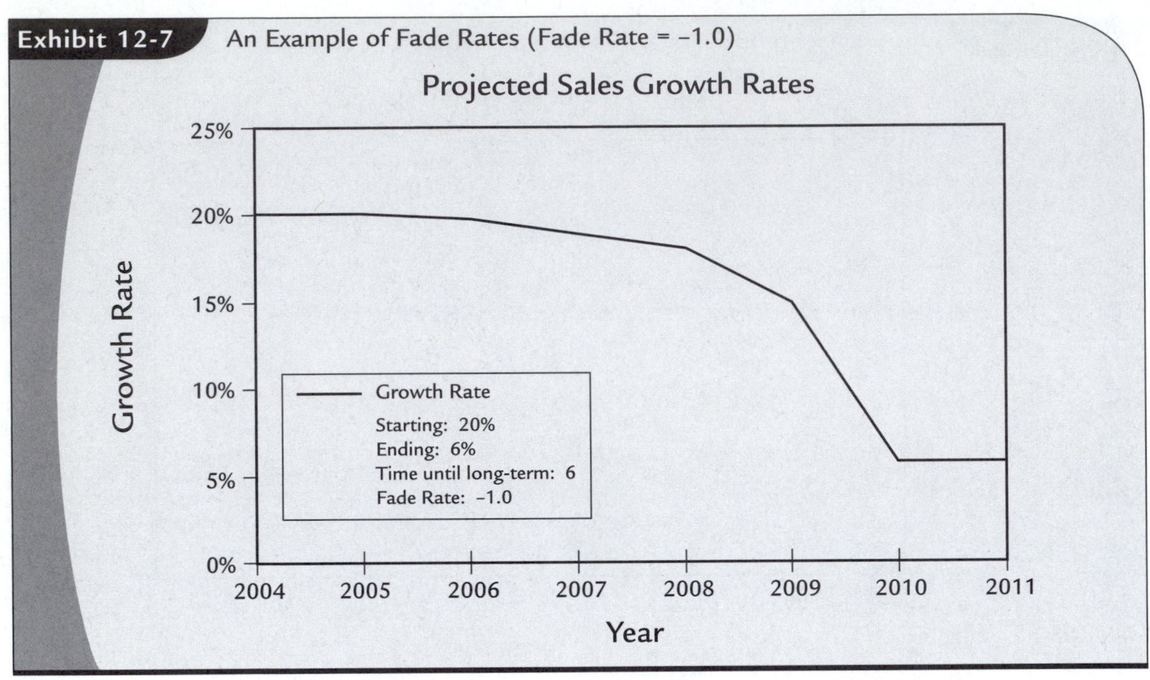

In summary, our spreadsheet provides a simple, easy way to generate reasonable patterns for sales growth, based on the analyst's judgment. The following section works through a realistic application of estimating these inputs for Home Depot.

Using Fade Rates to Forecast Home Depot's Growth Rates

The historical record of growth is often useful in predicting growth over the short term. In our experience, unless there are major acquisitions, very few companies dramatically increase their growth rate in the short-term, and very few have dramatic decreases (unless they have major asset dispositions). Therefore, you should begin by examining the recent trends in sales growth, as we did in Chapter 10 (see the *Condensed* sheet in the file ***Home Depot.xls***). As Exhibit 12-2 showed, Home Depot's 10-year average growth rate was 22.9%. However, the most recent year's growth rate was 8.8%, and the trend function indicated that the forecasted growth rate would be 11.5%. The historical data shows that Home Depot is still growing rapidly, but that the growth rate is slowing rather dramatically.

In addition to historical data, there are a number of different sources that provide analyses of companies and industries, and some of these are free, such as the one from Multex Investor that we described in Chapter 10. Exhibit 12-8 shows the analysts' forecasts of annual earnings. The mean estimate is $1.73 per share for the fiscal year ending in January 2004, with a 14 cent per share range of estimates (from $1.65 to $1.79) over the 28 analysts who participated in the survey. The mean predicted EPS

Exhibit 12-8 Analysts Forecasts of Earnings Per Share

	# of sets	Mean estimate	High estimate	Low estimate
Year ending 01/04	28	1.73	1.79	1.65
Year ending 01/05	24	1.96	2.10	1.75
LT growth rate	22	13.36	18.00	8.00

*Source:: **http://www.multexinvestor.com**, May 26, 2003.*

for the fiscal year ending in January 2005 is $1.96, which is a 13.3% increase, and the mean long-term predicted growth rate is 13.4%. All of this data suggests that, at least for the next several years, analysts believe that a growth rate on the order of 13%, is more likely than the historical average of 22.9%.

Notice that our historical analysis was based on the annual statements. If more recent data from quarterly reports is available, then we might want to include it in our analysis. We'll explain how to do this in a later section, but for now we'll ignore any quarterly reports.

Given the downward trend in Home Depot's past growth, we would usually begin our projections with a rate that is slightly lower than the rate in the most recent year. However, the *Hist Analys* sheet shows that the 2003 growth rate of 8.8% was much lower than growth rates in the previous two years (17.1% in 2002 and 19.0% in 2001). This suggests that Home Depot's 2003 sales were perhaps temporarily depressed by the economic recession and may rebound. Therefore, we initially chose a starting rate of 10% for the first year's projected growth in sales. This is quite a bit below the analysts' consensus forecast of 13.4% earnings growth, but we feel it is in line with recent developments in the economy and competitive forces faced by Home Depot.

As we explained earlier, the long-term growth rate for all companies will ultimately be in the range of 4.5% to 6.5%. But how do you choose a particular value in that range? If it is a company in a low-tech industry with few prospects for international growth, we generally choose a long-term growth rate close to 4.5%, or perhaps even lower. If the company is in a high-tech industry with lots of opportunities for innovation or if the company has strong prospects for international expansion, then we would choose a growth rate closer to 6.5%. Home Depot is in a low-tech industry in terms of its merchandise, but not necessarily in terms of its information technology and supply chain strengths. Additionally, we think it has good prospects for international expansion. So we chose a long-term sales growth rate of 5%.

How long will it take a company to reach the long term? Some mature industries, such as the cereal industry, are already in the long term. Other industries, such as broadband access, are in their infancy. Once again, we consider the degree of technology in the industry and the prospects for international expansion. Because we believe Home Depot has opportunities for international expansion, we chose 17 years as the time it will take for Home Depot's growth rate in sales to level off at its long-term rate of 5%.

How fast will Home Depot's growth fade from our projected starting rate of 10% to our projected long-term rate of 5%? We believe Home Depot has a strong brand identity and good opportunities for expansion, so we think its growth rate will fade slowly at first. Therefore, we chose a fade rate of –0.1.

Exhibit 12-9 shows our choices for the fade rate function and the projected growth rates. Notice that sales growth starts at 10% and fades to 5% over a 17-year period. Because the fade rate is less than zero, the growth rate fades more slowly in the early part of the forecast period than in the later years. Just as we showed in Chapter 10 for the *Hist Analys* worksheet, the *Input* worksheet also has graphing buttons that allow you to see the historical data and your forecast. The graph for Home Depot is shown in Part 4 of Exhibit 12-9. We have found that actually seeing our forecast in relation to the historical data provides a good reality check. In particular, it allows us to avoid "hockey stick" forecasts, in which there is a clear downward historical trend but a sharp upward projected trend. For Home Depot, we are forecasting a slightly higher growth rate in the near term as the economy pulls out of the recession, but a steady decline to the long-term rate as its market matures.

Choosing the Other Inputs Needed to Project Free Cash Flow

Recall that free cash flow is net operating profit after taxes (NOPAT) minus the investment in total net operating capital. The following sections explain how to forecast the items on the financial statements necessary to calculate free cash flow. However, before beginning, note a couple of rules of thumb, or default values, that we employ in the spreadsheet so that all of the inputs start off with values that are in some sense reasonable. With a few exceptions, the spreadsheet will set both the starting rate and the ending rate equal to the most recent rate.[1] In other words, the spreadsheet's default input values assume that the company will continue to perform in the future like it has performed in the recent past. The default time until the long term is 10 years, and the default fade rate is +0.10. This selection of fade rate gives a soft landing, as discussed earlier in this chapter.

As an analyst, you must use your own judgment to choose inputs that most realistically reflect the current situation for the firm, and these inputs may not be the same as the default values. For example, you may want to consider whether the long-term value for a given input should be somewhere near the historical average, rather than the most recent value, if you think that the firm's departure from the average is only temporary. In any case, you should use your knowledge of the firm, the industry, and the economy as a whole to guide you in selecting your inputs—don't just rely on the spreadsheet defaults!

Here's some more advice: Don't spend too much time or effort in refining an input parameter's estimate if it won't make a significant difference in the valuation result. The *Input* sheet shows the estimate of stock price at the top of the sheet (based upon the current set of inputs), so you can instantly see whether changing a

[1]The default inputs for sales growth are one exception. The default short-term rate is set equal to the most recent rate, but the default long-term rate is 5%. Other exceptions involve dividend ratios, debt ratios, and interest rates; we explain these later in the chapter.

Exhibit 12-9 The Fade Rate Function for Home Depot's Sales Growth Projections

Part 1

Inputs

Ratios for Pro Forma Analysis	Average	Trenc	Most recent	Starting rate	Long-term rate	Time until long term (years)	Fade rate
Year of analysis							
Ratios to calculate operating profit							
Sales growth rate	22.9%	11.5%	8.8%	10.0%	6.0%	17	-0.10

Part 2

Ratios for Pro Forma Analysis	Projected 2004	Projected 2005	Projected 2006	Projected 2007	Projected 2008	Projected 2009	Projected 2010	Projected 2011	Projected 2012	Projected 2013
Sales growth rate	10.0%	9.9%	9.8%	9.6%	9.5%	9.3%	9.1%	8.9%	8.6%	8.4%

Part 3

Ratios for Pro Forma Analysis	Projected 2014	Projected 2015	Projected 2016	Projected 2017	Projected 2018	Projected 2019	Projected 2020	Projected 2021	Projected 2022	Projected 2023
Sales growth rate	8.1%	7.8%	7.4%	7.0%	6.6%	6.1%	5.6%	5.0%	5.0%	5.0%

Exhibit 12-9 Part 4—Home Depot's Historical and Projected Growth Rates

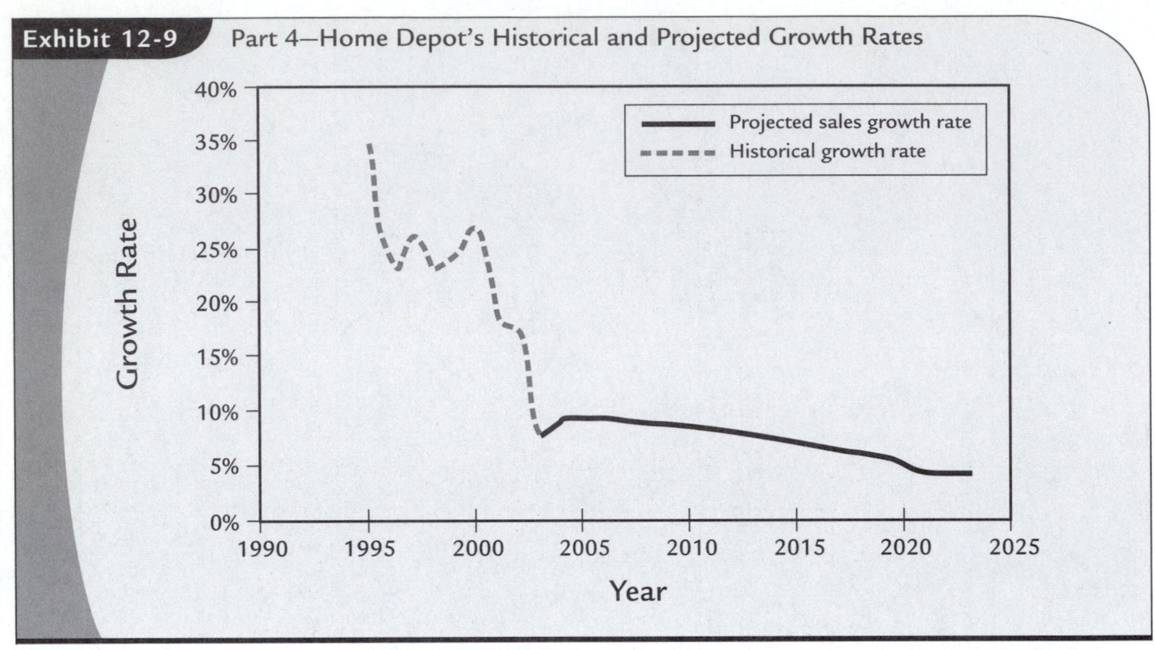

particular input has a significant impact on value. If the default input is pretty small (for example, as is usually the case with other long-term liabilities/sales) and small changes don't cause the estimated stock price to change very much, then just move on and spend your time and effort on choosing inputs that do have a large impact on value. In other words, don't sweat the inconsequential details.

Choosing the Inputs to Project NOPAT

The following items on the condensed statements are necessary for projecting NOPAT: COGS/sales, SGA/sales, and depreciation/net PPE. We also need an estimate of the tax rate, but we'll cover that later. As was the case when estimating sales growth rates, we can't know for sure how these critical value drivers will evolve over time, but here is how we think through the issues and choose inputs.

A company might currently have a great COGS/sales ratio, but this will attract competition, which, in turn, puts pressure on the profit margin. This might be due to a reduction in price or an increase in costs (perhaps caused by increased demand for specialized labor). In other words, we would expect that COGS/sales ratio for very profitable companies to fade to a sustainable long-term rate. You should use the same approach to estimate the COGS/sales ratios as you did for the growth rate in sales: (1) examine the company's historical COGS/sales ratios; (2) read analysts' reports on the company and the industry; (3) compare with similar ratios for other companies in the same industry; and (4) use your common sense. Exhibit 12-10 shows our choices for Home Depot, which we explain below.

Home Depot had a COGS/sales ratio of 67.4% in the most recent year. Although COGS/sales has been trending down, this is one of the ratios that suffers when competition heats up, and Home Depot is facing stiff competition as well as increasing

Exhibit 12-10 Inputs to Forecast NOPAT and Operating Capital for Home Depot

Inputs

Ratios for Pro Forma Analysis	Average	Trend	Most recent	Starting rate	Long-term rate	Time until long term (years)	Fade rate
Ratios to calculate operating profit							
Sales growth rate	22.9%	11.5%	8.8%	10.0%	5.0%	17	-0.10
COGS/sales	69.9%	67.5%	67.4%	67.4%	69.0%	10	0.10
SGA/sales	20.2%	20.8%	21.1%	21.1%	21.1%	10	0.10
Depreciation/net PPE	4.4%	5.3%	5.3%	5.3%	5.3%	10	0.10
Ratios to calculate operating capital							
Cash/sales	1.2%	3.1%	3.8%	1.00%	0.5%	10	0.10
Inventory/sales	14.1%	13.9%	14.3%	14.3%	14.0%	10	0.10
Accounts receivable/sales	1.9%	1.6%	1.8%	1.8%	1.8%	10	0.10
Other short-term operating assets/sales	0.3%	0.4%	0.4%	0.4%	0.4%	10	0.10
Net PPE/sales	27.7%	29.0%	29.5%	29.5%	29.0%	10	0.10
Other long-term operating assets/sales	1.2%	1.4%	1.6%	1.6%	1.6%	10	0.10
Accounts payable/sales	5.7%	6.3%	7.8%	7.8%	7.8%	10	0.10
Accruals/sales	4.2%	4.0%	4.3%	4.3%	4.2%	10	0.10
Other current liabilities/sales	0.5%	1.6%	1.7%	1.7%	1.7%	10	0.10
Ratios to calculate operating taxes							
Deferred taxes/net PPE	1.2%	1.7%	2.1%	2.1%	2.1%	10	0.10
Average tax rate (Taxes/EBT)	38.6%	38.6%	37.6%	38.6%	38.6%	10	0.10
Marginal tax rate	38.6%	38.6%	37.6%	38.6%	38.6%	10	0.10

market saturation. As competitors such as Lowe's grow, Home Depot will find it must either compete more aggressively on price—by offering a lower price and earning a lower margin—or it must compete on quality, which raises the unit cost of its products. In either case, competition will tend to force Home Depot's COGS as a percentage of sales up. We'll assume that CGS/sales will increase over the next 10 years from its current 67.4% to 69%. This should happen somewhat evenly, so we chose a fade rate of 0.0.

Home Depot's ratio of SGA/sales has increased quite a bit since 2000. We believe this has been a result of the expansion in the number of stores, the U.S. recession, and increased advertising in the face of competition. As its sales growth slows and the United States pulls out of its recession, Home Depot's same store sales may increase some, driving down SGA/sales, but at the same time, it will have to advertise more heavily to continue to grow. On balance, SGA/sales will probably not decline significantly, and so we project that it will remain at its current rate of 21.1% both in the near term and in the long term. Because the starting and ending rates are the same, the choice of time until long term and fade rate don't matter. Since we are relatively unsure of the accuracy of this forecast, once we have completed our base case scenario valuation, we should test whether our valuation is sensitive to variations in this ratio.

The final item for calculating "pre-tax" NOPAT is the ratio of depreciation to net PPE. Experience tells us that this ratio does not vary much from its long-term average unless the firm or industry undergoes rather dramatic technological change. We will accept our default values and keep the starting and ending ratio the same as the most recent value, which was 5.3% of sales.

Choosing the Inputs to Project Operating Capital

Exhibit 12-10 also showed the inputs necessary to project total operating capital. There are two ratios that are fairly large, inventory/sales and net PPE/sales. For inventory/sales, we chose a starting value equal to the most recent value (14.3%). Given recent advances in supply chain management software, we think it is likely that Home Depot's long-term ratio of inventory/sales will improve slightly to 14.0%.

Home Depot has been growing rapidly, and the U.S. economy has been in recession. These two factors have contributed to a lower than expected same-store sales and explain its recent increases in the net PPE/sales ratio. As growth slows and as the economy comes out of recession, we think this ratio will drop slightly. Therefore, we chose 29.5% as the starting ratio (which is the same as the most recent year) and 29.0% for the long-term ratio. We chose 10 years for the time to the long term and 0.1 for the fade rate. Home Depot's historical average is only 27.7%, and so our long-term ratio of PPE/sales may be overly pessimistic. We would reexamine our choice using scenario analysis once we have completed the base case.

Most of the other ratios that contribute to operating capital make relatively small contributions, and we usually accept our default values, with the starting and long-term ratios equal to the most recent value, 10 years for the time until the long term, and 0.1 for the fade rate.

Choosing the Inputs to Calculate Operating Taxes

The last section in Exhibit 12-10 shows the inputs necessary to calculate operating taxes: deferred taxes/net PPE, average tax rate, and marginal tax rate. We usually choose a starting and ending ratio for deferred taxes/net PPE that is equal to the most recent value, unless that ratio has moved substantially in the last 2 years. Because the deferred taxes/net PPE ratio is usually fairly small, the estimated value of the company isn't very sensitive to our choice.

Except for unusual circumstances, the historical tax rates for most companies should be in the range of 32% to 40%. If the most recent value is in that range, we usually choose a starting value for the Average Tax Rate that is close to the most recent year's rate, and in the absence of any compelling reasons we usually set the long-term rate to this value. If the historical rates are not in this range, then we usually set the starting value equal to the most recent value but set the long-term rate equal to 38% to reflect federal and state taxes. For Home Depot, the most recent year's rate was a full percentage point less than its historical average. Since this was an unusual year due to the economic downturn, we projected that Home Depot's tax rate would be equal to its historical average of 38.6% rather than the most recent value of 37.6%.

Unless we have information suggesting otherwise, we usually set the values for the marginal tax rate equal to those of the average tax rate.

Choosing Inputs to Complete the Projections

At this point, we have chosen all of the inputs necessary to project free cash flows. However, it is useful to project the completed financial statements because this will tell us how much additional external financing is required. This isn't necessary if all we want to know is the value of the company, but it provides important insights into the firm's future financing requirements. Exhibit 12-11 shows these inputs, which we will discuss later.

Specifying the Dividend and Capital Structure Policies

As we discussed in Chapter 8, most companies have one of the following dividend policies: (1) they pay out a percent of net income, or (2) they let dividends grow at a smooth rate.[2] We have chosen the second approach and will specify the growth rate in dividends. The spreadsheet default values are a starting growth rate in dividends equal to the starting growth rate in sales and an ending growth rate equal to the ending growth rate in sales. Using the defaults, the starting growth rate in dividends would then be 10%. However, Home Depot's current growth rate in dividends is 24.3%—which is very much larger than 10%. In this case we want to pick a starting value that is similar to the most recent rate, so we chose 24.0% for Home Depot's starting growth in dividends. We chose the long-term sales growth rate, 5%, for the long-term growth rate in dividends, 20 years until the long term, and a fade rate of –0.30.

[2]Chapter 8 also discussed the residual dividend policy. While many firms use this as a guide for setting the long-term dividend policy, most firms have relatively smooth growth in dividends in the short term.

Exhibit 12-11 Inputs to Complete the Projections for Home Depot

Inputs

Ratios for Pro Forma Analysis	Average	Trend	Most recent	Starting rate	Long-term rate	Time until long term (years)	Fade rate
Dividend and debt ratios							
Dividend policy: growth rate	29.50%	25.50%	24.20%	24.00%	5.00%	17	-0.10
Long-term debt/market value of firm	#N/A	#N/A	1.90%	1.94%	22.00%	15	0.10
Preferred stock/market value of firm	#N/A	#N/A	#N/A	0.00%	0.00%	1	0.00
Coupon rate on preferred stock	#N/A	#N/A	#N/A	0.00%	0.00%	1	0.00
Perm. component of ST debt/MV firm	#N/A	#N/A	#N/A	0.00%	0.00%	1	0.00
Ratios to calculate rest of income statement and balance sheet							
Nonoperating income/sales	0.14%	-0.04%	0.14%	0.14%	0.14%	10	0.10
Extraordinary income/sales	0.00%	0.00%	0.00%	0.00%	0.00%	10	0.10
Long-term investments/sales	0.42%	-0.71%	0.00%	0.00%	0.00%	10	0.10
Other long-term liabilities/sales	0.82%	0.79%	0.84%	0.84%	0.84%	10	0.10
Interest rates							
Interest rate on cash				0.00%	0.00%	10	0.10
Interest rate on short-term investments				1.30%	5.00%	10	0.10
Interest rate on all current debt				4.75%	4.75%	10	0.10
Interest rate on long-term debt				3.99%	3.99%	3	-1.00
Cost of capital and LT ROIC							
Weighted average cost of capital (WACC)				8.51%			
Long-term return on invested capital				8.50%			

Note: #N/A indicates that historical data is not available to make the required calculations.

As Chapter 8 explained, there are several ways to specify the amount of long-term debt in a firm's capital structure. We prefer to specify the long-term debt as a percent of the firm's market value, with market value approximated by the value of operations.[3] This ensures that the capital structure will be based on market values, which conforms to financial theory. You chose a target debt to market value ratio when you completed the *WACC* sheet, and this is the default long-term value on the *Inputs sheet*. The spreadsheet's default starting value is the most recent ratio of debt to market value, also obtained from the *WACC* sheet. We have no reason to make different choices, so we keep the default value of 1.94% for the starting ratio and 22% for the ending ratio. We're not sure how long it will take Home Depot to move to the target capital structure, so we chose a fairly high value, 15 years, for the time until the long term.

Home Depot has no preferred stock, either in its current capital structure or in its target capital structure as specified in the *WACC* sheet. Therefore, we input zeros for the percent of preferred stock in the capital structure and the rate on the preferred stock. Home Depot also doesn't have any permanent short-term debt in its current or target capital structure. Again, we input zeros for the percent of permanent short-term debt in the capital structure. If Home Depot had preferred stock or permanent short-term debt in its target capital structure, then we would have chosen inputs for them in the same way that we chose inputs for the long-term debt above.

Specifying the Nonoperating Items

The condensed statements have several items associated with Home Depot's nonoperating activities, and we must specify them to project complete financial statements. These include nonoperating income/sales, extraordinary income/sales, long-term investments/sales, and other long-term liabilities/sales. For most companies, such as Home Depot, these values are pretty small, and so we usually leave them at their default values, which are the their most recent values.

Specifying Interest Rates

To complete the projected statements, we need to specify the interest rates that a company pays and earns. An interest rate of zero is reasonable for cash, because most companies earn very little interest on their checking accounts.[4] For the rate on short-term investments, we go to the Yahoo!Finance or Federal Reserve web sites, as described in Chapter 11, and take a look at the current values for short-term Treasury securities (i.e., less than a year), commercial paper, and negotiable CDs. These rates are currently around 1.3%, and so we specified this as the starting value for the interest rate on short-term investments. Historically, short-term investments have earned a rate of around 5%, and so we chose 5% as the long-term value for the interest rate on short-term investments.

[3]Because free cash flows don't depend on the current amount of debt in the capital structure, there is no circularity resulting from making debt a percent of the value of operations. See Chapter 8 for details.

[4]The spreadsheet will allow you to enter another value if you think that is more realistic for a company you are analyzing.

For most companies, bank debt comprises the major portion of all current debt. Most banks charge an interest rate that is tied to the prime rate, which is currently 4.25%, as shown at the Yahoo!Finance site. Since a strong company like Home Depot usually can borrow at the prime rate, we chose 4.25% as our starting value for the interest rate on all current debt.[5] Note that the spreadsheet defaults to the rate you selected for short-term debt in the *WACC* sheet. As for the ending rate, the prime rate has averaged around 6%. Although the Federal Reserve may lower rates even further in the near term, rates will likely come up substantially as the recession draws to a close and as federal borrowing to cover the rapidly growing federal deficit competes for investors' funds. So we chose a higher rate, 6% as the ending rate. Again, we left the default values of 10 years until the long-term and a fade rate of 0.10.

Home Depot's existing long-term debt has a coupon payment of 5.375%, as we discussed in Chapter 11, so we chose this rate as the starting value for the interest rate on long-term debt. When calculating Home Depot's cost of debt in Chapter 11, we estimated a value of 4%, so we chose 4% as the long-term value for the interest rate on long-term debt. As Home Depot replaces its outstanding debt with new issues, it should realize a savings in interest costs. Here we should use 3 years as the time until long-term because we know that Home Depot's currently outstanding bonds will all mature by 2006. We chose a fade rate of –1.0 because we know the change in interest costs will be rather abrupt, as new bonds are offered to replace those that mature.

Completing the Inputs

Only two more inputs remain to be chosen. The first is the return on invested capital (ROIC) that we think Home Depot can earn on capital placed in service after the 20-year forecast period. We'll discuss how to choose this rate in Chapter 13, but for now just accept our input of 8.5%, which is the same as the WACC.

Finally, all of the valuations you have done in the previous chapters produce a stock price as of the date of the most recent financial statements used in the analysis. Home Depot's most recent financial statements were for its fiscal year ending on February 2, 2003. Thus, the predicted stock price is for that date. However, you would probably like to know the predicted price as of the current date, which we call the target valuation date. Therefore, we input 05/21/2003 for the target date because that was the date when we wrote this chapter.

If the company is publicly traded, it's nice to know how close the estimated intrinsic stock price is to the actual stock price. In Chapter 11, we explained how to find the actual stock price by using Internet resources. Recall that we found the price of Home Depot's stock on May 21, 2003, to be $30.62 per share.

Using Quarterly Data to Improve Your Inputs

The valuation model assumes that your historical data is from annual statements. But suppose the most recent annual statement was for February 2, 2003, and the current date is May 21, 2003, as it is for our analysis of Home Depot. In this situation, the

[5]Weaker companies typically pay 1 to 2 percentage points more than the prime rate, as discussed in Chapter 11.

quarterly report for the first quarter, ending May 4, 2003, might be available. Should you incorporate this additional information into your valuation?

First, remember that independent accounting firms audit annual statements, but not quarterly statements. Thus, quarterly statements do not undergo the same degree of scrutiny. In fact, companies occasionally revise quarterly statements later in the year. Thus, quarterly statements are only preliminary estimates.

Second, some firms have seasonal sales patterns. For example, over 40% of annual sales for Toys "R" Us occur in the quarter ending January 31. Many companies, including Toys "R" Us, also have distortions in their patterns of asset usage. For example, Toys "R" Us has about 45% more inventory in the quarter ending October 31 than in the other quarters. Therefore, for seasonal companies you should not project annual results by simply extrapolating quarterly results. Indeed, Home Depot is a company that we would expect to be seasonal because it's so closely related to construction and homebuilding activity.

If the firm that you are analyzing does not have a strong seasonal sales pattern, then quarterly results can be useful, especially if there have been two or three quarterly reports since the last annual report. We have prepared a spreadsheet to help you analyze the quarterly results, ***Quarterly Model.xls***. To use the spreadsheet, you should enter actual data based on the most recent quarterly reports in column B of the *Actual* worksheet. In particular, you should enter the cumulative year-to-date values for the income statement. For example, if sales in the first quarter were $80 million and sales in the second quarter were $100 million, you should enter their sum. You should also enter the cumulative values for the statement of cash flows. For balance sheet items, you should simply enter the amount shown for the most recent quarter. Finally, enter the most recent fiscal year results in column C of the *Actual* tab.

Your next step is to map this raw data into the financial statements shown in the *Comprehensive* worksheet by linking the cells in the *Actual* worksheet to the appropriate cells in the *Comprehensive* worksheet; see Chapter 9 for more details on mapping. Be careful because the raw data for quarterly financial statements often is presented differently than for annual statements. Be sure to map the quarterly data in a manner that is consistent with the way the annual data in ***Home Depot.xls*** is mapped. You must also enter the number of quarters in the *Comprehensive* worksheet.

The spreadsheet automatically maps the *Comprehensive* financial statements into the financial statements in the *Condensed* sheet. The *Condensed* sheet then calculates annualized ratios, based on the number of quarters. The sheet annualizes the ratios to make them comparable with the annual ratios shown in the *Condensed* sheet of the ***Valuation Model.xls***. For example, suppose sales for the most recent full fiscal year were $2 billion and cumulative year-to-date sales for the second quarter were $1.2 billion. The annualized sales are $2.4 billion ($1.2[4/2] = $2.4). Therefore, the annualized growth rate is 20% = $2.4/$2 – 1. A similar adjustment must be made for the asset-to-sales ratios; be careful to base these ratios on annualized sales.

When deciding on inputs for our actual valuation model, such as ***Home Depot.xls***, we usually look at the ratios from the ***Quarterly Model.xls***. If we have data for the third quarter of a nonseasonal company, then we place considerable weight on the ratios from the ***Quarterly Model.xls*** when choosing the starting inputs. For example, if the annualized growth rate is 20% based on 3 quarters, we will choose a starting growth rate very close to 20%. This ensures that our financial statements for the first year of our projection will be very close to the actual annual statement for the company's first full fiscal year that ends 3 months after the third quarter.

If there is only data for the first quarter, then we give little weight to the ratios from the ***Quarterly Model.xls***; in fact, we usually don't even look at the quarterly statements. If there are 2 quarters, then we use our judgment and place more weight than if there is only 1 quarter, but less than if there are 3 quarters.

At the time of this writing, only the quarterly statements for the first quarter of 2003 are available, and so we will not adjust our parameter estimates based on this limited information. However, if you go to this book's web site, you will find examples that do use the quarterly data.

Reviewing Your Choices of Inputs

Once you have completed choosing your inputs, your job is still not done. In general, you should have well-thought-out reasons if you choose inputs that differ from their historical averages or most recent values. Below are some reasons that might influence your choices for inputs. Take these, and any additional information you have about your own company, into consideration when choosing your inputs.

Reasons for higher sales growth than in the past and the resulting implications:

- Increased incentives to sales force. SGA as a percentage of sales will increase.
- Price reductions. COGS as a percentage of sales will increase (because per unit sales price is reduced).
- Product improvements. COGS as a percentage of sales will increase.
- Increased advertising. SGA as a percentage of sales will increase.
- More on-time deliveries or more items in stock. Usually this will increase inventory as a percentage of sales—but there are inventory management plans that some companies may be able to take advantage of that can reduce stock-outs without increasing inventory.
- Selling on better terms. Relaxing the credit policy will cause accounts receivable as a percentage of sales to increase.

Reasons for higher gross profit margins than in the past and resulting implications:

- Reduced labor costs through automation. This will require more net PPE as a percentage of sales.
- Reductions in SGA expense or COGS expense. Reductions in advertising or R&D may result in lower sales.

Reasons for lower inventories than in the past and resulting implications:

- Various inventory reduction plans, such as *just-in-time inventory management* and *supply chain management*. These can often achieve modest improvements with little cost and investment. However, significant reductions in inventory often require substantial investments in information technology, which will increase net PPE as a percentage of sales.

Reasons for lower accounts receivable than in the past and resulting implications:

- Tighter credit terms. These will reduce accounts receivable, but sales may decrease as a result.
- More aggressive pursuit of bad debts. This may reduce accounts receivable, but there is usually a cost for bad debt collections.

Reasons for lower net PPE than in the past and resulting implications:

- Company was not at full capacity in the past. If there is significant excess capacity, then sales can grow somewhat without much corresponding increase in PPE, which means the ratio of PPE to sales will decline until all of the excess capacity is used up.
- Outsourcing in-house manufacturing with contract manufacturing. The costs associated with paying for manufacturing the company once did in-house will often be reflected in increased COGS.

Avoiding an Error in Your First Year's Projections

Suppose a company has a ratio of accounts receivable to sales (AR/sales) of 0.15 in the most recent year, but has had a ratio of 0.07 historically. If you use the historical ratio, 0.07, for the projection in the first year, your sheets will indicate a very large increase in free cash flow for that year. For example, if sales were $300 million in the current year, then AR would be $45 million (based on the AR/sales ratio of 0.15). If you forecast sales of $310 million in your first year and have a ratio of AR/sales of 0.07, then your forecasted AR would be $21.7 million: $21.7 = $310(0.07). Taken by itself, this would mean that AR decreased by about $45 – $21.7 = $23.3 million, which would be a direct increase in FCF of $23.3 million in the first year of your projection.

Suppose sales are $320 million in the second year of your forecast. Continuing with a ratio of AR/sales of 0.07, the AR would be $22.4 million. The impact on FCF in this second year would be to lower FCF by $22.4 – $21.7 = $0.7 million. In other words, any time you have a large change in AR/sales, or any of the operating asset/sales ratios or the operating liabilities/sales ratios, you will have a one-time large change in FCF for that year. This is okay, if you really believe that a dramatic reduction in AR is probable, but it might happen by accident if you simply begin your projections by starting with the historical average ratio, which can be quite different from the most recent ratio. The moral is that, unless you have specific information that would warrant a significant departure from the most recent value for one of the inputs, use values at or close to recent levels for the input ratios. This is one of the rules of thumb described earlier in the chapter.

An example of a valid reason for departure from the rule of thumb in the case of AR/sales would be information that the firm was undertaking a significant change in its credit policy. (Any dramatic changes in important operating policies, at least for large firms, are likely to receive media attention, so even outside analysts may have valid information indicating such a departure.) Hence our rule of thumb for starting values: Unless you have specific credible information indicating something different, start the projections with a ratio that is close to the most recent ratio and let it fade to a value that reflects long-run expectations. Using this rule of thumb prevents unintended and implausibly wild swings in FCF during the first year of projections.

Spotting Errors

After we forecast our projected statements, we always check to see if the projections make sense. For example, if we forecast an increase in sales of 10% in the first year of our forecast, but we see a 40% increase in NOPAT, then we probably have an error (unless our analysis of operating characteristics leads us to expect that the company will be much more profitable.). The same is true for capital. For example, if sales grow at 10% and capital falls by 20%, then we probably have made a mistake in choosing some of our inputs. The same is true for net income. For example, suppose sales grow by 10%, NOPAT grows by 11%, but net income grows by 30%. In this case, the projected interest expense is probably wrong. If we had an ROIC for the most recent year of 12% but an ROIC of 1% in our first projected year, we probably have an error somewhere.

If we see such inconsistent and nonintuitive changes, we go to the projected income statements and balance sheets and look for big changes in individual items. Mistakes (especially typographical) often can be identified via large year-over-year changes in the affected item; for example, we might have intended to enter 20% as SGA/sales, but mistakenly typed in 200%. Therefore, when we have unexpected results for a particular year, the first thing we do is inspect the *Inputs* worksheet for a big change in one of the input ratios.

Summary

This chapter discussed the process of choosing inputs for projected free cash flow and for financial statements, including the use of scenario analysis to assess the impact of possible mistakes in input choices. We described the mechanics of forecasting financial statements, some basic rules of thumb, and some hints for spotting obvious errors in judgment or typing. We also explained how to use quarterly financial information to supplement the annual statements. We identified a number of useful Internet resources.

Understanding the mechanics of forecasting helps reveal the leverage points of valuation and the relationships between specific corporate operating policies and their financial consequences. It is helpful to benchmark the performance of the company being analyzed in very specific areas of operating performance, such as operating efficiency with respect to cost of goods, SGA expenses, and asset utilization.

As we discussed, a company's own past performance is an important indicator of its likely future performance. It is also helpful to understand the performances of close competitors or the industry as a whole. Such a comparative analysis helps best practices, and reveals opportunities for possible future performance improvements by the firm being analyzed. The appendix to this chapter has additional suggestions for a systematic overall approach to gathering information, as well as some additional specific data sources.

By demonstrating the use of the valuation model on Home Depot, we hopefully provided you with insight into the analyst's role in making plausible and consistent projections. The next chapter explains how to calculate the projected free cash flows and the intrinsic value of a firm's stock.

Spreadsheet Problems

12-1 Projecting the Financial Statements of Lowe's

This project is a continuation of the analysis of Lowe's begun in projects for Chapters 9, 10, and 11. This phase of the valuation of Lowe's is the full specification of the set of inputs required for FCF valuation. In completing this project, you will develop your own style of analysis, because you will be making subjective assessments of the relative importance of the various environmental factors and leverage points for Lowe's. No two analysts will get the same set of input estimates (or intrinsic value). As before, save the information you find useful by copying it into either a word processing document or spreadsheet document.

a. Using the suggestions in Appendix 12 as a guide, write up a three-tiered summary of important qualitative and quantitative factors that you feel will influence selection of input parameters for Lowe's. (You can be brief—this is primarily for your own use in selecting inputs.)
b. Historical averages for inputs have already been developed from the actual data entered into your Valuation spreadsheet for Lowe's in Projects 9-1, 10-1, and 11-1. Combining this information with a summary of factors resulting from step a, make a complete set of input projections for Lowe's.
c. List the key input variables about which you have significant uncertainty, along with a brief statement explaining the reason for uncertainties. These will be used later for scenario analysis and sensitivity tests.

12-2 Projecting Financial Statements

Pick another company (or one that your instructor assigns), and repeat the analysis required in Problem 12-1.

Appendix 12

Top-Down Analysis

Many analysts use a three-tiered approach to making projections: (1) they develop an understanding of the national and global economic environment relevant to the company being valued; (2) they research any important potential developments in the industry; and (3) they research the selected company, including strategy, core competencies, management, governance, and any other relevant factors. Following are some suggested resources for implementing this approach.

The Macro Perspective: Global and National

Top-down analysis should start with a forecast and discussion of the global and national economic environments. For example, does either the state of the economy in Europe or per capita GDP growth in the United States help determine demand for your product? If so, you need to find out what experts think about the outlook. Or perhaps certain inputs to your business, like petroleum products for the airline industry or interest rates for the construction industry, are determined globally. In such cases, there are expert forecasts available. Try the resources listed in Exhibit 12A-1 for starters.

Additionally, many libraries contain lists of web resources or online databases. For example, take a look at the Harvard University Baker Library:**http://www.library.hbs.edu/economics/general_resources.html**

The Industry-Level Perspective

Next, it is important to understand potential developments in your industry. A great resource is Standard & Poor's Industry Surveys, which contain up-to-date information and data on the outlook for specific industry groups. For example, two industry groups important to an analysis of Home Depot are Homebuilding and Specialty Retailing, of which a subcategory is Home Improvement Retail. For each industry category, a wealth of information is summarized, including:

CURRENT ENVIRONMENT
INDUSTRY PROFILE

- Industry Trends
- How the Industry Operates
- Key Industry Ratios and Statistics
- How to Analyze a Company

Exhibit 12A-1 Internet Forecast Resources

Global perspective	Web site
World Bank (economic research)	**http://econ.worldbank.org/**
International Monetary Fund	**http://www.imf.org/**
Foreign Policy Association	**http://www.fpa.org/**
United Nations (economic and social development)	**http://www.un.org/esa/**

National perspective	Web site
Federal Reserve Bank (statistical resources)	**http://research.stlouisfed.org/fred2/**
Donald Ratajczak	**http://www.westga.edu/~bquest/outlook.html**
Council of Economic Advisers, *Economic Report of the President*	**http://w3.access.gpo.gov/eop/**

COMPARATIVE COMPANY ANALYSIS

- Definitions
- Revenues
- Net Income
- Profit Ratios
- Balance Sheet Ratios
- Equity Ratios
- Per-Share Data

The database also includes a glossary and industry references.

Home Depot is in the subcategory called Home Improvement Retail, which includes the following companies:

BUILDING MATERIALS HLDG CP
HOME DEPOT INC
HUGHES SUPPLY INC
LOWES COS
SHERWIN-WILLIAMS CO

A Standard & Poor's industry survey is not free, but you may have access to a library that subscribes. (This is the case at many universities and public libraries.)

Many industry associations have web sites or publications that might also be quite helpful, especially if you are just starting to learn about the industry. Other web sites organize information by industry group, which provides a database for identifying major competitors and current news that is most relevant to the industry. Hoover's Online, **http://www.hoovers.com/**, which covers more than 300 industries broken into 28 sectors, is a good source.

The Firm-Level Point of View

Any worthwhile analysis will involve a discussion of important strategic factors for your selected company, including competitors, strategy, core competencies, management, and any other relevant factors. Some of this will be evident from your research on the industry perspective, but a lot more is only found by going down to company-level sources. Probably the first such source is the Management Discussion and Analysis (MDA) section of the company's own annual report. Also, check for company and industry-related news items using sources such as Lexis-Nexis, *The Wall Street Journal* Index, Factiva, and online Internet searches using your favorite search engine. Some of the Internet sources already mentioned in the chapter will give access to reports by professional security analysts. (Though these will typically be a bit dated, they may give you insights about critical drivers for the company.)

Another great company-level resource is the firm's proxy statement, which is the agenda for the firm's annual shareholder meeting. This document is required by securities law to be sent to stockholders prior to the annual meeting to inform them of important issues that will be discussed or voted on at the meeting. It can be found on the Securities and Exchange Commission's EDGAR database, **http://www.sec.gov/**, filed as form DEF 14A. But the proxy also contains other potentially critical information concerning the company's corporate governance. The law requires information about (1) company ownership (a list of shareholdings by managers and by any stockholder who owns at least 5% of the company's stock), (2) biographical information about candidates for the board of directors, and (3) details of compensation of the firm's top managers and its board of directors.

Chapter 13

The Valuation of an Actual Company: Home Depot

Introduction

In the last four chapters you learned how to put an actual company's financial statements into a usable format, how to analyze its current and historical financial position, how to calculate its free cash flows (FCFs), how to calculate its weighted average cost of capital (WACC), and how to project its financial statements. In this chapter, we'll show you how to finish the valuation analysis by estimating the intrinsic value of its stock. We start with some (necessary) technical details about calculating of the present value of free cash flows.

Horizon Value Methods

The value of a company is the present value of all future free cash flows, but analysts only forecast a finite number of years; for example, the file ***Home Depot.xls*** forecasts only 20 years. As we learned in Chapter 4, the last year in the forecast is called the horizon (which is the beginning of the steady state period). Recall that in Chapter 4, we found the current value of a hypothetical company, ACME General, by first estimating its horizon value, which is the value of all free cash flows beyond the horizon, discounted back to the horizon. Then we found the present value of ACME's horizon value and all of its forecasted free cash flows for the years up to the horizon. We repeated this process for Van Leer in Chapter 7.

For simplicity, we showed only one method for estimating the horizon value in those chapters. However, there are actually four possible ways to calculate the horizon value. The following sections explain the continuing value, book value, convergence value, and general value methods. We then apply the most appropriate one to Home Depot.

The Continuing Value Horizon Formula

Suppose our firm is growing at a constant rate at the horizon. In particular, sales and FCFs are growing at the same constant rate, which is less than the WACC. Suppose the ROIC for the last year in your forecast is 15%. In other words, the company is earning a rate of 15% on its existing capital. An important question to answer is: If the company has a WACC of 10%, is it reasonable to expect the company to continue earning 15% on its existing capital? The answer depends upon whether there are barriers protecting this company from the forces of competition so that it can earn a return in excess of its cost of capital indefinitely.[1] In other words, do we think future competition in the period after our last forecasted year will fail to drive down the company's ROIC as calculated at the horizon?

If we think the answers to these questions are "Yes" (meaning, the company will be able to earn a rate of return, ROIC, that is greater than its cost of capital for the foreseeable future), then we should continue to use the horizon value formula that we used for the hypothetical companies in Chapters 2, 4, and 7. Recall that this formula is

$$HV_T = \frac{FCF_T(1 + g)}{WACC - g}. \qquad \textbf{(13-1)}$$

where HV_T is the horizon value at year T.

This is called the continuing value horizon formula because it assumes that the ROIC for both existing and new capital will continue at the same rate as the company is earning at the horizon.

However, is it realistic for a company to earn such a high ROIC forever? After all, if the WACC is only 10%, surely an ROIC of 15% will attract the attention of competitors. The questions are: Will additional competitors actually enter this industry, and if they do, how fierce will the competition be?

Potential competitors face large barriers to entry in some industries. For example, one barrier to entry might be the required scale of the industry. Consider how difficult it would be to raise the funds needed to start a new company to manufacture automobiles. Of course, 5 years ago it seemed that this was true for microprocessors, but the extraordinarily high profits of Intel attracted other companies into that market. Several failed, but it appears that AMD will be successful.

Other barriers to entry include license requirements, such as those required to open another hospital in a specific geographic area. The absence of additional geographic locations can also be a barrier to entry, as is the case for snow ski resorts. Other nonreplicable sources of competitive advantage are patent protection and brand identity. For example, Coca-Cola has both patent protection and brand identity, while Disney has a strong brand identity. Sometimes a company's corporate culture can be a nonreplicable advantage, such as at Southwest Airlines.

In the absence of barriers to entry or nonreplicable sources of competitive advantage, competitors will surely enter an industry in which the ROIC is significantly greater than the WACC. This competition is likely to drive down the ROIC for all companies in the industry. In fact, if the markets are perfectly efficient (no barriers at all, so no sources of competitive advantage), then competition should drive the ROIC all the way down to the WACC.

If we decide that it is not reasonable to assume that the company we are analyzing can sustain the ROIC it has at the horizon, then there are a couple of approaches we can take. First, and probably best, we could reconsider some of our inputs in the

[1]"Indefinitely" implies a very long time, but our knowledge of discounting tells us that what happens in the very, very distant future is of little consequence to our present value calculations. So if we think that Microsoft will enjoy its competitive (or monopoly) edge for, say, 50 years, then for practical valuation purposes, its the same as assuming it will last forever, and the assumption that Microsoft's steady state ROIC exceeds its WACC would be reasonable.

forecast period so that the ROIC at the horizon is closer to the WACC. For example, given that one impact of competition is to reduce the profit margin by causing the product's selling price to decline, we might feel that it is reasonable to increase the long-term ratio of COGS/sales. Similarly, if we feel that the impact of competition would force the firm to increase its inventory so that it can respond more rapidly to customer orders, then increasing the long-term ratio of inventory/sales would be appropriate and would lead to a reduction in ROIC. This approach, modifying the inputs to the valuation model so that the long-term ROIC is closer to the WACC, is probably best in the sense that it forces the analyst to articulate the impact of competition.

However, another possibility is that the 20-year forecast period is simply not long enough to cover the evolving competitive environment facing the firm. We could increase the forecast period (i.e., the number of years before steady state is achieved) to 30 years, or even longer, and adjust the input ratios to reflect the influence of increasing competition during these additional years. In other words, the firm will not really reach its steady state during the first 20 years, and we should simply push the horizon out beyond 20 years.

But these two approaches, while perhaps intellectually satisfying, would be somewhat tedious in practice, especially when conducting sensitivity analyses, because we would have to continuously monitor the ROIC at the horizon for each scenario, and then decide exactly how the increasing competitive pressures faced by the firm will bring about a gradual reduction in ROIC. This task is complicated because competition can influence the firm's operating environment in many different ways. But the essential fact of competitive pressure, regardless of the particular form in which it is manifested in the firm's operating results, is that it brings about a reduction in ROIC. These difficulties suggest we look for a different approach. Fortunately, there are some other approaches that are much easier to apply and require the analyst to focus on the **long-term sustainable ROIC**, which is the ROIC that can be sustained in the presence of post-horizon competition. The following sections explain different formulas incorporating different sets of assumptions regarding the long-term sustainable ROIC, denoted $ROIC_L$.

The Book Value Horizon Formula

Suppose we feel that competition will be fierce immediately after the horizon. In particular, the ROIC on existing capital will immediately fall to the WACC, and the ROIC on new capital investment will also equal the WACC. Under these assumptions, it can be shown that the horizon value equals book value of capital as of the beginning of the horizon.

$$HV_T = Capital_T \tag{13-2}$$

To see this, think of a firm's value as consisting of the value of assets already in place and the value of future growth. If the ROIC on new assets is equal to the WACC, then the net present value (NPV) of all the new assets is zero. Therefore, future growth (i.e., adding new assets) doesn't add to the current value of the firm. Said another way, if the existing assets have an ROIC equal to the WACC, then the present value of the future cash flows that will be generated by the existing assets is just equal to the value of the assets themselves, which is the amount of invested capital. This gives us one of the most important lessons of valuation: Growth adds value to a firm only if ROIC exceeds WACC. If a firm's ROIC is less than its cost of capital, then growth destroys firm value, even if the firm is generating positive profits, positive free cash flows, and positive ROICs.

The Convergence Value Horizon Formula

Suppose we believe that due to sources of competitive advantage, the ROIC on existing capital can be maintained. However, suppose we also believe that competition will cause the ROIC on new capital added after the horizon to be equal to the WACC. In other words, all new investments are essentially zero net present value investments: They are worth exactly what they cost. This means the new investments don't add value to the firm. Thus, the horizon value is just the value of the free cash flows expected to be produced by the existing capital, given that the ROIC remains the same on the existing capital.

The present value of these free cash flows generated only by the existing capital is easy to determine. First, since there is no net investment, $FCF_{T+1} = NOPAT_{T+1}$. Second, since ROIC remains constant, $NOPAT_{T+1} = (ROIC_{T+1})Capital_T = (ROIC_T)Capital_T$. Thus $FCF_{T+1} = (ROIC_T)(Capital_T)$. Finally, since the existing capital can't increase and ROIC doesn't change, all of the FCFs from time T + 1 on are all the same, namely FCF_{T+1}. This is a perpetuity and the present value of this perpetuity is

$$HV_T = \frac{FCF_{T+1}}{WACC} = \frac{ROIC_T(Capital_T)}{WACC}. \tag{13-3}$$

Suppose the firm continues to grow, even though growth adds no value. What happens to the total ROIC over time? The total ROIC of the firm is the average of the ROIC on existing capital and the ROIC on new capital (which is equal to the WACC). Initially, the total ROIC for the firm is very close to the ROIC on the existing capital, because there is very little new capital relative to the existing capital. As the firm grows and adds new capital, the proportion of new capital to previously existing capital increases. As the proportion of new capital increases, the total ROIC gets closer to the WACC (which is the ROIC on new capital). Eventually, as the firm continues to grow, the proportion of new capital completely outweighs the previously existing capital, and the total ROIC of the firm converges to the ROIC on the new capital, which is the WACC. For this reason, the formula in Equation 13-3 is called the convergence value horizon formula.

The General Value Horizon Formula

Yet another possibility is that, due to sources of competitive advantage, the ROIC on *existing capital* will stay the same as in the last year of the forecast and that at least some of these sources of competitive advantage will continue into the future as the firm adds new capital. In other words, competition will result in a gradual reduction of the return on new capital, forcing the ROIC on *new capital* to fall to some long-term sustainable $ROIC_L$, which may be greater than the WACC. For example, in 2002 Coca-Cola had an ROIC of 17.5% and a WACC of 6.9%.[2] Due to its sources of competitive advantage (patent on its formula, brand identity, etc.), it is likely that competition will not be able to completely erode Coke's ROIC. An analyst might reasonably conclude that the long-term sustainable $ROIC_L$ for Coca-Cola is greater than its WACC and less than its current ROIC of 17.5%. Although this is only our opinion, a reasonable long-term $ROIC_L$ might be in the range of 12% to 14%.

Just as for the convergence horizon value formula, the total ROIC for the firm will eventually converge to the $ROIC_L$ on new capital as the proportion of new capital grows. The formula for the general horizon value is[3]

$$HV_T = \left[\frac{(ROIC_L - g)Capital_T}{WACC - g}\right] + \left[\frac{(ROIC_T - ROIC_L)Capital_T}{WACC}\right]. \quad \textbf{(13-4)}$$

Notice that the continuing value formula in Equation 13-1 and the convergence value formula in Equation 13-3 are special cases of the general value formula in Equation 13-4. In particular, if we choose a value for the long-term $ROIC_L$ equal to the forecasted value of $ROIC_T$ at the horizon, Equation 13-4 produces the same answer as Equation 13-1, the continuing value. If we let $ROIC_L$ equal WACC, then Equation 13-4 reduces to Equation 13-3, the convergence value.

The Horizon Value for Home Depot

Since it covers all the cases, we use the general value formula in Equation 13-4. For an application to Home Depot, see the file ***Home Depot.xls***. Recall from our discussion of the *Inputs* worksheet in Chapter 12 that one of the required inputs (cell F48) is the long-term return on invested capital. Our forecasted ROIC at the horizon (shown in cell W85 in the *Proj & Val* worksheet and in cell D4 of the *Inputs* worksheet) is 16.2%, which is very high compared to the WACC of 8.51%. We are sure that Home Depot won't be able to sustain the 16.2% ROIC. But we think it has some brand identity and stores with favorable geographic locations, so we think it will be able to sustain a long-term ROIC greater than its WACC. Therefore, we chose a value of 10% as our input for the long-term ROIC. This is shown in the *Inputs* worksheet in cell D48.

The Value of Operations for Home Depot

In previous chapters, we forecasted free cash flows, found the horizon value, and then discounted the horizon value and free cash flows to find the current value of

[2]Stern Stewart & Co., *The 2002 Stern Stewart Performance 1000*, supplied these figures.

[3]For a derivation of this formula, see M. Ehrhardt, "Corporate Valuation: Incorporating the Impact of Competition into the Adjusted Present Value Technique," *Journal of Applied Corporate Finance*, forthcoming.

operations. Suppose that we also wished to know the value of operations on dates other than the current date. For example, suppose we have the forecasted free cash flows and horizon value as shown in Exhibit 13-1. The current date is 2003. If the WACC is 10%, how can we find the forecasted value of operations in 2004, 2005, or on any other date?

In Chapters 4 and 7 we found the present value of the free cash flows and horizon value in one step.

$$V_{2003} = \frac{\$100.00}{(1 + 0.10)} + \frac{\$105.00}{(1 + 0.10)^2} + \frac{\$110.25}{(1 + 0.10)^3} + \frac{\$2{,}315.25}{(1 + 0.10)^3} = \$2{,}000 \quad \textbf{(13-5)}$$

But suppose we want the value of operations in a future year? There is actually a very easy way to do this, as shown in the *Val & Proj* worksheet in ***Home Depot.xls***. Here is how we would apply the approach to the data in Exhibit 13-1. First, the value of operations is the present value of all future free cash flows. If we want the value of operations for the year 2006, this is the same as the horizon value, which is the present value of all free cash flows beyond 2006 (and not including the FCF in 2006) discounted back to 2006. We can interpret the value of operations in 2006, V_{2006}, as the price at which we could sell the operations in 2006.

What is the value of operations in 2005? If we owned the operations at time 2005, we would be entitled to all the FCFs beyond 2005 (not including the FCF at 2005, since timelines assume that it was paid one second prior to our calculation of value). To simplify this, what would our cash flows be if we sold the company in 2006? We would get the 2006 FCF, and then we could sell the company for the 2006 value of operations. Therefore, the value of operations in 2005 can be calculated as our expected cash flows in 2006 discounted back one year.

$$V_{2005} = \frac{FCF_{2006} + V_{2006}}{(1 + WACC)} + \frac{\$110.25 + \$2{,}315.25}{(1 + 0.10)} = \$2{,}205.00 \quad \textbf{(13-6)}$$

We could make a similar calculation for the value of operations as of 2004.

$$V_{2004} = \frac{FCF_{2005} + V_{2005}}{(1 + WACC)} + \frac{\$105.00 + \$2{,}205.00}{(1 + 0.10)} = \$2{,}100.00 \quad \textbf{(13-6a)}$$

Finally, we can repeat the process to find the current value of operations as of 2003.

Exhibit 13-1 Finding the Value of Operations

	Actual 2003	Projected 2004	Projected 2005	Projected 2006
Horizon value				$2,315.25
Free cash flow		$ 100.00	$ 105.00	$ 110.25
Value of operations	$2,000.00	$2,100.00	$2,205.00	$2,315.25

$$V_{2003} = \frac{FCF_{2004} + V_{2004}}{(1 + WACC)} + \frac{\$100.00 + \$2,100.00}{(1 + 0.10)} = \$2,000.00 \qquad \textbf{(13-6b)}$$

Calculating the value of operations one year at a time is more time consuming if done by hand, but it is actually easier to program in a spreadsheet. In addition, it provides an estimate of the value of operations for each year in the forecast, which is a useful piece of information. Therefore, this is the approach we use in the valuation spreadsheet model.

The Half-Year Adjustment

Spreadsheets are powerful tools, but they are not an exact representation of reality. Our simplifying assumption is that all cash flows occur at a distinct point in time. For multiyear investments, we simplify the computation by using 1-year intervals as if these were the actual cash collection points. For example, many spreadsheets assume that all cash flows occur at the end of Year 1, Year 2, Year 3, etc. For example, if a company has a fiscal year end of December 31, and the most recent year's data was for 2003, then Year 1 corresponds to 12/31/2004. Of course, this is an oversimplification because we know that cash flows will occur throughout the year, and not just on December 31. We could easily change our spreadsheets so that each column corresponds to a quarter or a month instead of a year, but because we need at least 10 to 20 years of forecasts, this would create a rather large spreadsheet.

We follow the convention of having each spreadsheet column correspond to a year, but we make an adjustment to reflect the fact that we know cash flows are occurring throughout the year and not just on the last day of the year. If we assume that cash flows occur evenly throughout the year, then this means our estimate of the value of operations based upon year-end cash collection is understating the true value of operations. This is because most of a year's cash flows occur before the end of the year, yet we discount them as though they occur at the end of the year. Fortunately, there is a simple adjustment, the half-year adjustment, which treats the total yearly cash flow as if it occurs at mid-year.

Before adjustments, we calculate the value of operations as

$$V_{\text{Before Adjustment}} = \frac{FCF_1}{(1 + WACC)^1} + \frac{FCF_2}{(1 + WACC)^2} + \frac{FCF_3}{(1 + WACC)^3} + \ldots \qquad \textbf{(13-7)}$$

As we noted above, the cash flows occur throughout the year, not just at the end of the year. If they come in smoothly throughout the year, then this is equivalent to showing them as occurring at the middle of the year, on average.

So the true value, after we make this adjustment, is

$$V_{\text{After Adjustment}} = \frac{FCF_1}{(1 + WACC)^{0.5}} + \frac{FCF_2}{(1 + WACC)^{1.5}} + \frac{FCF_3}{(1 + WACC)^{2.5}} + \ldots \qquad \textbf{(13-8)}$$

Notice that the value after the adjustment is

$$V_{\text{After Adjustment}} = V_{\text{Before Adjustment}}(1 + WACC)^{0.5}. \qquad \textbf{(13-9)}$$

Therefore, the half-year adjustment is to take the value that you estimate under the assumption that cash flows occur at the end of the year and then scale it up by a half-year's growth at a rate of growth equal to the WACC.

Estimating the Value at Times Other than Fiscal Year-End

Our valuation model gives the value of the firm as of the end of the most recent fiscal year. That is the date of the most recent financial statement data and all projections are based on the assumption that we are starting from that date. For example, suppose the most recent end of a fiscal year is 12/31/2002. In that case, our model will give a price as of 12/31/2002. But suppose the current date is in the middle of the year, such as 8/15/2003. How do we find the value in such a situation?

Notice that 8/15/2003 is 227 days after 12/31/2002. (It is very easy to find the number of days between dates in a spreadsheet; simply subtract the first date from the second date.) The model assumes that the value of operations is growing at the WACC. So to find the value of operations as of 8/15/2003, we would apply the following formula.

$$V_{8/15/2003} = V_{12/31/2002}(1 + \text{WACC})^{227/365} \quad \textbf{(13-10)}$$

For example, if the value of operations on 12/31/2002 is $800 million and the WACC is 10%, then the value of operations on 8/15/2003 is $848.85 million [$848.85 = 800(1.1)^{(227/365)}$].

To find the stock price on 8/15/2003, we follow the same procedure as before: We add the value of investments to the value of operations to get the total value of the firm, we subtract the value of debt from the total value to get the value of equity, and then we divide by the number of shares to get the price per share. To implement this procedure, we need to know the value of investments, the value of debt, and the number of shares as of the target date. A simple way to find these values is to interpolate between the Year 0 values and the projected Year 1 values.

For example, suppose the 12/31/2002 value of investments is $30 million and the projected 12/31/2003 value is $45 million.

$$\text{Investments}_{8/15/03} = \$30 + [(\$45 - \$30)(227/365)] = \$39.33 \quad \textbf{(13-11)}$$

We follow the same procedure to find the value of debt as of 8/15/2003. For example, suppose the value of debt on 12/31/2002 is $300 million and the projected value for 12/31/2003 is $400 million.

$$\text{Debt}_{8/15/03} = \$300 + [(\$400 - \$300)(227/365)] = \$362.19 \quad \textbf{(13-12)}$$

In this example, the value of equity as of 8/15/2003 is $848.85 million (the value of operations) plus $39.33 (the value of investments) minus $362.19 million (the value of debt). Therefore, the value of equity is $525.99 million.

We need only the number of shares as of 8/15/2003 to find the price per share. There were 100 million shares on 12/31/2002, and if this number is unchanged on 8/15/2003, then the estimated price on 8/15/2003 is $52.60 = $525.99/100.

However, the number of shares outstanding does change from time to time due to stock splits, equity repurchases, and other events. You should always verify, if possible, the current number of shares outstanding. If the stock is publicly traded, this number can be found on the Profile page at Yahoo! Finance.

As described in Chapter 12, you can use the *Condensed* quarterly statements to find the amounts of investments and debt shown on the 6/30/2003 quarterly statements. You could then use these as estimates of the 8/15/2003 values. Alternatively, you might follow the same procedure we described above to find the 8/15/2003 values assuming that the 6/30/2003 values grow proportionately to the 12/31/2003 projected values.

Finally, you should always use the market values for investments and debt if you know them and if they are significantly different from the values reported on the financial statements.

The Valuation of Home Depot

Exhibit 13-2 shows the valuation data for Home Depot in the most recent year, the first 3 projected years, and the last 2 projected years; see the *Proj & Val* worksheet in the file ***Home Depot.xls*** for the full 20 years of data. Part 1 shows the calculations of forecasted free cash flow using the approach described in Chapters 10 and 12.

Part 2 shows the calculation of value. We begin by calculating the projected ROIC, which is 19.2% for the most recent year. It declines slightly in the first years of our forecast and then climbs slightly until it levels off at 16.2% in the last years of our forecast. As we explained earlier, we don't think Home Depot can maintain this high an ROIC indefinitely; we'll address this in just a moment.

Notice that we calculate growth rates for sales, NOPAT, operating capital, and FCF. As the first years show, the growth rates are quite variable. We expect this, since we are letting our inputs change during these years. However, all growth rates have leveled off to 5% by the last year in our forecast. Thus, we can use the horizon value formula. In particular, we used the general formula in Equation 13-4 and assumed a long-term sustainable ROIC of 10%. This is higher than the 8.51% WACC, because we believe Home Depot is building brand identity, but it is much less than the forecasted 16.2% because we believe competition will erode the ROIC over the long term. Using Equation 13-4, Part 2 shows a horizon value of about $189 billion.

If we go to cell W96 in the *Proj & Val* worksheet of ***Home Depot.xls***, we can see how sensitive the value of operations is to the choice of the assumed long-term ROIC. Changing $ROIC_L$ in cell D48 of the *Inputs* worksheet from 10% to the Year-20 forecasted value of 16.2%, the horizon value increases from $189 billion to $281 billion. Reducing the assumed $ROIC_L$ to the WACC of 8.51%, the horizon value drops to $168 billion.

As Part 2 of Exhibit 13-2 shows, the value of operations for the most recent year, which is the present value of all forecasted future free cash flows and the horizon value, is about $75 billion. Using the half-year adjustment of Equation 13-9, the value of operations is about $78 billion. Home Depot doesn't have many nonoperating investments, so its total value is also about $78 billion. After subtracting nonequity claims, in this case debt, and dividing by the number of shares, the estimated stock price for the most recent fiscal year-end, 2/02/2003, is $32.69 per share.

Exhibit 13-2 The Valuation of Home Depot

Part 1—Calculating Projected Free Cash Flows (thousands of dollars)

	Most Recent 02/02/03	Projected 02/02/04	Projected 02/02/05	Projected 02/02/06	Projected 02/02/22	Projected 02/02/23
Calculating Projected FCF						
Marginal tax rate	37.6%	38.6%	38.6%	38.6%	38.6%	38.6%
Reported income tax expense	$ 2,208,000	$ (2,481,880)	$ (2,705,304)	$(2,923,224)	$ (7,985,088)	$ (8,164,258)
Taxes reported but not paid	173,000	36,200	38,292	41,516	72,672	76,306
Actual taxes paid	2,035,000	(2,518,080)	(2,743,596)	(2,964,740)	(8,057,760)	(8,240,565)
Plus tax saved due to net interest expenses	13,913	27,081	8,062	6,874	232,671	464,388
Minus tax paid on nonoperating income	29,706	33,543	36,858	40,453	130,660	137,193
Tax on operating income	$ 2,019,207	$ 2,439,218	$ 2,638,217	$ 2,848,129	$ 8,014,426	$ 8,415,147
NOPAT/sales	3,810,793	3,973,782	4,295,743	4,637,998	12,936,606	13,583,436
NOPAT adjusted for extraordinary income	3,810,793	3,973,782	4,295,743	4,637,998	12,936,606	13,583,436
Operating current assets	11,852,000	11,271,117	12,298,610	13,412,267	41,870,088	43,963,592
Operating current liabilities	8,035,000	8,838,500	9,711,961	10,659,127	34,428,216	36,149,627
Net operating working capital	3,817,000	2,432,617	2,586,649	2,753,141	7,441,872	7,813,966
Operating long-term capital	18,094,000	19,903,400	21,820,057	23,898,130	76,344,644	80,161,876
Operating capital/sales	21,911,000	22,336,017	24,406,705	26,651,270	83,786,516	87,975,842
Investment in operating capital	2,082,000	425,017	2,070,688	2,244,565	3,989,834	4,189,326
Free cash flow (including extraordinary income)	$ 1,728,793	$ 3,548,765	$ 2,225,054	$ 2,393,433	$ 8,946,772	$ 9,394,111

Note: All calculations were performed in a spreadsheet model. Some calculations may not total exactly due to rounding.

Exhibit 13-2 The Valuation of Home Depot (continued)

Part 1—Calculating Projected Free Cash Flows (thousands of dollars)

	Most Recent 02/02/03	Projected 02/02/04	Projected 02/02/05	Projected 02/02/06	Projected 02/02/22	Projected 02/02/23
Free cash flow (including extraordinary income)	$ 1,728,793	$ 3,548,765	$ 2,225,054	$ 2,393,433	$ 8,946,772	$ 9,394,111
ROIC (NOPAT/ Beginning capital)	19.2%	18.1%	19.2%	19.0%	16.2%	16.2%
Growth in sales		10.0%	9.9%	9.8%	5.0%	5.0%
Growth in NOPAT		4.3%	8.1%	8.0%	5.0%	5.0%
Growth in operating capital		1.9%	9.3%	9.2%	5.0%	5.0%
Growth in FCF		105.3%	-37.3%	7.6%	5.0%	5.0%
WACC	8.51%	8.51%	8.51%	8.51%	8.51%	8.51%
Assumed long-term return on invested capital						10.00%
Horizon value						$189,478,001
Value of operations	$74,982,963	$77,816,333	$82,214,575	$ 86,818,792	$183,272,933	$189,478,001
Value of operations adjusted for half-year convention	78,108,874	81,060,362	85,641,959	90,438,118	190,913,266	197,377,013
Value of investments	65,000	3,310,972	7,072,393	10,861,449	9,455,180	0
Total value of firm	$78,173,874	$84,371,335	$92,714,352	$101,299,567	$200,368,447	$197,377,013
Value of all debt, preferred stock, and other nonoperating liabilities	1,812,000	2,109,008	4,355,968	6,635,818	44,104,746	49,054,539
Value of equity	$76,361,874	$82,262,327	$88,358,384	$ 94,663,748	$156,263,700	$148,322,474
Number of shares	2,336,000	2,336,000	2,336,000	2,336,000	2,336,000	2,336,000
Estimated price per share, end of fiscal year	**$32.69**	**$35.22**	**$37.82**	**$40.52**	**$66.89**	**$ 63.49**

Exhibit 13-3 shows the calculations for the target date of 5/21/2003. The intrinsic valuation for this date is $33.43. The actual stock price for Home Depot was $30.62 per share on this date.

How good an estimate is this? In other words, is an estimate of around $33 fairly accurate or not? To put that into perspective, consider the volatility of a typical stock, whose return has a standard deviation of about 35%. For a stock that starts the year with a price of $30, there is about a 16% chance the price at the end of the year will be below $19.50, and about a 16% chance that stock price will be above $40.50. In other words, stock prices are very volatile! Our experience in applying the FCF model to many different companies over the last 8 years indicates that most of the time the intrinsic valuation from the model is within 15% of the actual stock price. If the model gives us an estimated value within 15% of the actual stock price, then we think the model has done a very good job in the sense that it provides rational, fairly accurate intrinsic valuations (that is, if one believes that the financial markets price stocks fairly, on average). On the other hand, as investors, the valuations that most pique our interest are precisely those where the estimated intrinsic valuation is considerably different from the current market prices of the firms' stock.

Projections of Other Financial Measures

Although the estimated stock price is the bottom line in a valuation analysis, the projections also provide other useful information. Exhibit 13-4 shows some of this other data for Home Depot; see the file ***Home Depot.xls*** for the full 20 years of data.

Exhibit 13-3 Home Depot's Stock Price for the Target Date (thousands of dollars, except per share data)

Price per share on target date	
Fiscal year end	02/02/03
Target valuation date	5/21/03
Number of days from fiscal year end to target	108.00
Value of operations on target date	$ 78,970,816
Value of investments on target date	1,025,452
Total value of firm on target date	79,996,269
Value of debt on target date	1,899,882
Value of equity on target date	$ 78,096,387
Number of shares on target date	2,336,000
Price per share, target date	**$33.43**

Exhibit 13-4 begins with the most recent and projected estimates of economic profit (EP).[4] We define economic profit as

$$\begin{aligned} \text{EP} &= \text{NOPAT} - \text{Capital charges} \\ &= \text{NOPAT} - \text{WACC(Operating capital at the beginning of the year)}. \end{aligned} \quad \textbf{(13-13)}$$

In other words, EP measures the "profit" that the company generated during the year in excess of the "profit" that investors required at the beginning of the year. Given the high forecasted ROICs of Home Depot relative to its WACC, it's not surprising to see the large, positive projected EPs.

Market value added (MVA) is usually calculated as the difference between the market value of a company (based on its actual stock price) and the book value of the company. We define the projected MVA as the estimated value of operations (i.e., the present value of future FCFs) minus the total operating capital (at current book value).

$$\text{MVA} = \text{Value of operations} - \text{Operating capital} \quad \textbf{(13-14)}$$

Thus, our definition of MVA is a measure of the value added by the company's operations. As Exhibit 13-4 (and the *Proj & Val* worksheet in the file ***Home Depot.xls***) shows, Home Depot has a large current MVA of about $56 billion. In other words, Home Depot's managers have created $56 billion in value above and beyond the capital that investors have put into the business. Notice also that Home Depot's projected MVA steadily increases throughout the forecast period.

As we explained in Chapter 4, we don't put much credibility in comparative valuation approaches because they are just rules of thumb that don't provide insight into a company's operations. However, we do like to see how our projections conform to these rules of thumb, and so we show some widely used comparative measures in Exhibit 13-4. The first of these is the price/earnings ratio, often called the P/E (or just PE) ratio. For the current year, Home Depot's estimated P/E ratio is 20.8. Historically, the typical P/E ratio has averaged about 10 to 16, though in late 1990s, it was much higher. Home Depot's ratio is higher than the historical average, reflecting its high growth prospects and high ROIC. Although its P/E ratio is on the high side by historical standards, it is not out of line with the current P/E ratio for its industry (about 19) or the current P/E ratio for the typical firm in the S&P 500 (about 22.5).[5] Notice also that the projected P/E ratio declines throughout the forecast period as growth slows, until it is eventually within the normal range.

Another widely used comparative ratio is the market to book ratio, defined as the market value of equity divided by the book value of equity as shown on the balance sheets. Home Depot's ratio of 3.9 is consistent with the industry ratio of 3.4 and the S&P 500 ratio of 4.2.

We also report the Value/Sales ratio and the Value/EBITDA ratio. The value is the total value of the firm, and EBITDA is earnings before interest, taxes, depreciation, and amortization. We calculate EBITDA as operating profit plus depreciation. Home Depot's ratio is 11.6; Yahoo doesn't report the industry or S&P 500 ratios, so we have no easy method for comparison.

[4] This measure is closely akin to the measure known as economic value added, or EVA, which is the proprietary version used by Stern Stewart & Company.

[5] We obtained these from Multex Investor's ratio comparisons, as described in Chapter 12.

In Chapter 11, we stated that the target weights in the capital structure should be based on market values. Therefore, Exhibit 13-4 reports the market-based percent of the firm that is financed with debt. For Home Depot, this rate starts at around 2% and then increases to 22% by the end of the forecast period. This is the target ratio we specified when providing the inputs for Home Depot financial policies. Notice that the times-interest-earned ratio remains well above 4, indicating that Home Depot can easily support the increased debt. See Chapter 8 and the Chapter 13 appendix for more discussion on the role of capital structure in valuation.

Finally, the forecasted statements are helpful to the managers who are responsible for raising capital. Exhibit 13-5 shows a portion of the statement of cash flows from the bottom of the *Proj & Val* worksheet in ***Home Depot.xls***. First, notice that the bottom line shows that the net cash flow from financing activities is negative in the most recent year (2003) and is projected to be negative in each of the years reported in Exhibit 13-5. In other words, Home Depot is generating so much free cash flow that it has extra cash even after it pays its dividends. In 2003, Home Depot used most of this cash to repurchase equity (which is shown as a negative cash flow from Home Depot's perspective).

Recall from Chapter 12 that we balanced the sheets by either borrowing short-term or purchasing short-term investments, depending on the other projected assets and liabilities. If Home Depot doesn't have enough financing to support its growth plans, then it borrows short-term debt. Exhibit 13-5 shows that Home Depot's projected change in short-term debt is zero, which means that it doesn't have to add any short-term debt. If Home Depot has too much financing, based on its cash from operations and our assumptions about its capital structure and dividend policy, then we assume that it will use this extra funding to purchase short-term investments, such as marketable securities. As shown in 2004, we project Home Depot to purchase over $3.2 billion in short-term investments. Because we are assuming that Home Depot will increase the amount of long-term debt in its capital structure, the net effect of the increased debt and the large free cash flows is that Home Depot has over $3.7 billion in extra funding in 2005 that will go into short-term investments.

In fact, our projections show Home Depot borrowing $2.2 billion in 2005 and at the same time purchasing $3.7 billion in short-term investments. Let's consider the rationale behind this result. First, as we discussed in Chapter 11, Home Depot needs more debt in order to take advantage of the tax savings due to the deductibility of interest expenses. Put another way, Home Depot doesn't need the debt to finance its growth (because it has such strong free cash flows), but it does need the debt to reduce its taxes. Given that Home Depot will add the debt, then the question is how Home Depot will spend it. It is likely that its board will authorize additional stock repurchases in 2005 and subsequent years. Or perhaps Home Depot will make a major acquisition. As outsiders, we aren't in a position to make these decisions, and so we simply plow these extra funds into short-term investments. But as analysts, we can state with a high degree of certainty that Home Depot will in fact have surplus cash flow in the coming years and will have to make some decisions regarding its use.

Exhibit 13-4 Other Projected Data for Home Depot (thousands of dollars)

	Most Recent 02/02/03	Projected 02/02/04	Projected 02/02/05	Projected 02/02/06	Projected 02/02/22	Projected 02/02/23
Projected economic profit (EP)	$3,810,793	$2,108,839	$2,394,625	$2,560,635	$6,144,754	$6,451,992
Projected market value added (MVA)	$56,197,874	$58,724,345	$61,235,254	$63,786,847	$107,126,751	$109,401,171
Price/earnings ratio (P/E ratio)	20.8	20.8	20.5	20.4	12.3	11.4
Market to book ratio	3.9	3.6	3.3	3.1	3.3	4.0
Value/EBITDA ratio	11.6	11.4	11.6	11.7	8.1	7.6
Value/sales ratio	1.3	1.3	1.3	1.3	0.8	0.8
Times-interest-earned ratio	157.6	91.4	332.0	420.4	34.8	18.3
Long-term debt/value of operations		1.9%	4.4%	6.6%	22.0%	22.0%

Exhibit 13-5 Projected Financing for Home Depot (thousands of dollars)

	Most Recent 02/02/03	Projected 02/02/04	Projected 02/02/05	Projected 02/02/06
Financing Activities				
Change in short-term investments	$ 4,000	$ (3,245,972)	$ (3,761,421)	$ (3,789,056)
Change in long-term investments	0	0	0	0
Change in short-term debt	(5,000)	0	0	0
Change in long-term debt	71,000	247,908	2,193,585	2,221,971
Preferred dividends	0	0	0	0
Change in preferred stock	0	0	0	0
Change in other long-term liabilities	119,000	49,100	53,375	57,879
Change in common stock (par + PIC)	(1,452,000)	0	0	0
Common dividends	(492,000)	(610,080)	(756,398)	(937,640)
Net cash from financing activities	$ (1,755,000)	$ (3,559,044)	$ (2,270,859)	$ (2,446,846)

Of course, the projected cash flows for many companies aren't as large as those of Home Depot, and the projected statement of cash flows is a valuable tool in identifying the amount of future financing that will be required to support the company's operating plans.

Reverse Engineering/Scenario Analysis

Our estimated intrinsic value of $33.43 on the target date was based on our unbiased, best judgment regarding the future operating prospects of Home Depot. However, the actual price prevailing at the time of our analysis was $30.62. We often find it helpful to go back to our inputs and reverse engineer them until the estimated intrinsic value is equal to the actual price. We don't simply randomly change inputs, we go back to those inputs we were least sure about when we did our original analysis. For Home Depot, we felt fairly comfortable about our inputs for projected capital, but were unsure about the cost structure, particularly the long-term ratio of SGA/sales. Raising the long-run value of SGA/sales to 21.7% from our initial estimate of 21.1% will lower the intrinsic value estimate to $30.75. (Notice that the estimated stock price is shown at the top of the *Inputs* worksheet in ***Home Depot.xls***, making it easy to see the impact of a change in inputs.) This illustrates the sensitivity of the valuation of Home Depot to variation in its cost of goods, a result not too surprising for a low margin retailer. What this says to us as potential investors is that relatively small changes in one or more of our estimates of inputs to the Home Depot valuation puts the intrinsic value estimate at, or even below, the market price on the target date. This might cool our interest in Home Depot, even though the initial reaction to the $33.43 intrinsic value estimate may have been that the stock was a good buy. On the other hand, a small improvement in the cost structure causes a large increase in the estimated intrinsic stock price. So the investment decision boils down to how willing we are to bet on our input estimates!

Suppose, however, our originally estimated value was much higher than the current stock price, say around $45 per share, and large changes in our inputs were required to drive the estimated value down to its prevailing price. In this situation, given the same degree of confidence in our input estimates, we might conclude that the stock was underpriced, and represented a potentially valuable investment (a "good bet").

Sometimes the reverse might occur, in which case the model gives an intrinsic value that is much lower than the prevailing stock price. If it takes unreasonable improvements in our inputs to justify the prevailing price, then we might conclude that the stock is overpriced and sell it if the stock was already in our portfolio.

We have found that reverse engineering the inputs until the model yields the prevailing price is a nice way to do a reality check. If small changes in our first set of inputs, which were based on our best judgment, will cause the estimated price to equal the actual price, then we usually conclude that the stock is fairly priced. But if it takes implausible changes in our first set of inputs to justify the actual price, then we conclude the stock is mispriced.

Finally, reverse engineering has potential use by board members for setting targets in compensation plans. If we reverse engineer the inputs until the estimated value is equal to the actual stock price, then the projected statements reflect the market's expectations. If managers make decisions that lead to improvements relative to the projected statements, then the stock price and MVA should increase by more than investors expected. In other words, the managers will have created value and should be rewarded. Thus, we advocate using the projected financial statements of the reverse-engineered model to set targets in compensation plans. For example, suppose Home Depot were using a residual income type of compensation plan for its senior executives. The plan would compensate executives based on a target economic profit level. Our reverse-engineered model (the one with long-run SGA/sales at 21.7%) produced a projected economic profit for 2004 of $2.1 billion, and this is the target we would recommend in a compensation plan that uses EP.

Valuing a Company with a Changing Capital Structure

Suppose you know that a company will have a large change in its capital structure. For example, many highly levered companies plan on paying down the debt to a sustainable level over a period of years. If this is the case, then the WACC is changing for the company each year. Rather than try to estimate the correct WACC for each year, which is a very difficult task, we recommend using an alternative valuation method, called the adjusted present value (APV) approach. In the APV approach, you still project free cash flows, but you no longer discount them with the WACC. Instead, you follow a two-step procedure. First, you discount the free cash flows at the cost of capital the firm would have if it had no debt. The result is the value of operations that the firm would have if it were unlevered.

We know that interest payments will reduce the firm's tax bill. The amount of the reduction due to interest payments is called the tax shield of debt. The second step is to find the present value of the tax shield. When added to the previously calculated unlevered value of operations, the result is the value of operations for a levered firm. The advantage of the APV approach is that it can be used even if a firm has a nonconstant proportion of debt in its capital structure each year. See the appendix to this chapter for more details.

Summary

In this chapter, we showed you how to complete a valuation analysis, using Home Depot as an example. We started by discussing the logic of developing an appropriate horizon value for the firm. The horizon value should recognize the life cycle of the business and, in particular, the role of mounting competitive pressure as a firm and its industry approach maturity. The approach used in our FCF valuation framework is quite general, but it does require the analyst to give careful consideration to the evolution of competitive pressures as the firm matures.

We then worked through the complete valuation for Home Depot and saw how a number of potentially useful byproducts arise from the calculations, including calculations of earnings/price ratios and economic profit. We also get a set of projected statements of cash flow, which are particularly useful to an internal analyst for projecting the firm's needs for external financing and for planning future changes in dividend policy or stock repurchases.

We also discussed the notion of reverse engineering, that is, of discovering which assumptions regarding sales growth, profitability, and capital usage are required to justify the current market value of a company. Understanding the reasons why an estimated intrinsic value differs from the current stock price is an important dimension of the investment decision. We also saw how reverse engineering may be useful for internal corporate purposes, such as setting compensation targets.

Spreadsheet Problems

13-1 Valuing Lowe's

This project builds upon your expertise in using financial resources on the Internet. Start with the valuation spreadsheet for Lowe's that you created in Chapters 9, 10, 11, and 12.

a. Using your best judgment when selecting inputs on the *Input* sheet for Lowe's, what is your estimate of the intrinsic stock price? How does this compare with the actual price?

b. Reverse engineer your estimate by modifying inputs on the *Input* sheet (i.e., don't change your WACC inputs) until the estimated price equals the actual price. This will produce forecasts that are consistent with the market's expectations. Do you think the company can achieve these expectations, in other words, is the current price reasonable?

c. Describe the projected required financing. In particular, will Lowe's need to secure external financing, or will it have extra cash that it invests in short-term investments?

d. Suppose Lowe's can improve its operations. In particular, what happens to the current stock price if your long-term rates for the following ratios improve by one percentage point (i.e., if your estimate for COGS/sales is 65%, what is the impact of improving it to 64%)?
   1. Sales growth
   2. COGS/sales
   3. Inventory/sales

13-2 Valuing Another Company

Pick another company (or one that your professor assigns), and repeat the analysis in Problem 13-1, focusing on the following questions:

a. Consider the ROIC projections for the firm out through the end of the projection period. Are the ending values about what you would expect, given the likely impact of long-run competitive forces in the industry? Decide on your estimate of the resulting long-term sustainable ROIC.

b. Compare the intrinsic value estimate from your set of inputs to the target date market price of the firm's stock. Does the comparison suggest a buy or a sell?
c. Find price/earnings ratios for three of your firm's close competitors. Are these in line with the projected price/earnings ratio?
d. Now reverse engineer until you get a combination of inputs that would yield an intrinsic value estimate roughly equal to the current market price of your firm's stock. In light of your uncertainties about your initial inputs, how confident are you about tentative conclusion in part b above? Perform any other sensitivity tests that you feel are useful.
e. Make an outline for a 15-minute presentation of your conclusions about investment potential, or lack thereof, of your company. In the individual points within your outline, include a brief description of any exhibits you would use.

Appendix

13

The Adjusted Present Value Method

Until now, we have always found the value of a firm as the present value of its expected future free cash flows, discounted at the weighted average cost of capital. Recall from Chapter 11 that you must specify the capital structure of the firm to calculate its WACC, that is, you must choose what percent of the firm you expect will be financed with debt and what percent you expect to be financed with equity. Notice that this calculation assumes that the capital structure will remain constant in the future.

But what if your capital structure doesn't remain constant? This is the case for many firms. For example, a firm might currently have a high level of debt that it plans to pay off over the next 5 years. Or another firm, such as Home Depot, might have very little debt during its high-risk, high-growth phase, but decide to add debt gradually as it matures. Many other firms also have shifting capital structures, especially in the short run. Recall from Chapter 8 that of all the methods to make the balance sheets balance, only one method keeps the capital structure constant in terms of market values. The disadvantage of this method is that it requires either volatile dividend payments or frequent stock issues. Since many firms instead choose to have stable dividend payments and to avoid stock issues, this means their capital structures change in the short term. Therefore, you need to know how to estimate the value of firms with changing capital structures in the short term (i.e., the explicit forecast period prior to the horizon).

Before we plunge into the analysis, it is useful to think about the way in which debt affects the total value of a company. This is a complicated subject, but the next section does present a brief overview of capital structure theory.

Capital Structure and the Value of a Company

Let's start the analysis with a firm that has no debt. We call this an **unlevered firm**. The value of this firm is equal to the value of its equity. To keep the case simple, we assume the firm has no nonoperating assets. So the value of equity is just equal to the value of operations, which itself is the present value of the expected future free cash flows. Because the firm has no debt, the WACC for an unlevered firm is just its cost of equity.

Suppose we have another firm that is identical in every way, except that it is financed with a mixture of debt and equity. It has the same types of assets, the same customers, the same types of employees, and the same quality of management. Therefore, it has the same free cash flows as the levered firm, and these free cash flows are just as risky as those of the levered firm. So what is different between the levered and unlevered firm? Although they have the same free cash flows, they don't have the same tax bill. The levered firm pays interest, which it can deduct from its taxable income. Because the interest payments lower the taxable income, they also lower the taxes that the levered firm pays. In other words, the debt *shields* some of the firm's income from taxes. If D_0 is the amount of debt that the firm has at the current time, i is the interest rate on the debt, and T is the tax rate, then the company's tax savings will be $T(i)(D_0)$.

For example, suppose a firm has \$10 million in debt, an interest rate on the debt of 9%, and a tax rate of 40%. The firm will get to deduct a \$900,000 interest expense: \$900,000 = 0.09(\$10,000,000). This will save the company \$360,000 in taxes: \$360,000 = 0.40(\$900,000). Therefore, its tax shield due to debt is \$360,000. Notice that this is equal to $T(i)(D_0)$: \$360,000 = 0.40(0.09)(\$10,000,000).

Think of the pre-tax value of a firm as a pie. The government gets the first piece in the form of taxes, and investors get the remaining pieces. If a firm saves money each year by not paying as much in taxes, then the government's piece is smaller, making the investors' pieces larger. In other words, the tax shield adds to the firm's after-tax value. If the firm plans on having debt each year in the future, the current value of the tax shield is the present value of all the future tax savings due to deducting interests.

Therefore, we can think of the value of a levered firm as equal to the value of an identical but unlevered firm, plus the value of the tax shield due to future tax savings.

Too Much Debt and Bankruptcy Costs

It is certainly true that debt can have effects on the value of a firm other than just through the tax shield. For example, if a firm has an extremely large amount of debt, then the probability of bankruptcy can be quite large. As this probability of bankruptcy increases, some customers might choose not to buy the company's products, for fear that the company might later go bankrupt. As customers quit buying the products, sales fall (i.e., the growth rate in sales becomes negative), which makes the likelihood of bankruptcy even higher. This is exactly what was happening with Apple Computer in the early 1990s, before the return of Steve Jobs and the introduction of the iMac. In addition to the defection of customers, many software developers quit writing software for Apple, because they thought future sales might be lower. Customers recognized this, and many defected. Apple has had a phenomenal turnaround, but for many companies the mere *threat* of bankruptcy has actually precipitated bankruptcy itself. Enron is a perfect example. Although Enron did eventually reveal more debt than its financial statements indicated, its sharp drop in cash flows came about because other firms stopped participating in its energy trading operations. It was this loss of trading revenue, not the accounting fraud itself, that led to Enron's bankruptcy.

Future free cash flows are adversely affected if the threat of bankruptcy causes the sales growth rate to fall. But there are other ways in which the threat of bankruptcy hurts free cash flows. Suppliers become reluctant to extend credit, which causes accounts payable to fall. This hurts net operating working capital, which hurts free cash flows. With the threat of bankruptcy, many managers spend time preparing resumes or simply waste time while they worry about their futures. The same is true of hourly employees. This leads to a decline in productivity. All in all, these indirect bankruptcy costs can have a huge negative impact on free cash flows, which lowers the value of the firm.

If a firm actually goes through a bankruptcy, it inevitably incurs some direct bankruptcy costs. In a perfect world, if a firm missed an interest payment the bondholders could simply force the firm to file for bankruptcy. After the firm filed for bankruptcy, the courts would oversee a reorganization of the firm. In this reorganization, the old debtholders would exchange their old debt for new preferred stock and/or common stock in the firm. The old preferred stockholders would exchange their preferred stock for new shares of common stock. And the old common stockholders would exchange their existing shares of stock for a much smaller number of new shares, perhaps even no new shares at all. Notice that this perfect bankruptcy would simply be a reallocation of ownership. It would have no effect on the firm's free cash flows, so it would not affect the firm's value. It is true that the events leading up to the bankruptcy would certainly have reduced the firm's value, but the reallocation of ownership would not have affected it.

But it is not a perfect world, and the reorganization never goes smoothly. All of the involved parties hire lawyers, and of course that is a bad sign in and of itself! Bankruptcy lawyers are expensive, so the legal fees can be substantial. Also, often some of the assets are sold, and the sales price may be very low because there is a rush to sell the assets. These direct costs can be substantial, with many studies showing that they are in the range of 5% to 15% of the firm's prebankruptcy value.

Too Much Debt and Managerial Behavior

It also is possible that the debt itself can affect the behavior of senior management. On the one hand, having a lot of debt means that much of the firm's free cash flows must be used to make interest and principal payments. In other words, much of the free cash flow is precommitted. This "bonding" of the free cash flow can make managers less likely to squander the free cash flow on activities that don't really help the firm, such as perquisites (e.g., Lear jets, plush offices, extra staff) or glamorous but negative NPV projects (such as paying too much to acquire another company). As less free cash flow is squandered, the value of the firm goes up.

On the other hand, having a lot of debt can make senior managers too cautious for fear of missing an interest payment. For example, there can be projects that have positive expected NPVs, but that are very risky in the sense that the actual return might be very large and positive, or very negative. Because managerial reputation can be destroyed if the project's value turns out to be negative, many managers will choose to reject the project. Notice that this type of risk should not bother a well-diversified investor, who owns stock in many firms. If some projects in one firm turn out poorly, it is likely that some projects in other firms will turn out better than expected. With enough firms in the investor's portfolio, the investor can be reasonably sure of getting the expected NPV, even though the NPV for any single firm might be much higher or lower than expected. But managers are not so well diversified, with much of their direct wealth and their reputations (which indirectly lead to wealth) tied up in a single firm. Therefore, managers may avoid value-adding projects if they are too risky.

Valuation When Debt Is Moderate

For the rest of our discussion, we are going to assume that the level of debt is not so high that it triggers either direct or indirect bankruptcy costs and that it is low enough so that it has a negligible effect, for good or ill, on the behavior of managers. Under this assumption, the only effect of debt is due to the value of the tax shield.

Therefore, the value of a levered firm is the value of an identical unlevered firm, plus the value of the tax shield. The unlevered value of operations for a levered firm is the present value of the firm's free cash flows, discounted at the unlevered cost of equity. The value of the tax shield is the present value of the annual tax savings due to interest, discounted at some appropriate discount rate. Given the projected financial statements for a levered firm, it is easy to calculate the free cash flows and the annual tax shields. To find the value of the levered firm, we also need estimates of the unlevered cost of equity and the appropriate discount rate for the tax shields.

The following sections describe how to calculate the unlevered value of operations and the value of the tax shield.

The Unlevered Value of Operations

The value of operations for an unlevered firm is the present value of the firm's free cash flows, discounted at the unlevered cost of equity. But notice that the unlevered cost of equity isn't observable. When we measure beta for a firm, it is based on the stock returns of the firm, which already reflect the impact of leverage. In other words, all we can estimate is the levered beta (i.e., the beta of a levered firm) and the levered cost of equity (i.e., the cost of equity for a levered firm). Without getting into the technical details, here is how you should estimate the unlevered cost of equity.[1]

Suppose you can calculate the levered cost of equity, r_{SL}, for a similar firm (or for the same firm, if it is levered). Let r_{SU} denote the unlevered cost of equity, w_S denote the percent of the firm that is financed with equity, w_{LTD} denote the percent of the firm that is financed with long-term debt, i_{LTD} denote the interest rate on long-term debt, w_{STD} denote the percent of the firm that is financed with short-term debt, i_{STD} denote the interest rate on short-term debt, r_{PS} denote the cost of preferred stock, and w_{PS} denote the percent of the firm that is financed with preferred stock.[2] Then the unlevered cost of equity can be written as a function of the levered cost of equity.

[1]See P. R. Daves and M. C. Ehrhardt, 2002, "The Combined Impact of Growth and the Tax Shield of Debt on the Cost of Capital and Systematic Risk," *Journal of Applied Finance*, (Vol. 12, No. 2, Fall/Winter) 31–38.

[2]The weights should be based on the target capital structure, which is itself based on market values and not book values. See the discussion of the WACC in Chapter 11 for more details.

$$r_{SU} = w_S r_{SL} + i_{LTD} w_{LTD} + i_{STD} w_{STD} + w_{PS} r_{PS} \quad \textbf{(13A-1)}$$

For example, suppose you know the levered cost of equity for a company is 12% and that 40% of its capital structure is financed with long-term debt at an interest rate of 8%. The firm has no short-term debt or preferred stock in its target capital structure. Using Equation 13A-1, its unlevered cost of equity is

$$\begin{aligned} r_{SU} &= (0.6)(0.12) + (0.4)(0.08) \\ &= 0.104 = 10.4\%. \end{aligned}$$

Look in the file ***Home Depot APV Model.xls***. Select the *WACC* tab. Notice that this is similar to the *WACC* sheet in ***Home Depot.xls***, except it has an additional section to calculate the unlevered cost of equity. Notice that it also has a section for the post-horizon WACC, because we must specify the capital structure that we expect after the horizon. In other words, we must assume that the company will have a constant capital structure after the horizon even if it has a changing structure during the explicit forecast period.

Our first step is to calculate the unlevered horizon value, based on the FCFs that we expect beyond the horizon, the $ROIC_L$ that we expect in the long-term, and the unlevered cost of equity. We apply the general horizon value formula (Equation 13-4), except we discount at the unlevered cost of equity rather than the cost of capital. The result is the value of an unlevered firm at the horizon, $HV_{U,T}$.

$$HV_{U,T} = \left[\frac{(ROIC_L - g)Capital_T}{r_{SU} - g}\right] + \left[\frac{(ROIC_T - ROIC_L)Capital_T}{r_{SU}}\right] \quad \textbf{(13A-2)}$$

Next, we find the unlevered value of operations for each year. We do this exactly as in Chapter 13, except we use the unlevered cost of equity as the discount rate, rather than the cost of capital. We repeat this for each year until we find the unlevered value of operations as of the end of the most recent fiscal year. In other words, this is the value of operations that the firm would have if it had no debt.

The Value of the Tax Shield

The tax shield for any year is equal to the interest expense multiplied by the marginal tax rate. In other words, this is the amount of tax that the firm does not have to pay because it can deduct the interest expenses caused by debt. The value of the tax shield is the present value of all future yearly tax shields.

Before we can find the value of the tax shield, we must decide what rate we should use to discount the tax shield. Unfortunately, opinion is divided in the academic literature. Some argue that because the tax shield is being caused by the debt, the tax shield is just as risky as the debt. If this is true, then the appropriate discount rate for the tax shield is the interest rate on debt. Others argue that if the value of the unlevered firm goes up, then the firm will probably add more debt (i.e., it will base its capital structure on market values of equity, rather than on book values of equity). As the firm adds debt, its tax payments and tax shield will increase. Also, if the assets of the firm lead to a loss in any year, the company may have difficulty taking advantage of the tax deduction due to the interest expense. Therefore, the tax shield is about as risky as the firm's assets. If this is true, then the tax shield should be discounted at the unlevered cost of equity. We agree with the latter view, and that is what we do in our own valuation analyses.

The first step is to find the horizon value of the tax shield, which is the value of all yearly tax shields beyond the horizon, discounted back to the horizon. Unfortunately, the tax shield in the horizon year itself is not a very good indicator of these future tax shields, for two reasons.

First, we assume that the firm will have a constant capital structure after the horizon. This capital structure may differ from the capital structure prior to the horizon, and so the projected tax shields in the years leading up to the horizon may be different than the tax shields expected after the horizon.

Second, we specify the ROIC on new capital, which is the long-term $ROIC_L$ and may be different than the ROIC at the horizon; see the discussion leading up to Equation 13-4 for a detailed explanation. This has an impact on the amount of capital required to support operations, and this in turn affects the amount of debt in the post-horizon years. The tax shield at the horizon does not reflect the new level of debt required by this $ROIC_L$ on new capital, even if the capital structure does not change.

Fortunately, there is a relatively easy way to incorporate the effects of the new capital structure and the $ROIC_L$ on new capital, as shown in the following formula, where $HV_{TS,T}$ denotes the value of the tax shield at the horizon T and WACC is the weighted average cost of capital for the post-horizon period, based on the post-horizon capital structure.[3]

$$HV_{TS,T} = \left[\frac{(ROIC_L - g)Capital_T}{WACC - g} + \frac{(ROIC_T - ROIC_L)Capital_T}{WACC}\right] - HV_{U,T} \quad \textbf{(13A-3)}$$

The valuation model applies this formula to determine the horizon value of the tax shield. The value of the tax shield for the year prior to the horizon is the sum of the horizon value of the tax shield plus the tax shield at the horizon, discounted back 1 year at the unlevered cost of equity. The model applies this logic for all prior years, resulting in the value of the tax shield as of the end of the most recent fiscal year.

The levered value of operations is the sum of the unlevered value of operations and the value of the tax shield. The remainder of the spreadsheet is analogous to the calculations shown in ***Home Depot.xls***.

If you have a company with a changing capital structure, our advice is to value the company using the APV approach.

[3]See M. Ehrhardt, "Corporate Valuation: Incorporating the Impact of Competition into the Adjusted Present Value Technique," *Journal of Applied Corporate Finance*, forthcoming.

Index